Praise for David Callahan's

THE GIVERS

"Mr. Callahan offers critiques of the leading approaches to giving today. And he does so in a way that is highly readable to people who may never have billions (or even millions) to donate to causes. He also shows why the rest of us need to be more skeptical about the praise heaped on big donors."
—Paul Sullivan, *The New York Times*

"A detailed, judicious, and compelling analysis of an important and often ignored phenomenon: the impact of large-scale philanthropy on the United States in the twenty-first century."
—Glenn C. Altschuler, *The Philadelphia Inquirer*

"At issue for Callahan is not so much the impulse to give but outdated government incentives to mix giving with advocacy. This amounts, he says, to the wealthiest people having a louder voice than ordinary citizens."
—*TIME*

"[A] fascinating look into perhaps one of the least understood trends in the public square."
—*Booklist* (starred review)

"An intriguing look at the world of big-ticket philanthropy. . . . An eye-opening view of a vast sector of the economy that lies in the shadows but has undue influence, for ill or good."
—*Kirkus Reviews*

"A thoughtful call for transparency and oversight in the charity sector. . . . This striking, thought-provoking work is perfectly timed as American activists move to confront a new presidential administration."
—*Publishers Weekly*

David Callahan

THE GIVERS

David Callahan is founder and editor of *Inside Philan-thropy*, a digital media site that covers the world of giving by wealthy donors and foundations. Previously, he was a senior fellow at Demos, the national think tank he cofounded in 2000, as well as a resident scholar at The Century Foundation. His past books include *Fortunes of Change: The Rise of the Liberal Rich and the Remaking of America* and *The Cheating Culture: Why More Americans Are Doing Wrong to Get Ahead*. A graduate of Hampshire College, Callahan holds a PhD in politics from Princeton University. He lives in Los Angeles.

www.insidephilanthropy.com

THE

GIVERS

Wealth, Power, and Philanthropy

in a New Gilded Age

DAVID CALLAHAN

Vintage Books
A Division of Penguin Random House LLC
New York

FIRST VINTAGE BOOKS EDITION, MARCH 2018

Copyright © 2017 by David Callahan

All rights reserved. Published in the United States by Vintage Books,
a division of Penguin Random House LLC, New York, and distributed
in Canada by Random House of Canada, a division of Penguin Random
House Canada Limited, Toronto. Originally published in hardcover
in the United States by Alfred A. Knopf, a division of
Penguin Random House LLC, New York, in 2017.

Vintage and colophon are registered trademarks of
Penguin Random House LLC.

Library of Congress Control Number: 2016963048

Vintage Books Trade Paperback ISBN: 978-1-101-97104-8
eBook ISBN: 978-1-101-94706-7

Author photograph © Silvia Spross
Book design by Cassandra J. Pappas

www.vintagebooks.com

Printed in the United States of America
10   9   8   7   6   5   4   3   2

Contents

THE
GIVERS

Prologue:
The Great Power Shift

What wasn't to like?

On December 1, 2015, Mark Zuckerberg and Priscilla Chan pledged to use 99 percent of their shares in Facebook to make the world a better place. The occasion for this announcement was the birth of their daughter, Max, and the pledge took the form a letter to her—posted, naturally, on Facebook. It was sweet and earnest. More important, those shares were worth about $45 billion, enough money to do a whole lot of good.

Yet that vast pile of wealth also perfectly embodied the excesses of a new Gilded Age. It was an almost unfathomable sum, larger than the annual budgets of thirty-two U.S. states, and greater than the combined wealth of the bottom fifth of American households.

In their letter to Max, which Zuckerberg and Chan had worked on for weeks, even making last-minute changes at the hospital, the couple said that among their goals in giving away all their money was to "promote equality" so everyone has access to opportunity "regardless of the nation, families or circumstances they are born into."

Here was one kind of solution to an age of vast and vexing inequality: The richest of the rich could *give all the money back*. Who could possibly complain about such an act of generosity?

"Wow," wrote Bill and Melinda Gates, in a note of support to Zuckerberg and Chan. "The example you're setting today is an inspiration to us and the world." Warren Buffett added: "Mark and Priscilla are breaking the mold with this breathtaking commitment. A combination of brains, passion and resources on this scale will change the lives of millions. On behalf of future generations, I thank them."

As it turned out, though, not everyone lined up to thank the tech tycoon and his pediatrician wife for one of the largest philanthropic pledges in history. The backlash to the announcement was swift and surprisingly fierce. ProPublica's Jesse Eisenberg, writing in the *New York Times*, blasted the couple's choice to create a limited liability corporation, the Chan Zuckerberg Initiative, to handle their good works. That structure would allow them to avoid taxes, as well as oversight, said Eisenberg, since LLCs don't have to disclose their activities like traditional foundations. Eisenberg wrote that "we are turning into a society of oligarchs. And I am not as excited as some to welcome the new Silicon Valley overlords."

Other critics echoed these points, piling on with charges that Zuckerberg and Chan's "non-charity charity," as *The Atlantic* dubbed it, amounted to tax avoidance and an undemocratic power grab. The money should more rightfully go to government, some said.

The pushback was baffling to the young couple, who were barely in their thirties and saw themselves as anything but "overlords." Zuckerberg came from a fairly typical upper-middle-class family in Dobbs Ferry, New York, just north of Manhattan, the son of a dentist and a psychiatrist. Priscilla's background was far more humble. Her father had come to the United States after fleeing Vietnam in the 1970s and spending time in a refugee camp. He worked brutal hours running a Chinese restaurant in Boston, and her mother's hours were just as long. Priscilla was largely raised by her grandmother. During her four years at Harvard, she had worked at an after-school program serving low-income kids in Dorchester housing projects. As a pediatrician, much of her work was with underserved communities. "I work with families on the front lines," Chan told me. "My entire career has been about public service." Not long before giving birth, she had started a new primary school in the heavily Latino community of East Palo Alto, California. At Chan's urging, Mark had once taught a weekly class in East Menlo Park, another struggling corner of Silicon Valley.

Unlike many winners in the new economy, Zuckerberg and Chan had actually made the time and effort to cross America's vast income divide, helping out in a hands-on way. They were also deeply serious about doing their philanthropy well, consulting with numerous experts, trying to learn from their mistakes, and working to meld their very different strengths. "Mark is a great engineer and systems builder," Chan said. "He teaches me how to build organizations, how to think about scale. I teach him about what it's like to actually be on the front lines." They were determined to start giving early, and at a large scale, because it seemed like a waste not to put their wealth to good use sooner rather than later. As well, they wanted to have a long runway to get better at philanthropy. "We have an incredible opportunity."

Chan took the lead on many of the day-to-day tasks of building the infrastructure needed to give away billions. She saw the mission, in large part, as helping the part of America that she had grown up in—neglected communities where families were trying to struggle upward, or just survive, often against immense odds. "People are working as hard as they can, but there are systemic obstacles," Chan told me. That wasn't right. "We want everyone to have the same opportunities." Still, even as she and Zuckerberg earnestly set forth to give away more money than nearly anyone in history, they were being cast in a suspect light.

This wasn't the first time that Zuckerberg's giving had sparked a backlash. Starting in 2010, he had bankrolled a controversial effort to reform Newark's public schools that, to critics, showcased how ordinary citizens got elbowed aside as activist donors worked to reshape public institutions. In turn, Zuckerberg was hardly the first mega-philanthropist in U.S. history to be viewed with deep suspicion. Over a century earlier, John D. Rockefeller's proposed foundation had been denounced by the U.S. attorney general as "an indefinite scheme for perpetuating vast wealth" that was "entirely inconsistent with the public interest." Another U.S. official criticized the Rockefeller family's "huge philanthropic trusts as a menace to the welfare of society."

By the late twentieth century, though, these early criticisms of mega-givers had faded. As distrust of robber barons and their monopolies became a distant memory, so too did fears that philanthropy was yet another tool of oligarchical control—a "Trojan horse" in the plot against democracy, as the Rockefeller Foundation had also been called. In an America that celebrated the wealthy, and especially tech billionaires, the new age of charity was largely hailed as a good thing. The subtitle of a 2008 book on this phenomenon, "How Giving Can Save the World," summed up the uncritical hopes of the moment.

Then came the financial crisis and the bank bailouts, followed by a recovery in which the wealthy pulled even farther away from everyone else—to the point that the Forbes 400, a small enough group to fit into a ballroom, would come to hold more wealth than the bottom 61 percent of American households, with 194 million people. The rise of the Tea Party and Occupy Wall Street ushered in a new populist moment, one in which all elites—and especially the super-rich—came under new suspicion. Inequality in America, which had been growing since the 1970s, finally started to get the scrutiny it deserved. A dense treatise by the French economist Thomas Piketty, *Capitalism in the Twenty-First Century*—eminently ignorable in another era—shot to the top of the *New York Times* bestseller list.

This rising concern about inequality has been paralleled by a remarkable surge in new philanthropy. Zuckerberg and Chan were only the latest billionaires to make huge pledges to do good with their fortunes. Similar pledges, albeit on a small scale, have been coming at a steady clip, along with record-breaking gifts. Everywhere you look, new philanthropists seem to be pursuing big ambitions: to stop climate change, remake public education, build urban parks, eliminate malaria, end bias against LGBT people, find cures to Alzheimer's, and on and on.

It's hard to argue with some of these goals. Who doesn't want to extinguish Alzheimer's or malaria? But others are more controversial. If you don't favor same-sex marriage or charter schools or shutting down coal plants, you might not be too thrilled with how some billionaires have been deploying their money—subsidized, I should add, by your own tax dollars. In many ways, today's new philanthropy is exciting and inspiring. In other ways, it's scary and feels profoundly undemocratic.

The world of philanthropy is vast. It includes everything from parents chipping in for music classes at a local school to the global fight against HIV. Endless things can be said about the myriad efforts of private donors to tackle this or that issue. Are they prioritizing the right causes? Are they choosing the best approaches? Are charitable dollars being used in the most efficient fashion?

My own interest, though, is in the growing questions around the power of philanthropists to shape America. Just how much influence *are* the givers wielding these days, and to what ends? How should we feel about that clout here in the world's oldest democracy?

It's a good time to dig in on this front. Not only do philanthropists indeed have more power than ever before, as I'll show, but that influence is likely to grow far greater in coming decades. While civil society was a junior partner in the twentieth century relative to government and business, this is changing: Philanthropy is becoming a much stronger power center and, in some areas, is set to surpass government in its ability to shape society's agenda. To put things differently, we face a future in which private donors—who are accountable to no one—may often wield more influence than elected public officials, who (in theory, anyway) are accountable to all of us.

This power shift is one of the biggest stories of our time. Yet it's a hard one to tell properly for several reasons. Just figuring out what philanthropists are up to is no easy thing. Many funders, particularly the newer givers arriving on the scene with huge fortunes, don't reveal much about their giving, and nonprofit laws allow rivers of money to sluice through society in opaque ways. To give just one recent example, private donors put up millions of dollars in donations to influence U.S. policy toward Iran's nuclear program, including the fevered debate over the final deal reached in 2015. Yet we may never know exactly who all those givers were or how much money they gave.

At the same time, influence is a tough subject to get a handle on. Most of us understand the hard power that corporations have to shape how we live with new goods and services, just as we understand how government affects our lives with big policy shifts. But philanthropists often operate subtly, working behind the scenes to set agendas and shape decisions—backing ideas, research, and pilot projects. Even as they emerge as the new social engineers of our time, their fingerprints can be hard to see. Furthermore, philanthropy's rising power is not just about what's happening in the nonprofit sector; it's also about changes elsewhere in society—in the economy, politics, and government—that are boosting the *relative* clout of private givers. Connecting these dots is not always so easy.

Philanthropy in America is multifaceted. The bulk of charitable dollars take the form of modest contributions by millions of people, while another big piece is the giving of private foundations established by donors who are long gone. Giving by corporations is also sizeable.

This book has a narrower focus. It looks just at major living donors. It describes the unprecedented giving by these people, and seeks to explain who they really are. Why do they give? What do they want? How do they think? I look at the ever more sophisticated ways their wealth is being deployed to shape society—and link that trend to the decline of government. Most of all, I try to get a fix on just how much influence the givers are having, where, and with what effects on the rest of us.

One answer to these questions is that the closer you look at the new philanthropic power elite, the more you'll see that this group is increasingly diverse and often quite divided on the biggest issues of the day. Even in education, supposedly dominated by a monolithic set of right-of-center funders like the Walton family, you'll find givers with a wide range of views—not to mention donors whose views keep evolving, as we'll see in the cases of both Mark Zuckerberg and Bill Gates.

The picture this book paints of a heterogeneous new power elite is reassuring in some ways. Nearly all readers will find philanthropists who share their values, even as they may learn of more donors to fear. To me, though, the key point is not which team of philanthropists are winning or losing on this or that issue; rather, it's how these givers are becoming more powerful while ordinary Americans struggle to get their voices heard at all.

Today's big philanthropy is arising in an era when the wealthy already seem to control so much territory in America—whether it's politics through their campaign contributions or ownership of the tech and media companies that shape our culture. Now, through their giving, they are wielding even more influence.

This is deeply troubling. But, as I show, a simple narrative about plutocratic power is the wrong way to understand big philanthropy. Things are more complicated, given the flow of new money to empower people working on issues like climate change, poverty, and criminal justice. Even if you worry about inequality, it's hard not to feel hope as super-empowered, high-minded givers look to solve problems in ways that get around partisan gridlock or dated ideas or entrenched interest groups.

The truth is that democracies just aren't so good at some things—like tackling over-the-horizon threats, for example. And, in many instances, today's philanthropists are zeroing in on precisely those problems that our political system has fumbled or shyed away from. We need people with big plans, a drive to make a difference, and the money and power to do so, even if they sometimes get behind bad ideas. We want philanthropists to have lots of freedom to deploy what Warren Buffett has called "society's risk capital." The givers can attack challenges with a freedom and agility that public officials could only dream of—which is one reason why philanthropy has been called "society's passing gear."

Still, as more mega-donors emerge, with any number of grand ambitions, we need to ask much harder questions about the accountability of philanthropy, which operates outside of familiar checks and balances. While CEOs can be overthrown by shareholders, and senators rejected by voters, nobody can stop billionaires from using great wealth to push their schemes for society, however misguided. That power, it must be emphasized, has little to do with meritocracy. You may need at least some intelligence and talent to amass great wealth; but anyone who's rich can be a major philanthropist, regardless of his or her qualifications for this role. And just because you're good at making money doesn't mean you'll be any good at giving it away. Nor does an embrace of philanthropy mean that someone is looking out for society as a whole. Giving, as we'll see, can be yet another tool to advance partisan goals and class interests. In effect, it can be a way of taking.

The bigger risk here, though, is not that the mega-givers will make mistakes or feather their own nests. Rather, it's that their rising power will further push ordinary Americans to the margins of civic life in an unequal era when so many people already feel shoved aside by elites and the wealthy.

Decades ago, in the early postwar era, scholars like C. Wright Mills worked to gain an understanding of a new ecosystem of power that included major corporations, government, and the military. Today, and going forward, no explanation of who runs America will be complete if it doesn't reckon with the rise of big philanthropy—and the givers behind it.

1

The Coming of Big Philanthropy

As Michael Bloomberg prepared to step down as mayor of New York City, after twelve years on the job, he said that among his goals after leaving office was to start running outside again, which hadn't been practical with a security detail while mayor. He also said he wanted to "sleep in a bit." Bloomberg had spent years waking up at six a.m. and working till ten p.m. or eleven p.m. at night. Just after leaving office, in January 2014, he and his partner, Diana Taylor, headed off to Hawaii and New Zealand for a two-week vacation—his first real vacation in over a decade.

Later, as Bloomberg settled into his post-mayoral life, it became clear that he wouldn't be relaxing much. Bloomberg soon plunged back into the day-to-day management of his massive media company, Bloomberg L.P. In less than a year, the CEO of the company, Daniel Doctoroff, would be gone as Bloomberg reasserted his control.

Bloomberg also turned to philanthropy in a bigger way after he left office. Even as he amassed great wealth, starting in the 1980s, Bloomberg had always planned to give away most of that money. He lived extravagantly, to be sure, owning a private jet and some thirteen properties around the world by 2013—which included estates in London, Bermuda, the Hamptons, and Westchester County—but he gave on an equally large level.

Bloomberg had no interest in an older model of philanthropy, whereby business titans waited to the end of their lives or left the job to their heirs.

Instead, he believed in giving as much as he could while still alive, a logic he pushed to other donors.

Bloomberg once recalled how, in the 1990s, he talked to a wealthy benefactor who planned to leave Johns Hopkins University $50 million upon his death. "But I asked him: Why wait? Why deny financial aid to this generation? Why deny a possible cure for a disease to this generation?" The donor changed his mind, giving all the money immediately. Over many years, Bloomberg himself channeled some $1 billion to Johns Hopkins, his alma mater. In a 2010 public statement about his giving intentions, Bloomberg had written "that the reality of great wealth is that you can't spend it and you can't take it with you."

Bloomberg's fortune is vast indeed. When he started his media company, which came to dominate the market for financial data, he covered many of the start-up costs himself, drawing on a large severance package he had gotten from his former Wall Street employer, Salomon Brothers. Later, Bloomberg bought back stakes in his company from other early investors. As a result, he ended up owning 88 percent of a company that now has nineteen thousand employees and $9 billion in annual revenue. During his years as mayor, the value of the company had grown steadily. Bloomberg was worth just under $5 billion as he took office in 2002. By the time he left, that figure had soared to $33 billion. Within two years of leaving City Hall, his wealth had climbed higher still, to over $40 billion.

That kind of money isn't easy to give away. For example, if Bloomberg gave as much annually as did the legendary Rockefeller Foundation, it would take him almost three centuries to dispose of his fortune. To make any dent in giving away his wealth, Bloomberg has to give on the level of Bill Gates or George Soros, who rank among the world's top mega-donors.

Bloomberg had been an active philanthropist before becoming mayor, and he started giving more once at City Hall. Among other things, he gave many millions to nonprofit groups around the city—giving that some saw as a naked effort to co-opt critics and bolster his power. Bloomberg offered a more benign explanation: he was simply using private funds to pay for priorities that the city couldn't afford. Regardless, never before had a major public official in the United States so adroitly used philanthropy to advance his agenda—just as Bloomberg set a new record for spending his own money to get elected in the first place.

Bloomberg also quietly built up the infrastructure for his philanthropy during his years in government. He bought a $45 million Beaux-Arts mansion on 78th and Madison Avenue in 2006 to house his foundation, and in 2010, he appointed his longtime aide Patricia Harris as CEO of Bloomberg Philanthropies, a job she took on even while still working at City Hall. Harris led the push to organize and staff the foundation over subsequent years—getting ready for much bigger giving to come.

In 2013, his last year in office, Bloomberg quietly gave away around $450 million—an amount nearly as great as the Ford Foundation's annual grantmaking. Big chunks of that money went to finance a global version of the "nanny" agenda that Bloomberg had pursued as mayor. He put up millions of dollars for a worldwide push against smoking, as well as an effort to reduce traffic deaths in poorer countries. Bloomberg also gave big to combat climate change. In 2011, he had given the Sierra Club its biggest gift ever—$50 million to try to shut down coal-fired power plants around the United States.

After he left City Hall, Bloomberg moved even more aggressively with his philanthropy. Within a month, he announced a $53 million commitment to fight overfishing and reform fishing practices. That issue might sound obscure to most people, but not to Bloomberg. As he said in making his gift: "While billions of people depend on fish for food or income, only 13 percent of the world's fisheries are safe from being over-fished, presenting serious environmental and public health challenges. Data shows the world's severely threatened fish populations can rebound if fishing is properly managed."

Billions of hungry people, disappearing healthy food, and—best of all—data-driven solutions. This was Mike Bloomberg's kind of issue.

A month later, Bloomberg put up $10 million to help prevent children from accidentally drowning in Bangladesh. And the big numbers would keep coming. In fall 2014, Bloomberg announced he was putting another $125 million into work to cut the global carnage of traffic deaths. His foundation also rolled out an initiative to support public art in U.S. cities, on top of tens of millions of dollars Bloomberg had already donated to the arts. Meanwhile, additional grants bankrolled efforts to help cities in the United States and other countries become more innovative.

There was more, too. During his first eighteen months out of office,

Bloomberg doubled down on his giving to the Sierra Club to fight coal plants, expanded his global fight against smoking, and pledged $50 million to support global reproductive health and rights.

As mayor of New York, Bloomberg was famously obsessed with data, and with identifying practical ways to improve life in the city. As a philanthropist, he's also driven by a keen pragmatism. Whereas many billionaires are drawn to the hardest problems or the trendiest causes, Bloomberg operates in a more utilitarian way when deciding where to put his biggest money—crunching the numbers to figure out how his giving can do the most good.

Neither of the two biggest causes he has invested in over the years—reducing tobacco use and improving traffic safety—register much in the glittery precincts of philanthropy, but Bloomberg has picked two real winners. Smoking kills six million people worldwide every year, which is far more than AIDS and malaria put together. That number is projected to rise to eight million by 2030. A funder who bends this curve even slightly can save untold lives, which is why Bloomberg has so far poured at least $600 million into the cause. The same goes for road safety, where the body count is also huge: 1.25 million people die annually from accidents and tens of millions are injured. His foundation estimates that some 125,000 lives will be saved as a result of Bloomberg's investment of more than a quarter of a billion dollars in road safety activities across the world. Sounds like a bargain, right? Meanwhile, Bloomberg's quest to shut down coal-fired power plants—a cause to which he's now given over $130 million—is a twofer: shuttering such plants reduces carbon dioxide emissions but also lowers old-fashioned air pollution, saving lives. In early 2015, Bloomberg estimated that 5,500 lives annually were already being saved because of coal plant shutdowns in recent years.

Bloomberg is a savvy philanthropist in another way: He understands that influencing government is often the best way to get things done and focuses much of his giving on leveraging changes in public policy.

In a sweeping statement of his philanthropic strategy in early 2015, Bloomberg wrote: "Some still see philanthropy as an alternative to government. I see it as a way to embolden government." He went on: "Governments have the authority to drive change in ways that philanthropic organizations cannot. By leveraging our resources, and forming partnerships with government, philanthropic organizations can help push those changes forward." That mind-set, said Bloomberg, was "at the heart of everything" that his foundation did.

In 2014, Bloomberg's annual giving totaled $462 million. The following year, it totaled $510 million. With tens of billions of dollars to give away, this gusher of donations isn't likely to stop anytime soon.

Bloomberg has a reputation as a nonpartisan pragmatist, even as he's taken on climate change and gun violence, and he doesn't strike many as a scary figure. He is not feared the way that progressives fear the Koch brothers or conservatives fear George Soros. But the plain facts about Bloomberg are actually rather unnerving: One of the world's wealthiest men has openly said that he plans to spend the bulk of his fortune to influence government policies, not just in America but around the planet.

If you don't know much about philanthropy—and few Americans do—you may have imagined that Michael Bloomberg's run as a power player would end when he stepped down as mayor of New York. Of course, nothing of the kind was true. He simply pivoted to pull other levers of influence. Bloomberg, who used his great wealth to buy his way into office, now turned to using that wealth to push changes that could have more impact on the lives of more people than anything he did as mayor.

Bloomberg will give away billions in coming years at the same time that any number of great fortunes are harnessed to philanthropy. And just as few Americans are following what New York's ex-mayor is doing, neither are they paying attention to what some of the nation's other wealthiest people are up to—or the degree to which they're deploying their fortunes to have a say over the great issues of the day. That power, I should add, doesn't just rest in the hands of those giving wealth away. It also is wielded by the people the givers entrust with their money, whether it's largely unknown foundation staff like Patricia Harris—who's been called one of the most powerful women in the world—or equally unknown heirs, like the three children of Warren Buffett, who together give away a larger sum every year than Michael Bloomberg. The philanthropic elite now emerging is not just more influential than most people realize; it's more extensive, commanding a growing array of institutions that reach into nearly every corner of American society.

THE NEW WEALTH

There are two parts to the story of the great power shift unfolding in U.S. society. One part is about the rising tide of philanthropic giving; the second is about the declining ability of government to solve big problems and provide public goods.

Let's start with the new private money.

For all the philanthropy we've seen in recent years, it's nothing compared to what lies ahead.

To many of today's billionaires, mega-giving is the logical endgame to careers spent amassing such vast fortunes that philanthropy is the only real place the money can go. A similar phenomenon played out a century ago, when the historic fortunes of the early industrial age amassed by Rockefeller, Andrew Carnegie, and others were used to endow large foundations that went on to wield huge influence in America and the world. This time, though, everything is bigger—both the wealth and the clout that comes with it.

How much money are we talking about? More than you think.

Even if you're generally aware of the crazily large fortunes piling up at the very tippy top of the income ladder in our second Gilded Age— say, because you thumb through the Forbes 400 special issue now and again—chances are that you still don't realize just how big the fortunes at the top have become. Or how much bigger they are likely to get.

Take Bill Gates and Warren Buffett. They're long-familiar figures, as two of the richest men in America. But if you haven't been paying attention, you may not have noticed that both have gotten *much* richer over the past decade. Buffett added $25 billion to his fortune between 2005 and 2015. Gates added even more, pushing his net worth to nearly $80 billion.

And these fortunes may rise even further. While Gates still owns large amounts of Microsoft stock, he has largely deployed his fortune in private venture capital investments that could bring substantial returns as they mature in coming years. Buffett, meanwhile, has lately been making a string of bold acquisitions that could boost Berkshire Hathaway's fabled stock even further into the stratosphere down the line.

Or consider Mark Zuckerberg. Amid the uproar over his plans to give away $45 billion in Facebook stock, almost nobody mentioned an obvious point: The actual amount could end up being far greater than that. While

Facebook's 2012 IPO was famously a disaster, its stock began a quiet upward tear in 2014, eventually soaring to over $100 a share. The smart money snickers that Facebook is overpriced and that the tech bubble will burst any day now. And maybe it will. But if the value of Facebook ever comes close to that of other top tech giants (like Google or Apple), Zuckerberg, who owns a huge stake in the company, will be far richer than he is today.

Gates, Buffett, Bloomberg, and Zuckerberg aren't the only billionaires who've gotten much wealthier in the past decade—a period, by the way, when the median net worth of all U.S. households fell thanks to the housing crash. The fortunes of the wealthy have kept soaring across multiple industries and through the ups and downs of the business cycle. New-economy billionaires have gotten much richer—Larry Ellison added $40 billion to his wealth between 2005 and 2015, Jeff Bezos added $42 billion—but so have titans of the old economy. David and Charles Koch, for example, had a combined net worth of $9 billion in 2005. In 2015, that figure stood at around $85 billion, a huge gain that helps explain why the Koch brothers have had plenty of extra cash to pour into politics and philanthropy lately. Phil Knight of Nike gained $17 billion in new wealth during the decade. Sheldon Adelson, the casino mogul, doubled his wealth to $26 billion.

Much has been said about why so few people have come to have so much money, fortunes that defy comprehension and rival the GDP of some countries. A confluence of factors—globalization, technological change, and public policies favoring capital—have worked together to create this second Gilded Age, boosting the wealth of the Forbes 400 by nearly 2,000 percent since 1984. It's a fascinating story, and an outrageous one, too. Even as the U.S. economy stopped working for most ordinary people long ago, the piles of wealth at the very top have kept growing larger and larger. America's political class has either actively abetted this shift or nipped lamely at the juggernaut of runaway inequality.

At this point, though, the scandal of how the income chasm grew so wide is less intriguing than the question of what will become of today's fortunes going forward.

Michael Bloomberg was exactly right when he said about great wealth that "you can't spend it and you can't take it with you." This comes from a man who's done a pretty impressive job of spending money, from sinking over $250 million into a political career to snapping up multiple estates. But when you have billions of dollars there's no way you can dispose of more than a tiny fraction of it through even the most feverish personal excess. Nor can your heirs consume such wealth, even if you have a lot of them and they are huge spenders. Passing great fortunes to the next generation just kicks the question down the line of what will eventually come of that wealth. One day, it will have to be consumed in some fashion.

Philanthropy is an obvious solution here. For the richest of the rich, it may feel like the *only* solution.

Of course, philanthropy is attractive to the wealthy for a wide range of other reasons beyond necessity. I'll dig into the varied motives behind their giving throughout the book, but one point to stress at the outset is just how prevalent the philanthropic impulse is among today's upper class and just how many of these people are turning to giving in an organized way.

From 2003 to 2013, according to one study, itemized charitable contributions from people making $500,000 or more increased by 57 percent, while itemized contributions from people making $10,000,000 or more increased by 104 percent over the same period. Some 30,000 new private foundations have been created since 2000, along with 185,000 donor-advised funds, which offer a simpler way to channel money to charitable causes. That explosive growth is likely to continue in coming decades amid the greatest wealth transfer in U.S. history. One study has predicted that nearly $60 trillion will be transferred from American estates between 2007 and 2061, with $27 trillion of that money going to charity. Another study estimated that affluent baby boomers alone will donate $6.6 trillion to philanthropy over the next twenty years.

Numbers like this speak to just how many U.S. households have the capacity for substantial giving. While it's pretty obvious that a billionaire would have some spare cash to give away, plenty of other people do, too.

A 2015 study found that nearly 70,000 individuals living in North America have assets of $30 million or more—a huge jump from just a decade ago. It found that some 5,000 households had assets of over $100 million. These figures include just liquid, investable assets (not real estate). Lots of Americans, in other words, have the resources to combine a lavish lifestyle with serious giving, and a growing number of today's wealthy are doing exactly that.

New philanthropists are helped along by an ever growing complex of consulting firms and management services. The charitable arm of Fidelity is the top leader in this regard. Its advisors can handle every aspect of a client's philanthropy, from identifying which causes to support with what strategies, to actually cutting the checks. Working with over 100,000 donors, Fidelity handled $3.1 billion in giving in 2015—making it the second largest grantmaking operation in the world, after the Gates Foundation. Schwab Charitable moved just over $1 billion in the same year, nearly twice as much money as the Ford Foundation gave.

Meanwhile, community foundations—where the wealthy have historically looked for help with their giving—are bigger and wealthier than ever, almost doubling their annual grantmaking since 2010. Grants made through the Silicon Valley Community, where Zuckerberg and other tech stars stash their cash, nearly doubled in just one year alone, between 2014 and 2015—soaring to $816 million.

As the great wealth of a new Gilded Age is harnessed to philanthropy, what will that mean for the rest of us? Will it mean faster strides in "advancing human potential and promoting equality," which are the goals that Mark Zuckerberg and Priscilla Chan have laid out? Or will it deepen and entrench what many already see as a new era of American plutocracy?

I'll explore these questions from many angles in the pages ahead. A starting point to grasp, though, is that the emergence of big philanthropy is adding a new wrinkle to how we understand inequality in our second Gilded Age. Mainly, people have talked about the great fortunes at the top as a symptom of a yawning economic chasm. Now, with the wealthy turning to philanthropy on an epic scale, those fortunes need to be seen in a new light: They are becoming powerful drivers of a range of agendas. Many of today's richest Americans, we can already see, will wield a lot more influence over how the rest of us live as they give away their money than they ever wielded while making it.

How will this influence be used? How is it being used already?

THE BIGGEST GIVEAWAY IN HISTORY

If big philanthropy had a nerve center, it would be the Office of Philanthropic Partnerships at the Bill and Melinda Gates Foundation, which occupies a pair of modern V-shaped buildings in downtown Seattle. There, a small team coordinates the Giving Pledge, an effort to galvanize greater giving by the world's richest people and, as important, to help them to have maximum impact with their money.

More than 150 people have joined the pledge, which was publicly unveiled by Bill Gates and Warren Buffett in 2010. Zuckerberg has done so. So has Mike Bloomberg, as well as a who's who of other billionaires—among them Paul Allen, Richard Branson, Elon Musk, and David Rockefeller. Only Americans were part of the pledge at first. Now it includes billionaires from sixteen countries. Every year, members gather for an annual retreat to swap insights and hear from experts on different topics.

Fostering more philanthropy became a goal of the Gates Foundation early on, driven by the logic that new giving by other donors was a key to making a dent in the gargantuan problems the foundation was tackling, like global poverty and disease. Bill and Melinda Gates also had a strong personal interest in encouraging new donors, as did their close friend Warren Buffett. Because of the vastness of their wealth, all three had been forced to think carefully about the challenges of disposing of so much money. (Buffett's easy solution was to pledge most of it to the Gates Foundation.) Yet in the course of hobnobbing with other billionaires, the Gateses and Buffett came to see that many of America's richest people had yet to figure out what they would ultimately do with their money. The three thought more needed to be done to get those folks to focus on that critical question. Buffett had the idea for an organized effort, one that would draw in other top philanthropists to help proselytize for greater giving, starting earlier in life.

"The sooner, the better" is Bill Gates's view of when the wealthy should start giving. But he didn't always think that way. "I didn't do much philanthropy in my 20s and 30s," he recalled to an interviewer. "I didn't believe in weekends, vacations. So philanthropy wasn't the only thing I didn't believe in. I was just fanatical." While building Microsoft, Gates could go days working nearly around the clock. To keep up with the boss, some programmers kept sleeping bags under their desks.

When Bill and Melinda were still dating, Gates told her that he planned to give away all the wealth created by Microsoft—but only after he turned sixty (in 2015). He hated the idea of trying to both run a big company and oversee a foundation at the same time. Later, though, Gates would regret his tunnel vision. "I wish I had had a basic awareness of the different living conditions around the world," he said.

A trip to Africa with Melinda in 1993—his longest vacation ever—started to broaden his horizons. The couple went for a safari, to see wild animals, but were deeply moved by the challenges faced by the people on the world's poorest continent. Walking on a beach on Zanzibar, they had their first real discussion about how, exactly, they might give away a historic fortune.

Over the next few years, Bill sped up his timetable for giving as he learned more about the appalling state of global health. He and Melinda were shocked to read a news story about rotavirus, which causes severe diarrhea and kills hundreds of thousands of children every year. Melinda would recall: "We thought 'Well, that can't be.' In the U.S. you just go down to the drugstore."

Ever the geek, Bill dug into the data, poring over the World Bank's World Development Report, among other publications. He came to see how little he knew about global health. Previously, he had thought that "there wouldn't be a disease I never heard of that was killing over half a million children a year. And that if there were, all the drug companies would be working on it." He had also thought that by the time he did eventually go into philanthropy, "all the really important stuff would already be addressed" and he'd "have to struggle to find something really impactful." But once he read that report, he saw that there were huge, obvious problems to be solved—and many lives that could be easily saved. "It just jumped out at me."

The Gateses began global grantmaking in the late 1990s, as co-chairs of their foundation. Bill has described his partnership with Melinda as the third great collaboration of his life—the first being with Microsoft co-founder Paul Allen, the second with the company's long-serving CEO, Steve Ballmer. Never before had a husband-and-wife team worked so closely in giving away so much money. John D. Rockefeller's wife, Laura Spelman Rockefeller, had died twenty-two years before her husband—whose main partner in giving, in any case, was Frederick T. Gates. Andrew Carnegie's wife, Louise, was a peripheral figure as he disposed of his vast steel fortune. But the Gateses, like many wealthy couples today, have made their mammoth-size philanthropy a truly joint project.

"We come at things from different angles. And I actually think that's really good," Melinda has said. "So Bill can look at the big data and say I want to act based on these global statistics. For me, I come at it from intuition. I meet with lots of people on the ground. And Bill has taught me to read up from that to the global data and see if they match. And I think what I've taught him is to take that data and meet with people on the ground."

Patty Stonesifer, a Microsoft executive, was another key player in the mix, as the first CEO of their foundation. Years later, as she wrapped up her work in that role, Stonesifer was part of the discussions with Bill, Melinda, and Warren about how to galvanize bigger, earlier philanthropy by the super-rich. When she stepped down from her post, in the fall of 2008, she took on a special assignment for the trio: to see if an initiative could be developed to spur such giving.

Robert Rosen, a former White House aide under President Bill Clinton and senior staffer at the Gates Foundation, was also drawn into this exploration, as was Olivia Leland, a Harvard grad who had come to the foundation in 2007 from the global development world.

The years before the 2008 financial crisis saw a huge increase in wealth accumulation—with the net worth of the Forbes 400 hitting an all-time high of $1.57 trillion in 2007—and these towering piles of money were the backdrop for the Gates conversation on how to spur new philanthropy. There was a recognition, Rosen told me, of "an incredible opportunity in terms of having an impact on society by just the amount of wealth that could be transferred. We'd been through a cycle of an enormous growth of wealth, and that money had the potential to be invested in philanthropic efforts that had the potential to benefit society."

"Potential" is a key word here, because the Gates team well knew that, absent advance planning, great fortunes could end up locked away in trusts or hit by steep estate taxes and never reach philanthropy at a scale that might otherwise be possible. One analysis of estate tax filings found that in 2007 just 12 percent of all estate wealth for that year went to charitable bequests. Meanwhile, in the same year, the four hundred biggest taxpayers in the United States gave away about 8 percent of their earnings, for a total of $11 billion.

The big question was how to boost both these numbers—how to channel more estate wealth to philanthropy but also induce greater "giving while living." Making that happen required that more of the richest people in the world really focus on their philanthropy, which wasn't always easy. Many were super-busy. Others didn't want to deal with sticky family issues. "There are a lot of reasons why people put off thinking about philanthropy," Bill Gates has said. "It makes you think about your will, and what you're going to do with your wealth."

Also, it can be challenging and time-consuming to do philanthropy well—especially in a large-scale, high-impact way. The Gateses themselves had made a number of missteps over the years. People had to be prodded to give more, but they also needed help in doing so wisely.

As Stonesifer's exploration unfolded, looking at how the super-wealthy approached giving, the team saw three kinds of people. There were some who were already "being incredibly generous and having tremendous impact," said Rosen. There were others who had the right intentions and were actively giving, but "weren't seeing the results and impact one might hope." And then there was a third group "who hadn't yet found their pathway to engage, or if they had, were doing it at a scale that maybe could be magnified quite substantially."

Rosen was being diplomatic in this description. In fact, among America's ultra-rich, there were—and are—a shockingly large number of people who've barely given away any money at all. In a *New York Times Magazine* article in 2006, the philosopher Peter Singer had called out U.S. billionaires for not giving enough even as millions of people died from preventable diseases in poor countries. Singer had even gone after the wealthy who were giving at a large level, including Bill Gates himself, for not doing as much as they could. (Singer wondered aloud why Gates was living in a 66,000-square-foot house valued at over $100 million when that money could be used to save more lives.)

You didn't have to agree with Singer's metrics of obligation to see that he had a point. The increase of wealth at the top of America had gotten obscene—especially compared to how little of that money was being used for the benefit of society. Something had to be done.

But what? After kicking around ideas internally for a while, the Gates team decided to put that question to a broader group. Warren Buffett had been mulling who might be part of the discussion, keeping a file of "Great Givers." The Gateses also had names of people they thought would be interested.

In March 2009, Bill Gates and Warren Buffett sent a jointly signed letter to David Rockefeller, saying that the two had been talking about philanthropy and wanted to get a dozen or so "like-minded people around one table to broaden the discussion." They asked Rockefeller—then ninety-five, and the surviving patriarch of one of the most philanthropic families in history—to co-host the conversation in New York. Rockefeller agreed. Invitation letters soon went out to such billionaire philanthropists as Eli Broad, Ted Turner, Charles Feeney, George Soros, Pete Peterson, Oprah Winfrey, and Michael Bloomberg. Some of these people, such as Feeney and Bloomberg, had already said publicly that the bulk of their wealth would go to philanthropy.

Most of those invited to the meeting agreed to come, and in May, a group of a dozen or so convened for an afternoon and dinner at the President's House at Rockefeller University in New York. Going around the table, everyone shared their story of how they'd gotten into large-scale giving—along with some of the emotional challenges they'd encountered along the way. Buffett would say after the meeting that it made him feel like a psychiatrist.

Later, over dinner, the group discussed how to increase giving, batting around different ideas. That same topic would be chewed over at a second dinner in November 2009, held at the New York Public Library, as well as a third dinner in December, at a swanky hotel in Silicon Valley. Another recurring theme was anxiety among some participants—about whether they could handle the demands of giving so much or ensure that their money would be well spent.

One idea that eventually gained traction was a campaign that asked the super-wealthy to take a pledge to engage in large-scale philanthropy. The concept, said Rosen, was to "have people make a substantial commitment, and put it out there as a model for others to follow." Eventually this jelled further, into a "Giving Pledge"—to eventually donate at least half of one's wealth to philanthropy. That share was always seen as a minimum or floor. The pledge wouldn't be legally binding, but rather a statement of intent. Only billionaires would be asked to join this ultra-exclusive new club.

Buffett and the Gateses began making calls to sell the pledge in June 2010, getting in touch with seventy or eighty people—a sizeable slice of America's billionaires. George Kaiser, an Oklahoman who'd made his fortune in oil and finance and was a huge fan of the pledge idea, pitched in to help sell it, as did the eBay billionaire Jeff Skoll. Those who said yes were asked to submit letters that would appear on a website. Buffett and the Gateses took the Giving Pledge public in June 2010, which attracted more commitments, and by the time they rolled it out officially in a press conference in August, forty families and individuals had signed on.

The list included many of those who'd been part of the initial dinners, plus many others. Some of the names had long been fixtures on the Forbes 400, like Ronald Perelman, T. Boone Pickens, George Lucas, and Larry Ellison. Others were less familiar, like John and Laura Arnold, a young couple giving away a finance fortune, and Tashia and John Morgridge, whose giving was powered by money John had made running Cisco, the tech company. The pledgers represented nearly every major sector of the economy: finance, tech, entertainment, real estate, retail, and oil and gas.

Just a few months later, in December 2010, it was announced that another seventeen people were joining the Giving Pledge, including Mark Zuckerberg and Priscilla Chan. The campaign would grow from there, eventually going global and coming to include some 150 signatories. *Fortune* would call it the "biggest fundraising drive in history."

BIG MONEY LOOKING FOR BIG IMPACT

Although the Giving Pledge would become well-known, and was even featured on *60 Minutes*, the actual mechanics of the campaign have received little attention. From the start, the idea was not just to get America's richest people to promise big bucks for charity; it was also to help these pledgers to give effectively.

Olivia Leland became the first director of the Giving Pledge, working with a small staff to forge a community out of a far-flung group of billionaire philanthropists who, for the most part, didn't know one another. Leland would hold that position during the project's formative years, through 2014. She was succeeded by Rob Rosen.

The effort to build community has had several components. Staff bring together pledgers in an annual conference, as well as in smaller sessions and conference calls at other times. Rosen told me that the Gates Foundation has aimed to find ways to connect pledgers "through a shared learning environment so that they could be inspired and supported to find the particular areas where they wanted to be engaged and supporting mechanisms to help accelerate that and have greater impact."

Given their wealth, pledgers are grappling with the challenge of giving on an outsized scale. But the basic questions they confront are shared by philanthropists at many levels. One question, said Rosen, is "to what?" Donors often need help figuring out what causes or issues to contribute to. A second question is "how?" Donors want to know how to choose a vehicle for giving, set a strategy, and measure results. A third area where pledgers need support, one that is fuzzier than the first two but still crucial, is how philanthropy fits in with the rest of their lives.

All these issues get attention at the annual retreats, which usually take place in late spring and attract over half of the pledgers. The first retreat was held in 2010, the year the pledge launched, and there was uncertainty as to whether such conferences would make sense, given how busy people were. The retreat took place at Miraval, a luxury resort in the desert outside Tucson, Arizona. Leland said it was a bit awkward at first, since most participants were strangers to one another—and yet some of the billionaires were well-known figures. That meeting showed that pledgers did, in fact, have a strong appetite for shared learning—especially among those newer to philanthropy. The retreats have been going strong ever since.

These events take place over a day and a half that is jammed with presentations and discussions. The matter of where to give gets taken up in panels that dive into specific issues, looking at the ways philanthropic dollars can make a difference. One year a top topic was supporting scientific research, an area that generated a lot of interest and led to a follow-up session after the retreat. Conversations about how to give are also a staple of the retreats—including, at one session, a staged debate for and against creating foundations that exist in perpetuity.

Meanwhile, the bigger question of where philanthropy fits into people's lives always comes up. Giving away billions of dollars is no easy task, and some pledgers struggle with the work required to fulfill their commitment of giving so much to charity. "Actually making sure the resources are deployed to have great impact is a challenge to figure out, and it takes significant time and effort," said Rosen.

One thing to understand about the Giving Pledge is that even most of those who joined years ago have made little or no dent in disposing of their fortune. Despite all the attention the pledge has gotten, its full effects are unlikely to be felt for years to come. Much bigger giving than we've yet seen by these billionaires is required for them to meet their commitments.

This gusher of new money will transform philanthropy in coming years. The U.S. billionaires who've signed the Giving Pledge have almost as much money as the combined assets of *all* the U.S. foundations that now exist, over ninety thousand of them. The joint net worth of just Gates and Buffett alone is greater than the assets of the top twenty-five U.S. foundations (excluding Gates's own foundation). And while these two men have succeeded in orchestrating the Giving Pledge, both now have a lot more money than they did in 2010, as do most of the others who joined the pledge early on. Getting rid of that money will be no easy thing.

Bill and Melinda Gates have said they will give away all the money in their foundation within twenty years of when the last one dies, at which point the foundation will close its doors. Right now, that sum—along with their private investments—amounts to around $120 billion. But if you add in the money Buffett has pledged to the Gates Foundation, we're talking about an even higher figure—over $150 billion. At some point, moving money at this scale will likely require the world's biggest foundation to get even larger, increasing an annual grantmaking level that already far exceeds that of any other funder by a large margin.

As the Giving Pledge fully plays out, though, the Gates Foundation is unlikely to remain such a lonely giant. Oracle founder Larry Ellison was among the first batch of pledgers, revealing in his letter that years earlier he had already earmarked 95 percent of his wealth to go into a philanthropic trust when he dies. If the tech billionaire died tomorrow, the Lawrence Ellison Foundation could soon emerge as an entity on a par with the Gates Foundation. George Soros didn't sign the Giving Pledge, but has indicated that the Open Society Foundations will absorb the vast bulk of a fortune that currently stands at $26 billion and that, given his investing record to date, could be much larger by the time Soros dies. Then there is the financier Carl Icahn, worth some $17 billion. In joining the Giving Pledge, Icahn wrote that he'd decided years earlier that "substantially all of my assets would be used to fund a charitable foundation." When it one day comes into being, that foundation may be bigger than the Ford Foundation.

Mike Bloomberg hasn't expressed much interest in leaving behind a large foundation and instead has been on a tear to give while he's still alive. The problem is that he's not yet giving nearly enough. For all his big gifts in the past few years, he'll need to get money out the door at a much faster rate to ever fulfill his Giving Pledge. Bloomberg would need to give over $1 billion a year for three decades straight to do so—that is, assuming he doesn't get richer over time, as he has in the past. Zuckerberg, who may well get much richer in coming decades, faces an even more monumental challenge in disposing of his Facebook fortune.

Gifts by living wealthy donors constitute less than a quarter of all annual charitable giving, which totaled $373 billion in 2015. The rest comes mainly from ordinary individuals, private foundations, and corporations—which is a reminder that there's a lot else happening in philanthropy beyond this book's focus on the ultra-rich. In particular, legacy foundations—including big national players like Ford and MacArthur, and funders who are locally focused—play a big role in shaping what's happening in the nonprofit sector, yet I don't cover their activities in this book. I should also stress that it's not yet clear whether the new wave of giving by wealthy donors will increase the overall level of charitable giving in the United States, which has remained stuck for decades at around 2 percent of GDP.

What is clear is that this growing river of money will dramatically expand the size and influence of a new power elite of living donors that already wields enormous clout. One analysis by the scholar Kristin Goss found that nearly half of America's top two hundred philanthropists—including many Giving Pledge members—have expressed an interest in shaping public policy. The pages ahead dive into the many ways they are already doing exactly that.

GOVERNMENT DOWN

In fall 2010, the same year the Giving Pledge launched, Republicans took control of both houses of Congress and a majority of statehouses. The new majorities, brought to power by Tea Party activists and record campaign spending by wealthy donors, set out to enact sweeping cuts to government spending. The next several years in Washington would see recurrent budget battles and brinksmanship, including a shutdown of the federal government and a near default on the national debt. When the smoke had cleared, though, Congress had enacted long-term budget cuts totaling over $3 trillion. As a result, the funds that the federal government has available to try new things and solve problems—not to mention sustain basic services—are now forecast to shrink steadily through the foreseeable future.

The ax has fallen in recent years across every area of discretionary spending, from scientific research to Head Start to environmental protection. In 2016, the share of the federal budget going to non-defense domestic discretionary spending, measured as a percentage of GDP, shrank to 3 percent. One analysis stated: "The share of national income going to these programs—in education, science, infrastructure, environment, medical care for veterans, human services, homeland security, and other fields—is rapidly approaching the lowest level (measured as a share of the economy) in at least five decades."

The last time federal officials had so little discretionary money to work with, relative to the size of the nation's economy and population, Dwight Eisenhower was in the White House. But more cuts are predicted, and bigger ones, too. Non-defense discretionary spending is projected to fall to 2.2 percent of GDP by 2024—a long slide from a high of over 5 percent in the 1970s. And the decline is likely to continue for decades.

Quite apart from the legacy of the Tea Party, the public sector is facing intense fiscal pressure from two long-term trends. First, mandatory spending on seniors is set to explode as more and more boomers retire and start relying on Social Security and Medicare. Outlays for these and other entitlements is projected to nearly double in the next decade alone to more than $4 trillion annually. Second, interest payments on America's vast national debt will spike upward, to $900 billion annually by 2026, nearly four times higher than current levels. By 2046, it's projected that— absent major reforms—mandatory spending will consume 21 percent of GDP, about the same level as *all* federal spending in 2016.

Things won't be much better at the state level, where many employee pension systems have been woefully underfunded, and now face long-term shortfalls of nearly $1 trillion, according to a 2015 study by the Pew Charitable Trusts. Top cities are also in the red, like New York, which had $46 billion in unfunded pension liabilities in 2014. States and localities have loads of other debt, too, thanks to the liberal use of bond measures over many years—and all told now have $3.7 trillion in outstanding debt.

Even if big reforms do happen—say, a combination of tax hikes and spending cuts—the discretionary resources that government can deploy to tackle social or environmental problems are likely to keep falling for many years to come. In future decades, government is likely to spend much of its money cutting checks for seniors and bondholders.

Meanwhile, philanthropic giving is projected to keep rising as far as the eye can see, at least in raw numbers. And if such giving also rises as a share of GDP, beyond 2 percent, it could equal or surpass the percentage of national wealth going to federal non-defense discretionary spending within the next few decades, which would be a striking milestone. Following World War II, government was always the richer, more powerful actor in partnerships with philanthropy—the sector that could take the ideas incubated with private funding and bring them to scale. In a future that's already arriving in some areas, as we'll see, it may be philanthropy that is often holding the fatter checkbook.

A fiscal squeeze isn't the only problem facing government. Public institutions often aren't effective change agents because of lumbering bureaucracies and political dynamics that have grown ever more dysfunctional. While decades of conservative assaults have badly damaged public agencies, signs abound of a deeper calcification of government—which the journalist Jonathan Rauch has described as "demosclerosis." In Rauch's telling, the public sector is no longer so good at innovation. "The way for governments to learn what works in a changing world is to try various approaches and quickly abandon or adjust the failures: trial and error," Rauch writes. But that's become harder to do as myriad interest groups have become ever better at defending failed or unnecessary programs— from anachronistic farm subsidies to ineffective urban enterprise zones. "In Washington, every program is quasi-permanent, every mistake is written into a law that some vested interest will defend furiously. The result is that as the old clutter accumulates, government cannot adapt." Rauch wrote these words more than two decades ago. Things have only gotten worse since then.

In the past few years, trust in government has sunk to new lows amid spectacular failures and fresh reminders of public sector impotence. Just look at the problems revealed in the Veterans Administration or the bungled rollout of Healthcare.gov, a linchpin of Obamacare. Or look at California's efforts to build a high-speed rail system, an obvious need for a sprawling state choking in traffic. Finding the money to cope with ever ballooning costs has been only part of the challenge; equally daunting for the state has been overcoming lawsuits and environmental challenges to the rail line. Jerry Brown, the state's Democratic governor, has run into similar obstacles in trying to get more affordable housing built. Any number of other big public plans around the country have also struggled in recent years. As Philip Howard has written in his book *The Rule of Nobody,* this tends to happen because "no official has authority to make decisions." Instead, he writes, "Government is run by millions of words of legal dictates, not by the leaders we elect or the officials who work for them."

There remain plenty of bright spots in government, especially at the local level, where dynamic mayors are doing neat things. Overall, though, the public sector is not as inviting as it once was to people who aspire to make change.

Plenty of Americans still want to heed JFK's famous call to give back to their country. But many of the most ambitious would rather be on the payroll of philanthropy than the public sector.

One defense offered by today's mega-donors for their activist giving is that they're helping America get around demosclerosis—whether by out-flanking interest groups like the fossil fuel industry and teachers unions, or by financing the risky experiments that elected officials won't touch. This can-do mentality helps explain why the givers have so many champions even as a growing chorus of critics warn of creeping plutocracy. Ultimately, though, the power of the purse is the main factor that's moving philanthropists into the driver's seat of American life.

It should be pretty obvious why shrinking public resources and dyna-mism translate into more power for private philanthropists: because they're the people to whom social change makers and others will increasingly turn to finance new initiatives and existing services. Already this dynamic is playing out in multiple arenas like education, science, environmental conservation, and health care. If you have a big idea for improving society, chances are you'll get further by hitting up a billionaire to back it than by lobbying elected leaders. In fact, increasingly public officials themselves are turning to a private donor class to finance new projects.

This shift is occurring against the backdrop of another long-standing and better-known trend: the growing dominance of the wealthy over politics, which has reduced the voice of ordinary people when it comes to who gets elected and what laws get passed. In his 2012 book, *Affluence and Influence: Economic Inequality and Political Power in America*, the scholar Martin Gilens compared the preferences of different income groups with actual policy outcomes in Washington, D.C., to confirm an obvious point: that the responsiveness of elected leaders "is strongly tilted toward the most affluent citizens." Gilens found that the "preferences of the vast majority of Americans appear to have essentially no impact on which policies the government does or doesn't adopt." In his 2008 study, *Unequal Democracy*, Larry Bartels found that low-income Americans were especially impotent, writing: "The preferences of people in the bottom third of the income distribution have no apparent impact on the behavior of their elected officials."

Studies like this help explain why so many Americans have come to view U.S. society as rigged in favor of the rich: *Because it is,* and more people are catching on. One 2016 survey found that 65 percent of respondents agreed that "the economic system in this country unfairly favors powerful interests." Other polls have found the same thing, showing that Americans have grown deeply worried that the upper class has too much power.

Now, with the rise of big philanthropy, the wealthy are using an ever wider range of levers to turn their money into influence.

Some say this isn't a problem because the givers back a diversity of views, including the voices of low-income groups and environmental activists who otherwise wouldn't be heard. There's much truth to this, as we'll see later in the book. But research has also documented that the rich diverge sharply from the general public in how they view key issues. That's especially true when it comes to economic policy.

One survey, funded by the Russell Sage Foundation, found that the general public was much more likely than the wealthy to favor a higher minimum wage, expanded tax credits for low-income workers, and job creation efforts by government. The wealthy, for their part, are more prone to favor spending cuts to close budget deficits and to support free trade than is the general public. And they are far *less* likely to agree with a majority of Americans that the economic system is rigged in their favor. That 2016 survey mentioned earlier found that only 38 percent of respondents making over $100,000 a year thought the economic system was unfair, compared to 60 percent of middle-income people. Which makes sense: If the status quo is working just fine for you, you're less likely to question it. Meanwhile, on social issues, like gay marriage and abortion, and also on the environment, the affluent tend to be more liberal than the general public.

The rich really are different from the rest of us. And, lately, philanthropy has become a more popular and powerful way for them to advance views that aren't necessarily shared by their fellow citizens.

One other thing: even as more wealthy donors charge into the nonprofit sector, ordinary Americans—struggling with stagnant incomes and rising costs—have reduced their own giving, according to some analyses. A 2016 study of tax data found that since 2005, "charitable giving deductions from lower-income donors have declined significantly, and have been declining at almost the same rate that contributions from higher-income donors have increased. While itemized charitable deductions from donors making $100,000 or more increased by 40 percent, itemized charitable deductions from donors making less than $100,000 declined by 34 percent." Along with the rise of broader inequities in our new Gilded Age, civil society itself has become ever more dominated by the upper class.

These trends are troubling in a nation that prides itself on its egalitarian values. Yet the details of how the new philanthropy is actually affecting people's lives and U.S. society are complex. In some cases, the wealthy are wielding this power in ways that further reinforce their dominance—financially, politically, and culturally—and you don't need to look very hard to find self-interested giving. In other cases, their money is going to empower marginalized people, amplify new voices in the public square, or make headway against problems that have stymied elected officials. Often, what's happening is a murky mix. Even when wealthy donors are expanding debates, true to the spirit of pluralism, we can't forget that it's they who are choosing *which* voices and ideas get extra juice.

Cheerleaders for philanthropy see nearly everything the givers do as positive, while critics can be just as myopic and, at times, paranoid. The deeper I've dug into today's mega-giving, the more I've come to feel whiplashed between hope and fear. This is a trend that is profoundly exciting and inspiring—but also very scary if you're worried about civic equality in the world's oldest democracy.

2

Who Are These People?

Maybe twenty years ago, there was still such a thing as a philanthropy "establishment." It was centered in New York, with outposts in places like Chicago and Boston, and very much shaped by august institutions like the Ford and Rockefeller foundations, along with the Carnegie Corporation. There weren't many big funders on the West Coast or in the Southwest, and only a few individual mega-donors who were active.

Then, all hell broke loose. First came the rise of West Coast philanthropy in the late 1990s, with the emergence of several giant foundations rooted in tech wealth and bearing such names as Hewlett, Packard, and Gates. Next, a growing array of living mega-donors started to arrive on the scene, loaded with cash from boom times—not just in tech, but in finance, retail, media, real estate, and other areas. Many did things their own way—sometimes creating professional foundations, other times not. A massive gift from the publishing magnate Walter Annenberg in 1993 to improve public schools and, four years later, Ted Turner's $1 billion pledge to boost the United Nations, presaged a new era in which the super-rich deployed huge sums of money to achieve very specific goals. (With ever more wasted along the way, as some said about Annenberg's record education gift, which left hardly a trace in its wake.)

In just the past decade, the world of philanthropy has grown even more crowded with newcomers, further splintering it and ensuring its lack of any cohesive, shared mind-set. In turn, that fragmentation reflects what has happened with America's upper class as a whole. The stamped-ing wealth boom of recent decades, spread across many industries and regions, hasn't just vastly expanded the ranks of the rich; it's greatly diversified who these people are and how they think.

The wealthy are still almost entirely white, yet otherwise they are an ever more varied bunch. And so are the biggest givers.

Among today's top philanthropists are millennial techies who don't remember a time before the Internet—and octogenarian real estate bar-ons who grew up during the Great Depression and have never sent an e-mail. There are donors who didn't go to college—and those with a raft of degrees. There are those who got rich in a few short years, and those who've spent many decades building their fortunes. Some givers were born on third base, while many others are tapping self-made wealth.

Women have always played a huge role in philanthropy, but today that role is larger than ever, and an unprecedented number of women donors are giving away their own money or inherited wealth, as opposed to their husband's.

Today's philanthropists come in every political stripe, from far-right libertarian donors to progressive Democrats—with most somewhere in between. They are diverse in other ways, too. You'll find Christians and (many) Jews, and mega-donors from all parts of the country—well beyond the new economy hot spots.

Southwest oil money may sound like yesterday's news, but these for-tunes are now bigger than ever before—powering a growing wave of giv-ing that, among other things, is reshaping cities like Houston and Tulsa. In Chicago, old money and new money are working together to create a philanthropy boom town. The north woods of Maine have been roiled by controversy as one of the state's richest women has used her fortune to buy vast swaths of wilderness and push for a new national park. A top donor in Missouri has given millions to remake education and public policy in that state, while the heir to a chain of retail stores has used his grantmak-ing to move North Carolina's politics sharply to the right. The biggest arts philanthropist in America has focused her giving not in New York or Los Angeles, but in Arkansas. In Colorado, which is now home to five bil-lionaires with a combined net worth of nearly $40 billion, philanthropy is surging as never before. The same can be said about Washington State, which has twice as many billionaires today as it had a decade ago—and also more jockeying for influence among the super-rich on such issues as education and guns.

It's not so easy to generalize about all these people or their giving. There's an old saying that "if you've seen one foundation, you've seen one foundation," which reflects how idiosyncratic philanthropy often is and the diversity of causes and approaches that donors get behind. Lately, that's become all the more true.

WHY THEY GIVE

The path that donors take to large-scale giving can be wildly different. William Ackman, who became a billionaire through hedge funds, told me that he decided to become a philanthropist in college, long before he had any money, after reading the social justice theorist John Rawls. Another hedge fund billionaire, John Arnold, told me that his philanthropic journey began at a checkout aisle of the supermarket, when he saw a magazine touting the "fifty best nonprofits in America." Arnold, who was making a lot of money and thinking about giving back, bought the magazine and made his first $25,000 donation to one of the groups on the list. Still another finance billionaire, Steve Cohen, was slowly drawn into ever larger giving over many years. He shrugged when I asked him about a $275 million pledge he'd recently made, for veterans' mental health, his biggest ever. "It just seemed right," he said. His son, Robert, had served as a U.S. Marine in Afghanistan and had tipped Cohen off about the epidemic of suicides among returning soldiers.

Herb Sandler, a retired banker, told me about growing up Jewish on New York's Lower East Side and instinctively siding with the underdogs of the world. Later, after making a fortune in banking, he would act on his social justice beliefs in a big way. Eli Broad, the billionaire benefactor in Los Angeles, described to me his urge to give back to a city that has been so good to him. Shelby White, another philanthropist who directed millions to her hometown—in her case, Brooklyn—suggested something similar to me.

Robert Schulman, who'd gotten rich from hedge funds, said that his turn to giving flowed from the simple fact that he and his wife, Nancy, had more wealth than they needed. "We realized we had enough money," he told me. "We had an apartment in the city and a big house in Westchester. I was not interested in private planes or private boats.... Our children and our children's were not going to want for an education or a retirement."

Schulman said that, for many driven businesspeople, money is a "way to keep score." At some point, though, the actual usefulness of having more declines sharply. "The marginal utility of going from being worth twenty-nine million dollars to being worth thirty million is entirely different from the marginal utility of going from being worth one million to two million," he said. "The marginal utility of going to thirty million is close to zero. It's not going to change anything.... You can only eat at one good restaurant a night." As the money calculus changed, Schulman and his wife found themselves drawn more into philanthropy, eventually creating their own charity to help survivors of domestic violence and at-risk youths.

When the Giving Pledge started, one smart move of the Gates team was to ask each pledger to submit a public letter declaring their intentions. Olivia Leland, in coordinating the pledge, was struck by how seriously joiners took these letters, often going through many drafts to get them exactly right. The result is a growing treasure trove of quite personal documents that offer insights into the motives of some of America's biggest philanthropists.

Several themes run through the letters, starting with the sense of gratitude that Eli Broad mentioned. People who've done extraordinarily well are often very grateful to the institutions that have helped them along the way, as well as to the broader society in which they've thrived.

Brian Chesky and Joe Gebbia, the founders of Airbnb, who met at the Rhode Island School of Design, each described how that school had opened up their sense of possibility. Both aim to use some of their billions to ensure such experiences for others. "I want to devote my resources to bring the moment of instantiation, when someone who has an idea sees it become real, to as many people as I can," wrote Gebbia.

The hedge fund billionaire Glenn Dubin captured the sentiment of many pledgers in writing that "philanthropy is my way of giving thanks to the opportunities I had had and my personal attempt to perpetuate the American Dream." Priscilla Chan told me something similar, saying about her rise from an immigrant family to become a successful doctor: "I would never have had access to all those opportunities were it not for all

the people who supported me along the way. . . . I wanted to give back."
The idea that "with wealth comes responsibility," as another pledger put
it, is voiced often by top givers. One global study of high-net-worth individuals found that for nearly half who engage in philanthropy a "sense of
responsibility" is a top motive.

Another theme in the pledge letters is a keen awareness among these
billionaires of just how lucky they've been and, by contrast, how many
people are unlucky. Warren Buffett has famously attributed much of his
success to "winning the ovarian lottery"—that is, being born as a white
male to middle-class parents in an America on the cusp of the postwar
boom. George Kaiser, the son of Jewish refugees from Germany who had
gone into the oil business in Oklahoma, said much the same thing: "I
suppose I arrived at my charitable commitment largely through guilt,"
he wrote. "I recognized early on, that my good fortune was not due to
superior personal character or initiative so much as it was to dumb luck.
I was blessed to be born in an advanced society with caring parents. . . .
As I looked around at those who did not have these advantages, it became
clear to me that I had a moral obligation to direct my resources to help
repair that inequity."

Many pledgers point to their parents' generosity to explain their own
commitment to giving. Sidney Kimmel, who made his fortune in apparel
before moving into the entertainment industry, wrote: "I learned as a
young boy that sharing with others is the right thing to do, a lesson I
observed from my father's willingness to share even our meager means
with those less fortunate." Pete Peterson remembered his father, who
owned a Greek diner, "feeding countless numbers of hungry poor who
came knocking on the back door of his restaurant." Lynn Schusterman
wrote: "I was raised in a household in which giving back was a core value.
One of my fondest childhood memories is holding my father's hand as he
visited less fortunate elderly people who had no one else to care for them."

The study of the global wealthy mentioned earlier found that the most
often cited reason for giving was "personal fulfillment," and that point
comes up a lot in pledge letters. Peterson wrote: "As I watched and learned
from my father's example, I noticed how much pleasure his giving to others gave him. Indeed, today, I get much more pleasure giving money to

what I consider worthwhile causes than making the money in the first place. As I checked with other philanthropists, I found this was a very common experience." Indeed, it is. Bill Ackman wrote: "Over the years, the emotional and psychological returns I have earned from charitable giving have been enormous. The more I do for others, the happier I am. The happiness and optimism I have obtained from helping others are a big part of what keeps me sane."

The psychological returns from philanthropy are well documented. "It is a fact that givers are happier people than non-givers," wrote Arthur Brooks, an expert on giving who now leads the American Enterprise Institute. Brooks cited a range of research, including studies that have shown how giving affects one's brain chemistry, producing a "Helper's High." The positive mental returns from giving explain how initial modest philanthropy can snowball into something much bigger. Bill Gates has expressed deep satisfaction in a vast philanthropic enterprise that, to the outside, can look rather joyless and technocratic. "It's the most fulfilling thing we've ever done," Bill Gates has said about his and Melinda's large-scale giving.

Ed Scott, who made a fortune in Silicon Valley, in the unsexy niche of "middleware," told me about the immense pleasure he got from his first real gift. He made it through his church, after his pastor spoke one Sunday about a congregant who was a low-income single mother. A waitress, she struggled to get around by bus and juggle the demands of caring for two children, one of whom was disabled, while working eight-hour shifts. Listening in the pews, Scott and his wife thought the solution to her woes was pretty obvious: she needed a car. So the Scotts anonymously donated money to buy her a minivan. They learned in a later sermon how it had transformed her life. "I saw things differently from that point forward," Scott said.

Before then, Scott had been laser-focused on his business career. "My goal was one thing: make money. That's all I thought about. I was just like everybody else. I was interested in going to work, getting the stock options, and getting the big hit. If anyone had told me to care about something else, I would have said, 'Get out of my face. You're crazy.'"

But after he sold a company he had helped start and scored a few other big hits, Scott was set for life—and then some. "I made more money, way more, than I ever thought I'd make in my wildest dreams." Scott had only a limited interest in spending that money on personal things. He told me: "I realized that unless you're a very greedy person, you can't actually spend more than ten or fifteen million dollars on yourself." So, starting with the minivan, he began to give away his extra money, and in larger and larger amounts, eventually becoming a leading donor to groups fighting global poverty and disease.

Other top philanthropists have spoken of their giving with a mixture of obligation and practicality—namely, that if you've somehow ended up with the means to try to solve big problems, you'd better get cracking.

The eBay billionaire Pierre Omidyar and his wife, Pam, wrote in their pledge letter: "Our view is fairly simple. We have more money than our family will ever need. There's no need to hold on to it when it can be put to use today, to help solve some of the world's most intractable problems." The Facebook co-founder Dustin Moskovitz wrote: "As a result of Facebook's success, I've earned financial capital beyond my wildest expectations. Today, I view that reward not as personal wealth, but as a tool with which I hope to bring even more benefit to the world." Paul Allen, the Microsoft co-founder, said much the same thing: "I believe that those fortunate to achieve great wealth should put it to work for the good of humanity." He added: "In recent years, I have felt a growing sense of urgency about the mounting challenges confronting our planet. Through my giving, I seek to tackle climate change, prevent dangerous epidemics, save Earth's most iconic species from extinction and restore our oceans to health, before it's too late."

Melinda Gates has said simply: "It's the right thing to invest back in society if we want to have an equitable and just world, and if you've been lucky enough to have some extra wealth and income."

The sociologist Paul Schervish at Boston College has long explored how the wealthy think and why they give. He's said that, whereas most of us accept that we can't much change the world around us, and so we live within existing institutions, the wealthy are far more likely to believe they actually *can* change the terms of society. "Great expectations and grand aspirations occupy people across the financial spectrum," Schervish writes. "What is different for wealth holders is that they can be more legitimately confident about actualizing their expectations and aspirations."

Schervish describes this as a sense of "hyperagency," which he calls "the fundamental class trait of the rich," and a key to understanding these people—and their philanthropy.

That sense of hyperagency can certainly be found in the Giving Pledge letters, many of which are filled with proud details of the impact that pledgers have already had with their giving. "One of the most memorable moments in my life was at a charity dinner I was attending for a breast cancer cause," wrote Ronald O. Perelman, who'd made his billions through a sprawling conglomerate. "A woman approached me and said, 'I just wanted to say thank you—because of you my sister is alive.'"

Perelman went on to describe the backstory: About how he'd met a cancer researcher, Dennis Slamon, who was doing groundbreaking work but was unable to find enough funding for a critical study. "The idea of funding this immediately appealed to me. I have always been interested in giving to projects that may not get done otherwise. . . . I asked Dr. Slamon what he needed and then told him to get to work." The result of that research was Herceptin, a breakthrough drug for treating certain types of breast cancer.

Other philanthropists tell similar stories—about seeing a problem or opportunity and then taking action that makes a difference. Ed Scott recalled to me how he convinced an international aid group he worked with, Compassion Africa, to begin a more aggressive testing and treatment program for the HIV-infected children it worked with, many of whom were expected to die. He put up $750,000 as seed funding for the effort, which included hiring a top immunologist. Other donors eventually followed. Scott believes his intervention ultimately saved numerous lives.

Few ordinary people will ever have such an experience—of knowing that other people are living because we did something to give them that chance. When giving has impact, the empowerment that comes from it tends to spur greater giving.

Laura Arnold—who along with her husband John, a former hedge fund manager, has given away over $700 million since 2011—told me that the amazing thing about having a foundation is that you can move beyond grumbling privately about the problems you read about in the newspaper. "We love the fact that we're able to do something about it," Arnold said. "Instead of just being outraged, we try to channel that outrage into a solution that we think is constructive and a better alternative.

Alexandra Cohen, who's also helping give away a multi-billion-dollar hedge fund fortune, told me she had the "best job in the world" because she doesn't have to be an idle bystander to suffering or misfortune. She can take action and "make a difference in someone else's life." Like so many philanthropists, Cohen learned to give from her parents—or more, precisely, her working-class mother, who always had an eye out for needy neighbors in their impoverished Puerto Rican neighborhood in Manhattan. Cohen came to be the same way when she grew up, with a reflex to help solve people's problems. Yet now—thanks to her marriage to Steve Cohen—she has an almost fantastical ability to do so. That might entail giving $3,000 to a waitress down on her luck at her favorite IHOP, as Cohen once did. Or giving $50 million to build a new pediatric emergency department at New York Presbyterian Hospital.

The Cohens haven't signed the Giving Pledge, but are likely to give away much of their wealth—which now stands at $13 billion. That pile is three times greater than the Rockefeller Foundation's endowment. It will almost certainly grow larger still in coming years.

Anyone with a bit of spare cash can read a story in the paper—about, say, gun violence or melting ice caps—and then write a check to an outfit working for solutions. What's different about the rich is that they can give on a scale, and with an impact, that most people can't imagine. Schervish writes: "Those of us who are not wealthy pool our charitable gifts with those of others, and many of our gifts are anonymous. But wealth-holders, instead of simply being participants in a charitable effort, can create new charitable organizations or operating foundations on their own. What takes a social movement for ordinary people to accomplish, wealth-holders can do relatively single-handedly. They don't just find worthy charitable causes; they found them."

That said, even the wealthiest donors—if they're smart—know there are acute limits to their power. You might imagine those rarefied annual retreats that bring together Giving Pledge members as suffused with hubris. But Melinda Gates has described people's attitudes in those meetings as "very humble." She explained: "If you're in the area of philanthropy, the problems are so large and you know you're only a small piece of trying to figure this out."

A final motive for big-league giving worth flagging is that many wealthy people aren't keen to see much of their fortunes one day going to estate taxes—or, maybe even worse, being passed down to their children.

No billionaire has spoken out more strongly than Warren Buffett about the corrosive nature of inherited wealth. As early as 1986, Buffett told *Fortune* magazine that the ideal amount of inheritance to leave your kids was "enough money so that they would feel they could do anything, but not so much that they could do nothing." That sum, he estimated at the time, was probably a "few hundred thousand dollars." Later, when Buffett pledged most of his wealth to the Gates Foundation, he said: "I'm not an enthusiast for dynastic wealth, particularly when 6 billion others have much poorer hands than we do in life."

Bill and Melinda Gates read the *Fortune* article before they were married, and agreed strongly with Buffett. Bill has written: "Melinda and I are strong believers that dynastic wealth is bad for both society and the children involved. We want our children to make their own way in the world. They'll have all sorts of advantages, but it will be up to them to create their lives and careers."

Mike Bloomberg has been even more forceful on this point: "Inheriting too much money at one time destroys initiative, distorts reality, and breeds arrogance." Another billionaire, John W. Jordan II, echoed that sentiment in his Giving Pledge letter: "While I have taken care of my children and want them to enjoy comfortable lives, I do not believe that those who provide their offspring with luxuriously upholstered lives serve them well but rather saddle them with a terrible burden. The trappings of extreme wealth are quite dangerous if not intelligently and responsibly directed. . . . We all know second and third generation wealth where the recipients were actually born on third base but think and act like they hit a triple."

The core motives that the rich have for giving help explain the "why" of their philanthropy. But the context of their lives plays a huge role in explaining the "how" of that giving.

The sociologist Francie Ostrower spent years in the 1990s looking into this area, first as a graduate student and later as a professor at Harvard. Elite philanthropists, she wrote in her book *Why the Wealthy Give,* "live in a milieu in which giving is the norm, and characterize philanthropy as an obligation that is part of their privileged position." Ostrower detailed the many ways that the wealthy are pulled into giving through a web of organizational and social ties.

An attention to status is definitely part of the equation. Philanthropy functions as "a mark of class status that is connected to elite identity," Ostrower writes. How giving plays out, though, in terms of what donors support, depends on the affiliations they have. For example, Jewish donors have their own strong networks, with set norms and favored causes.

Schervish makes similar points. Donors are often spurred by a sense of identification with others, he writes, starting with people most like themselves, which is why so much charity tends to flow to institutions that donors have a direct connection with, particularly religious institutions, arts organizations, and schools. But identification can also take the form of empathy for the less fortunate, especially for donors who've struggled at points in their life.

One way to get a handle on the newer philanthropists—and how they wield influence—is to look at how they got rich in the first place. When the wealthy get into giving they tend to turn to friends for guidance, who are often peers in their industry. They may kick in for the same causes, use the same philanthropic advisors, and embrace the same approaches as others around them. If you want to better understand today's new donors, a good place to begin is with the philanthropic tribes they belong to.

TECH PHILANTHROPISTS

No industry is producing more big new donors these days than tech, which has spawned enormous fortunes in an era of rapid digital breakthroughs and expanding global markets. Who are these people and how do they think about philanthropy?

The first thing to understand is that there have been two waves of tech philanthropy. The first was in the 1990s, when some of the top fortunes of the early computer boom were harnessed for giving. Bill Hewlett and David Packard both endowed massive foundations, and in 2000, another industry pioneer, Intel's Gordon Moore, gave $5 billion to create a foundation. That same year, the Bill and Melinda Gates Foundation was launched, seeded with a $27 billion gift from the couple. Gates's early partner in founding Microsoft, Paul Allen, had started a foundation in 1988 but stepped things up as the new century began with big giving for brain research. Pierre Omidyar and Jeff Skoll of eBay were two other tech winners who turned to large-scale philanthropy during this period, as did Quark founder Tim Gill and GeoCities founder David Bohnett, both with a focus on LGBT rights.

Steve Case, the co-founder of AOL, started his foundation in 1997, with his wife, Jean. Michael Dell, the PC computer billionaire, also worked closely with his wife, Susan, to create a foundation that got going in 1999. Another tech titan turned philanthropist from that go-go era is John Morgridge, who built Cisco Systems into a giant in the 1990s—and then sank the bulk of his winnings into a foundation he ran with his wife, Tashia. The couple who had founded Cisco, Sandy Lerner and Leonard Bosack, made far less money than Morgridge did—and ended up giving most of it away. Irwin Jacobs, the billionaire who founded Qualcomm in the 1980s, also went on to become a major philanthropist. A range of other early tech winners also became donors, like Mitch Kapor, the founder of Lotus.

The second wave of tech philanthropy has unfolded since about 2010. That was the year Mark Zuckerberg made his $100 million pledge to improve Newark's schools. Two other Facebook billionaires soon joined Zuckerberg in large-scale giving: Sean Parker, who set up a major new foundation in 2015 and has emerged as a large-scale donor to medical research; and Dustin Moskovitz, who is moving growing sums of money through the foundation he set up with his wife, Cari Tuna. The couple plan to give away all their wealth while they're still alive.

Facebook riches have also been channeled to philanthropy through Jan Koum, who put aside $600 million in a donor-advised fund after scoring a huge windfall from the sale of WhatsApp to Facebook in 2014. That same year, Oculus co-founder Brendan Iribe gave $31 million to the University of Maryland, which he had dropped out of, after selling Oculus to Facebook. Jim Swartz, whose firm, Accel, was one of the earliest investors in Facebook, is now deeply engaged in philanthropy with his wife, Kathy.

Meanwhile, the billionaire founder of Salesforce, Marc Benioff, has lately emerged as a leader of the tech philanthropic community in the

Bay Area, working with his wife, Lynne, to make huge gifts for hospitals and seeking to rally other donors to give more in the region. Benioff is also pushing tech start-ups nationwide to set aside a chunk of their firm's equity for philanthropy, as he did when founding Salesforce. Both the Google co-founders, Sergey Brin and Larry Page—who together have a net worth of more than $75 billion—have started setting aside sizeable chunks of wealth for philanthropy. Brin parted with $850 million between 2011 and 2014, funds that helped build up a large foundation and support a wide array of causes. Page, who gave away $177 million in 2014 alone—including $15 million in emergency funds to combat Ebola—has also been quietly building up a major foundation, which is named after his father. It now has well over $1 billion in assets. Eric Schmidt is a third Google billionaire plowing big bucks into philanthropy, working with his wife, Wendy, to sound the alarm on environmental threats, among other interests.

Any number of other tech people are also giving, at varying levels, such as Twitter co-founders Evan Williams and Jack Dorsey; PayPal co-founder Peter Thiel; the venture capitalist Marc Andreessen; the angel investor Ron Conway; LinkedIn founder Reid Hoffman; and Tesla's Elon Musk, who's giving interests include taming the "existential threat" posed by artificial intelligence. Beyond these big names, plenty of other tech winners have lately been turning to philanthropy, such as Mike Krieger, who started Instagram. Along with his wife, Kaitlyn, Krieger is putting money behind criminal justice reform, among other issues. The couple has been helped along in this work by the philanthropic operation piloted by Cari Tuna and Dustin Moskovitz.

Quite a few of today's younger tech donors are in touch with one another and, increasingly, have a shared outlook on philanthropy.

For starters, most believe in starting to give early. "People wait until late in their career to give back. But why wait when there is so much to be done?" Zuckerberg said after he joined the Giving Pledge in December 2010. "With a generation of younger folks who have thrived on the success of their companies, there is a big opportunity for many of us to give back earlier in our lifetime and see the impact of our philanthropic efforts."

Zuckerberg made his first big gift before Facebook even went public, and he's not the only tech entrepreneur who is turning to philanthropy while still very much engaged in business. More wealthy techies want philanthropy to complement their careers, as opposed to something they turn to later, after they've made their bundle. And they're being egged on by other techies to give early. "There's no better time to start than the present," wrote Sean Parker in an essay on "philanthropy for hackers" in the *Wall Street Journal*, around the time he put $600 million into his foundation.

This sense of urgency stands in sharp contrast to the past. Early tech titans like Bill Hewlett and Gordon Moore waited until retirement to ramp up their giving. Bill Gates didn't establish his foundation until after he'd been running Microsoft for over twenty years.

Not so today's techies. And it's not just that the younger tech donors want to start earlier; many want to move faster, too, with some aiming to give away all of their money in their lifetimes. These folks aren't interested in creating foundations that exist in perpetuity, long a common choice among donors.

Why the focus on moving big money sooner rather than later? The top reason is to have more impact. In particular, tech donors like Dustin Moskovitz have stressed the value of deploying resources early to solve problems that will otherwise grow and become harder to solve later.

This readiness to give early, and give big, is already amplifying the influence of tech philanthropists, as we've seen with Zuckerberg—a person, of course, who already wields immense power through a business that reaches 1.7 billion people. In earlier times, a young entrepreneur would never have tried to shake up K–12 education with a $100 million gift just six years after starting his company. But get ready for more of that kind of thing.

Another trait of tech philanthropists that amplifies their influence is how they scout out causes. In Silicon Valley, you often make your fortune by solving a problem that nobody else has solved—or, ideally, is even working on. Many techies are bringing the same mind-set to their philanthropy. "I talk to a lot of clients about identifying the gaps," said Nick Tedesco, who works at JPMorgan Chase's Philanthropy Center in San Francisco and advises emerging donors. Before that, he was with the Giving Pledge team at the Gates Foundation, where he came to know many top philanthropists and their different styles.

Tech donors are less interested in fortifying existing institutions and causes, and more intent on "putting their philanthropic capital into underfunded areas," Tedesco told me. They ask "Where is there a lack of funding and where can my funding have an impact." These givers also put a big focus on "catalytic philanthropy. People are looking to back systemic philanthropy that attacks problems at their root causes and not just treat the symptoms."

The hunger to change whole systems is nothing new in philanthropy. The earliest entrepreneurs who become philanthropists, including Rockefeller and Carnegie, were chasing the same goal with their money. And the staff of plenty of legacy foundations, like Ford, think in similar terms. That said, most of today's philanthropists aren't so ambitious and, instead, tend toward a more cautious, stewardship approach to giving. They direct money to universities, hospitals, art museums. Or they gravitate to groups already well along in trying to solve established problems, whether it's curbing climate change or reducing HIV infections.

Tech philanthropists do some giving along these lines. But their main interest is in leveraging their money to create change on a grand level. That these donors think in such grandiose ways has made them an easy target of critics, often from philanthropy's old guard. Making change is not like creating software, say veteran funders—who've often been quick to cluck their tongues when efforts funded by Bill Gates or Mark Zuckerberg founder on the shoals of social complexity.

Tech donors aren't daunted by such disapproval. In their day jobs, failure is commonplace: nearly all tech superstars have at least one dud start-up or product under their belt. If something doesn't work, you learn what you can and try something else. There's even a conference, FailCon, dedicated to dissecting efforts that flopped.

While older foundations are hardly allergic to risk, and get a bad rap as invariably cautious, tech donors are more ready by disposition to embrace the adage that philanthropy "is society's risk capital." When they swing, they're more apt to be eyeing the fence. Some are looking for the philanthropic equivalent of a "unicorn" (a start-up that attains at least a billion-dollar valuation). This trait makes them more potentially powerful in society, and certainly more disruptive—in ways good and bad.

Another hallmark of Silicon Valley culture that the new donors bring to their philanthropy is a focus on learning from others and collaborating. As competitive as the tech world is, it's also a hugely collaborative place, where information flows widely and people build on one another's ideas. "Tech entrepreneurs understand the many is better than the one," Tedesco said. And as these people embrace philanthropy in a big way, they are looking to their peers for guidance and are engaged in lots of talking and comparing of notes.

Such collaboration is hardly unique in philanthropy but it's worth spotlighting to better understand how this community is evolving with their giving. It's not just that many more dollars are flowing out of Silicon Valley aimed at changing the world; it's that many more conversations are happening within it about how best to do that.

Many techies like to think they are on a grand mission to improve life on earth with new breakthroughs, and so philanthropy is a natural fit with their worldview. But the moral blind spots of these leaders can be enormous. For instance, Facebook and Google—companies that were founded by active philanthropists and that also engage in extensive corporate charity—have both engaged in elaborate tax avoidance schemes using offshore subsidiaries. Apple, which has lately been celebrated for its big turn toward philanthropy under CEO Tim Cook, is an even worse offender, pioneering new forms of tax avoidance that have allowed it to stash billions in profits in foreign tax havens, outside the reach of the U.S. Treasury.

One analysis found that Apple's tax avoidance schemes allowed it to avoid $2.4 billion in taxes in 2011 alone. Microsoft, Yahoo, Adobe, Netflix, and other tech companies have used the same strategies—resulting in huge losses in government revenue at a time when budget cuts are hurting many of the people and causes that tech philanthropists say they want to help.

WALL STREET WEALTH

Finance is another industry where vast new fortunes have been minted in recent years—a quarter of U.S. billionaires have made their money in this sector—and now big philanthropy has begun to follow.

You might think of this turn as signaling the emergence of a kinder, gentler finance sector, and partly that's so. Supposed greedheads are happily parting with far more of their money than most people might ever imagine. But philanthropy is also giving U.S. financial elites one more way to wield influence, expanding their reach into new areas of American life, such as education and public policy. No picture of Wall Street's immense power these days is complete without a grasp of the new, high-octane philanthropy emerging from this world.

For a long time, the hedge fund star George Soros was one of the few well-known philanthropists from finance. Then Warren Buffett emerged with his huge pledge to the Gates Foundation in 2006. By this time, too, the Robin Hood Foundation, which was started in 1988 to channel Wall Street donations to anti-poverty groups, was becoming far more visible, holding annual galas that raked in tens of millions of dollars.

More recently, a growing torrent of money has been coming from a wide array of finance donors. Over two dozen industry leaders have signed the Giving Pledge, including the top hedge funders Jim Simons and Ray Dalio—both of whom have ramped up their giving in recent years, parting with hundreds of millions of dollars. Between the two of them, though, they still have another $30 billion.

Then there is Stanley Druckenmiller, a retired hedge funder who gave away over $75 million in a recent year and has quietly built up a foundation with over a billion dollars in assets. Among other things, Druckenmiller is the single biggest backer of the Harlem Children's Zone. Julian Robertson, a billionaire in his eighties who was once known as the "Wizard of Wall Street," has been giving away as much as $100 million a year, with big checks going to environmental groups and education reform outfits. Denny Sanford made his fortune in credit cards and now is getting rid of it at a rapid rate, giving away nearly a billion dollars in the past decade. Charlie Munger scored big as Warren Buffett's partner—big enough that he's given away over $200 million since 2013. Steve Cohen has stepped up his philanthropy in the years since he survived a federal probe of insider trading at his hedge fund, giving away hundreds of millions of dollars, with his wife, Alex, taking the lead.

David Gelbaum has quietly given away much of his hedge fund fortune to liberal groups like the Sierra Club and the American Civil Liberties Union (ACLU), as well as to conservation and veterans' causes. Steve Schwarzman, the private equity billionaire, has made huge gifts that include $300 million for a U.S.-China scholars exchange program. David Rubenstein, another private equity winner, has been called a "patriotic philanthropist" because he has focused some of his giving on monu-ments, buildings, and documents of historic significance. Tom Steyer is a retired California hedge funder who has lately become a major player on climate policy. Paul Singer has bankrolled right-wing think tanks among other causes. John Paulson is the hedge funder who gave $400 million to Harvard and, before that, $100 million to the Central Park Conservancy.

Beyond these many philanthropists from finance, there are still others, including some of the billionaires already mentioned: John Arnold, a for-mer Enron trader who started a hedge fund and then retired to focus on philanthropy that aims to improve education, public pensions, health care, and more; Pete Peterson, whose money comes from private equity and is focused on public policy; Sanford Weill, the former head of Citi-group, who has given away more than $1 billion, mainly for hospitals and medical research; Herb Sandler, the progressive philanthropist who made his money from a savings and loan association; and Bill Ackman, who became a billionaire through his activist hedge fund investing and who now is taking an equally activist approach to philanthropy. A number of billionaires from finance have become well known for their support of charter schools and education reform groups, including Charles Schwab, Stephen Mandel, and Paul Tudor Jones. Jones had founded a charter school in the Bedford-Stuyvesant section of Brooklyn, New York, and later helped start the Robin Hood Foundation.

I could name many additional donors coming out of finance, like Jeremy Grantham, Seth Klarman, Louis Bacon, George Roberts, Glenn Dubin, Kenneth Griffin, Michael Milken, Henry Kravis, and Leon Black. What generalizations might we offer about this crowd, and about Wall Street philanthropy as a whole?

For starters, the scope of giving by finance leaders is surprisingly large. These people have a reputation for greed, and a zeal for making money that is so intense that ethics may fall by the wayside. That reputa-tion is well deserved, but philanthropic currents have long run through this world, and they've grown stronger in recent years. The growth of the Robin Hood Foundation, Wall Street's favorite charity, is a good barometer of what's been happening. That group pulled in $195 million in contributions in 2015, up from $64 million in 2005. Many of the largest financial firms have robust employee giving programs, and some have even required employees to contribute. Bear Stearns, the investment firm that collapsed in 2008, compelled employees to contribute 4 percent of their bonus money every year to charity. Goldman Sachs may well have produced more major philanthropists than any firm on Wall Street. Goldman givers include Henry Paulson and Larry Linden, both of whom focus heavily on the environment.

The biggest of the new finance donors, by far, are emerging from hedge funds and private equity—which makes sense, since that's where the greatest fortunes have been made. Yet even the most active of these philanthropists, like Simons and Dalio, have barely scratched the surface of their fortunes. Others take a more traditional approach, of leaving philanthropy to the end of their lives. Carl Icahn, as mentioned, has only given modestly so far, but has said that nearly all his money will go to charity. Then there is someone like David Tepper, who's worth $11 billion and has been an active philanthropist, but not yet at a level that can make a dent in his fortune. In short, whatever giving we're seeing now from Wall Streeters is nothing compared to what lies ahead.

(Here and throughout the book, I use the term Wall Street broadly, since finance is very much a national industry, and in the past decade it's grown greatly in places outside New York—as has the philanthropy fueled with finance dollars.)

This industry hasn't become just more national in the past decade or so; it's became more cerebral. A lot of the new finance money has been made using sophisticated strategies to predict the markets, and the hedge fund world in particular has some notably intellectual billionaires. Soros is the best known in this regard, as the author of numerous books and articles. Jim Simons ended up with $15 billion by parlaying his math genius into trading gains; he's the most successful of the so-called "quants" who have proliferated in finance, using quantitative skills to master markets. Plenty of other finance billionaires have gotten rich primarily by monetizing their intellectual prowess. Also key to this crowd's success has been predicting trends, using leverage, and being willing to make risky bets.

These traits help explain a few features of finance philanthropy: first, many of these donors understand complicated areas that involve science, such as climate change and medical research; second, they appreciate the importance of research and the role of expertise; third, they are often drawn to sophisticated grantmaking strategies developed with expert input; and fourth, some are ready to put big money behind efforts that may well fail. In these respects, the finance donors have some similarities with the techies.

Many philanthropists from Wall Street are quite ideological. They rank among the biggest backers of Washington think tanks and hard-hitting advocacy groups, as we'll see later in the book. They tend to have a keen faith in the power of markets to solve problems, which can drive their giving in various ways—most notably, the outsized support by Wall Streeters of the school choice movement. You can also see their belief in markets in other areas, like the environment, where they've sought to create new financial incentives for ecological progress, and on global development, where some see a huge potential for social enterprises to combat poverty, for example, through helping small farmers make more money.

These examples aside, Wall Street donors overall tend to be more drawn to a stewardship model of philanthropy than are the techies. For all the cowboys in finance, people mainly get rich in this industry by posting strong returns year after year, while steadily expanding the pile of money they're working with. That's different from tech, where you score big by conquering unsolved problems or blowing up existing industries. Finance types are more comfortable with the status quo, and a lot of their giving goes to boost elite universities, arts institutions, hospitals, and land conservation trusts. Compared to techies, they're more into charity than change.

Finance philanthropists are conservative in other ways, too. Traditional gender roles are more pronounced in this sector—in ways that play out in giving. Often, it's the men who make the money and the wives who give it away, dealing with day-to-day details when it comes to where to give and how much. While their husbands ascend to the pinnacles of finance, the wives climb to the peak of the social sector. Joan Weill may be the best example of this, serving on innumerable boards and committees of top nonprofits in New York, like the Alvin Ailey American Dance Theater, even as her husband became a leader in banking. This division of labor remains a good old-fashioned recipe for how to become a power couple. Still, it's best not to read too much into the fact that the wives often hold the checkbooks. Nearly all philanthropic couples set the overall direction of their giving jointly.

A last point about Wall Street philanthropy: Even more so than tech, the generosity of this community is marked by moral contradictions. Many of these donors have gotten so rich to begin with thanks to a financialization of the U.S. economy that some analysts believe has been a key driver of inequality. Instead of primarily serving the real economy as it once did, the argument goes, finance has come to focus more on its own profits—siphoning wealth *away* from the real economy and into the pockets of extravagantly paid middlemen.

Then there's the fact that massive wealth accumulation by many of finance's biggest winners—in hedge funds and private equity—has been fueled by historically low tax rates on capital gains for the past two decades, not to mention the "carried interest" loophole that has exempted some of their earnings from taxation as regular income. These tax policies cost the government many billions in revenue even as Washington budget cutters whack programs benefiting the same populations that, say, the Robin Hood Foundation seeks to help. Of course, the financial world also played a leading role in crashing the U.S. economy in 2008, with vulnerable low-income communities taking the biggest hit.

Yes, Wall Streeters are indeed giving at a record level—but with little acknowledgment of their role in fueling some of the problems their philanthropy is trying to solve.

When you look closely at today's top finance donors, you'll find that few of them, as individuals, had much to do with the meltdown of 2008 and many would be fine with paying higher taxes. Still, you can understand why the largesse of these folks doesn't exactly generate universal acclaim. Many Americans hold the far upper class, and especially Wall Streeters, responsible for the nation's deep economic woes—and aren't impressed when they sprinkle around a sliver of their vast winnings for charity. Nor is there universal enthusiasm when the crowd that brought us derivatives and synthetic CDOs sets out to fix public schools or end poverty in Africa.

TITANS OF THE OLD ECONOMY

Tech and finance have produced most of the largest fortunes in the past two decades, and in both sectors, creative and hard-driving leaders have often scored the biggest rewards. In turn, many of these people bring intense, restless energy to their philanthropy. Some come to wield far more influence through giving than they ever did in business—an important point to remember in thinking about wealth and power these days. What people do with their billions can affect society much more than how they made that money.

The titans of the old economy—rising in sectors like energy, real estate, and retail—have also become richer than ever during recent boom times, and many of them, too, have lately turned to philanthropy on an unprecedented scale, with implications for the rest of us. These donors are often less creative in their giving, but they well understand how to turn money into power.

The explosion of new wealth in the old economy over recent years is a story that has gotten little notice, with so much attention focused on Wall Street and Silicon Valley. In fact, these gains have been striking. As mentioned earlier, the Koch brothers have added some $70 billion to their combined fortunes since 2005 as the value of their industrial conglomerate has soared. That wealth exemplifies the riches that can still flow from such "dirty" businesses as oil refining and petrochemical production. While the Kochs have famously converted some of their wealth into hard political influence, through election spending, they've actually had greater impact by backing a wide array of libertarian and conservative policy institutes over many years. (More about that later.)

The wealth of the Walton family has also grown by an additional $70 billion or so since 2005, thanks to a rise in Walmart's stock, which helps explain why the Walton Family Foundation has moved to greatly expand its giving for charter schools, as well as to put in place a huge new environmental program. In fact, the Waltons now rank among the very largest green philanthropists in the United States—exerting a very different kind of influence here than in education, with a big focus on preserving rivers and waterways.

Look through the ranks of the Giving Pledgers and you'll find several oil tycoons who have far more money now than they did fifteen years ago (although less than they did five years ago, before oil prices crashed). One is Harold Hamm, who plans to devote his billions to fighting diabetes. He's bringing enough new money to this area to be a potential game changer. Another is Richard Kinder, an energy billionaire who is busy putting his stamp on Houston, exemplifying an approach to philanthropy that's popular among many old-economy billionaires—which is to focus locally and help remake particular cities and regions.

That's the strategy of George Kaiser as well, who also got his start in oil and later moved into finance. Now he's one of the most influential people in Oklahoma thanks to his philanthropy, which touches many corners of that state and particularly Tulsa. Eli Broad made his fortune in homebuilding and insurance—and has used it to help shape modern Los Angeles, as I'll discuss in more detail later.

In Boston, Amos Hostetter Jr., who founded an early cable television company in 1963, is the single biggest philanthropist in town, working with his wife, Barbara, through the influential Barr Foundation, which pumps money into education, the arts, and more. Philip Anschutz—who started out in oil and went on to build a corporate conglomerate—is now the top philanthropist in Colorado, supporting hundreds of nonprofits in Denver and across the state. In Chicago, Lester Crown became a billionaire by diversifying his father's material services company (think gravel) and now controls stakes in diverse companies, including the Chicago Bulls. Through his eighties, Crown remained a pillar of the Chicago establishment, a role solidified by his family's growing philanthropy, which touches many parts of life in the city. Arthur Blank made his fortune as the co-founder of Home Depot—and now ranks among the top philanthropists in Atlanta, a city where he also wields influence as owner of the Atlanta Falcons football team.

Most of these people are older, some in their eighties, and they've taken an old-school path to influence. They've made their money over many decades, not in a flash of inspiration in sectors with red-hot growth. They've devoted both their time and their wealth to issues in their communities—and have, in the process, emerged as key power players. Their philanthropic giving has often worked in tandem with political donations and civic leadership roles—a familiar recipe for influence that nowadays is fueled by ever more money, along with more ways to turn wealth into power.

These old-school types aren't interested in dazzling anyone with their creative brilliance. Some, like Hostetter, operate well out of the spotlight, exercising clout without leaving visible fingerprints—at least that the average citizen can see. Some don't mind being known as bulldozers. Eli Broad is highly visible and, by his own account, a man who will readily be "unreasonable" to get his way. That ability to twist arms served him well in building two Fortune 500 companies.

There is a big difference between getting rich over decades in the old economy, by building sprawling corporations or real estate empires, and getting rich quickly in tech or finance, where vast wealth can be generated with fairly small organizations, like hedge funds or Internet businesses. Big companies are more complex and bump up against a wider range of players in society. This path to wealth can entail endless wheeling and dealing—including with politicians and regulators—which results in a strong understanding of how power works across different sectors of society. So while old-economy barons may lack fancy new ideas for creating systemic change, they do know how to get stuff done—including against formidable odds.

One corner of the old economy to watch closely is real estate, where some tycoons are turning to big-time giving after decades of assembling vast property portfolios. In California, John Arrillaga and Richard Peery, two billionaires who made a fortune by becoming the biggest commercial landlords in Silicon Valley, are now emerging as one of the top philanthropists in that region, along with John Sobrato, another local real estate billionaire. In New York City, aging real estate barons like Stephen Ross, Leonard Stern, and Jerry Speyer have long exercised influence over the city's politics and development patterns. Now, as they step up their philanthropy, they're looming large in Gotham in other ways, too.

BUSINESS LESSONS

Nearly all the new mega-givers who have emerged in the past fifteen years have made their fortunes in business. But that background plays out in different ways for different donors. Some see the skills and mindset they used to build their wealth as all-important in shaping how they dispose of it. Sean Parker, for instance, has argued that technologists like himself will be successful in philanthropy to the degree they stay true to a "hacker" philosophy, which includes an anti-establishment bias, a belief in data, and "a nose for sniffing out vulnerabilities in systems." If they operate this way as philanthropists, which Parker intends to do, they could have a huge impact.

Many of the new donors embrace a venture investing mind-set. They believe that, to succeed as philanthropists, not everything they try has to work out. Rather, what they need are a few major hits—breakthroughs that can more than compensate for whatever flops occur along the way. Philanthropists who have made their money by placing big bets, like the hedge funder Bill Ackman, apply some of the same criteria they have used in investing to evaluating possible grants.

Other donors have sought to bring management strategies they used in business to solving social problems. Eli Broad, as I'll discuss later, has sought to improve public schools by recruiting and training new leaders for K–12 systems. Herb Sandler, who built a banking fortune with his wife, Marion, partly through acquiring other companies, shares Broad's focus on identifying and empowering strong leaders. Sandler is also a fanatic for due diligence, investigating philanthropic opportunities with the same rigor that allowed him and Marion to avoid missteps as they assembled a sprawling savings-and-loan empire. Michael Dell's foundation, based in Austin, Texas, and chaired by his wife, Susan, puts a big emphasis on data and metrics—both hallmarks of Dell Computer, which beat competitors in the PC market by keeping operating costs low and being a leader in supply chain efficiency. Larry Linden, the former Goldman Sachs partner mentioned earlier, has used his understanding of complex financial deals to pioneer new ways to preserve large swaths of rain forest. His small Manhattan-based foundation is a leader in conservation finance and environmental markets.

There are obvious risks when star business leaders turn to philanthropy, thinking they have some special edge over those who've come before them in trying to solve social problems. Just because you've built a Fortune 500 company or invented new software or beat the S&P doesn't mean you'll have the faintest clue about helping third-graders learn to read or bringing drinking wells to Africa.

The smart donors coming from business are acutely aware of this pitfall. "I'm not a person who says 'I built a great business therefore I know how to build a great philanthropy,'" Glenn Hutchins, a successful private equity investor, told me. "I'm very mindful that they are two very, very different kind of things."

Hutchins's father had worked overseas on issues of agriculture and rural poverty, and Hutchins himself grew up being taught that helping others was just what "you always did." But, watching his father, he'd also learned that tough problems weren't solved overnight by smart outsiders who parachuted in. "You need to have some degree of humility and perspective on which of your skills are applicable and which are not."

Many philanthropists could use more of Hutchins's humility. Chances are, though, that they'll end up plenty humble after they've been giving for a while. The more ambitious donors are, the more likely they are to fail as they take on dauntingly complex problems. There may be no philanthropist, for example, who has failed more often and more spectacularly than Bill Gates. The fact that he's unfazed by missteps that have cost hundreds of millions of dollars may reflect how he experienced even greater failures leading Microsoft, such as spending big to develop new products that flopped or missing out on the rise of Internet search engines. "Google kicked our butts," Gates once said. Gates learned to be philosophical about mistakes, saying, "Success is a lousy teacher. It seduces smart people into thinking they can't lose." He is hardly alone among philanthropists, many of whom had failures in their business careers before coming to philanthropy.

Whatever the exact background of the new donors and whatever their learning curve turns out to be as philanthropists, a common thread among them is that they tend to have a strong sense of empowerment, or hyperagency. They have enough money to try to make change in society, and they know it. What's more, they often feel an obligation to put that power to use.

Such people are not new in America. But what's different now is that, in this second Gilded Age, there are so many more of them than ever before. Hyperagency has met mass hyperaffluence, and nearly every corner of society is being affected as these trends converge in philanthropy.

The rapid growth of a new, much larger class of empowered donors adept at using private wealth to shape public life would be an unnerving shift in any democracy. But what's especially troubling at this moment in American life are the divergent trajectories of the wealthy and the general public when it comes to a sense of civic efficacy.

Even as more members of an expanded upper class have come to feel more sure of their ability to make things happen, many ordinary Americans feel the exact opposite way: skeptical that their voice matters or that democratic institutions can solve problems. Barely half of U.S. citizens bother to vote, and well over a third don't identify with either political party. Distrust of government has lately stood near an all-time high. A 2012 survey found that 48 percent of respondents agreed with the statement: "People like me don't have any say about what the government does."

The empowerment gap between the wealthy and the general public wouldn't be as troubling if the economic and social views of the donor class tracked closely with how ordinary Americans see the world. But, as discussed in the last chapter, that's not the case; the wealthy often want different things for society than their fellow citizens do.

And the rift goes deeper. A common take on Donald Trump's rise in the 2016 election cycle is that he channeled rising public anger at a cosmopolitan elite who many believe has come to dominate American life. That elite is real and, at its very center are the new philanthropists—economic winners who are adept at converting wealth into power by bankrolling armies of experts and advocates. For all their noble motives, the mental distance between the givers and tens of millions of Americans who feel shut out of today's progress could hardly be greater.

Whether you agree with the goals of particular donors is less important than what all this means for U.S. democracy—and the cohesion of our society.

3

Grandmasters

When Republicans forced historic spending cuts after retaking the U.S. Congress in 2010, Tea Party insurgents got most of the credit. Yet well before that earthquake election, curbing the budget deficit had emerged as a major priority of official Washington—even as many economists warned against cutting spending when the nation was still recovering from the 2008 financial crisis, with unemployment over 9 percent, and even as poll after poll showed that most Americans wanted their elected leaders to focus on creating jobs, not cutting the deficit.

So how did fiscal austerity end up on top of the national agenda? Part of the answer lies in the laser-focused philanthropy of Pete Peterson, a financier who was among the first signers of the Giving Pledge and who has given a large fortune over many years to sound the alarm about long-term federal budget deficits.

Peterson had been at the first dinner of billionaires that Gates and Buffett convened in New York, and he didn't need much persuasion to join the Giving Pledge. He'd been giving big for years, and already planned to devote most of his fortune to philanthropy.

When Peterson joined the pledge in 2010, he cited his humble roots in explaining his motivation. His father had come to the United States as a penniless seventeen-year-old immigrant and built a successful Greek restaurant, yet had always sent money back to poor relatives in Greece and helped the hungry in his community. As well, said Peterson, his father had understood the concept of "enough" when it came to personal consumption. That example had stuck with Peterson. But his own notion of how to give back couldn't have been more different from his father's. Peterson focused his philanthropy in the lofty realm of public policy.

In the 1990s, he co-founded and helped fund the Concord Coalition, a high-powered advocacy effort to draw attention to deficits. Peterson took out full-page ads in the *New York Times* warning of fiscal calamity and also wrote several books on the subject. Along with George Soros, Peterson may be the most published billionaire in America. He's also among the best connected in elite circles, with ties to both Democrats and Republicans. He served as commerce secretary under Richard Nixon and was CEO of Lehman Brothers for a decade after that. For over two decades, he chaired the Council on Foreign Relations, perhaps the most august of elite institutions and a major recipient of Peterson largesse. He also served a stint as the chair of the Federal Reserve of New York, another exclusive domain.

By any measure, Pete Peterson amassed considerable power during his long career in finance and government. But his greatest influence has come from his philanthropy, particularly his major giving over the past decade. Three nonprofit institutions bear his name: the Peterson Institute for International Economics, a top Washington policy group he has chaired for years and that was renamed after he gave it $50 million in 2006; the Peterson Center on Healthcare, which he founded with a $200 million gift to reshape U.S. health care; and the Peter G. Peterson Foundation, which is run by his son, Michael.

Peterson established his foundation in 2008, after he scored a windfall when the private equity firm he'd helped build, Blackstone, went public. Peterson pledged a billion dollars to the foundation, putting his new wealth behind his longstanding goal of curbing long-term budget deficits. (He also bought a $37.5 million apartment on Fifth Avenue, suggesting the concept of "enough" was a relative term.) Peterson's gift made headlines, and he won accolades for his "generosity"—never mind that the money went to amplify his own public policy views—as opposed, say, to conquering some dread disease. Most media coverage of philanthropy doesn't make much distinction among charitable gifts—and nor does the

IRS for that matter. You get the same tax deduction whether you donate to a genuine charitable cause, say a food bank, or donate to a think tank with an ideological agenda.

The Peterson Foundation got up and running as the U.S. economy coped with the aftermath of the fiscal crisis of 2008, which sent federal deficits into the stratosphere as tax receipts fell and the government engaged in stimulus spending to prop up economic demand. The specter of trillion-dollar budget gaps—temporary though they were—frightened many Americans, both in and outside Washington. The Peterson Foundation spent millions to fan these fears, helping finance deficit watchdog groups, as well as projects at a range of think tanks and public education by the Peterson Foundation itself.

By 2010, Peterson-backed work was all over Washington, sounding the alarm about the growing national debt—and lending mainstream credibility to conservative calls to slash government spending, which, again, many top economists saw as misguided given the weak recovery. Even Peterson himself, a centrist in his views, didn't favor immediate big budget cuts that could harm near-term growth. Rather, he saw the rising deficit fears as an opening to push long-term entitlement reforms, with those cuts phased in gradually. Few Tea Partiers were so subtle in their thinking.

In February of 2010, in response to growing concerns about the deficit, President Obama created the National Commission on Fiscal Responsibility and Reform. While the panel was co-chaired by two former public officials, Alan Simpson and Erskine Bowles, and almost entirely composed of members of Congress, its staff came from elsewhere. The *Washington Post* would report that the salary of one of the top staffers, Ed Lorenzen, was paid by the Peter G. Peterson Foundation, while that of another staffer, Marc Goldwein, was paid by the Committee for a Responsible Federal Budget, which got much of its funding from the Peterson Foundation.

The Simpson-Bowles Commission issued its recommendations in December 2010, proposing to reduce deficits through some tax increases but mainly through spending cuts, with a big focus on the reforms to Social Security and Medicare that Pete Peterson supported. After the commission had finished its work, its co-chairs helped launched a high-profile advocacy effort called the Campaign to Fix the Debt, which included television ads and was primarily financed by the Peter G. Peterson Foundation.

The Simpson-Bowles Commission, and the PR blitz that followed, cemented the deficit as a top issue in Washington in 2011 and 2012—even as unemployment remained stubbornly over 8 percent. As it turned out, though, deficit reduction didn't go anything like Peterson or thoughtful fiscal hawks had hoped. With Tea Party hardliners calling the shots in Congress, even threatening to default on the national debt, and Washington gridlocked, deficits were cut through mandatory across-the-board spending cuts—while putting off the kind of entitlement reform that Peterson favored and sidestepping the tax hikes recommended by the commission. As the ax fell everywhere, including on vital areas like scientific research, Simpson and Bowles called the forced cuts "mindless."

Peterson wasn't pleased with the outcome either, complaining that Washington was not yet "talking about the underlying problem that confronts the long-term future." But he vowed to push on with his funding on deficits and debt. He has the money to sustain that crusade for many years to come. In 2016, *Forbes* estimated Peterson's net worth at $1.6 billion—most of which, if Peterson is good to his word, will go to philanthropy.

THE HIGHEST GROUND

In the popular imagination, philanthropists make their mark by giving money to cure diseases, bankroll college scholarships, build art museums, and so on. That is partly true. But for some donors, there is no greater prize than influencing the overall thrust of national politics and policy. You can see why, too: If your wealth can shape which big ideas are ascendant in public life, you can influence so much else that happens in America.

Wealthy donors have long used philanthropy to wage ideological warfare and contest the highest ground of U.S. politics. What's different now is that a far greater number of rich people are deploying more money to this end than ever before, and with greater sophistication. These days, if you're wealthy and determined to shape the broad direction of American life, you pump money into elections through campaigns and super PACs. But you'll also recognize that bankrolling public policy outfits—at both the national and the state level—can often be a far more powerful lever for swaying debates on big questions like the size of government or the causes of poverty or how much to regulate business. Even better, such spending is tax deductible.

The nation's top think tanks have lately been reeling in more billionaire backers, as the wealthy have come to have a stronger appreciation of just how influential these institutions are. New money is also flowing to legal groups, leadership training institutes, media watchdogs, and other outfits designed to wage big-picture ideological warfare. This type of philanthropic giving doesn't get nearly the attention that other giving does, but arguably it has the most influence in shaping the direction of U.S. society as a whole.

The think tank was invented in the twentieth century to offer objective analysis of complex issues. Now, though, think tanks often operate as the motherships of ideological movements on both the left and the right—weaving together a jumble of values and ideas into a coherent story and actionable policy agenda. The best ones excel at framing the terms of public debates and putting specific ideas on the national agenda (or knocking other ideas off).

Lately, the most popular think tank among the ultra-rich is the American Enterprise Institute (AEI), a conservative policy group based in Washington, D.C., that's over seventy-five years old.

One way to understand AEI's ties with the wealthy is that it's the *smart* conservative think tank inside the Beltway. If you're a rich right-winger who, say, made your fortune opening car dealerships in the Sun Belt, you might give to the Heritage Foundation, with its Tea Party leader, former U.S. senator Jim DeMint, and its simple black-and-white view of how the world should work.

If you're a wealthy libertarian who believes that the free market can solve nearly all problems, you give your money to the Cato Institute, which was founded in 1974 with seed money from Charles Koch and remains heavily bankrolled by him and his brother David.

But if you have a Wharton MBA and got wealthy with algorithm-based trading strategies, or complex leveraged deal-making, AEI is probably the place for you, with its brainy president, Arthur Brooks, and a building stocked with PhDs. At least nine billionaires have given money to AEI in recent years, boosting its budget upward by tens of millions of dollars. During President Obama's two terms in office, AEI's revenues climbed 120 percent, hitting a record high of nearly $55 million in 2015.

That funding surge isn't so surprising. Conservative groups rake in money when Democrats hold the White House, and the reverse is true when a Republican president is in office. (At the left-wing *Nation* magazine there's a saying: "What's bad for the nation is good for *The Nation*.") But the boom times at AEI have also had a lot to do with Brooks's leadership. Brooks gets that conservatives can seem oblivious to poverty and inequality, and he wants to change that. In a long piece in *Commentary* in early 2014, he said that the poor were being left behind in America and that "conservatives and advocates for free enterprise" need to build the "social-justice agenda that America deserves." Brooks has been pushing for AEI to come up with conservative-friendly ways to address poverty and inequity, and he has made AEI a hot spot for younger intellectuals on the right who favor a less Darwinian policy agenda.

Brooks might seem to be an unlikely candidate to be running a big Washington policy outfit. His first career was as a French horn player, and he didn't go to college until he was thirty, enrolling at Thomas Edison State College, in Trenton, New Jersey. Later, after getting a PhD he became a professor at Syracuse University, becoming an expert on charitable giving. He had had little managerial experience before he was tapped to run AEI, and his knowledge of fundraising was mainly theoretical. His scholarly insights, though, turned out to be powerful; Brooks had learned from his research that charitable giving makes people happier, and is a key way they express their values. He knew that appeals that connect with donors at this higher level, rather than in a transactional way, were likely to be most successful. The case for giving to AEI that he stresses to potential contributors, Brooks explained to me, is "not I need you to give me money so I can do stuff." Rather it's that "AEI is a machine. You put your money into one end of the machine and out the other end magically comes an expression of your values."

As for those values, Brooks told me that since taking over AEI in 2009, he has emphasized to everyone in AEI's orbit—staff and donors alike—that "we're really in the business of pushing opportunity down to the people who need it the most." That mission sounds like the exact opposite of what you might imagine that AEI would be up to, with a board of trustees long dominated by CEOs and Wall Streeters. But Brooks is a fervent believer that conservative ideas offer the best hope for raising up those at the bottom of society, and he's put this claim at the forefront of AEI's brand. He said: "I ask our staff every year to have an examination of conscience at night where they ask themselves 'did all of my work go for the benefit of those with less power than me?' And if the answer is no, you're not doing it right. And if the answer is yes, get a good night's sleep and come back ready to fight." Brooks wants AEI to be high-minded in other ways, too. "We try not to violate standards of civility in the way we pursue the competition of ideas," he told me, "understanding that the competition of ideas is not a holy war of ideology."

All this sounds a bit far-fetched for a think tank that has long been the home of Charles Murray, one of the more controversial intellectuals of recent decades, and that has regularly offered a platform for Republican leaders, including former vice president Dick Cheney, to engage in fierce attacks on Democratic policies. The partisan hawk John Bolton, who's a resident fellow at AEI, once called President Obama a "small man" and "one of the most narcissistic individuals to ever hold that job." Meanwhile, AEI scholars routinely stand up for Wall Street and back cuts to any number of supports for low-income Americans. Brooks himself has argued in favor of lowering the minimum wage, a view not widely shared among the disempowered class that he imagines AEI defending.

While AEI is indeed civil-minded and mild compared to places like Heritage, it's more ideologically hard-hitting than it was during its first few decades in operation—exemplifying a trajectory of the Washington think tank world as a whole.

AEI was created in 1938 by group of businessmen led by Lewis H. Brown, who wanted a research center to promote the virtues of "a system of free, competitive enterprise"—virtues that they believed had become marginalized in universities, where many professors were enthralled with a socialist economic model that at the time was thriving in the Soviet Union. From its beginnings, the American Enterprise Institute would have close ties to top corporate executives, but it operated in the vein of policy institutions of the day such as the Russell Sage Foundation and the Brookings Institution, with a focus on sober and careful research.

For much of the twentieth century, think tanks like AEI and Brookings were pretty sleepy places. But things started to change in the 1960s, as Brookings helped advance the liberal war on poverty—becoming so linked to Democrats that an aide to President Nixon once proposed fire-bombing it. Then, starting in the 1970s, a new wave of aggressive conservative philanthropists from the business world began pouring money into think tanks with an eye to rolling back the New Deal and the Great Society, along with the new environmental and consumer protection regulations. In a widely circulated 1971 memo, the head of the U.S. Chamber of Commerce, Lewis F. Powell Jr., then a corporate lawyer (and later a Supreme Court justice), called on business to fight back in an organized way against a "broad attack" on American free enterprise. Two years later, in 1973, the beer magnate Joseph Coors contributed $250,000 to establish the Heritage Foundation and continued to fund it through the Adolph Coors Foundation. Richard Mellon Scaife was another founding donor, and in its first year, Heritage attracted board members from Chase Manhattan Bank, Dow Chemical, General Motors, Pfizer, Sears, and Mobil.

Over the next few decades, conservative philanthropists scaled up not just Heritage, but also the Cato Institute and an array of right-wing think tanks, legal groups, leadership institutes, and policy journals. Some of these same donors also put pressure on AEI to move rightward, which it did starting in the 1980s, offering a home to hard-hitting neoconservative thinkers like Irving Kristol and Jeane Kirkpatrick.

This new infrastructure helped the Right wage a war of ideas that fueled Ronald Reagan's policies and, later, those of the Gingrich Congress. Perhaps the biggest victory of conservative think tanks was knocking off the federal welfare entitlement in 1996, after millions of dollars were poured into research arguing that much social spending just made poverty worse. Charles Murray's 1984 attack on the welfare state, *Losing Ground*, was financed by conservative donors. These institutions also had major influence during the presidency of George W. Bush. The neoconservative foreign policy vision behind the Iraq War was partly formulated in a think tank effort, the Project for the New American Century.

The Obama presidency catalyzed yet another upsurge of conservative think tank philanthropy, as new legions of business donors rallied to fight what they again saw as a sweeping attack on the free enterprise system. Quite a few of these donors, though, looked quite different from the philanthropists that helped create the Heritage Foundation and the Cato Institute. Some had reasons for being drawn to the high-brow American Enterprise Institute.

Back in the 1980s, many of America's wealthy had made their money in manufacturing or real estate or retail. Since then, a shift toward a knowledge economy has produced an explosion of billionaires who got rich in finance or tech by monetizing their intelligence and advanced degrees. That change in how wealth is created helps explain why AEI is doing so well these days.

The Heritage Foundation and AEI push many of the same positions— among them, keep taxes on rich people low and cut social programs for the poor—but AEI does so in a more nuanced, sophisticated way. You won't find any Tea Party types floating around the building (although you might run into Dick Cheney in the elevator).

AEI's positioning as a kinder, smarter conservative think tank plays well in the more cosmopolitan reaches of the upper class, with highly educated wealthy donors who oppose tax hikes and regulation, but nevertheless worry that there's too much poverty and too little social mobility. These same people also tend to be turned off by simplistic ideological appeals and shrill rhetoric. They want to win policy struggles with superior logic, not the think tank equivalent of negative ads, which is what places like Heritage often traffic in, along with a heavy dose of anti-liberal jingoism.

"Basically everybody in AEI's world is politically conservative, but they believe that this vision of lifting people up is the best way to get it done," says Arthur Brooks. "And they want to be able to do that while feeling good about it, and not hating people on the political left who think they have a better way of helping people. . . . That's been the magic."

While Heritage claims to have 700,000 donors, AEI's sizeable budget comes from under 1,500 contributors who give an average of $35,000 a year. Around 65 percent of its revenues come from individual donors, and Brooks works hard to cultivate these supporters. In 2015, he made 90 out-of-town trips and gave 179 speeches. Brooks believes that getting people excited about AEI's vision and scholarship is the best way to reel in contributions, as opposed to an outright "ask" or a red meat ideological appeal. "We don't sell de facto membership in the conservative movement," Brooks told me. "We don't do anything like that. We appeal to people who are just super interested in ideas, and who believe that ideas have huge consequences." This is a niche offering in the Washington policy bazaar, and Brooks has played to it, stressing AEI's intellectualism at every turn, in an unspoken contrast to other think tanks on the right.

"Virtually my whole board has spent some time in graduate school doing something like classics, philosophy, something in the social sciences," Brooks says. "They all have these weird backgrounds. They're basically intellectuals who wound up running hedge funds, private equity firms, who became CEOs. But they never lost their love for ideas and their belief that ideas are what propel the world forward."

A perfect example is Bruce Kovner, a Manhattan-based billionaire and retired hedge fund manager who epitomizes conservative cosmopolitanism and has been on AEI's board for decades, including six years as its chair.

Kovner was born into a Jewish family with immigrant roots. His grandparents had fled the pogroms in Russia and Poland in the late nineteenth century, eventually ending up in Brooklyn. Kovner grew up in the suburbs of Los Angeles, where his father moved when he was young. He was a young Democrat and his hero was President John F. Kennedy. "The popular idea at the time was that the Democrats and FDR were committed to fairness and the Republicans were committed to greed," Kovner would recall. "I grew up in that kind of household." He attended Harvard on a scholarship, studied at the Kennedy School of Government as a grad student, and worked as a writer and cab driver. He dabbled in investing on the side, from his one-bedroom apartment on 57th Street in Manhattan, speculating on commodity prices, interest rates, and currencies, before becoming a trader at the Commodities Corporation, which had been started by economists from MIT and Princeton. Kovner was very successful there, and went on to found his own firm, Caxton Associates, in the early 1980s. That firm helped pioneer new kinds of advanced techniques to understand and profit from financial markets, including mastering derivatives.

Starting with an initial investment of $10 million, nearly half of which was Kovner's own money, Caxton earned around $3 billion in profits in its first decade, with a gross trading return of 55.6 percent per year. By the time he retired in 2011, Kovner was worth $5 billion.

Kovner didn't turn to the right as a result of getting rich. He moved to the right long before that, at Harvard in the 1960s, under the influence of Daniel Patrick Moynihan, then a professor at the university, whom Kovner would call "one of the most important influences of my life." Kovner says of Moynihan: "He explained how the war on poverty of the mid-sixties was not extinguishing poverty, but creating bureaucratic dysfunction and a class dependent on welfare." Kovner recalls that as a big revelation. "I came from a background where the mere intention to eradicate poverty was a badge of honor, sufficient to do the job. I learned that good intentions are not enough. I learned economics."

Kovner joined the AEI board in 1989, at the invitation of its president at the time, Chris DeMuth, whom he knew from Harvard. Before DeMuth got in touch with him, Kovner hadn't spent much time thinking about think tanks or AEI. But the more closely he looked at AEI, the more he liked it. "I realized that AEI stood for two of the core principles in my life. First, defending the vision of America as a place committed to free enterprise and personal liberty. Second, the necessity of a serious and assertive military and foreign policy that would defend America in a dangerous world."

Kovner is typical among conservatives in that he views free enterprise as the most powerful tool to fight poverty and ensure meritocratic outcomes. "We know that the free-market economy has lifted hundreds of millions, if not billions, of people from poverty," he's said. "I want to support institutions that promote those policies."

As it happens, though, hedge fund managers like Kovner have benefited in big and direct ways from the definition of free enterprise that outfits like AEI put forth. For example, scholars at AEI have vigorously defended taxing capital gains at a much lower rate than earned income, a bifurcation that yields huge benefits to the wealthiest Americans, who are much more likely to derive their income from investments. AEI scholars have even defended the much-derided loophole on carried interest, which allows hedge funds and private equity groups to define fees generated by investing other's people money as capital gains, as opposed to regular income derived from performing a service.

Scholars at AEI have also opposed stronger regulation of Wall Street, despite the rise of a "shadow banking system" starting in the 1990s—one that includes asset management firms like hedge funds with a strong appetite for risk yet subject to little oversight. Many accounts of the 2008 financial crisis implicated this system in helping bring down the economy. But AEI scholars have contested this view, and one wrote: "The calls from regulators and others for additional regulation of so-called 'shadow banks' are a rush to judgment. . . . To impose additional regulation on the shadow banking or securities system would add costs that will impair economic growth." AEI scholars have tended to blame government, not Wall Streeters—who largely pay their salaries—for the financial crisis.

Like many top hedge fund managers who have become billionaires in recent decades, Bruce Kovner made his fortune in an era when financial regulations were being dismantled in Washington and taxes on capital gains reduced to record low levels, with policy groups like AEI helping to accomplish these goals. Kovner got rich primarily because he brought smart new approaches to investing, but the ascendancy of laissez-faire ideas starting in the 1980s helped him get richer than he might have otherwise.

Arthur Brooks dismisses the idea that financial self-interest might be a motivator for AEI's donors. "It would be a really, truly terrible cost-benefit calculation for a donor to give a million dollars to a think tank hoping that somewhere down the line that that think tank would actually result in changed policy and lower that person's taxes," he says. The connection between ideas and legislative action is too "roundabout," and there are more direct ways to lobby for one's financial self-interest other than giving to think tanks. "It's a terrible investment. And those guys didn't get rich with bad investments."

Further, Brooks doesn't think that winning favorable treatment by public officials is even much on the minds of AEI's donors, many of whom have so much money that a little more isn't going to make a difference. They happily live in high-tax places like New York City and California, as opposed to maneuvering for every last financial edge.

"A lot of our donors think their taxes are too high, but as a matter of principle, they're not that worried about their own taxes," Brooks says. "They're offended by a sprawling, mediocre, huge, all-encompassing blob of a government that they think is suffocating initiative and excellence. That's what they really bridle against. In point of fact, my donors care less about the money than it might appear." Brooks might have added that most people come to their ideological beliefs early in life, well before they start rising in their careers, a point also true of philanthropists—Bruce Kovner being one example. Wealth offers a way to promote long-held views; it's less likely to account for these views.

To Brooks, the ideal AEI donor is not someone looking for near-term policy wins in Washington, and he doesn't promise that kind of return. Rather, he's looking for donors who understand "that ideas can have a slow burn impact—get into the culture, get into the media, get into the conversation, sometimes get into politicians' brains."

Regardless of what AEI's backers may be thinking, there's no denying that wealthy donors are far more likely to align themselves with think tanks that side with corporations and Wall Street in policy fights. Meanwhile, groups that stand up for lower-income Americans—like the Center on Budget and Policy Priorities—have a much harder time attracting affluent backers, and tend to be smaller in size. Most of their money comes from liberal foundations where the original donor is long dead (and quite possibly rolling in his grave), while raising big money from individuals can be an uphill climb. The more structural a think tank's critique of capitalism, the harder time it has cultivating major donors. Unsurprisingly, wealthy Americans who have benefited from the economic status quo are less interested in challenging it.

That imbalance mirrors a broader tilt in Washington and in state capitols; the wealthy have more powerful representatives in these places than do citizens lower on the economic ladder. This tilt has grown ever more pronounced since the 1980s, as political scientists such as Kay Schlozman and Jacob Hacker have shown, amid the decline of unions and an explosion of business trade groups and lobbyists—underscoring E. E. Schattschneider's famous remark that the heavenly chorus of American pluralism "sings with a strong upper-class accent." The expansion of conservative think tanks like AEI is a key part of this story.

The class tilt is likely to keep growing, too. Thanks to recent boom times, and historically low tax rates, the wealthy now have more spare cash than ever before to put behind their economic views, which tend to be more conservative than those held by ordinary Americans. Investing in think tanks may indeed be a "roundabout" way to achieve policy change, as Arthur Brooks notes, but putting money elsewhere—say, behind presidential candidates—carries its own pitfalls. Just ask all the mega-donors on the right who gave at a record level to elect Mitt Romney in 2012, only to watch Barack Obama prevail. Four years later, no big donors on the Republican side were able to stop Donald Trump from winning the GOP nomination.

In contrast to the crapshoot of electoral politics, investing in think tanks offers a reliable and proven way to slowly change policy and culture over time—and without the high-profile controversies that can come with partisan giving, which is often a concern to wealthy donors who also run businesses. This helps explain why, in early 2016, reports leaked out that Charles and David Koch were shifting their attention away from federal electoral campaigns and back toward philanthropy. The brothers, wrote *National Review,* "had always believed that building the intellectual foundation for libertarian ideas in think tanks and universities—and supporting important public-policy initiatives at the state and local levels—paid greater long-term dividends than spending on elections." Now, tired of being publicly vilified in ways that hurt their sprawling company, Koch Industries, they were inclined to shift back to that focus.

Whatever the Kochs choose to do, a torrent of new money is already flowing into think tanks on the right, and not just AEI. The Heritage Foundation's revenues have, in recent years, cracked the $100 million mark for the first time. In 2013, Heritage landed the largest gift in its history: for $26 million. A year later, AEI pulled in its largest ever gift, when one of its board members, Daniel D'Aniello, gave $20 million for a new building. It was Brooks's finest moment yet as a fundraiser.

D'Aniello is the billionaire co-founder of the Carlyle Group, the famed Washington-based private equity firm. He grew up in a struggling Italian Catholic family in a Pennsylvania coal-mining town—his single mother never earned more than $6,000 a year—before attending Syracuse University on a scholarship and getting an MBA from Harvard Business School. After that, D'Aniello worked his way upward in corporate America, first at TWA and then at PepsiCo and Marriott. He founded the Carlyle Group in 1987 with a colleague from Marriott and three other partners, backed by $5 million from investors. These days, Carlyle has nearly $178 billion in assets under management, and the three founders still with the firm, including D'Aniello, have a combined net worth of nearly $10 billion.

D'Aniello is no former social science grad student like Kovner, but is instead the kind of values-driven donor that Arthur Brooks describes. And he explained his record gift to AEI in terms of his worldview and life experience. "Promoting and protecting free enterprise and opportunity is personal for me," D'Aniello said. "It's what enabled my firm to grow and thrive and I want all people to have the same shot at achieving the American Dream."

Brooks got to know D'Aniello when Brooks was still a professor at Syracuse and D'Aniello sat on its board of trustees. Both men love Syracuse because it sees itself as a top tier school for the everyman, as opposed to the prep school crowd. They became friends and, later, found themselves working closely together at AEI, with D'Aniello becoming vice chair of the AEI board. The billionaire came to take a keen interest in AEI's quest for a new headquarters, and finally stepped up to help in a decisive way.

While D'Aniello's motives for bankrolling AEI's expansion seem pure enough, his backstory is not entirely about the unalloyed triumph of free enterprise. A long line of critics of the Carlyle Group have argued that the firm, which has employed many former top U.S. government officials, epitomizes "access capitalism." Former defense secretary Frank Carlucci, who joined the firm as chairman in 1992, helped orchestrate some of its biggest early paydays, investing in Pentagon contractors. Other former officials who helped Carlyle prosper at the lucrative nexus of government and industry have included James Baker, Richard Darman, and former president George H. W. Bush.

In fairness to D'Aniello, this kind of thing has gone on since the days of the Roman Republic, and today's access game is played by people of all ideological stripes. In a not-so-virtuous cycle, political ties can be used to win preferential treatment by government—in the form, say, of low tax rates or favorable regulations or lucrative contracts—that leads to greater riches and the ability of business winners to spend yet more money currying the favor of the political class.

If you want to understand "why the rich get richer," as the saying goes, Washington, D.C., is one place to look. Two political scientists who did just that, Jacob Hacker and Paul Pierson, concluded in their book *Winner-Take-All Politics* that the clout of wealthy interests in the nation's capital has been a bigger driver of inequality than the usual suspects of globalization and technological change. In turn, a massive concentration of wealth at the top of the income ladder has armed the upper class with even more resources with which to wield political power.

Philanthropy is playing a growing role in this feedback loop, as more givers with deeper pockets bankroll think tanks that have the ear of top officials.

Most ordinary people have limited options for being heard in a noisy public square. They can start petitions or send tweets or write letters or engage in other activities aimed at influencing policy. Citizen activists do occasionally have impact—think of the leaders of the Tea Party or Black Lives Matter—but they are wielding slingshots compared to the wealthy. If you're rich, you can pay the salaries of policy experts to advance your beliefs within the corridors of power. You can underwrite books and magazines to sway broader audiences. You can support lawyers who use litigation to achieve change. You can finance pop-up PR blitzes, like the Campaign to Fix the Debt.

Some two hundred people are now working in the new Daniel D'Aniello Building that houses the American Enterprise Institute, a short cab ride away from a White House where some AEI scholars used to work—and may one day work again when Republicans are back in charge there. Fittingly, the Beaux Arts–style building once housed luxury apartments, including one for Andrew Mellon, the industrialist and banker who parlayed his wealth into a post as U.S. Treasury secretary during the 1920s, where he pushed through sweeping tax cuts for the rich.

D'Aniello hasn't signed the Giving Pledge and doesn't plan to. It's too public and showy, he's said. "It just didn't fit," he told the *Washington Post*. Anyway, he's also said that the pledge requirement to give away at least half one's wealth sounds too modest. "If you're only going to give away 50 percent of your wealth . . . *c'mon* . . . I'm going to do much more than that." Since D'Aniello is currently worth nearly $3 billion, it would seem that dramatically higher levels of giving lie ahead. That sounds like good news for AEI.

Despite all the money conservative think tanks have raised in recent years, much more is on the way.

MARRYING POLICY AND POLITICS

Gifts to policy groups often go hand in hand with other kinds of giving that aims to have influence. Many top backers of right-wing think tanks are also major contributors to Republican Party committees and GOP-aligned super PACs. This overlap is nothing new, and you also see it on the left, but it's soared in recent years, and some of the newer donors coming on the scene are pulling all levers with particular gusto.

A leading example is Robert Mercer, another brainy guy who made his fortune in finance. Growing up, Mercer was obsessed with computers, learning to code in high school, back before personal computers existed. After receiving his PhD in computer science from the University of Illinois, he worked at IBM, where he developed speech recognition programs. In 1993, Mercer joined Renaissance Technologies, the hedge fund founded by math whiz Jim Simons, which employed quantitative models based on mathematical and statistical models to predict movements in the market. It was a smart career move; Renaissance became one of the most successful hedge funds of all time. (More about Jim Simons later in this book.) Mercer rose to become co-CEO of the firm. In some recent years, he's earned over $100 million.

Starting in 2012, Mercer emerged as one of the right's top political donors, giving $5.4 million to conservative candidates and outside groups. He gave even more in the 2014 election cycle: $9.2 million. Mercer contributed more money that year to a Koch-created outfit, the Freedom Partners Action Fund, than did the Koch brothers themselves. In 2016, he was the single biggest donor during the presidential primaries, pouring over $13 million into Ted Cruz's super PAC. (That Cruz didn't win underscores how campaign donations can disappear down the drain; the contributors to Jeb Bush's campaign got an even worse return on their investment.) Later, he helped bankroll Donald Trump's campaign.

Shrewdly, though, Mercer is a diversified investor when it comes to pursuing influence. The Mercer Family Foundation, which is run by his daughter Rebekah, has given many millions to conservative policy groups—donations that the media has largely ignored even as the *New York Times* breathlessly reported in 2015 on Mercer's new kingmaker status as a political donor. That's not unusual: Despite the well-known influence of think tanks, there is little coverage of the river of philanthropic money that goes into these institutions—almost all in the form of tax-deductible gifts.

Mercer has backed a wide array of policy groups that put forth a broad vision for a conservative America, as well as detailed plans for curbing taxes and regulation. In a recent year, big money went to the Manhattan Institute, the Heritage Foundation, and a host of state-based think tanks, including the Center for the Defense of Free Enterprise in Washington State and the Goldwater Institute for Public Policy in Arizona. Conservative philanthropists often favor state groups, because grant money goes further there. They also love pounding on the mainstream media for alleged "liberal bias," which is why Mercer has given millions to the Media Research Center, which says its mission "is to bring balance to the news media." Another recipient of one of Mercer's biggest gifts has been the Federalist Society, a group that reports that it has "created a conservative and libertarian intellectual network that extends to all levels of the legal community."

Mercer money has also flowed to a newer group, the Government Accountability Institute, where Rebekah has sat on the board. The institute says its mission is to "expose crony capitalism, misuse of taxpayer monies, and other government corruption or malfeasance." Mainly, though, GAI is a platform for Peter Schweizer, author of the book *Clinton Cash*, an attack on Bill and Hillary Clinton's finances that was carefully timed for the 2016 election cycle. Much of its work has focused on investigating the Clintons, along with the Clinton Foundation. This kind of thing—501(c)(3) nonprofits that are de facto partisan attack dogs—is increasingly common.

Nearly all of Robert Mercer's policy giving has been to groups with a broad ideological agenda, as opposed to a focus on any specific issue. Many conservative funders give the same way, seeing investing in multi-issue think tanks and leadership development institutes as the best way to move public debates by influencing the overall narratives around the economy, social policy, and national security.

Think tanks are natural partners for political parties and candidates, which also put forth sweeping visions, and there's a long history of politicians relying heavily on think tanks to do the heavy intellectual lifting of creating policy positions. This has been especially true of Republicans, who have fewer friends in academia than the Democrats. The Heritage Foundation famously supplied the new Reagan administration with a detailed plan for governing in 1981, the first of many policy blueprints it developed to guide Republican officials. A long list of GOP stars have spoken at its galas.

LIBERAL MONEY PUSHES BACK

For many years, conservative donors were largely alone in grasping the clout of think tanks. While these funders built up places like Heritage, AEI, and the Cato Institute into powerful policy battleships, liberal philanthropists tended to direct their money to specific causes—writing checks to advocacy groups working on such single issues as the environment, abortion, or LGBT rights.

Starting in the late 1990s, though, more leaders on the left started to worry that a grab bag of causes didn't add up to a compelling liberal vision for America. And, with Republicans firmly in control of Congress, swept into power by the intellectual Newt Gingrich and his big picture "Contract with America," liberals fretted about how the right was winning the war of ideas.

In 1997, a philanthropy watchdog group published an in-depth report by Sally Covington, *Moving a Policy Agenda: The Strategic Philanthropy of Conservative Foundations,* on the right's public policy investments over the previous two decades—documenting just how much funding was quietly flowing to such work and how much influence it had at both the national and the state level. A follow-up report on *Moving a Policy Agenda* (which I wrote) showed that conservative donors had pumped well over $1 billion into just the top twenty think tanks on the right during the 1990s, and that these organizations had grown more sophisticated at waging battle in the political arena, in close concert with Republicans, on issues like Social Security, Medicare, taxes, and education. "Many operate like 'extra party' organizations," I wrote, "adopting the tactics of the permanent political campaign."

A key finding of these reports was that conservative philanthropists were investing in the ideal levers of influence in an era when voting rates were low and mass movements were weak. With elites making more decisions in America, while ordinary citizens were checking out of civic life, efforts to sway high-level policy debates with research and ideas paid big dividends. Whoever could win the larger ideological battles could win everything else.

Covington had some sharp words about the failure of big foundations like Ford to adapt to this new reality. She wrote: "Conservative funders see themselves as part of a larger movement to defeat 'big government liberalism' and they fund accordingly, but mainstream foundations prefer to make modest, on-the-ground improvements in specific neighborhoods. As a result, mainstream foundations increasingly operate within the larger policy assumptions and parameters that conservative funders help shape."

While Covington's report got wide attention among liberal funders, few of these foundations were interested in going head-to-head with conservatives in the war of ideas. However, such intellectual combat did appeal to some of the major new wealthy donors that emerged on the left during George W. Bush's first term as president.

Foremost among these were Herb and Marion Sandler, a couple who had become billionaires after moving to California in the 1960s and building up Golden West, a savings-and-loan association, over forty years.

Herb had grown up Jewish on New York's Lower East Side and become a lawyer. He was working at a small firm in Manhattan—where, by his description, he was "really a nobody"—when he met Marion Osher, a Wellesley grad with an MBA. Osher was among the few female securities analysts on Wall Street, where she had become the leading expert on the savings and loan industry. "She was a superstar," Herb told me.

Through her research, Marion had come to view the S&L industry as an overlooked area primed for growth. With financial help from her brother, Bernard, she and Herb bought Golden West Savings, a small bank in Oakland with just one branch, for over $3 million in 1963. Marion had a keen understanding of which S&Ls did well, and why, and the couple scaled up the bank in a careful, deliberate way. Acting as co-CEOs, they kept costs low and built a conservative loan portfolio, while also experimenting with new products, like adjustable-rate mortgages. After going public in 1968, they made a series of acquisitions and ultimately turned Golden West into one of the largest thrift banks in the United States. They would eventually sell out to Wachovia in 2006, at the height of the housing boom, for $24 billion—walking away with $2.4 billion.

The Sandlers first turned to philanthropy in a serious way in 1988, after nearly two decades of accumulating wealth. "I had never had any money," Herb said. "So for me this was astonishing."

The spark for philanthropy was the death of Herb's brother at the age of sixty-two. That event focused the couple on "what life was really about," and they began thinking hard about what they might do with their wealth—ultimately deciding they wanted to give most of it away. The Sandlers made sure their two children, James and Susan, were part of that decision, as many wealthy couples do when they consider large-scale philanthropy. Such inclusion doesn't just reduce the likelihood of conflict later on; it's a chance to create a true family project that can span generations.

The Sandlers aimed to give away money with the same deliberate rationality with which they had made it. Together with their kids, they worked with a flip chart to think through priorities. Everyone came with lists, and everyone had a veto over final choices. "It had to be something that interested everyone," Herb said. Another criterion was that giving had to focus on big problems and promise to materially improve people's lives.

The first decision to emerge from this process was to support Human Rights Watch, a group that fights injustice around the world, then still in a formative growth period. It wasn't a surprising choice. Even as the Sandlers grew wealthy, they never drifted from their liberal worldview. "I had always identified with the underdogs," Herb said of his growing up. His father gambled on horses and was forever in debt. The family lived in publicly subsidized housing. Marion's parents were more affluent, but that hadn't always been the case. They were Jewish immigrants from Lithuania and Russia who had owned a hardware store before they did well in real estate.

To Herb, the fact that he and Marion had ended up wealthy had as much do with "luck and timing" as anything else. He knew that many other people weren't so fortunate. "The world is an incredibly unfair place," Herb said, adding, "I can't stand powerful people taking advantage of vulnerable people."

In the following years, the Sandlers' early philanthropy came to include big investments in health and also basic science. But gifts to make society more fair would remain a constant. And, always, the family operated with a keen eye for places where their money could make a decisive difference. They wanted to make things happen that wouldn't otherwise happen.

After George W. Bush took office in 2001, the Sandlers started focusing on public policy in a bigger way. Believing that more needed to be done to save America from an ascendant right wing, they became preoccupied with the question of why conservative ideas had become so influential in the first place.

After some digging, the Sandlers learned how savvy right-wing funders had bankrolled groups like Heritage and AEI to shift the terms of national policy on issues such as welfare, regulation, taxes, and the role of government as a whole. Herb, in particular, spent hours doing Internet research to trace the funding and see why the right had done so well. He read *Moving a Policy Agenda*, along with the 1971 "Powell memo" that had laid out a long-term game plan for moving U.S. public policy to the right.

Soon enough, the Sandlers came to embrace the wisdom of backing visionary think tanks rather than supporting narrow work on specific issues, as so many liberal donors were doing. The next question became where, exactly, to put their money.

From their years in business, the couple were big believers in due diligence, and they brought this mind-set to their exploration of think tanks, a world they knew little about. They embarked on an extended listening tour of the liberal policy universe, which included sessions with top staff at existing think tanks. Marion Sandler became well known for asking brusque questions while knitting during meetings, coming across more as a grandmother than as a veteran business executive—until she opened her mouth.

The Sandlers weren't impressed with what they found as they made the rounds, coming away disinclined to back any of the existing policy institutes on the left. A better path, they decided, would be to create something new from scratch—a think tank that could someday rival Heritage or AEI. And so the Sandlers began looking for an entrepreneurial leader whom they could bankroll to build a high-powered Washington think tank, a quest that eventually led them to John Podesta, who had been Bill Clinton's chief of staff, among other roles.

Podesta had been noodling around with his own ideas for creating a new progressive policy center and struck the Sandlers as a promising candidate to trust with millions of dollars. In keeping with their belief in due diligence, the couple talked to over two dozen people who had worked with Podesta in government. The reports on him were so positive that Herb was sure there had to be a catch: "I was prepared to dislike him." Eventually, though, the Sandlers became convinced that all the rave reviews were true. They committed an initial $20 million in funding to Podesta, on the condition that he take on the job of building the new think tank full-time. It would be called the Center for American Progress (CAP).

Over the following decade, CAP emerged as the flagship progressive policy shop in Washington, drawing donations from many other wealthy donors. The billionaire hedge fund manager Tom Steyer contributed at a major level, as did Glenn Hutchins, a successful private equity investor who had done a stint in the Clinton administration before moving on to the hugely successful Blackstone Group. Both Steyer and Hutchins joined CAP's board, which also came to include another mega-donor, the Swiss billionaire Hansjörg Wyss.

Funding also came to CAP from the Democracy Alliance (DA), a network of wealthy progressives co-founded in 2005 by Rob Stein, a former Clinton aide. Five years after Covington's report came out, Stein put together a hard-hitting PowerPoint presentation on the influence of conservative policy groups and a growing right-wing media establishment led by Fox News. Stein's PowerPoint galvanized a strong response among top Democratic donors, who came together to launch the Democracy Alliance, whose partners began giving millions of dollars a year in gifts to organizations recommended by the DA's staff. CAP was among the biggest grantees.

As it grew, CAP hewed to the influence model of the big conservative think tanks. It invested as heavily in communications and legislative outreach as it did in research, fielding a large staff that focused on connecting its policy work to public officials and the media. And, like places such as AEI, it developed strong ties to partisan politicians. When Barack Obama took office in 2009, numerous CAP staffers joined his administration. Eventually, John Podesta himself went to work for Obama, leaving the management of CAP in the hands of Neera Tanden, a former aide to Hillary Clinton.

Meanwhile, the Sandlers also embraced the dual-track giving model that so many wealthy conservatives followed, making major political contributions in addition to bankrolling policy groups. They were among the biggest donors in the 2004 election, joining other billionaires in a push to oust Bush from office. They would never give as much again, but did remain major political donors.

CAP isn't the only think tank that receives grants from the Sandler Foundation, which is based in San Francisco and run by Herb and his children, as well as a small staff, giving out tens of millions of dollars annually. (Marion Sandler died in 2012.) Funds also flow to other top policy groups, including the Center on Budget and Policy Priorities and the Center for Responsible Lending, which the Sandlers also helped create (along with the investigative journalism shop ProPublica). In 2013, the foundation began bankrolling a new scholarly center in Washington to research the link between inequality and economic growth, taking on the long-standing argument that efforts to temper inequalities inevitably slow the economy. The Washington Center for Equitable Growth is all about supporting academic research, distributing tens of thousands of dollars in grants for rigorous studies, but it was founded with a close eye on politics, looking to bolster Democratic arguments for "middle-out economics"—the idea that reducing inequality and boosting the middle class is a key to faster growth. Heather Boushey, the center's first director, told me the goal is to "integrate this work into the policy process and knit it into a larger picture of the economy."

The logic behind the center was compelling for a funder like Herb Sandler, who was always on the lookout for ways to leverage his gifts: If a shift occurred in the macroeconomic debate over inequality, it would be easier to win policy battles on a range of issues, such as raising the minimum wage and reforming tax policy.

NEWCOMERS

Not every philanthropist keen to sway public policy wants to join an ideological team. Some see the arms race between left and right think tanks as precisely what's wrong with politics—and aim to bust this duopoly.

So it was that, in the early spring of 2015, Sean Parker and Ron Conway, two Silicon Valley veterans, helped to launch a new policy center in Washington called the Economic Innovation Group. "It's time for a paradigm shift in the way we think about growth, investment, and job creation," said Steve Glickman, executive director and co-founder of the group. "Important voices are missing from the policy debate, and Washington is mired in the same, stale conversations."

Parker had made his career disrupting yesterday's industries, initially through Napster and then as the first president of Facebook. Conway was a legend in the valley for his long string of savvy angel investments in breakthrough companies.

Just two years earlier, Conway had told the *New York Times*: "I really don't have a lot of interest in national politics, and it's because I'm a skeptic . . . I don't want to spin the wheels and not get anything done." But apparently the temptation of backing a start-up gunning to change business as usual in the nation's capital was more than he could resist.

Conway and Parker were outsiders in Washington, which was exactly the point. Who better to upend existing policy models than the folks who had invented stuff like Google?

"It's time for those of us in the tech community to look beyond the borders of Silicon Valley, and to think long term about solutions to broader national challenges," said Parker. "Our approach to public policy should leverage the lessons we learned as technology entrepreneurs and investors: take big risks, seek out innovative solutions, and don't shy away from big problems."

New money stampeding into town with grand plans is an old story in Washington, and this was the second such foray by techies that Parker had helped launch. Along with Mark Zuckerberg, Bill Gates, and others, he had also been a co-founder of FWD.us, an immigration advocacy effort started in 2013 that was widely seen as clumsy and ineffective.

Parker said that Silicon Valley's leaders had learned from that effort. "There is a genuine idealism to FWD's mission," he told *Politico*, "but its early tactics were perceived cynically. The right approach is probably more cautious and prudent." Parker added, though, that mimicking the tactics of existing Beltway policy shops was definitely not the answer, since those groups had become "shills" for the party line. He said that if the Economic Innovation Group was going to be successful, it "needs to be a neutral and honest broker."

Rachel Pritzker is another philanthropist who has sought to move beyond existing ideological paradigms by backing new ideas.

Pritzker told me that she's been involved in philanthropy "my whole life." It was something "instilled in my family." That would be the famous and sprawling Pritzker family, which includes eleven billionaires and has a combined net worth of some $30 billion—originally derived from the Hyatt hotel chain, but pumped up by various other investments over the decades. Today, so many Pritzkers are involved in philanthropy that it can be hard to keep them all straight.

Rachel belongs to the fourth generation of Pritzkers, and like many younger philanthropists, she's intent on doing things differently.

Her first major foray into giving was during the early 2000s, when she became a founding board member of the Democracy Alliance. Pritzker was galvanized by the PowerPoint presentation given by Rob Stein, documenting the enormous power of conservative groups and media outlets. She was struck by Stein's point that progressives "were losing because we weren't winning hearts and minds," and plunged headlong into helping create the DA, investing time and money to get the organization going. She also served on the board of Media Matters for America, a group that pushes back against right-wing media outlets like Fox News.

The Democracy Alliance focuses heavily on near-term policy and political battles, with a keen eye on the electoral cycle. After a time, though, Pritzker found her own attention shifting to a different set of challenges, the kind that often can't get traction in the politics of the moment. "I wanted to think longer term and focus more on original problem solving ideas," she said. And to do that, she felt she needed to get out of Washington, D.C., and the way its endless, zero-sum ideological warfare locked people into narrow worldviews. Pritzker moved to the Bay Area and, as she remembered, "started hanging out with people who were having big and bold conversations."

Among the kindred spirits she connected to over time were the cofounders of the Breakthrough Institute, Ted Nordhaus and Michael Shellenberger, who'd made a name for themselves by advancing iconoclastic ideas, most famously through their essay, "The Death of Environmentalism." The Breakthrough Institute has described itself as a "paradigmshifting think tank committed to modernizing environmentalism for the 21st century," and it lists "audacity" and "imagination" as among its core values. The place is the antithesis of a typical Beltway policy shop, and Pritzker loved it, becoming one of its biggest donors and the chair of its advisory board.

Pritzker also tapped her family fortune to set up her own foundation, the Pritzker Innovation Fund, which works mainly on climate and energy issues, with the goal of developing and advancing "paradigm-shifting ideas to address wicked problems."

Pritzker describes "wicked problems" as problems "without easy solutions." They aren't just complex problems; they are extraordinarily complex problems.

Climate change, along with sustainable energy use, is the top wicked problem on her fund's agenda. While there are some clear ways to make progress in this area—like, say, raising the price of carbon to change incentives around energy use—the larger, more daunting challenge is ensuring that all of humanity—some 9 billion people eventually—will have access to energy without creating an ecological catastrophe. Pritzker told me that even the very basic question of how much energy humans need to have a high-quality life has not been as closely analyzed as you might think. To her, this is a perfect example of where smart philanthropy can make a difference by underwriting new intellectual work, which is the main focus of the Pritzker Innovation Fund, with grants going to think tanks and policy research. Pritzker's view is "that new ideas can create paradigmatic shifts in approaches that break through polarization and gridlock by changing the terms of debate."

In other words, Rachel Pritzker is another philanthropist who believes that ideas are the ultimate leverage point. Use your money to change the conversation and you can change everything else.

Many top philanthropists have never given a dime to think tanks and never will. They don't like the thought of writing checks to a bunch of policy wonks and PhDs when their cash could go to more direct efforts to solve problems. Think tank work can seem awfully detached from the real world.

Yet anyone who looks more closely can see how policy groups help orchestrate what happens on any number of issues that concretely affect the lives of millions of people.

The billions invested in conservative think tanks, starting in the 1970s, helped move U.S. public policy to the right, ushering in an era of low taxes, deregulation, and cuts to government programs. Eventually, though, those investments triggered a response, with a new set of wealthy progressive donors emerging to push back against inequality, using some of the same funding tactics perfected by right-wing philanthropists.

Still, in general, far more money is going into policy work friendly to corporations and Wall Street. For example, the two national think tanks that directly stand up for workers—the Economic Policy Institute and the National Employment Law Project—together had revenues of under $15 million in a recent year. That's less than half the money raised annually by the Cato Institute, the libertarian think tank that dreams of abolishing the U.S. Department of Labor (along with plenty of other federal agencies) and is heavily backed by Wall Street donors, as well as the Koch family. AEI and Heritage, in turn, are far bigger than Cato.

This ongoing imbalance of power, though, shouldn't obscure the fact that big changes have occurred in think tank funding in the past fifteen years. More wealthy progressives like Herb Sandler have arrived on the scene—a trend that underscores how the upper class is increasingly diverse in its ideology. Class and politics don't line up as neatly as they once did, in an earlier era when industrialists slugged it out with labor unions. Many of the new rich are highly educated knowledge workers who grew up, and live, in blue America and favor a strong government that invests in public goods like education, scientific research, and infrastructure. They wish the public sector was more nimble and effective, but they're not anti-statists and they don't mind paying higher taxes. In fact, such billionaires as Warren Buffett and Reed Hastings have publicly campaigned for tax increases—Hastings even published an op-ed in 2009 titled "Please Raise My Taxes."

Others, like Nick Hanauer, an early investor in Amazon, have strongly argued that inequality hurts the economy—by undermining middle-class buying—and poses a profound threat to social stability. Hanauer wrote in a widely read 2014 article in *Politico* that the "model for us rich guys here should be Henry Ford, who realized that all his autoworkers in Michigan weren't only cheap labor to be exploited; they were consumers, too." If America took dramatic steps to reduce inequality, Hanauer predicted that people like him would "most certainly get even richer." On the other hand, if income gaps kept growing, he envisioned "pitchforks coming." He wrote: "I have a message for my fellow filthy rich, for all of us who live in our gated bubble worlds: Wake up, people. It won't last."

Overall, the wealthy remain more conservative than ordinary Americans on issues like labor policy, regulation, and taxes. But there are now enough rich liberals engaged in philanthropy to ensure that the far upper class isn't a monolithic bloc backing conservative and centrist viewpoints. That is translating into a far more robust war of ideas.

We hear a lot about how politically polarized America is these days. What we don't often hear is that, like the rest of us, the wealthy are also more divided than ever. This means that even as the new philanthropic power elite has come to wield ever more influence, that clout is rarely directed in any one, uniform direction when it comes to the great issues of the day.

4

Super-Citizens

Not long before Thanksgiving 2014, readers of the *New York Times* learned that a new island park was going to be built in the Hudson River off the West Side of Manhattan, in Chelsea. Plans for the 2.4-acre park, built on Pier 54—where the Titanic survivors had returned to New York—called for walkways, lawns, and three performance spaces. It would be the most ambitious new park in New York in years, costing around $170 million. The majority of that tab would be picked up by the media mogul Barry Diller and his wife, the fashion designer Diane von Furstenberg.

The couple have offices within walking distance of each other, not far from the Hudson. Diller is in the stylish white glass building across from Chelsea Piers that he had Frank Gehry design for his company, IAC. The building is a few blocks from the site of the new park, which was quickly dubbed "Diller Island." The corporate headquarters for Furstenberg's company are in the Meatpacking District, on 14th Street.

The neighborhood has changed dramatically in recent years, from the days when transvestite prostitutes worked the cobblestone streets and a biker's bar was among the few nightspots. The Meatpacking District has become an upscale destination, with the High Line Park—a striking public space built on an abandoned elevated rail line—bringing in throngs of tourists. Real estate values have gone into the stratosphere.

Diller and Furstenberg were the biggest donors to the High Line, a park financed largely with private donations that stretches through much of West Chelsea, starting just below 14th Street and ending at 34th Street. The other top backer of the park was the Pershing Square Foundation, which is run by the billionaire hedge fund investor Bill Ackman and his wife, Karen. The High Line has transformed a neighborhood once known for auto repair shops and self-storage spaces. As the park was completed in stages, new glass apartment towers sprang up on either side, with two- and three-bedroom units going for millions of dollars. One journalist wrote: "The High Line has been to usual gentrification what a bomb is to bottle rockets." In 2015, the Whitney opened its new art museum on Gansevoort Street—an expensive move downtown paid for by a stable of wealthy donors. The museum drew even more visitors to the neighborhood. Longtime Chelsea residents complained as yet another corner of New York was turned into a playground for rich people and tourists.

Diller Island will amp things up even further. Sitting like a flying saucer in the Hudson, and visible from both the High Line and the Whitney, it will be yet another draw for outsiders. "I have always liked the idea of public art and public places, and that's just been growing in me over decades," Diller would say later, about why he backed the project. "It isn't going to cure world disease. But it's totally worthwhile."

Diller and Furstenberg were early signers of the Giving Pledge, and Diller in particular is a big fan of the group's annual retreats. "I don't think there's another group like it anywhere—a room full of very complex personalities—of drive and aspiration—of ego and curiosity—all engaged in wanting to help solve problems for others," Diller wrote, in a letter to Bill Gates and Warren Buffett. Diller liked the retreats so much that he offered to help pay their costs, only to be assured that the Gates Foundation had things covered. He and Furstenberg have given away millions through their foundation, spreading grants around in both New York and Los Angeles, to an array of causes that includes the arts, human rights, human services, and environmental conservation. But the commitment for Pier 54 was far bigger than anything that had come before.

The announcement of the new park triggered instant controversy. It had been planned in secrecy by the Hudson River Trust, which enlisted Diller and then quietly got buy-in from Governor Andrew Cuomo and Mayor Bill de Blasio. Community members on the Far West Side and their elected representatives learned about Diller Island along with the rest of the readers of the *New York Times*.

One element of the project that raised hackles was that the park, which would also require $40 million in public funds to be completed, would actually be controlled by Barry Diller himself, who had recruited a high-powered group to lead programming for the park's event spaces. Critics also questioned how public funds for parks were being allocated. In New York's poorer neighborhoods, hundreds of parks had fallen into disrepair and badly needed upgrades. Yet Diller had succeeded in orchestrating a project that would draw millions of government dollars for a park in one of Manhattan's wealthiest areas, a neighborhood that already had two major parks—the Hudson River Park and the High Line. What sort of way was that to make decisions about public spaces?

Welcome to the era of "super-citizens," where philanthropists are literally reshaping the geography of our cities. Barry Diller's projects have been small in comparison to what billionaires are backing elsewhere. In Houston, the energy pipeline magnate Richard Kinder and his wife, Nancy, are tapping a multi-billion-dollar fortune to remake parts of that city. They're helping finance a transformative 150-mile system of urban trails called the Bayou Greenways, one of the largest parks projects in the United States. The Kinders' money has also gone to other parks projects throughout the city. Like Diller and Furstenberg, the couple signed on to the Giving Pledge early on. It was not a tough decision since they had decided years earlier to give away 95 percent of their wealth. Much of that giving is focused on Houston, the city that Rich Kinder credits with enabling him to make his fortune—with its open, entrepreneurial culture. "In Houston, you are what you achieve," the couple wrote in their Giving Pledge letter. Beyond new parks, the Kinder Foundation is pouring millions into the city's schools, hospitals, and social service organizations.

Not far away, in Tulsa, Oklahoma, the billionaire George Kaiser is spending even more lavishly. Like Kinder, Kaiser believes that parks are a key to vibrant cities, and is underwriting a vast riverfront park in Tulsa that may be even costlier than the Bayou Greenways. Kaiser is giving $350 million for the project, dubbed "A Gathering Place for Tulsa," the largest sum ever committed by a private philanthropist to a public park. Kaiser is so rich that he didn't need to bother with getting government to pick up part of the tab. His foundation is not only paying to build the park, it will pay to maintain it.

George Kaiser's money is reaching into other parts of Tulsa, too. A liberal in a deep red state, he has pumped millions into building state-of-the-art early education centers that serve low-income children, and given even more to help set up health clinics in schools and public housing projects. In his Giving Pledge letter, Kaiser wrote that America had failed to live up to the ideal at the core of its social contract, equal opportunity. Kaiser's solution is to use his own funds to "help those left behind by the accident of birth." He wrote: "If the democratically-directed public sector is shirking, to some degree, its responsibility to level the playing field, more of that role must shift to the private sector." Kaiser knows that he can't remake all of U.S. society, no matter how many billions he has. So he's focused narrowly on the goal, as his foundation puts it, of making "Tulsa the best city for children to be born, grow and succeed."

In San Francisco, two wealthy funders—the Haas family and the billionaire Stephen J. Bechtel—were instrumental in transforming part of the Presidio, a former military base near the Golden Gate Bridge, into a national park. Bechtel gave $35 million to the effort. Meanwhile, the tech billionaire Marc Benioff has, along with his wife, Lynne, led an ambitious push to improve Bay Area hospitals, giving $200 million for new facilities in San Francisco and Oakland. Benioff has also worked to rally tech companies behind local anti-poverty efforts, rounding up donations from firms widely criticized for boosting inequality to new heights in the region. His company, Salesforce, has made improving local schools a top philanthropic priority, giving millions in grants and organizing its employees to volunteer their time tutoring kids in subjects like math and science.

In Boston, the Barr Foundation, created by cable TV billionaire Amos Hostetter Jr. and his wife, Barbara, has emerged as one of the most influential institutions in the city, public or private. It has given hundreds of millions of dollars in grants, with this money flowing to nonprofits working in every corner of city life. Former Barr staffers have become top officials in city government. Among other things, Barr has been a leading player in helping orchestrate an "arts renaissance" in Boston, arguably wielding as much power in the city's cultural sector as any public agency. The Hostetters' foundation is also deeply involved in K–12 education and transit issues. The couple, who live in a historic mansion on Beacon Hill, keep a low profile in Boston, but they are widely seen as among the most powerful people in the city.

In Chicago, money given by the Pritzker family is shaping many areas of city life—to the point that one of those heirs, J. B. Pritzker, has been called the "other mayor of Chicago." In Cleveland, the Gund family has poured millions into civic projects aimed at revitalizing a famously battered industrial city. It put funds into revitalizing the city's public square, as well as assorted other projects, including parks. Not far away, in Detroit, a coalition of the top foundations in America pooled over $800 million to save the city from bankruptcy. One foundation involved in Detroit, Kresge, is even helping underwrite a new light rail system downtown.

SHAPING HOW WE LIVE

Power comes in many forms in public life. But one of its most tangible manifestations is the ability to shape the communities in which millions of people live. And now, more than at any time in memory, philanthropists are exercising such power—not just by financing parks, but by underwriting the physical expansion of top universities and hospitals, as well as major cultural institutions. A few miles north of Diller Island, gifts by two billionaire donors to Columbia University Business School, totaling $225 million, are helping fuel a transformation of West Harlem that has pushed out some long-time residents and businesses. One housing advocate called the sprawling new campus Columbia is building "a quintessential, if extreme, example of how difficult it is for communities to be heard when powerful institutional neighbors propose development or redevelopment." That's all the more true when such neighbors are backed by billionaire donors. Across town, on Roosevelt Island, some $600 million in gifts from three philanthropists is helping create a science campus for Cornell University.

Of course, remaking urban public school districts has also been a top project of the new philanthropists. In New York, the Fund for Public Schools has raised more than $350 million since 2002. Smaller efforts of donors, in the Big Apple and elsewhere, have included pushing for bike lanes and building public libraries and gardens and swimming pools. Some of the most ambitious projects of private donors are done in partnership with government, with the result that philanthropists have become more deeply enmeshed in the machinery of civic life.

Much of this philanthropy gets celebrated without many second thoughts. Parks, libraries, and museums make cities livable; top universities and medical research centers make them great, attracting talent from around the world. What's not to like?

Maybe a bunch of things, as the case of Diller Island suggests—from who is making choices over public life to who actually benefits from those choices.

What's happening in cities like New York and Houston is a microcosm of a broader power shift whereby private donors—who are both more numerous and more wealthy—are stepping into a vacuum created by the decline of the public sector. New York mayor Bill de Blasio may not be able to find much money for big new projects, but Barry Diller can.

Here, too, though, the story isn't a simple one. Yes, it's troubling to see such public power in the hands of private individuals; on the other hand, donors like Diller and Kaiser are bringing badly needed new resources to boosting America's cities at a time when more people are embracing urban life. Their projects often bypass the grueling process of waiting for funds to be appropriated—assuming money can be found at all—and then waiting for the gears of public agencies to slowly grind forward. The givers can get things done, and fast.

What's more, while private donors like Diller appear alarmingly unaccountable, public officials haven't always been so accountable themselves.

Robert Moses, who famously transformed the New York area with highways, bridges, and parks, did so in part by amassing unprecedented power as an appointed government official and using it in authoritarian ways. In fact, much of the urban renewal of the mid-twentieth century wasn't so pretty, as government reshaped cities through massive highway and housing projects. The Federal-Aid Highway Act of 1956 was a powerful tool in this regard, giving state and federal government control over new highways, including the power to smash those roads through urban neighborhoods using eminent domain. Urban renewal projects dreamed up by public officials remade numerous cities in the 1950s and 1960s, at times in destructive ways as vibrant communities were destroyed or relegated to the shadows of elevated highways.

Philanthropy was sometimes involved in these big makeovers, although typically in a supporting role, with government agencies mainly driving the action. John D. Rockefeller III may have chaired the private fundraising effort that raised tens of millions of dollars to complete Lincoln Center, the performing arts center in New York City, but the project was Moses's idea. It was he who appointed Rockefeller to the job and invoked the power of eminent domain to seize sixty-seven acres of land and demolish blocks of Upper West Side tenement buildings that housed some three thousand families, most of them African American.

In Pittsburgh, the philanthropist and real estate developer Richard King Mellon—an heir to the great Mellon industrial fortune—was instrumental in instigating the massive demolition and redevelopment projects that transformed downtown Pittsburgh in the 1950s. He also pushed for urban renewal as a supporter of the American Council to Improve Our Neighborhoods, which promoted redevelopment. But government funds were indispensable for the massive projects that Mellon envisioned. In many other cities, philanthropy played little or no role in a broad refashioning of urban life during the 1950s and 1960s. This was a golden age for men like Moses and Edmund Bacon, another top urban planner who served for decades as the leader of the Philadelphia City Planning Commission, remaking that city to the point that he is sometimes referred to as "the Father of Modern Philadelphia." Elsewhere, it was mayors who had the grandest urban visions, such in Chicago, where Richard J. Daley orchestrated any number of major construction projects during his twenty-one years as mayor, including O'Hare International Airport and numerous expressways.

Today, there are plenty of visionary public officials aiming to reshape cities, but they often have fewer resources to work with. Pension outlays have been swelling in many cities, crowding out other priorities. Federal assistance to urban areas, in decline for decades, fell even more sharply after Congress made sweeping budget cuts in 2011. Aid to localities from federal programs—for job training, water safety, transportation, law enforcement, and more—has dropped across the board.

Funding for parks has been among those areas hit by recent budget cuts—not that there was much federal aid of this kind left to pare down. A few decades ago, from the mid-1960s through 1981, Congress had appropriated an average of $626 million per year to the Land and Water Conservation Fund (LWCF) program, in 2007 inflation-adjusted dollars, which helps finance the creation of parks, including urban ones. Between 1982 and 2007, however, the program averaged less than one-tenth that amount, or $61.9 million per year. In 2015, Congress moved to eliminate the LWCF program altogether. Among its powerful opponents in Washington: the Heritage Foundation, which published a strong policy brief that year calling for its permanent elimination.

The memo's author was Nicholas Loris, a young policy wonk who was the Herbert and Joyce Morgan Fellow at Heritage's Thomas A. Roe Institute for Economic Policy Studies. Herbert Morgan, the philanthropist who endowed Loris's fellowship, made his fortune in real estate law in the South. Heritage describes him and his wife as "longtime proponents of free enterprise and limited government." Thomas Roe, who funded the institute where Loris worked, had gotten rich by parlaying the company he inherited from his father into a Fortune 500 conglomerate. Before Loris came to the Heritage Foundation, he worked for the Charles Koch Charitable Foundation. There are a lot people like Loris in Washington these days.

Through relentless attacks on government over the past four decades, conservatives have pursued the dream of returning to a time—before the New Deal and World War II—when the public sector played a much smaller role in American life. Among other things, they have argued that private charity did a much better job of fighting poverty in the nineteenth century than big government did in the twentieth century. And they've suggested that public goods like museums and libraries are best financed by the private funds. Many libertarians go further, suggesting that schools and parks should also be funded privately.

The Right has come nowhere near to achieving its vision, but it's made some real progress, squeezing government funding for things like the arts, parks, libraries, and public universities. Elected officials of both parties, but particularly Democrats, have also helped weaken local government by not putting aside enough money to properly fund public pensions and entitlements for the elderly. Now the costs of these obligations is soaring. New York is a good example: city outlays for pension costs rose to around $8 billion in 2015, or 11 percent of the budget, up from 2 percent in 2000. Thanks to the Wall Street boom during some of this period, Mayor Michael Bloomberg still managed to increase public spending, including on parks, but in December 2013, Bloomberg warned that rising pension and health-care costs threatened to doom urban government in coming decades. "It is one of the biggest threats facing cities," Bloomberg said in his final speech as mayor, "because it is forcing government into a fiscal straight jacket that severely limits its ability to provide an effective social safety net and to invest in the next generation." Or to spend money on parks.

These fiscal woes, whoever is to blame, have opened up more space for people like Barry Diller to make their mark on public life. Indeed, the strains on government have escalated at precisely the moment when a generation of aging billionaire titans like Diller, who started assembling their fortunes in the 1980s, are now looking to dispose of this wealth through philanthropy. That timing is fortuitous in some respects, with more private donors stepping up just as public agencies are finding themselves tapped out; but it's also alarming, raising questions about who is in charge of our cities.

What's happening in Kalamazoo, Michigan, offers an unsettling glimpse of what the future of urban governance might look like. That former industrial city has long struggled with fiscal woes, and in 2016, Mayor Bobby Hopewell turned to a wealthy friend, William Johnston, for help in closing a growing budget gap. Johnston, who chairs a wealth management company, widened the conversation to include William Parfet, the retired CEO of a drug company and a local philanthropist. Eventually, the two men pledged $70 million over three years to help stabilize the city's budget, finance a reduction in property taxes, and bankroll new programs to reduce poverty and spur growth.

The mayor and other officials hailed the gift as transformational, and stunning in its generosity. It was indeed both of those things. Two wealthy patrons with deep ties to Kalamazoo were coming to its rescue at a moment of dire need. But, unmistakably, the gift also marked a shift in power away from the city's elected leaders toward private donors. Likewise, when a group of foundations orchestrated the even bigger bailout of Detroit, they secured a larger say over that city's future.

The past offers some clues about what these new power arrangements may look like. Super-citizens were familiar figures in the pre–New Deal era, before the rise of a stronger government, when private money loomed much larger in public life. Andrew Carnegie bankrolled libraries in cities around the country, among them New York: he gave millions to the New York Public Library—which had been created by Gilded Age philanthropists—to construct sixty-five branch libraries around the city. New York's earliest major cultural institutions were also the projects of nineteenth-century business titans, as was the case in many cities. Higher education, too, in America was dominated by wealthy donors—before public universities were invented.

Private philanthropists also largely called the shots when it came to aiding the poor, which mostly fell to nonprofit charities. Settlement houses, one of the main anti-poverty tools of the time, were privately funded by wealthy donors and staffed by volunteers. Emergency food and financial support came from churches or civic associations.

The United States is unlikely to return to this era of truly small government. Too many Americans believe in a strong public sector, and quite a few are pressing hard to expand government further. Still, there's little question that government will be doing less in coming decades, and we're already moving into new terrain, in terms of who provides public goods. With government stepping back, philanthropy is stepping forward—and occupying a bigger seat at the table of power than at any time in the past century.

A FORGOTTEN BOROUGH

Not long before Barry Diller and Diane von Furstenberg made their giant gift to create a rarefied island park off Chelsea, Mayor Bill de Blasio had announced a new city effort to refurbish some thirty-five parks in overlooked city neighborhoods. This initiative only scratched at the problem of crumbling parks in poorer parts of the city. At least two hundred parks around New York were in a decrepit state, and some of the city's poorest neighborhoods had no parks at all. De Blasio had vowed to promote "parks equity" as a candidate, and now he was trying to deliver as mayor. The total he'd managed to pull together to spruce up some three dozen parks amounted to $130 million—the exact sum, coincidentally, that Diller and von Furstenberg pledged for their one 2.4-acre park in one of the city's most affluent neighborhoods.

Before that gift, the biggest pledge ever to New York public parks had been John Paulson's gift of $100 million to the Central Park Conservancy (CPC) in 2012. The billionaire hedge funder lives less than half a block from the park, in a 28,500-square-foot mansion on East 86th Street. And while Central Park had already become a shining jewel thanks to some $700 million in private donations since the 1980s, Paulson was moved to chip in even more.

The Central Park Conservancy has flourished for obvious reasons. The city's premier park borders the wealthiest neighborhood in the city, the Upper East Side, and over the years, CPC had become a fundraising powerhouse. Its board of trustees includes numerous heavyweights from finance who live near the park, like Paulson, and its huge success is a classic example of how the wealthy give to organizations that directly enhance their lives.

Yet it would be wrong to settle on a reductive narrative of self-interest in explaining the new parks philanthropy being driven forward by supercitizen donors. For starters, Central Park is hardly just a playground for the rich; it also borders Harlem and draws people from all over the city—and the world. Elsewhere, philanthropists have invested in parks with a close eye on equity concerns. The huge Bayou Greenways project in Houston that the Kinders are financing is designed to connect to nearly every neighborhood in the city, with the goal of getting people out of their private cars and backyards and into a public space that's accessible to "all the people from the huge melting pot that is Houston." It's estimated that six in ten Houstonians will live within a mile of the Greenways when the park is finished. George Kaiser's ambitious waterfront park in Tulsa is also designed to benefit everyone in the city.

Meanwhile, in New York, not every wealthy philanthropist was sold on the idea of giving ever more money to Manhattan's parks. One major donor, Shelby White, set her sights instead on reviving public spaces in Brooklyn—a borough that the moneyed elite seldom visited even as it began to gentrify.

White is the widow of Leon Levy, a Wall Street investor who left the bulk of his fortune to a foundation when he died in 2003. She's a familiar type in the annals of philanthropy: the woman who outlives her wealthy husband and finds herself charged with disposing of his fortune once he's gone.

A former journalist, White created the Leon Levy Foundation from scratch, building up a small staff and grantmaking operation. And although she had long lived a Manhattan life of wealth and privilege, she had never forgotten where she came from, which was a Jewish immigrant household on Flatbush Avenue in Brooklyn. When White found herself in control of a sizeable foundation—one with assets of around half a billion dollars—she decided she'd give back to the borough of her youth.

"I was a Brooklyn girl, and wanted to do stuff for my hometown," White told me. To decide where to put money, "I went to the places I had gone as a kid." First among them was Prospect Park, which like Central Park is a masterpiece designed by Frederick Law Olmsted. "Prospect Park was my childhood park. I lived a block away. I did everything there. I went rowing, I went horseback riding, I had my first cigarette. I really loved Prospect Park."

In the early 2000s, though, the park was sinking into neglect. The city wasn't putting up the funds to properly maintain it, even as parks spending increased during the early years of Bloomberg's tenure, and it didn't have wealthy patrons. The Prospect Park Alliance lacked the juice of the Central Park Conservancy, with its Masters of the Universe board. "There were so many people doing stuff for Central Park," White recalled. "There was nobody doing stuff for Prospect Park."

White decided to help right the scales, making a $10 million gift in 2008 for Prospect Park restoration work. It was the largest gift ever for the park—or any public institution in Brooklyn.

With improvement in Prospect Park moving forward, White looked around at the other pillars of her childhood community. The Brooklyn Public Library, headquartered in a landmarked Art Deco building on Grand Army Plaza, was struggling. The Leon Levy Foundation gave it a $3 million grant designed to move the library into the twenty-first century, with new information technology. The Brooklyn Botanic Garden, just a few blocks away, was also in poor shape, coping with crumbling infrastructure. White directed a $7 million grant toward building a new water system for the garden—hardly the sexiest destination for a major gift, but one that was badly needed. These were both record-level gifts.

White gave money to two other Brooklyn mainstays, too: the Brooklyn Museum and the Brooklyn Academy of Music. Up in the Bronx, big gifts went to make improvements to the New York Botanical Garden. To this day, the Leon Levy Foundation remains the largest private donor to New York's outer boroughs.

One other philanthropist who made a stir in Brooklyn, but not in a good way, is Joshua Rechnitz, a forty-something hipster heir with a love of bicycle racing. In 2012, Rechnitz offered up what was then the largest gift ever to a New York City park: $40 million to build a velodrome racing track in the new Brooklyn Bridge Park. The offer was quickly accepted by the public-private entity overseeing the new park, only to set off head scratching and controversy.

Most people don't even know what a velodrome is, and understandably so: racing single-gear bikes without brakes on a banked indoor track ranks among the more esoteric sports. The heyday of velodrome racing was over a century ago, at which time it drew huge crowds to tracks throughout New York and elsewhere. Rechnitz dreamed of throngs of people once more cheering on cyclists racing indoors at speeds of up to forty-five miles per hour. He had formed a nonprofit, Velodrome NYC, and had been scouting for locations before focusing on the Brooklyn Bridge Park. His proposed facility would have seating for 2,500 spectators, and be housed in a fieldhouse that would accommodate other recreational activities.

After the novelty of Rechnitz's historic gift wore off, the backlash began. Some wondered why a rich guy with obscure tastes got to dictate how a sizeable piece of the new park—as large as a football field—was used. "The number of people who really want it you can count on the fingers of your left hand," wrote one community critic of the racetrack. "What is it doing in our park? Why help the city build a huge stadium in a tiny waterfront park for this quaint, obscure, bizarre sport?" Other locals worried about the additional traffic the velodrome would bring to the cobblestone streets of Brooklyn Heights, and wondered why Rechnitz's gift had been accepted without more input from the community. As Brooklynites thought about their hopes for the borough's first major new park in decades, a velodrome was pretty much the last priority that came to mind. Private money, not public interest, was shaping a park that was supposed to be for everyone.

Rechnitz fought back against the critics with a team that included lawyers and architects. He finally abandoned his plans in 2013, although not because of community opposition, or so he said. The costs of the project had kept rising. And even after Rechnitz pledged an additional $10 million, it wasn't enough. He was wealthy, but he was no Barry Diller. Nor, in his style, was Rechnitz a Shelby White, who had focused her giving on Brooklyn institutions valued by the entire community.

White's giving did raise a troubling question, though: Why was her philanthropy needed at all? What kind of great city can't properly maintain an Olmsted jewel like Prospect Park or meet the basic infrastructure needs for the Brooklyn Botanic Garden, which draws a million visitors a year? "In this country, we don't really fund public infrastructure and public spaces as we do in other countries," Emily Lloyd, the head of the Prospect Park Alliance, told the *New York Times* in 2013. "It's always a huge stretch."

Lloyd's point wasn't quite right. There once was a time—before the Reagan years—when government *did* fund infrastructure and other public goods like parks at a higher level. But that era was now past, and the money that *was* flowing wasn't allocated fairly. When Wall Street was booming, Bloomberg had increased spending on parks, but with an approach that relied on public-private partnerships—and bypassed many parks that private players didn't care about. So it is, wrote Michael Kimmelman in the *Times*, that some city parks have been "reduced to the status of beggars."

CITY OF WEALTHY ANGELS

In the 1920s, downtown Los Angeles was among the top metropolises in America. It was dubbed the "Wall Street of the West" thanks to all the banks and other financial institutions clustered on Spring Street in ornate office buildings, while grand hotels, theaters, movie palaces, and department stores lined other streets. The city's rail lines were more extensive than New York's, with 1,100 miles of track.

Within a half century, though, LA's downtown had become a case study in urban decline—doomed by the rise of the automobile and suburbanization. Many of the big businesses were gone, along with the theaters and department stores. The area became best known for having one of the largest concentrations of homeless people in America, on Skid Row.

Today, the homeless still camp en masse on Skid Row, but now they share Downtown Los Angeles with throngs of hipsters, tourists, and museum goers. Rebranded "DTLA," the area has moved to the forefront of urban gentrification. A key driver of that shift has been the area's transformed cultural institutions. These include the Los Angeles Philharmonic, housed in a spectacular Frank Gehry building sheathed in a stainless-steel skin that opened in 2003; the Los Angeles County Museum of Art, which was transformed starting in 2004, with new buildings and collections; and the Museum of Contemporary Art, founded in 1979 and greatly expanded since, which has one of the top collections of modern art in the world.

Then there is the latest addition to the downtown cultural scene: another museum of modern art, which opened in the fall of 2015, called the Broad. It holds the collection of Eli and Edythe Broad, who paid $140 million to have the museum built. The Broads' art holdings—some eight thousand works, by such artists as Jasper Johns, Jeff Koons, Roy Lichtenstein, and Andy Warhol—has been valued at over $2 billion. Now anyone can see many of those pieces, free of charge.

Eli Broad was one of the men who helped doom Downtown Los Angeles in earlier times. He made the first chunk of his fortune starting in the 1960s by mass-producing suburban homes, as a co-founder of KB Home, which became the largest homebuilder in the United States. Broad later went on to make an even bigger fortune by transforming an insurance company into a financial powerhouse, SunAmerica—which he would sell to AIG for $18 billion. He is the only person to have created two Fortune 500 companies.

Los Angeles has been the prime locus of Broad's giving, and he's done more than any private citizen to transform downtown, putting up many millions of dollars and generating loads of controversy along the way.

Broad grew up in Michigan, the son of Jewish immigrants from Lithuania. His father, who was a socialist, ran a five-and-dime store in Detroit; his mother was a dressmaker. Broad went to Detroit public schools and then to Michigan State University, where he majored in accounting. After he graduated, he became the youngest certified public accountant (CPA) in Michigan history. Broad went into housebuilding to make more money, and—with his partner, Donald Kaufman—pushed into a growing market by building cheaper houses. Their big idea was to cut costs by selling houses without basements. "We were always at the lower end of the market," Broad told me. Eventually, Broad and Kaufman moved to the fast-growing West, first to Arizona and then to Los Angeles.

As Broad became wealthy, he wanted to give back in Los Angeles, a city famous for allowing people to invent new paths forward for themselves, including many Jewish newcomers who felt shut out of the power structures of the East. Broad said about LA: "It's a meritocracy. It's been very good to me business-wise. It's given me an opportunity to do things I couldn't do in other cities because I didn't have the right political background, family background, religious background, and so on."

From his earliest days as a philanthropist, Broad was never interested in just writing checks. Instead, he was keen "to create things that didn't exist before or to make existing institutions better," as he described it. And one thing that didn't exist in Los Angeles when Broad moved there in the 1960s was any sense of an urban center, or many of the institutions that might anchor such a center. LA had no opera or ballet, and little in the way of theater. Its art museums were anemic, with almost no modern art. There wasn't much mystery as to why downtown was empty and desolate: no one had any reason to go there. "This city was a hundred suburbs trying to find a city," Broad said, repeating a familiar cliché about the sprawling metropolis.

A key date in downtown LA's renaissance is 1979, when the philanthropist Marcia Simon Weisman started the push to create the Museum of Contemporary Art (MoCA). Weisman pledged both cash and art from her private collection to create the museum. Eli Broad was among the early donors, putting up $1 million for the MoCA, along with Max Palevsky, who had made his fortune as an early tech entrepreneur. Broad did more than contribute to MoCA: he led a fundraising campaign that raised $13 million. MoCA would open downtown, on Grand Avenue, in 1986. Broad was named "founding chairman."

The following year, Lillian Disney, the widow of Walt Disney, made a $50 million gift to create a concert hall—for the Los Angeles Philharmonic, also on Grand Avenue. After construction stalled due to funding problems, Eli Broad stepped forward to lead a new fundraising effort in partnership with Mayor Richard Riordan. The Disney family and the Disney company would ultimately kick in around $110 million for the project. Broad's own contributions to what became the Walt Disney Concert Hall were around $25 million.

Meanwhile, Broad kept giving to the MoCA as it expanded, with his donations ultimately totaling over $15 million. He also exerted huge influence over the museum after it encountered hard times in 2008 and Broad stepped in to bail it out. As well, Broad has been a big player in developing the Los Angeles County Museum of Art, giving nearly $60 million to construct a new building for the museum, which opened in 2008. He is a "lifetime trustee" of the LACMA.

Broad was also instrumental in creating the Grand Arts High School in downtown, which was inspired by similar schools elsewhere, such as New York's LaGuardia High School of Music & Art and Performing Arts, which was immortalized in *Fame*. The project exemplified Broad's hands-on approach to philanthropy. He helped lead the effort to sell the city's education administrators on the idea of an arts high school, and then, once the school was approved, Broad helped pay for an architectural competition for its new building on Grand Avenue—one that would complement the other new institutions he had helped create.

Eli Broad has often drawn criticism for his dominant role in the arts in Los Angeles, with others in that world complaining about his heavy-handed, controlling tactics. Broad, for his part, has complained at times that not enough donors were stepping up to help turn LA into a modern metropolis through grand cultural projects. The city, he has said, shouldn't be a "one-philanthropist town."

There were other arts donors in LA, of course—a community that has collectively helped mobilize hundreds of millions of dollars over the decades to revitalize the city's cultural scene—but none have had the deep pockets or drive of Broad. One reason for his outsized influence has also been the weakness of public funding for the arts. In 2003, the budget of the California Arts Council was cut more than 90 percent, and it has never fully recovered. The state now ranks almost last in the nation in public funding for the arts. The lack of government money has meant that private arts funders like Broad have had more clout in setting the cultural agenda in California.

Another area in Los Angeles where Broad has exerted influence is public education. In August 2015, readers of the *Los Angeles Times* learned that the Broad Foundation was secretly working on a plan to dramatically expand the scope of charter schools in the city. A month later, more details emerged: The foundation was teaming up with other deep-pocketed education funders, including the Walton Family Foundation, in a push to move over half of all schoolchildren in Los Angeles into charter schools.

By the time this plan emerged, Eli Broad had already given hundreds of millions of dollars for education reform efforts nationwide. Among his major aims has been to draw talented people into education leadership positions through the Broad Academy, which trains administrators to run urban school systems. The larger goal of Broad's education-related giving has been to break what he calls "a tired government monopoly." Like other big donors to charters, such as the Fisher family, which made its billions from the Gap clothing stores, Broad believes the competition posed by charter schools will force traditional public schools to step up their game.

Broad came over time to the idea of remaking LA's school system with charters. When he first became involved in education in Los Angeles, in the 1990s, he focused on making changes within the existing system by seeking to influence the Los Angeles Unified School District. "But nothing changed. We have very strong teachers unions here," Broad told me. He added that he had nothing against unions—"I'm from a union family"—but he did have a problem with detailed collective bargaining agreements that stipulate what teachers will and will not do, and make it very hard to fire teachers. Charters are widely favored by education reformers as a way to get around teachers unions. "Looking at how we had tried to change things," Broad said, "I came to the conclusion that the only way to make things happen would be to have more school choice, more competition, more charter schools."

Over the past decade, the Broad Foundation has helped turn Los Angeles into a center of the charter school movement. Broad has pumped millions into this effort, backing efforts at both the state and the city level to spread charters. His foundation has been one of the biggest donors to the California Charter Schools Association, the top advocacy group pushing for laws more favorable to charter schools, and he's backed other groups that focus on swaying policy in Sacramento.

Broad's political donations in California have worked in tandem with his philanthropy: He was a major donor to Arnold Schwarzenegger, who was a fervid champion of charters as governor. Broad also gave heavily to candidates running for state superintendent of public instruction, a pivotal post shaping education policy in the state. As with his arts projects downtown, Broad has pulled multiple levers of power to reshape education in LA—levers only available to the super-rich.

By 2015, LA had more kids in charter schools than any other city, with over two hundred charters serving over a hundred thousand students. The new plan backed by Broad and other funders, called the Great Public Schools Now Initiative, aimed to more than double that number, adding 260 new charter schools over a period of just eight years. Broad and the other philanthropists hoped to put up $490 million to fund the expansion.

It was a breathtaking plan, the most ambitious push ever by charter school advocates. If the effort succeeds, it will create one of the biggest shifts in any urban education system in decades—one largely orchestrated by private money. And while the Broad Foundation won't say what share of the total cost it will shoulder to make this expansion happen, the sum is likely to be in the tens of millions of dollars. A memo outlining the plan, obtained by the *Los Angeles Times*, said that donors planned to set aside $21.5 million to deal with the political hurdles to creating more charter schools. This money would go, among other things, to fund a legislative strategy to "undo regulatory interference" with charter schools. It would also be spent to mobilize pro-charter parents in low-income communities, which has been a key strategy of charter backers.

Broad and the other funders already had a strong start in this regard: For several years, they had been backing Parent Revolution, an organization that advocated for charter schools in Los Angeles and beyond. The group's name might suggest support from a groundswell of local activists. In fact, just a few philanthropies provided most of its budget. Between 2012 and 2014, the Broad Foundation had given the group nearly $1.5 million. The Laura and John Arnold Foundation gave it even more, $4.5 million, and the Walton Foundation had kicked in big, too. Beyond parents, the Broad Foundation had an eye on the media. It was among several pro-charter funders that gave $800,000 to fund a new education reporting project by the *Los Angeles Times*—money the beleaguered paper accepted despite the obvious conflict of interest posed by the gift.

Finally, Eli Broad and other wealthy donors—including Michael Bloomberg, Doris Fisher, and members of the Walton family—personally made $2.3 million in campaign contributions in 2015 to a pro-charter PAC that aimed to influence the LA school board elections. Four seats on the seven-member board, which would have a big say over the fate of the Broad charter plan, were up for grabs.

The donations by pro-charter funders, which turned the school board race into the most expensive in the nation, weren't revealed until months after ballots had been cast. This wasn't the first time that mega-donors had poured money into a local school board race in the United States. In recent years, pro-charter philanthropists have also sought to influence school board races in New Orleans; Bridgeport, Connecticut; and Denver with campaign gifts. Broad has been among the contributors helping "nationalize" local school board races, as one study put it. Previously, teachers unions had been the main donors in such races, usually at small levels. Broad and other donors to education-related elections see themselves as leveling the playing field, although in the 2015 school board races in LA, they outspent the unions by over $1 million as they sought to set the stage for the biggest expansion of urban charter schools ever.

The political hurdles to what was quickly dubbed the "Broad Plan" soon became evident, when the city's top teachers union came out in opposition. United Teachers Los Angeles (UTLA) president Alex Caputo-Pearl said, "We're going to make every effort that we can to organize against the expansion of what are essentially unregulated non-union schools that don't play by the rules as everybody else." Caputo-Pearl also told the *Times*, "We're concerned about anything Eli Broad is involved with."

In September 2015, when the Broad museum opened on Grand Avenue, the teachers union led a protest. "Invest in public schools, not billionaire vanity projects," said one sign. But it wasn't just the unions who had qualms about the plan. Some observers questioned the rush to expand the city's charter schools when the existing charter schools were achieving what the *LA Schools Report* called "mixed" results. In January 2016, the LA school board voted 7 to 0 for a resolution aimed at checking the Broad Plan.

Diane Ravitch captured the sentiments of many critics of education-reform philanthropy when she wrote about the LA plan: "The really important question is why a billionaire should be allowed to buy half of a public institution. If Eli Broad didn't like policing in Los Angeles, could he buy half the police force? If he thought the public parks were not well run, could he buy half of them? Why should he be allowed to buy half the children in LAUSD?"

In truth, Broad and the other funders behind his charter plan were thinking well beyond the students in LAUSD. The memo detailing their plan stated: "Los Angeles is uniquely positioned to create the largest, highest-performing charter sector in the nation." Broad told me that the goal is a "model that can be emulated in other cities. It's not just about us."

As for his critics, Broad doesn't worry much about them. He's famously not concerned with being Mr. Nice, unlike his wife, Edythe, who has many admirers. "My wife is not as aggressive as I am," Broad said. "I'm respected, and she's loved."

Edythe has little interest in education philanthropy, which Broad said is "not pleasant work." He adds: "She wonders why I spend all this time and energy on something that is frustrating where you can't make rapid progress."

Even as he and other unelected private donors work to improve LA's public school system, Broad disputes the idea that there is anything undemocratic about his tactics. Like many philanthropists throwing their weight around in public life in ways that ordinary citizens can't imagine, Broad sees himself as expanding the dialogue, not dominating it. "I think everyone is getting heard. We're getting heard, the philanthropists. The unions and administrators are getting heard. Overall, we're creating debate."

Broad, who is in his early eighties, told me he is "working harder than ever." So far, he's given away more than $4 billion and plans to give billions more.

Not long before he was elected mayor of New York in 2001, Michael Bloomberg ran into his old friend Vartan Gregorian on the street in New York. Gregorian led the Carnegie Corporation, which was among the oldest foundations in America, and one with close ties to nonprofits in the city. Gregorian told Bloomberg that these groups were reeling as a result of the attacks of September 11 and an economic downturn. Could Bloomberg do more to help them out, using his vast personal wealth?

Bloomberg agreed, and soon sent over a very large check to Carnegie, which the foundation was free to use as it saw fit. More big checks followed after Bloomberg took office, arriving each December, with the sums rising into the tens of millions of dollars.

Carnegie spread the money far and wide, to hundreds of nonprofits around the city, particularly arts and cultural groups. Ultimately, by 2010 more than $200 million would flow from Bloomberg through this program. And while the grants were made by Carnegie, and Bloomberg stayed anonymous, it was widely known that the mayor had quietly become one of the largest private funders of nonprofits in the city.

An inspiring story of generosity? Certainly, as the money proved a crucial lifeline for many groups during tough times. But this giving was also deeply unsettling, particularly to Bloomberg's political rivals, who didn't have anything like his resources with which to buy influence around the city. The *New York Times* reported that when Bloomberg was pushing the City Council to revise the city's term limits law, to allow him to run for a third term as mayor, his "aides asked several groups that had received Carnegie grants to lobby for the change publicly." Others, presumably, didn't have to be asked: They knew who their sugar daddy was.

The change to the law was ultimately approved, allowing Bloomberg to run for a third term in 2009. It would be his toughest race yet, but Bloomberg eked out a narrow victory over Democratic challenger William C. Thompson. He spent $103 million on his final race for office, or about $183 per vote.

The following year, Bloomberg pulled the plug on the Carnegie grants program for city nonprofits.

5

Disrupters

Sean Parker grew up in suburban Virginia, outside of Washington, D.C. He learned to code at a young age after his father, who had been chief scientist at the National Oceanic and Atmospheric Administration, taught him how to program on an Atari 800. His fascination with computers led the FBI to his door when he was a teenager, after he hacked into a Fortune 500 company. (As a minor, he was let off with community service.) Parker won the Virginia state science fair after creating a web crawler and did so well financially in high school, working for D.C.-area tech companies, that he decided to skip college.

Parker became a hero in the hacker world after 1999, when he and Shawn Fanning created Napster, a music-file-sharing service. Napster was wildly popular with music lovers, attracting tens of millions of users and fundamentally disrupting the recording industry. It was equally unpopular with music creators, and was eventually shut down by lawsuits. Parker's next project, the networking site Plaxo, also did well—but he was ousted after differences with the venture capitalists who controlled the company.

Then, in 2004, Parker hooked up with Mark Zuckerberg and became the first president of Facebook. Parker saw the transformative potential of the business even as Zuckerberg himself still hedged his bets, working on a side project called Wirehog. "Sean was pivotal in helping Facebook transform from a college project into a real company," Zuckerberg later told *Forbes*. Parker recruited Peter Thiel as the company's first investor and, during subsequent investment rounds, helped structure Facebook so that Zuckerberg had complete control of its board. Parker had learned the hard way what can happen when venture capitalists hold power over young entrepreneurs. As it turned out, though, Parker would be ousted from Facebook by the company's financiers after he was arrested in 2005, on a cocaine charge that was later dropped.

Parker walked away from his short involvement at Facebook with enough stock to later become a billionaire while still in his early thirties. He bought multiple homes in California, as well as a $20 million townhouse in Greenwich Village and traveled on private jets. He filled closets with expensive suits and eyeglasses and shoes. His 2013 wedding, amid the redwoods in Big Sur, with guests wearing costumes created by the *Lord of Rings* costume designer, reportedly cost millions of dollars to orchestrate.

Yet even if Parker had gone on spending at this rate through his lifetime, he would only have scratched the surface of a fortune estimated at $2.4 billion in 2016. Besides, Parker saw big problems that he wanted to help solve, starting in the area of health. He had struggled all his life with food allergies, which can produce terrifying and life-threatening anaphylactic allergic reactions. Parker was interested in other health threats, too, like cancer. And he was fascinated by the failure of medicine to conquer such challenges. He said about food allergies at one point: "This should be a curable disease but all we've done is put Band-Aids on it. We've been treating symptoms for 100 years."

Parker believed that one key to making big medical breakthroughs—not just on allergies and cancer, but on many other problems, such as diabetes and arthritis—lay in the autoimmune system. Any number of diseases come about because the immune system goes sideways and attacks the body's tissues, rather than doing its proper job, which is to keep us healthy. "A huge amount of costs in the healthcare system goes toward treating these diseases that have, at their root, an immunological component that needs to be addressed," Parker said. And yet there was reason to believe that this is what Parker would call a "hackable problem," drawing on new research on immune mechanisms.

In 2015, after a flurry of big gifts for autoimmune research, Parker stepped things up further, announcing that he was setting aside $600 million to create the Parker Foundation, with a big focus on the life sciences.

The goal was to orchestrate new breakthroughs that would "accelerate novel immunotherapies and treatment strategies." In April 2016, Parker got more focused, committing $250 million to launch the Parker Institute for Cancer Immunotherapy, an effort that brings together researchers from a half dozen of the top U.S. cancer centers in a collaborative search for breakthrough cures to cancer. It was one of the biggest pledges ever made by a private donor to cancer research.

The federal government spends around $5 billion a year on cancer research. Big Pharma invests even more. By comparison, Sean Parker's grant of $250 million to advance cancer immunotherapy is not a lot of money. How much progress can a philanthropist wielding a slingshot hope to have against a disease that kills eight million people a year worldwide?

That question will be answered in time. But to Parker, this is a prime area where philanthropy can make a difference. Government tends to be risk-averse in funding biomedical science, with the National Cancer Institute gravitating toward sure-thing research delivering incremental gains, not breakthrough cures. "The agencies responsible for funding most scientific research don't encourage scientists to pursue their boldest ideas," Parker said. Meanwhile, cancer researchers tend to work in silos, spread out across institutions that don't talk to one another, guarding findings that ideally should be shared and built upon. Those same researchers also spend too much time writing grants instead of running studies with the freedom to pivot easily as new information comes in. "These web-like layers of bureaucracy don't just make it hard for scientists to do their best science, they make it hard for scientists to do science at all," Parker said. The Parker Institute aims to do things differently—and accelerate breakthroughs as a result.

Fighting dread diseases ranks among the oldest priorities of philanthropy. Much of John D. Rockefeller's giving focused on this area a century ago. In fact, researchers backed by the oil titan's money were the first to identify autoimmune diseases, and that was just one among many breakthroughs made possible by Rockefeller wealth. Legions of philanthropists would follow in Rockefeller's footsteps in bankrolling medical science. Health, along with education and the arts, remains among the most well-established philanthropic causes.

Yet as Sean Parker plunged into large-scale giving, he didn't look to philanthropy's past for role models. Rather, he turned to the tech world where he'd made his fortune. "The Parker Foundation will apply the lessons learned from Silicon Valley start-ups to our philanthropic initiatives," he said. "We must move fast, make concentrated bets based on our convictions, have the courage to make mistakes and learn from them."

In a *Wall Street Journal* essay, he went further, putting forth a manifesto that rejected the old ways of giving and arguing that a new breed of tech donors should follow in the path of hackers as they gave away their fortunes. "Hackers are popularly considered to be troublemakers, but they are also dedicated problem solvers, as interested in discovering holes in systems as they are in exploiting them for personal gain," Parker wrote. "By identifying weaknesses in long-established systems, they have successfully disrupted countless industries, from retail and music to transportation and publishing." Now it was time for wealthy techies to do the same with their philanthropy.

In Parker's view, the great fortunes of outsiders like himself and his fellow hackers stand as an "aberration in history." These were never people who aspired to join the establishment or elite society. And now that they're rich they should have no interest in following a conventional model of philanthropy, Parker said. "It's important for hackers to embrace the values that made them successful in the first place: skepticism of the establishment and a desire to provoke or upend it."

In his essay, Parker aimed to sum up his own emerging philanthropic worldview and that of his peers, and rally others behind it. For starters, he said, the new tech donors aren't going to wait until later in life to give. "The only way to avoid the pitfalls of philanthropic decay is to deploy resources quickly, in response to current problems. This means spending down all of your philanthropic assets during your own lifetime." One of the worst things the new donors could do would be to build large, cautious foundations that exist in perpetuity, like Rockefeller and Carnegie did. "Hacker philanthropists must resist the urge to institutionalize and must never stop making big bets," Parker said. He also described new donors like himself as drawn to "hackable problems"—those ready to be solved and where a donor could bring the leverage and competitive advantage needed to succeed.

Finally, Parker said that tech donors shouldn't be afraid of politics, and he cited George Soros, Michael Bloomberg, and Charles Koch as prime examples of philanthropists who extended their reach through investments in public policy. Wrote Parker: "It is possible to engage in politics and advocacy for the public good."

THE NEW WAY

Sean Parker's manifesto generated some pushback from the philanthropy establishment, which took offense at his view of foundations as "antiquated institutions" whose leaders were mainly focused on "preserving the resources and reputations of the institutions they run."

These critics had a point. Many of the legacy foundations like Ford and Carnegie were indeed lumbering bureaucracies with sky-high overhead, but they were still scoring some big wins. Ford, for example, was one of the largest funders of the successful push for LGBT rights. The Robert Wood Johnson Foundation had a major hand in the enactment of the Affordable Care Act. The Rockefeller Brothers Fund—an outfit founded over seventy-five years ago—played a key behind-the-scenes role in helping orchestrate the historic 2015 deal to end Iran's nuclear program.

But if Parker was too flippant in his dismissal of established philanthropy, his manifesto captured the outlook of many newer philanthropists, and not just those from the tech world. Younger donors from Wall Street—like hedge fund billionaires John Arnold and Bill Ackman—are also giving early in life with a keen focus on investments that can be disruptive and produce systemic change. Some wealthy heirs, like Dave Peery, the son of a California real estate mogul, think along the same lines, and are revamping family foundations to move beyond the traditional charitable model and push for larger reforms in society.

The quest for the big play—philanthropic bets that produce major change—isn't just animating younger donors, either. Eli Broad thinks the same way. Broad may be the archetype of the traditional white-haired civic power broker, who comes from the old economy and pumps millions into museums and local schools. But, remember, he made his fortune as an entrepreneur who disrupted first the home-building industry and, later, the stodgy backwater of annuities. Broad has said he approaches medical research, an interest he shares with his wife, "the way a venture capitalist approaches investment—look for promising new ideas and put up seed money that can be leveraged."

That outlook led him in 2001 to the field of genomic medicine, which—

like autoimmune research—may hold the key to making progress against a whole range of diseases. He and his wife put $600 million into creating a center for genomic research, the Broad Institute, that brought MIT and Harvard together in a historic collaboration. The success of the institute would eventually attract $825 million from another philanthropist, Ted Stanley. When Sean Parker began putting together his cancer immuno-therapy effort, one person he turned to for advice was Eric Lander, the president and founding director of the Broad Institute. Lander ended up sitting on the board of the Parker Institute.

FasterCures, the research organization created in 2003 by another older philanthropist, Michael Milken, also foreshadowed the impatient approach that Parker would bring to immunotherapy. Milken, who noto-riously made his fortune in the fast-paced world of finance in the 1980s, had been appalled after he got prostate cancer at how long it took for new drugs and medical advances to get to ordinary patients. His goal with FasterCures has been to create a harder-charging medical world, one that operates more like the dynamic business sector where Milken earned bil-lions before being convicted for insider trading.

In short, donors like Sean Parker are anything but new to philan-thropy. What's changed is that philanthropists intent on spending fast to find breakthroughs or achieve disruptive change are more numerous than ever before, especially among the ranks of younger entrepreneurs emerging as major winners from tech and finance. While a handful of bil-lionaire philanthropists like Parker and Zuckerberg get all the attention, below them is a growing army of wealthy donors who think the same way and are turning to giving in a hands-on, activist way. They don't want to just support "causes." They want to solve problems—big ones. They want their money to make a decisive difference.

That makes sense given how you achieve major wealth in today's econ-omy, which is often by looking at what everyone else is doing and then doing something different. You find the need that hasn't been met or bet on the trend that nobody else sees or find a way to do things better, faster, and cheaper. And, if you're really successful, your innovation disrupts entire industries—forever changing how things are done, which is what Napster did to the recording industry.

A standard question that venture investors ask would-be entrepre-neurs is, what problem are you trying to solve? A next question is, how are you going to solve that problem on a large scale? And then, how will you navigate the risks needed to pull off your vision? People who've answered those questions in business, succeeding in a big way, are often well suited for high-impact philanthropy—and today there are record numbers of donors emerging with entrepreneurial backgrounds.

This has no precedent in history. Although huge piles of wealth have long been created by successful entrepreneurs—Henry Ford was a classic entrepreneur, and so was John D. Rockefeller—it's only recently, in the past few decades, that the culture of entrepreneurship has become a pervasive feature of an American business world that not so long ago was ruled by the "organization man." Since the beginning of the dot-com era, entrepreneurialism has been operating on steroids, producing vast fortunes at a faster pace, as business cycles have sped up. Now, this same energy is increasingly being harnessed to giving away money on a large scale, marking a major turn in the annals of philanthropy.

Why does this shift matter so much? Because it's amplifying the impact and power of philanthropists at a time when their clout is growing due to other forces, such as the increased scale of giving and the decline of government. It's not just that so much *new* money is arriving these days in philanthropy; it's that so much *impatient* money is arriving. More donors, like Parker, are turning to philanthropy at the height of their careers, bringing the same entrepreneurial drive to their giving that made them winners in business. What's more, as apostles of "giving while living," many aim to deploy their philanthropic capital earlier and more aggressively than previous generations of donors.

Parker isn't alone among these new donors in believing that the entrepreneurial class has unique problem-solving abilities with which to tackle the challenges facing humanity. While it remains to be seen whether this view is well-founded, such optimism is exciting at a moment when there is no shortage of difficult problems to solve. Lots of super-empowered problem-solvers, it might seem, are exactly what the world needs right now.

But, just as clearly, this is a scary thing. These newcomers often know little about the complex problems they aspire to solve—yet may have too much hubris to recognize it—which raises an obvious risk of screwups. Making a bundle in software or short trading doesn't mean you'll know the first thing about, say, K–12 education, and it's easy for misguided philanthropists to do a lot of damage (more about that later). Overconfidence is a dangerous thing when combined with great wealth and little in the way of accountability. Some newcomers are well aware of these risks and tread carefully; others operate more brashly.

Also worrying is the way that the rising confidence of the donor class stands in stark contrast to how most Americans feel when it comes to their ability to shape society—which is increasingly disempowered. These trends are not entirely unrelated. The more active the rich have become in injecting their money and preferences into public life, the less that ordinary people may feel they can compete and the more they may tend to withdraw.

RAMPING UP

Dustin Moskovitz, the Facebook co-founder, is among the successful entrepreneurs who have lately entered philanthropy with big money and big ambitions. He's also a reassuring example of a donor who is moving forward with a fair degree of caution and humility.

In the mythology of Facebook's founding, Chris Hughes and Eduardo Saverin are often cast as kids who just got lucky by rooming with Mark Zuckerberg at Harvard. Moskovitz, though, was a programmer and a key player in Facebook's development. He did much of the heavy lifting to found the company as its first chief technology officer and then vice president of engineering. It was Moskovitz who oversaw the young techies who built out Facebook's architecture in its formative years. He left Facebook in 2008, walking away with enough stock to become a billionaire—one of the youngest in the world. As those shares have climbed in value, Moskovitz's fortune had surpassed $10 billion by 2016.

Moskovitz has viewed his vast and unexpected wealth with a certain detachment. He had gone to public schools in Ocala, Florida, the son of a psychiatrist father and a mother who was a teacher and an artist. Moskovitz met Mark Zuckerberg on his first day as a sophomore at Harvard and within a few years was rich beyond imagination. His fortune was far greater than he could ever need or spend on himself, and was amassed so quickly that he didn't even think of it as "his" money; he was more inclined to refer to it as "the" money. He saw himself as a steward of capital that "belongs to the world," and should be used as a tool to make that world a better place.

Moskovitz decided early on that he would give away all "the money" and do so in his lifetime. "I don't intend to amass capital and then leave it to another generation," he told an interviewer on the eve of Facebook's IPO in 2012. "I expect not to have it by the time we get to the end of our lives."

Moskovitz's partner in this effort is his wife, Cari Tuna, a former reporter for the *Wall Street Journal* who quit journalism in 2011 to take on the job of building the couple's foundation, Good Ventures, while Moskovitz remained engaged in the tech world through Asana, a company he co-founded.

Like her husband, Tuna comes from an ordinary upper-middle-class background. She was born in Minnesota and grew up in Indiana, where both her parents were doctors. She attended that state's first charter school, and then went on to Yale, where she majored in political science and wrote for the school paper. She was working for the *Journal* in the Bay Area when she met Moskovitz, who by then already planned to give away his Facebook billions. Together, they decided that Tuna would spearhead that mammoth job, even though she had never managed staff and had no background in philanthropy. Something similar, though, could be said about any number of young entrepreneurs who stumbled into ambitious leadership roles in the tech world. "It would have been very hard for someone else to do it," Tuna told me. "Dustin and I have a very trusting relationship which allows me to be here [at Good Ventures], representing our values, and working on a day-to-day basis."

Moskovitz and Tuna knew that giving away billions of dollars in their lifetime wouldn't be easy, and so it was imperative to begin early. "If you're thinking about giving away money at that kind of volume, you need to start learning now," Moskovitz said in 2012. "It will take us a decade just to get to full capacity." There would be plenty of time for trial and error along the way.

Moskovitz shares a number of traits with other entrepreneurs who've turned to philanthropy in recent years. Like many of these people, he is giving early in life, while very much still involved in business, as opposed to leaving the big giving to later. He also has no interest in endowing a foundation that will exist in perpetuity, doling out grant money in small increments. He wants to deploy capital quickly by "identifying the causes where we can make the most leveraged contributions."

Moskovitz and Tuna, who signed on to the Giving Pledge in 2010, see big gains from front-loading their philanthropy. "It will hopefully never be as inexpensive as it is now to help people," Tuna told me, referring to the many places where philanthropic dollars can buy big results. For example, for just a few thousand dollars, today's donors can save a human life by giving for anti-malaria bed nets. Investing in vaccinations is another cheap way to have an impact. In effect, said Tuna, it's a buyer's market right now for philanthropists who want to make a difference, with plenty of low-hanging fruit to choose from in a world awash with needless suffering and preventable deaths.

Further, giving money today can help solve problems early that will only be more expensive to tackle later. The cost of a bed net or vaccination is infinitely cheaper than the cost of taking care of people who become sick with malaria or other diseases. In a different way, helping poor households build financial assets can lead to a host of benefits that come when people have some wealth. "Giving now puts people in a better position to help themselves and others," said Tuna. "The good we do now compounds over time."

Many foundations, designed to exist in perpetuity, aim to preserve their endowments by only spending the income from their investments, often around 5 percent a year. Tuna and Moskovitz see that approach as too limiting. "If we were only giving 5 percent for the rest of our lives, we would have so much less to work with to address the problems of our time." Mark Zuckerberg and Priscilla Chan are among many younger mega-givers who believe the same thing. Few of these donors want any money to be left over by the time they die.

Moskovitz and Tuna share another common trait of today's activist donor class: They're intent on using their money to make things happen that otherwise wouldn't, looking to invest in "important areas on which we could have an outsized impact long-term." In other words, they're not keen to kick in funding to existing, popular causes; instead, they want to invest their money in places that can be decisive.

And where, exactly, might those places be? This can be a daunting question for newcomers to philanthropy who are intent on being strategic.

To find answers, Tuna embarked on a long string of conversations, starting after she quit the *Wall Street Journal*, that took her to a slew of foundations and nonprofits. She met with leaders in the quest for an AIDS vaccination and also sat down with people who ran the sprawling philanthropic operation of Pierre Omidyar, the founder of eBay. She met with top academics to talk about how their philanthropy might improve research, and with the head of the ACLU, Anthony Romero, to talk about investing in public policy and advocacy.

Tuna and Moskovitz studied how Bill Gates and George Soros were doing their giving, and also listened closely to the advice of Paul Brest, the chief of the giant William and Flora Hewlett Foundation, who had become a spokesman for strategic philanthropy. Herb Sandler—the retired banker who has underwritten liberal think tanks and groundbreaking medical research—became another source of advice.

Young Silicon Valley philanthropists have a bad rap in some quarters for being dismissive of all funders who've gone before them. That's overblown, and Tuna and Moskovitz aren't the only new tech donors who have turned to the powers that be for guidance. Zuckerberg made a point of talking to veteran funders as he ramped up his education giving—for example, visiting Eli Broad at his home in Brentwood with Facebook's chief operating officer, Sheryl Sandberg, for a conversation that lasted for hours.

As it turned out, though, one of the earliest, most important connections Cari Tuna made was with a young Harvard grad who had left his hedge fund job hoping to lead a revolution of sorts against the charitable establishment. That would be Holden Karnofsky, executive director of GiveWell, a nonprofit he co-founded in 2007 to evaluate charities. Karnofsky is a believer in effective altruism, which stresses that philanthropic dollars should be directed in ways that best improve the world. Effective altruists like philosopher Peter Singer argue that it's wrong to give money for, say, the symphony, when those same donations, made to the right organizations, could save human lives.

Tuna had read Singer's 2009 manifesto for effective altruism, *The Life You Can Save*, while still at the *Wall Street Journal* and was deeply influenced by his ideas. The book focuses on global poverty, and how even modest donations go a long way toward alleviating suffering in poor countries. All this made tremendous sense to Tuna, who came to see "global health and development as a good fit for philanthropy. Dollars just go so far in improving the lives of low-income people." Bill and Melinda Gates had come to the same conclusion in the late 1990s, as they first embarked on large-scale giving.

Still, the big question for donors is knowing which groups really are using money most effectively to improve the world—particularly in remote regions like Africa, which are utterly foreign to most philanthropists. How could a donor sitting in Silicon Valley or Manhattan know whether a nonprofit working in Senegal or Tanzania was actually getting the results it claimed? That's where GiveWell came in. It searched around for groups that seemed to be doing the greatest good, analyzed them as rigorously as was feasible, and then recommended the very best of them to donors.

Not everyone is keen on effective altruism and its fiercely utilitarian logic. But Tuna, who was already sold on this approach, was thrilled to hook up with GiveWell, and began working closely with the group to sort through the myriad choices that she and Moskovitz confronted as they set out to give away billions. In fact, Tuna liked GiveWell's methodology so much that she offered Karnofsky and his staff space at Good Ventures' offices in San Francisco, which are downtown with views of the harbor. Eventually, they formalized their collaboration in a joint effort, the Open Philanthropy Project.

Tuna and the new team spent months and months researching potential areas of giving, along with ways to give. They made a list of all the causes they might support, and dug into the details.

Three criteria emerged to guide their choices: importance, neglectedness, and tractability. Tuna wanted to address big problems where there was the clear potential to make a difference, but which other funders tended to overlook. The goal was to focus "on where our money can go the furthest," she said.

Tuna and the GiveWell staff also agreed that taking risks—lots of risks—was essential. They viewed grantmaking as similar to the venture capital business. Tuna explained to me: "A lot of philanthropy's biggest successes have come from funding work that wasn't obviously going to succeed and could easily have failed, but ended up having enormous impact." Good Ventures embraced a "hits-based" approach to giving— that is, the goal is to score some major hits, without fretting about the misses. "We expect to fail a lot," Tuna said. "But a few of the things we support will have, we hope, enormous impact—and enough to make up for the failures."

Two of Good Venture's first grants went to organizations that GiveWell ranked above all others—$500,000 to the Against Malaria Foundation, and $250,000 to the Schistosomiasis Control Initiative, which advances deworming in poor countries. Good Ventures also put money into another global NGO that GiveWell strongly touted, a group that engaged in cash transfers to poor people in Africa called GiveDirectly. The simple premise of this operation is that what people need most to escape poverty is, well, *money*. With just a little extra cash, a poor family in a place like Kenya could buy a cow or farming tools or start a small business—investments that could help them build other assets and climb upward from poverty.

GiveDirectly's approach was supported by a growing body of research. Yet it was an odd duck on a global development scene where most funding went to things like building schools or drilling wells or vaccinating children—funding that was channeled through a vast complex of international aid organizations. GiveDirectly offered a way around these middlemen, and that approach struck a chord in Silicon Valley, where any number of successful ventures were based on "disintermediation." Maybe it was possible to cut the anti-poverty industry's market share the same way that, say, web companies like Travelocity had nearly wiped out travel agencies. A broader mantra of the valley is to empower individuals over institutions, and Cari Tuna saw the same need here: "Governments and donors spend tens of billions of dollars a year on reducing poverty, but the people who are meant to benefit from the money rarely get a say in how it's spent," she would write.

Six months after Good Ventures made its first grant to GiveDirectly, it made a far bigger second one, of $500,000. And just a year after that, Moskovitz and Tuna made their biggest bet as philanthropists, giving $7 million to GiveDirectly.

Others from the tech world also got behind this group, including another Facebook co-founder, Chris Hughes, who joined its board and threw a party in San Francisco in 2013 to introduce his tech friends to GiveDirectly. Another believer was Jacqueline Fuller, a former Gates Foundation executive who ran Google's philanthropic arm. At Hughes's party, Fuller shared a story of the time she approached her superiors about supporting GiveDirectly. She explained the NGO's philosophy and the response she received was "You must be smoking crack." Google did, however, get on board with a $2.5 million donation.

In 2015, Good Ventures made an even bigger bet on GiveDirectly: $25 million—the foundation's largest grant yet. Tuna announced the investment in a blog post in which she imagined a future in which billions of dollars in global aid is redirected away from inefficient middlemen and given directly to the poor.

Meanwhile, Moskovitz and Tuna have also given big to push major changes in the United States. They've devoted millions to fueling efforts at criminal justice reform, as well as backing work to improve the welfare of farm animals. Drug policy reform has been another cause, which they've bankrolled with both grants and campaign donations, emerging as among the biggest supporters of 2016 ballot initiatives to legalize marijuana. (A cause that Sean Parker also strongly embraced, giving over $7 million to pass an initiative in California.) The 2016 election cycle saw Moskovitz and Tuna emerge for the first time as mega Democratic donors, with the $35 million in gifts to super PACs. That same year, as Facebook's stock continued to climb, Moskovitz's fortune climbed to more than $12 billion.

As for how those billions will ultimately be deployed, the plan is continuing to take shape. Tuna told me that they'll give away a growing stream of money as they get a better fix on where it should go. She said that the goal is to "give sooner rather than later, as soon as we can give confidently."

When the couple's philanthropy is fully up and running, and hits what Tuna calls "peak giving," they'll be giving out hundreds of millions of dollars a year.

CATALYTIC

Over the past decade, over fifteen thousand new foundations have been established in the United States. Most exist only on paper, without staff or websites, and plenty of donors manage to give away a lot of money without much infrastructure. Wall Street types seem especially averse to building up foundations. Explaining why he hasn't hired much help, even as he gives on a large scale, Bruce Kovner said, "I have resisted forming a larger organization because bureaucracies have a way of creating their own agenda. I would rather keep my strategic priorities limited and clear—and then personally make sure that they are being accomplished without mission drift."

Another explanation for why Wall Streeters stay lean is that they're used to investing huge amounts of money, many billions of dollars, and so the much smaller numbers involved in philanthropy don't seem very daunting. Still, as any number of philanthropists have learned the hard way, giving away money wisely isn't easy. That's all the more true if you want to leverage your funds to achieve large-scale change—something that many mega-givers from finance are also keenly interested in these days.

Wall Streeters understand leverage for the obvious reason that it's how you make money in finance, or at least a lot of money. You take piles of capital that isn't yours, place bets, and leverage more capital to place even bigger bets. If all goes well, you end up like Bill Ackman, the billionaire hedge funder known for his activist investing.

Ackman would be a good model for a novelist looking to update *Bonfire of the Vanities*. He has a prototypical Master of the Universe profile, except that he lives on the Upper West Side, not the Upper East Side. Ackman was born in 1966 and grew up in Chappaqua, an affluent Westchester County suburb of New York, the son of the chairman of a commercial real estate mortgage brokerage. He went to Harvard for both his undergraduate degree and his MBA, starting his own hedge fund straight out of business school. Ackman has had some major ups and downs as an investor, but is now safely a billionaire—a label he doesn't like. "Billionaire sounds like it's someone who's all about the money," he once said. "The only thing money has meant to me is independence." As for that independence, Ackman owns a house in the Hamptons and a Gulfstream jet, along with an apartment in the Beresford on Central Park West, bought for a record-setting sum. On Wall Street, he is known for his sharp-elbowed moves and titanic clashes with other investors, as well as his cockiness. In an interview with *Vanity Fair*, Ackman said that in high school he bet his father $2,000 that he would get a perfect 800 score on his verbal SAT. The bet was called off, but decades later, Ackman still talked about it. He's that kind of guy.

One of Ackman's detractors is the preeminent corporate lawyer

Marty Lipton, who argues that activist hedge funder investors—whom he's called "Alpha Wolves"—are partly to blame for America's economic stagnation because they've forced corporations to embrace short-term thinking. Ackman takes the exact opposite view—that investors like him push firms to improve—and once publicly challenged Lipton to debate the subject, an offer that was rejected. "It would be beneath me," Lipton said. This little skirmish is one of many that have unfolded between Ackman and his critics in recent years. He's also battled financier Carl Icahn about the company Herbalife, which Ackman shorted and called a pyramid scheme. When Ackman's hedge fund suffered a 20 percent loss in 2015, after being up 40 percent the year before, some people were surely thrilled by the news. (Even with the steep loss, the fund's base management fee ensured over $500 million in compensation for Ackman and his team that year—a standard practice that conjures up the saying "heads I win, tails you lose.")

What doesn't quite fit with this brash picture is Ackman's long-time interest in philanthropy. Ackman has said that some of his earliest memories were of his father exhorting him to give back. He took that advice seriously, and began donating money as soon as he began making it in his late twenties, with his first hedge fund. Another influence Ackman cites is John Rawls, the philosopher, whom he read at Harvard. Rawls famously argued that society should be organized in a fashion that ensures fairness for anyone born into any position. To Ackman, one implication of Rawls's ideas was that those born to privilege had an obligation to redistribute some of that wealth. "I thought I would be very successful," he told me. "And I decided that, if that were true, I would be as successful as I could be and then reallocate the resources in the way that I thought made the most sense." Along with his wife, Karen, a landscape architect, Ackman has given away tens of millions of dollars through the Pershing Square Foundation.

If Rawls were still alive, he'd surely shudder at the thought that voluntary giving by billionaires is any kind of solution to record levels of inequality. Whatever the case, the Ackmans are emblematic of a new generation of donors who are changing the face of philanthropy. They jumped into big-time giving early in life, rejecting the old model of making money first and giving it away second—just like a lot of other emerging donors. Also like many newer donors, the Ackmans have rejected an old-style, passive approach to philanthropy. While they write some checks to Harvard and other well-established institutions, their bigger focus has been on putting money where it can play a catalytic role in improving America and the world.

"I'm a big believer that philanthropy is about solving problems," Ackman said. He doesn't view nonprofits as the best tool to solve problems—in his book, that would be business—but he does see a role for philanthropic dollars "where there isn't a for-profit solution to the problem." Because the Pershing Square Foundation doesn't have huge resources—say, like the Ford Foundation—the Ackmans and their small staff are drawn to opportunities where their money can be pivotal in some way, leveraging change that would not otherwise occur. Often, that means investing in fledgling initiatives, where early money can help get a promising new effort off the ground. "We're not going to move the needle in some massive organization that raises $500 million a year," Ackman said. "But in a start-up we can. . . . You can help make these organizations grow very quickly."

Paul Bernstein, the first president of the Pershing Square Foundation, shared with me a telling anecdote about an early conversation he had with the Ackmans when discussing the new job. He asked them if they had an interest in giving for HIV/AIDS, which Bernstein had worked on for years and which was (and still is) ravaging Africa. The Ackmans said such funding wasn't in the cards because of all the work already being done in this area. "They didn't see where they could be catalytic." For some new donors, even a reliable path to saving lives is less appealing than the big play that can disrupt some existing system in a way that improves the world.

In a standard model of philanthropy, a donor chooses a set of priorities—like protecting the environment or conquering a dread disease—and starts writing checks to groups working on those issues. The Ackmans do some funding like that, but tend toward a different, more opportunistic approach. Instead of being guided by a list of causes, the Pershing Square Foundation takes an open-ended approach, scouting for "programs that are catalytic for social change and meaningfully improve people's lives."

From his decades of financial investing, Ackman believes he has a keen sense of which ideas and leaders are likely to succeed. He says that the basic ideas behind venture investing, which he learned at Harvard Business School, guide his decisions in both his hedge fund and philanthropy. "To me the most important thing is the person running it," Ackman said, about sizing up an opportunity. The other top questions are "what's the problem, how big is it, and what is the probability that they'll be able to solve it."

After due diligence by his staff, Ackman often makes giving decisions quickly. "In twenty minutes, I can decide. I meet the entrepreneurs; I make a judgment about the business plan." That was the case when Amy Bach came in to pitch her organization, Measures for Justice, which she started in order to make better use of data to "flag systemic problems in the justice system" that result in disparities and injustices. Her idea is that comparing how different local governments are doing on criminal justice indicators and holding them accountable for their performance is key to driving reform. "No data, no change" is the group's motto.

Bach approached Pershing Square because the Ackmans have a keen interest in justice issues. They'd been big contributors to the Innocence Project, and to Human Rights Watch, where Karen sits on the board. Bach arrived seeking $600,000, which was a big ask. She ended up getting much more. "In this meeting, we were just blown away," Ackman recalled. "And we said, 'Look, how much would you need to do this on a really accelerated time frame where you don't have to spend all your time fundraising?' She said, 'I don't know, let me think about it.'" The foundation ultimately made a $3.1 million grant to Measures for Justice. "I think it's going to become one of the most important organizations in terms of criminal justice reform," Ackman said.

The search for people with a big vision who "really could change the world," as Bernstein put it, also led the Pershing Square Foundation to heavily back Andrew Youn, a Yale grad with an MBA who lives in Rwanda and co-founded the One Acre Fund, which aims to bolster the productivity and income of small farmers in Africa and beyond.

When the foundation first got behind One Acre, it served maybe 10,000 farmers. Now it's serving over 200,000—which Youn still sees as a prelude to much bigger things to come. The fund predicts that it will serve one million farmers by 2020, and that it will keep growing. Why is this vision exciting to Bill Ackman? Because farming is the dominant economic activity of the world's poor. A model that can be expanded—

giving farmers more financing and better training, along with market insights to maximize their profits—could be transformative for millions of people. Youn is the kind of person the Pershing Square Foundation likes to get behind.

The same can be said about Cory Booker. In 2010, Ackman joined Mark Zuckerberg in backing an ambitious bid by then Newark mayor Booker to improve that city's public schools. Ackman had been a political contributor to Booker for years, when the mayor came to the Pershing Square Foundation with a proposal for helping underwrite his sweeping reforms. Ultimately, Ackman contributed $25 million to the effort. "Newark was really about betting on a person, and the person there was Cory Booker," Ackman told me. "Cory Booker was someone I had known for a long time and had enormous confidence in. We had the mayor of the city. We had [Governor Chris] Christie on board. And I made a five-minute decision to be supportive, with the details left to the Foundation for Newark's Future to work it out." That was the organization established by Zuckerberg's gift "to provide the 'shot in the arm' necessary to create systemic change in the city's educational system," as the foundation has described its mission.

Much has been written about the Newark effort, including Dale Russakoff's *The Prize: Who's in Charge of America's Schools?* The reform push generated strong community backlash and one of the nastiest fights over urban education in memory. Critics saw it as another example of the kind of arrogant, top-down education philanthropy that had created polarization and chaos in other cities, including New York and Washington. The Newark reform effort, which parents and teachers in the city only learned about when it was announced on the *Oprah Winfrey Show,* seemed to confirm the worst fears about a new era of big philanthropy—that too often wealthy donors, not ordinary citizens, would be driving the agenda in key areas of public life.

PUSHING GOVERNMENT

Ackman wouldn't be pounded for the Newark episode the way that Zuckerberg was, but he was the second largest donor to the effort. Both he and the Pershing Square Foundation president at the time, Paul Bernstein, later defended the effort—which Bernstein called "incredible, brave, bold, risky and ambitious." Also, counter to some claims, Bernstein insisted it was not mainly about tearing down the city's existing public school district and replacing it with charter schools. The reform was an "attempt to address the entire system and improve it, not destroy it," Bernstein told me, noting that the biggest beneficiaries of private money were the district and its schools, and particularly teachers. Money did go to charters, Bernstein said, doubling the number of Newark students attending them (to 40 percent), but "I was excited to be involved in Newark precisely because it was a break from the charter versus district polarization. . . . There was substantial work to enhance existing schools."

Ackman told me that "Newark has worked out a lot better than the press has suggested," and there's some truth to that. Between 2010 and 2015, for example, the graduation rate in the city rose from 56 percent to 69 percent. The dramatic expansion of charters in the city has also given many students access to better schools than district choices. Yet by other measures, not much has improved in Newark's education system, even as school closings and other disruption upended the routines of thousands of students and parents.

The Newark reform push is often described as a project driven by unelected philanthropists. In fact, though, this effort was catalyzed by the popular Booker—after he was reelected mayor with 59 percent of the vote—and made possible with support by another public official, Governor Christie. Philanthropic dollars allowed the reform to be as ambitious as it was, but the donors weren't mainly calling the shots—to their considerable frustration at times. One takeaway for Ackman was to be wary of situations you can't control. Just as Ackman in his day job doesn't like investing in pooled funds run by other investors, he doesn't like writing checks to nonprofit intermediaries and hoping that everything turns out okay. "We like investing directly. I'd rather pick one organization at a time than give to some omnibus organization."

The main mistake of the Foundation for Newark's Future, in Ackman's view, was that it didn't put enough money into charter schools, which were the most successful element of the reform effort. Like many of the new philanthropists, Ackman believes deeply in the disruptive power of charters. He told me: "Charter schools aren't necessarily better than public schools; the best charter schools are. And to the extent that the KIPP [the national charter network] academies of the world grow at relatively rapid rates, I think it will have a big impact. And it has a disruptive impact. If you have a school where the kids are way better performing than the public school across the street, that puts a lot of pressure on the city and a lot of pressure on the teachers and the union to solve the problem."

To critics, though, charters can often have the opposite result: hurting public schools by draining away financial resources and the best students. Another critique of charters, based on emerging research, is that while the best ones do boost test scores, they don't transform the lives of poor and minority kids over the long term—for example, by increasing later earnings. One reason may be that socioeconomic conditions outside of schools have far more impact on young lives than whatever happens *inside* of schools, a common argument of liberal critics of education reformers.

But to Ackman, the charter revolution is still just getting started. He likens the role of charters to activist investors (like himself) who use their stake in companies as leverage to push management changes that boost earnings. "The share of investors who are activists are a very small percentage of investors in the markets, but have had an enormous disruptive impact on the performance of corporate America," Ackman said. "And I think the same thing can happen with charter schools."

A broader point, made by Ackman and other mega-givers, like Michael Bloomberg and John Arnold, is that philanthropy can have its greatest impact when it helps to scale up experiments that change how government operates. Even as critics accuse billionaires of trying to privatize education, parks, and other areas of public life, these donors often see their job quite differently—as pushing a calcified public sector to step up its game and developing new solutions for government to invest in.

Ackman is no anti-statist ideologue, but like many business leaders, he's not so hopeful about public institutions. "Unfortunately, there are very few governments around the world that are efficient, effective, not corrupt, and where there's a continuity of high-quality leadership," he said. Still, he sees philanthropy not as replacing government, but as improving it. "I think philanthropists can be a positively disrupting force in creating some high-quality institutions and examples that can push the government in the right direction," Ackman said. Melinda Gates has made a similar point: "All philanthropy can do is take the risks, show the way forward, do the big bold experiments. . . . But then it takes government to scale them up."

John Arnold also talked about the ability of philanthropy to finance experiments and take risks, in ways that government can't. "There are absolute constraints on what a political entity can do, just because of the nature of how politicians are elected, and the incentive systems that most politicians have," Arnold told me. Philanthropy's strength, Bill Gates has said, is "taking a long-term view, which the political system isn't likely to do."

Eli Broad put the point this way: "Neither Bill Gates nor I have to worry about getting fired. We take big risks in pursuit of big rewards."

There's no question that democratic institutions have their shortcomings when it comes to solving problems. Public officials have few incentives to take risks and many reasons to play it safe. Government agencies can be slow and lumbering. New elected officials come and go every few years, undermining continuity of leadership. Well-organized interest groups often have the power to block policies that benefit the broader public. Operating outside of political oversight, philanthropy offers the promise of shortcuts. It can be, in the memorable words of Paul Ylvisaker, a former Ford Foundation executive, "society's passing gear."

Yet Broad's comment about how he and Gates can't be fired goes to the heart of the concerns many Americans have about today's philanthropists: They can throw around their money however they want, including in ways that may negatively affect the rest of us, and there's nothing we can do to take away that power if it's abused. Further, as the resources in the hands of philanthropists get bigger, so, too, will the scale of their experiments to reshape society—along with the trauma inflicted when things go wrong.

Major donors gunning for disruptive change tend to shrug off the risk of failure. It's part of any process for solving problems, they say. Ackman told me he was "really comfortable with failure . . . I'm sure there is some new mistake we haven't yet made that we'll make in the future. But as long as we learn from it, it's fine."

Many business leaders, especially in tech, embrace this same ethos—and the arrival of more of these people in philanthropy is leading to more risk-taking. That's a good thing in some ways, and scary in other ways. When a start-up fails, money is lost and people need to find new jobs. When an experiment in remaking urban education fails, it can cause major dislocation in the lives of families. That happened not just in Newark, but in New York City and in many other places when the Gates Foundation poured $2 billion into a national push to break up large high schools and shift students into small schools—only to later abandon this strategy.

Sean Parker, Dustin Moskovitz, and Bill Ackman are only three of the many newer philanthropists who are also keen on financing disruption. Well before this wave of givers came along, Jeff Skoll, the eBay billionaire, had set out to back visionaries worldwide seeking to change entire systems, whether it's how girls are educated in Afghanistan or how health care is delivered in America. Skoll's foundation remains dedicated to this mission, convening an annual conference of social entrepreneurs every year.

It's not surprising that so many donors have lately followed in Skoll's footsteps, given how many of these people have made their fortunes. What's open to question is whether a focus on individuals with visionary ideas, like Cory Booker or Andrew Youn, is really the best way to bring about disruptive change. While entrepreneurs loom large in the business world, creating new products and services that disrupt entire industries—sometimes in the space of just a few years, as in the cases of Uber and Airbnb—societal change often comes about in different ways.

Catalysts for systemic change, history shows, are social movements that unite masses of people who are unhappy with a current system and set out to transform it. The civil rights movement is one obvious example; the women's movement is another. More recently, the Tea Party—a decentralized movement led by no single figure—had a huge impact on politics and policy. Likewise, Black Lives Matter, which emerged after a police shooting in Ferguson, Missouri, operating mainly as a far-flung virtual network, has had a big impact, driving a new national conversation about race and concrete reforms to policing practices across the United States.

Systemic change also often happens over time, through the collective efforts of many different stakeholders working toward a shared goal. The sharp decline in teen pregnancy rates over the past decade is one example. No single visionary led the charge to tackle this problem; rather, a great many people and institutions have played a role—which has also been true for major progress against problems like traffic deaths and smoking.

Meanwhile, it's hard to think of many social entrepreneurs who've succeeded in bringing about change on a truly large scale in recent decades. Some of the best examples of such people—like Wendy Kopp of Teach for America or Mike Feinberg of KIPP—have built up organizations that are important, but still quite small compared to the scope of the problems they are tackling.

The reality of how social change happens is one reason why breathless talk of "disruption" by new donors tends to annoy veterans of the philanthropy world, who've been around long enough to know that pick-and-shovel work is what's often needed to make changes in society. Also irritating to these veterans is the charge that the older legacy foundations don't know how to push big ideas to overhaul society and that the Sean Parkers of the world have a new, better formula. Many professional grantmakers, often derided as "bureaucrats" or "philanthropoids," would argue that people like themselves, who've come up through the nonprofit sector, have a keener grasp of how to create systemic change in areas like education or health than rich techies and finance guys who parachute in with their "bold" ideas.

Who's right in this debate? It may not really matter. A beauty of philanthropy is its diversity and how decentralized it is. When it comes to any big problem, you'll find a multiplicity of funders working different approaches, guided by different theories of change.

This experimentation and endless competition of ideas is not always so constructive, with funders often reinventing the wheel or working in isolation from one another. But it's promising in other ways, in that donors are forever trying new things, increasing the overall odds of success.

The diversity of philanthropy is also reassuring if you're worried that today's mega-giving is elevating some particular ideology. The new elite emerging may indeed have growing power, but they're also shooting off in a growing number of directions—and, not infrequently, working at cross-purposes to one another.

Modern philanthropy is not an organized system governed by any single set of ideas or group of leaders who are all on the same page. That said, one thing is clear about this rising power center in American life: Ordinary people have little influence over what it does.

6

Leverage Points

In early 2014, an extraordinary trial unfolded in a Los Angeles courtroom. For two months, a state superior judge heard testimony in a civil lawsuit charging that California's job protections for ineffective public school teachers resulted in poor and minority students being deprived of equal access to education, a guaranteed right under the state's constitution.

The main target of the lawsuit was teacher tenure, which grants permanent employment to California teachers after just two years on the job. The suit also challenged statutes that made it difficult to fire teachers, even those who were incompetent, and it took aim at rules that prioritized teacher seniority above all else—even effectiveness—when layoffs had to be made, the so-called "last in, first out" statutes.

The picture painted by the suit was damning: teachers in California were winning job protection well before they could be properly evaluated, and then became nearly impossible to fire in a system that seemed designed to protect deadwood instructors. It was a great setup for the teachers, critics said, but a lousy deal for students. Education reformers had been making this very point for years, yet never before had the argument reached a state court.

The plaintiffs in the suit were nine students who attended California's public schools around the state. The case, *Vergara v. California,* was named after a teenager, Elizabeth Vergara, who claimed that her education and broader life prospects had been hurt by bad teaching. She and her fellow plaintiffs were a diverse and poised group, who proved good at staying on message in talking to the media. One reason for this is that they had been carefully recruited as plaintiffs in a suit backstopped by top-notch PR specialists. The lead co-counsel for the plaintiffs in the case was Theodore B. Olson, who had been solicitor general of the United States under George W. Bush, as well as a top official in the Reagan Justice Department. Olson had argued sixty cases before the U.S. Supreme Court, including the *Bush v. Gore* case that decided the 2000 election. He'd long been closely involved with the Federalist Society, the powerful legal group underwritten by conservative foundations.

Beyond Olson, *Vergara v. California* was litigated by a prestigious team of lawyers from Gibson, Dunn, & Crutcher—a global firm with over a thousand attorneys—whose more typical clients included giant corporations like Amazon, Viacom, and Intel. Olson's co-counsel was Marcellus McRae, a Harvard Law School grad and one of the firm's hotshots.

So how did all this legal and PR firepower come to be arrayed behind a lawsuit challenging teacher employment laws? The answer lies in the activist philanthropy of a Silicon Valley entrepreneur, Dave Welch.

Welch is something of an accidental combatant in the education wars. He grew up middle class with six siblings in Maryland, where he attended public schools. He was fascinated by science as a kid and went to college in Delaware before going on to get his PhD in electrical engineering from Cornell. From there it was on to Silicon Valley, where he spent the next three decades working in the fast-moving field of fiber optics. For many years, he helped build a company called Spectra Diode Labs, or SDL, where he did pioneering work, coming to hold scores of patents and publishing numerous technical articles. He was a star in the rather obscure field of optical engineering in the 1990s, winning an array of awards. Welch was also enmeshed in the business side of SDL, negotiating major corporate acquisitions. He made a fortune when SDL was acquired by JDS Uniphase for $43 billion just before the stock market crashed in 2001. Welch went on to co-found his own Silicon Valley company, Infinera, manufacturing optical telecommunications systems. In 2011, the Optical Society of America presented Welch with its highest award, saying that his "work has played a key role in the important advances we're seeing in the bandwidth, intelligence, and other capabilities of optical networks today, and will pave the way for future communication systems breakthroughs."

Welch is no billionaire and not well known outside his industry. He's one of the many entrepreneurs in Silicon Valley who never make the Forbes 400 list and fly well beneath the radar—yet end up with more money than they need.

Along with his wife, Heidi, Welch created a foundation in the late 1990s. One of their biggest causes was the environment. They made low-six-figure grants to the Natural Resources Defense Council (NRDC), and Welch joined the board of the group. He and Heidi came to underwrite a new fellows program at NRDC, aimed at finding novel ways to harness market forces to reduce greenhouse gas emissions.

Dave Welch's other big cause is education. Like a lot of winners in the new economy, Welch climbed to success and riches by mastering specialized skills through long years in classrooms and labs. In turn, the businesses he's built have relied on brainy employees who've also spent years honing their cognitive firepower. Welch is part of a highly degreed upper class that sees education as all-important to opportunity, and it's no coincidence this issue looms so large for today's new philanthropists.

Many of Welch's early education donations went to public and private schools in Silicon Valley, where he and his wife were raising three children. Over time, he grew engrossed by education policy and was especially appalled at how hard it was in California to get rid of incompetent teachers. Welch isn't just worried that kids are being deprived of effective teachers, which research shows is the most critical in-school factor that affects student outcomes. He worries that kids are also being permanently damaged by bad teaching. "We're harming a lot of individuals, taking away their passion to learn," he told me. "There's something grossly wrong and probably illegal about it. If it isn't illegal, it should be."

Looking more closely at state teacher employment policies, though, Welch came to believe that they were stacked in favor of teachers. "Of the education code in California, the vast majority of it doesn't actually address the issues of did the child learn, and does the child have the right to learn," Welch said. In contrast, these laws *do* offer detailed protections for teachers. Rules that safeguard teachers' jobs "are all well and good concepts," Welch said, "as long as they're consistent with the outcome of the child. If they're inconsistent with the outcome of the child, then we've got a system that is not there for the child."

Many education philanthropists, frustrated by this system, have looked to do an end run around it, scaling up a parallel universe of charters and nonprofits that serve needy kids. Welch didn't see that approach as very effective. While he values what such givers are doing, he said, "the primary funder, by far, is the government. And the leverage of making the government's money in the education system work better is huge, substantially more impactful than the value of philanthropic dollars. So then you ask the question of how do I get the government's money to be more efficient?"

The most obvious answer—to work for change through the California state legislature, which sets the laws governing teacher employment—struck Welch as a "dead end," since this was the same body that had enshrined the idea that "adult rights are superior to children's rights."

Welch was likely right on this score, given union power. For years, the California Teachers Association has lavished money and attention on the state's elected representatives. CTA has been the single biggest campaign contributor in California since 1998, making over $200 million in donation to hundreds of candidates and dozens of ballot initiatives. It's also been one of the top spenders on lobbying in Sacramento, right up there with the oil industry. Going up against that kind of influence was no easy thing.

This left the court system, which Welch believed could be a powerful ally for his cause. The key here was how California's constitution guaranteed the right to a quality education. If a lawsuit could show that this right was being infringed upon by poor teachers, and the laws that protected them, the legislature would be forced to revise those laws.

To develop such a suit, Welch founded a nonprofit, Students Matter, in late 2010, funding it through his foundation. After intensive research and preparation, the group was ready to file its lawsuit in May 2012. It was a scary moment for Welch and his wife, and they talked through the risks of going forward. Once a suit was filed, litigation could drag on for years, possibly leading all the way to the California Supreme Court. If no other donors lined up to help back the suit, the couple would be on the hook for all its costs not covered by pro bono legal help. They discussed what this might mean for their finances. "That is a significant cliff to jump off of," Welch told me. "You can't decide halfway through that you're not going to finish. From a philanthropy point of view, I had never done anything like that." The couple decided to go for it.

Vergara v. California did indeed take years to wind its way through the courts—first to trial and then two appeals that the led to the state's highest court. California's two biggest teachers unions did their best to stop the challenge, joining the suit as defendants in 2013, calling its allegations "meritless." The trial got under way in January 2014, and over four weeks the legal team for the students presented testimony about how hard it was to fire bad teachers through a process that could take as long as a decade, and the negative effects of allowing them to stay in the classroom. The defense pushed back, both in the court and in the media, rebutting the allegations of *Vergara* one by one. Joshua Pechthalt, president of the California Federation of Teachers (CFT), called tenure critical to protecting "teachers' freedom to teach all points of view necessary for critical thinking," and said that lengthening the probation period beyond two years would amount to the "elimination of tenure" since half of all teachers "quit before they hit the five-year mark."

Other commentators saw *Vergara* as focusing on the wrong problem. "Getting rid of these bad laws may do little to systemically raise student achievement," Dana Goldstein wrote in *The Atlantic*. "For high-poverty schools, hiring is at least as big of a challenge as firing."

Another critique of the obsession with bad teachers is that most school principals are far less concerned with firing the teachers at the bottom, which tend to be a small fraction, than boosting the performance of those in the middle. One education researcher wrote: "Instead of working to erode collective bargaining agreements or promoting other policies that assume teacher negligence—like test-based accountability—we should be channeling our energies into building teacher capacity."

In June, the court ruled in favor of the plaintiffs: "Evidence has been elicited in this trial of the specific effect of grossly ineffective teachers on students," wrote Judge Rolf M. Treu. "The evidence is compelling. Indeed, it shocks the conscience." He went on to write in scathing terms that teacher tenure disadvantaged students, that the "tortuous process" for dismissing teachers was unwarranted, and that seniority rules—which Treu called "unfathomable"—were also harmful. In a sweeping victory for the plaintiffs, he declared that all the statutes challenged by the suit violated the constitutional right to equal education.

Vergara sent shockwaves through the education world and beyond. "The ruling opens a new chapter in the equal education struggle," editorialized the *New York Times*, praising the verdict. Reformers were jubilant, and quickly set about planning similar suits in other states. The most visible of these plotters was Campbell Brown, the former CNN anchor turned education reformer. Brown hoped to take down teacher tenure in New York State, recruiting philanthropic support for her effort. Brown wouldn't reveal the source of her money, nor was she legally required to. Lawsuits started gestating in other states, too, and the cause attracted the support of the famous liberal constitutional scholar Laurence Tribe, who called on fellow progressives to rally around the *Vergara* ruling, writing that "the right to unionize must never become a right to relegate children to permanent second-class citizenship."

Teachers unions were apoplectic about *Vergara*. It was one of the biggest victories yet by the business philanthropists these unions had come to view as their mortal foes. As the unions saw it, *Vergara* was just the latest example of how rich private individuals were hijacking public education. "It's discouraging when people who are incredibly wealthy, who can hire America's top corporate law firms, can attempt to drive an education agenda devoid of support from parents and community," said CFT head Joshua Pechthalt, after Judge Treu's ruling.

Nearly two years later, CFT and the California Teachers Association led the cheering when a California appellate court unanimously struck down *Vergara*. CTA called that ruling a "stinging rebuke" to an effort led by "wealthy anti-union 'education reformers.'" The union reaffirmed the practice of granting teachers tenure after two years, along with the "last in, first out" rules. In any case, it said: "The legislature is the place for policy decisions like this, not through court cases brought by phony front groups created by PR firms and millionaires."

Meanwhile, Students Matter moved quickly to petition the California Supreme Court to review the case. "Every student deserves a great public education; yet California's education laws make this impossible," Dave Welch said in a statement. But in August 2016, that court—while sharply divided—said it would let the appellate court ruling stand. *Vergara* had reached its last stop. In another statement, Welch pledged that the "fight was not over."

Welch didn't accomplish his goal, but the influence he has sought to wield over public policy in America's biggest state is eye-opening. Welch doesn't have anything like the resources of a Bill Gates or Eli Broad, yet by focusing a few million dollars on a pivotal issue, teacher employment laws, and using a key lever of change—litigation—he mounted a strong challenge to an entire body of legislative law enacted by elected state representatives. That doesn't sound like how democracy is supposed to work.

On the other hand, the way that teacher contract law got made in Sacramento over many years isn't how democracy is supposed to work, either, and it's naive to imagine that public education was some pure zone of civic life before zillionaire philanthropists came along. In fact, education policy in the United States has been saturated with interested money for decades, mostly from unions, who've often coopted their overseers in government with heavy political spending. As education-reform philanthropists see things, they're simply leveling the playing field—in favor of low-income minority students for whom nobody is speaking.

Regarding *Vergara* itself, Welch rejects the idea that it was some end run around democracy. "I think it's the exact opposite," he told me. "The courts are there for individuals' rights. And sometimes those rights are abused by the legislature. . . . we used the tools of a functional democracy to highlight that there's a problem and to present the facts."

COURTS OF WEALTH

Private philanthropy has been backing litigation to change public laws for at least sixty years. Like Welch, many funders have seen this as both a cost-effective leverage strategy and, in some cases, as the only path forward to make change. Like Welch, too, they have placed great hope in judicial institutions that are supposed to focus on the facts and don't answer either to interest groups or to small-minded voters holding up the forward march of progress.

In the 1950s, philanthropists supported the long and expensive litigation battle that culminated in the landmark *Brown v. Board of Education* case that struck down school segregation. The Field Foundation, established by a department store heir, backed the NAACP Legal Defense Fund, which spearheaded the case. In turn, the powerful arguments made in the *Brown* suit were based in part on research into the negative effects of segregation by the Swedish social scientist Gunnar Myrdal, who published his findings in 1944 in *An American Dilemma*. That study was supported by the Carnegie Corporation. Later, starting in the 1970s, liberal funders backed litigation in the states to push for equitable funding of public schools. Fueled by millions of dollars in grants, lawsuits sought to get around self-interested white suburban voters who were blocking a fairer distribution of education funds to help minority communities.

Over time, liberal foundations and philanthropists also built up an entire infrastructure of legal groups that used litigation to advance policy goals related to civil rights, women's rights, and consumer and environmental protections. The environmental group, NRDC—which was founded by young idealistic lawyers in 1970 with backing from the Ford Foundation—has long been among the top practitioners of public interest litigation, winning a string of court victories in recent decades. These days it has a budget of more than $100 million a year.

So, while one progressive critic decried Welch's *Vergara* suit as "a blatant effort to legislate from the bench, keeping parents and educators out of education policy decisions," it is actually the Left—backed by private funders—that invented public policy litigation.

Conservative philanthropists have embraced this strategy, too, scaling up their own network of legal groups starting in the 1980s and creating the Federalist Society to help ensure a supply of right-minded lawyers who could staff such operations—not to mention judges who would be favorable to conservative lawsuits.

A lawyer named Clint Bolick was among the pioneers of this field. He founded the Institute for Justice in 1991 with backing from Charles Koch, who liked the idea of a "national law firm for liberty" and pledged five years of seed funding. Bolick moved fast to diversify his base of funders, which proved easier than he anticipated. "No one had really tried to get individual donors invested in litigation," Bolick said later. "And it turned out that donors were very moved by the stories of the people we represented." IJ has now litigated more than two hundred cases, including five before the U.S. Supreme Court. Among other things, it has provided legal muscle for the school choice movement, defending voucher programs that channel public dollars to private and parochial schools. Ninety-two percent of its funding comes from individuals. One of IJ's biggest donors, before he died, was the Wall Street investor Robert Wilson, who gave millions. A wealthy futures trader, William Dunn, has been another key backer.

Health care is one area where investments in litigation have lately paid dividends for the Right. After the Affordable Care Act was passed in 2010, conservative legal groups mounted a major effort to challenge the constitutionality of the law. A leader in this work was the Cato Institute, the libertarian think tank financed by David and Charles Koch, as well as other funders that included the billionaire media mogul John Malone. Also pushing the legal attack was the Pacific Research Institute, which got money from Robert Mercer, among many donors. Additional groups lending brain power to the legal assault on the ACA included the Reason Foundation, American Civil Rights Union, and the Individual Rights Foundation. All were financed by wealthy donors, as well as by foundations set up by previous generations of businessmen, like the Lynde and Harry Bradley Foundation.

This well-financed legal push led to the U.S. Supreme Court's hearing two cases challenging the constitutionality of the Affordable Care Act. Both had the potential to affect the health-care choices of many Americans. In the first case, which challenged a linchpin of the law, the individual mandate, the Court upheld the constitutionality of the mandate—but ruled that states didn't have to expand Medicaid coverage to more low-income people, which the law also stipulated. As a result of that ruling, over twenty states withheld coverage that was supposed to be offered under the ACA. Some eight million low-income people slated to be eligible for Medicaid found themselves out of luck.

In 2016, the right's litigation network also succeeded in getting the Supreme Court to hear a case challenging the right of public-sector unions to collect "fair-share" fees from non-members. In many states, workers who opt out of public-sector unions still have to pay dues. Barring that practice would deal a major blow to such unions; this has long been a goal of conservative philanthropies as part of a broader strategy to "defund" the Left. The strategic thinking is simple enough: Since public-sector unions provide major firepower for progressive causes and Democratic candidates, reducing their financial resources will weaken the Left on a range of issues.

Perhaps no conservative funder has spent more to weaken public-sector unions than the Bradley Foundation in Milwaukee, whose former president, Michael Grebe, was close to Scott Walker, the Republican governor who made his name by seeking to curtail the collective bargaining rights of public-sector unions in Wisconsin. Bradley has been one of the top funders of the Center for Individual Rights, which brought the suit challenging "fair share" fees. The Bradley Foundation has also supported at least eleven organizations that submitted amicus briefs for the plaintiffs in the case.

And who were those plaintiffs? Nine California public school teachers who had declined to join the California Teachers Association. The lead plaintiff in the case, Rebecca Friedrichs, told reporters: "Increasingly I saw that many of the things the union bargained for actually made my job as a teacher harder. Because of tenure laws, it is almost impossible to fire incompetent, and sometimes even abusive, teachers. And because of seniority-based layoff policies—last-in, first-out—which the union has negotiated, newer teachers are the first to go regardless of how good they are."

Those words sure sound familiar. And although *Friedrichs v. California Teachers Association* wasn't connected in any way to the *Vergara* suit, the two litigation efforts made clear just how many funders are looking to the courts to advance their agenda.

Just six months before *Friedrichs* reached the U.S. Supreme Court (which, in a tie vote, let union dues stand), philanthropists backing a litigation strategy scored one of their biggest victories ever in 2015 when a legal push heavily financed by LGBT-rights funders triumphed in the Court in securing marriage equality.

That legal breakthrough, which set off celebrations in gay neighborhoods across the United States, was years in the making. Part of the backstory here involves Chuck Williams, a wealthy donor who in 2001 made a $2.5 million gift to establish the Williams Institute, a center for LGBT scholarship at UCLA Law School. It was the biggest donation ever for academic work of this kind, and Williams went on to give the institute another $10 million. A half-dozen other individual donors have made gifts of between $1 million and $5 million to the institute, which has also pulled in a steady stream of grants from foundations. This money has allowed the institute to do groundbreaking legal work arguing for advances in LGBT rights.

Over time, the Williams Institute emerged as the legal nerve center for the push for marriage equality. It built up a staff of twenty scholars, who pumped out law review articles and policy studies and filed amicus briefs in crucial marriage equality cases as they wound their way through the nation's courts. Its scholars also served as expert witnesses in multiple cases relating to marriage rights for same-sex couples, including every case heard before the Supreme Court. Numerous federal courts cited the institute's research in striking down bans on same-sex marriage.

One notable victory by the Williams Institute was in helping mount the legal challenge against Proposition 8, the California ballot initiative that eliminated the rights of same-sex couples to marry in that state. In his decision striking down Prop 8 in 2010, two years after it passed, U.S. District Judge Vaughn R. Walker cited Williams Institute research more than thirty times.

The Williams Institute is a small operation. It's attracted only a sliver of the hundreds of millions of contributions that have gone to push the LGBT cause over the past decade. But Chuck Williams and the institute's other backers have gotten a huge bang for their buck by focusing laser-like on legal battles. *The Advocate* has called the Williams Institute "the most important LGBT group you've never heard of."

Chuck Williams isn't a lawyer himself, or an academic. He's a businessman who spent years as a corporate executive. When he became a philanthropist, he was determined to give in a hands-on way to the issue he cared about most: discrimination against LGBT people. After scouting out the field of nonprofits in this area, Williams became convinced that what was missing was a respected think tank that focused on LGBT legal and policy issues—one that would be seen as non-political and credible. The movement had enough activist organizations. It needed to get more sophisticated. To change minds, Williams said, "you need to have sufficient clarity of logic and research that supports that logic."

The marriage victory served up yet more evidence that litigation is a powerful tool in advocating for stronger rights, ensuring constitutional protections that may not yet be accepted by public opinion. But litigation can also be useful in getting around other obstacles to policy change, offering a way to bypass legislative bodies that are too timid to act on controversial issues or that have been captured by interest groups. Environmentalists backed by wealthy donors have often used the courts to overcome the lobbying and electoral might of industry, which was Dave Welch's strategy with *Vergara*. With the odds stacked against reform in Sacramento, where teachers unions ruled, he rightly saw that the most promising path to change was through the judicial system.

Philanthropists look to high-leverage strategies like litigation to press their causes because they often don't have much money in the grand scheme of things. While mega-billionaires like the Koch brothers—who have a combined net worth of over $80 billion—may have the resources to sway elections or hire armies of lobbyists, few wealthy donors have that kind of money. Funders are especially mindful of their limited resources, in relative terms, when they go up against powerful interest groups or take on large national challenges. In these cases, philanthropists need to think very strategically about how to move their agenda.

SMARTER POLICY

Nearly all strategic philanthropists put a big focus on influencing government policy. Litigation is one way to do that. Another is to pilot new ways of solving problems—or to draw attention to ideas that do work but haven't yet attracted strong government backing.

Right now, among today's new mega-givers, John and Laura Arnold are leading exemplars of this approach.

John was born in 1974 and grew up in an upper-middle-class household in Dallas, where he attended public school. He went to Vanderbilt University, studying math and economics. After college, he got hired by Enron, in Houston, starting as an oil analyst and then trading in natural gas derivatives. He was so good that he made an $8 million bonus in 2001, the year of Enron's spectacular collapse—money he used to seed his own energy hedge fund, Centaurus, in 2002. He was even more successful there, achieving returns for his fund in one year of 317 percent and becoming America's youngest billionaire in 2007. Like so many of Houston's wealthiest residents, Arnold would move to the swanky neighborhood of River Oaks, where he and wife, Laura, built a 20,000-square-foot modernist home designed by New York architect Alexander Gorlin—after tearing down a historic mansion called Dogwoods.

Arnold made his fortune through old-fashioned speculation backed by sophisticated research, looking for good values in the energy market. But he distinguished himself by a willingness to make gigantic bets. When he cashed out of the hedge fund business in 2012, retiring at thirty-eight, he was worth around $3 billion.

In his new life, Arnold turned to a different kind of betting as he and Laura became full-time philanthropists—launching the foundation that bears their name and staffing it with an ever growing cadre of expert staff. Laura had quit her job first, in 2006, to devote her time to philanthropy. She had grown up in Brandon, Florida, and excelled academically. She went to Harvard for college, then to the University of Cambridge for a master's degree in European studies, and from there to Yale for a law degree. She had spent time in corporate law and worked at an energy company—but found herself pulled toward philanthropy as the family fortune swelled.

The couple doesn't have one of the larger piles of the new Gilded Age, but they have plenty of wealth, most of which they hope to give away in their lifetime. The Arnolds were early signers of the Giving Pledge, and like a lot of pledgers, they have explained their motivation in terms of reciprocity. They attribute their success to the opportunities given to them by society and have voiced a responsibility to help others have the same opportunities—a narrative that implicitly rejects a libertarian storyline of how great wealth is created, centered on heroic individuals. Like Dustin Moskovitz, the Arnolds see their fluky, outsized fortune in a utilitarian light, "as an instrument to effect positive and transformative change."

Even more than many of the new philanthropists, the couple is intent on leveraging their giving in strategic ways. They aren't interested in incremental change. They want to move aggressively, take big risks, and give in a hands-on way. The Arnolds also want to be nimble and opportunistic. They have avoided fixating too much on specific issues and have instead scouted out places where their money could achieve major change.

When the couple began their giving, they found that search frustrating. Making the rounds at nonprofits, listening to pitches, they weren't sold by many of the claims they heard. "Everybody was super-nice," Laura recalled of those meetings. "They're all trying to save the world and everything is great and everyone is super-optimistic. Everyone was pumping up their success, saying we're serving more people, and doing more things."

But much of it wasn't convincing to the Arnolds. "There was something about that narrative that never sounded right to us," John told me. Laura cited education technology as one area where "you see this lack of rigor and emphasis on anecdote in a lot of how nonprofits promote themselves. It all felt a little soft to us. . . . We just started not trusting what we were hearing." The biggest reason it all felt fishy, Laura said, was that "the problems weren't getting better. They were getting worse despite enormous investments in areas such as education."

During his years as an investor, John Arnold had become an avid consumer of studies and data. Now, as he approached large-scale giving, he dug into potential social investments with the same skeptical eye and due diligence he had brought to big financial bets—only to find this new terrain far more complex. "We were hoping there was an easy answer," John told me, as in "let's find the five best social programs and we can write a check, and don't have to put much time or effort or work into this process." Yet as they started researching various problems, they found it wasn't so easy to "find the best or determine what was even effective. . . . The more you read, the more research you did, the less you seem to know about what works and what doesn't."

The Arnolds did find various organizations they wanted to invest in during their early years of giving, especially in education. John Arnold's very first major donation was a $25,000 check to KIPP, the charter school network, and much bigger money would flow to KIPP over time. The Arnold Foundation also gave to many of the other stalwarts of the education reform movement, including Teach for America, the New Teacher Project, and the Charter School Growth Fund. They emerged as leading backers of the effort to revamp the New Orleans education system in the wake of Hurricane Katrina, giving millions to it.

Reforming public pensions was another area the Arnolds came to early, as they ramped up their philanthropy. That issue exemplified a key kind of problem the Arnolds were interested in: situations where perverse incentives created bad outcomes for society. "Looking at pensions, we saw that the actors sitting at the negotiating table had similar incentives, which is make a lot of promises for the future, but let's not pay for it today," John said, referring to the elected politicians and the public-sector unions that were calling the shots on pensions. "And those incentives ran counter to the public's interest. But nobody was expressing a voice or giving heft to the interests of the public."

With his Enron background and hedge fund wealth, John Arnold quickly attracted criticism for his work on pension reform. Enron's bankruptcy had destroyed $2 billion in employee retirement savings and had also badly hurt a number of public pension funds, which lost $1.5 billion as their Enron stock became worthless. Critics saw Arnold as another Wall Street conservative who was hostile to unions and wanted to downsize government in favor of a pro-market agenda that shifted ever more risk onto ordinary people—for example, by replacing secure defined-benefit retirement plans with riskier defined-contribution plans such as 401(k)s.

In fact, Arnold was open to a variety of ways to bolster public pension systems. He didn't insist that there was a one-size-fits-all solution to the financial woes that were playing out in different ways in different places. The most important thing, to Arnold, was opening up the pension debate and tackling a challenge that the political system, with its short-term focus, had handled so poorly—most notably, with legislatures failing to make adequate contributions every year to ensure that public pensions would be properly funded in coming decades.

The pension work led the Arnolds to think more broadly about what they describe as "inefficiencies" in how society is managed. "Getting involved in that issue led us to see other areas where the actors involved in a problem had incentives that ran counter to the best interests of society," John said.

In a mission statement for their foundation, the Arnolds came to define their goals in ambitious terms: "Our strategy is to systematically examine areas of society in which underperformance, inefficiency, concentrated power, lack of information, lack of accountability, lack of transparency, lack of balance among interests, or other barriers to human progress and achievement exist."

That was quite an agenda. But identifying top problem areas was only part of the challenge of improving U.S. society; the other part was finding solutions that really worked, backed by solid evidence. This wasn't easy. The more the Arnolds explored the policy world, the more they came to believe that much of the intellectual edifice underpinning the social and public sectors was flimsy. They felt that a lot of bad research was driving both philanthropic and government funding, with billions going into approaches that weren't backed by rigorous evidence.

To the Arnolds, a key to making progress on many problems in society is, in effect, stronger due diligence. If nonprofits and governments only invested in well-tested solutions that truly make things better, they would have dramatically higher impact. This basic idea—that do-gooders need to be far more rigorous to succeed—came to be the most important driver of the Arnolds' philanthropy. They see achieving such change as the ultimate form of leverage.

Like other high-minded philanthropists before them, the Arnolds fantasize about a policy world where reason prevails, trumping age-old human foibles. And they have specific ideas for how to ensure that reason does triumph, starting with the use of better methods, to find out which ideas government should get behind.

One organization they began backing was the Coalition for Evidence-Based Policy, a small outfit in Washington, D.C., that had long labored away in relative obscurity. For years, it badgered federal agencies to fund only social policy interventions that had been proven to work through randomized controlled trials—the same kind of vetting researchers use for new drugs or medical treatments. The coalition's persistent complaint was that a "lot of what is funded by government is probably not producing the hoped-for outcomes," its founder, Jon Baron, told me. Over time, Baron's group got different agencies to see the light, but it was a tough slog.

This wasn't a left or right cause, and compared to whales like the Heritage Foundation or the Brookings Institution, the Coalition for Evidence-Based Policy was a minnow in the Washington policy world. Yet the Arnolds believed supporting this kind of work could have far greater impact than wading into the familiar battles of ideology that tended to consume the capital. They were such keen fans of the group that in 2015 the coalition was merged into their foundation, becoming its Washington outpost. Jon Baron became part of a growing team at the Arnold Foundation trying to move evidence-based decision-making to the heart of how government works.

This effort is highly opportunistic, looking to make progress wherever possible. As Laura said: "We're almost indifferent as to whether or not the issue is homelessness or education or nurse-family partnerships, as long as the conversation has evolved from judgments based on intuition to judgments based on some sort of evidence that is credible." Big Arnold grants went to back more rigorous policy experimentation in such areas as hunger, health-care delivery, prescription drugs, education, workforce development, poverty reduction, and juvenile justice. Meanwhile, the foundation staff sifted through mountains of evaluations of various social programs. These reviews tended to underscore how money was often going to support interventions of marginal effectiveness. However, the team also found some real winners: programs proven to make a real dent in such challenges as improving high school graduation rates and increasing employment.

The upshot of all this work was a tantalizing glimpse of a very different future of social policy—one where governments and nonprofits religiously followed the evidence, shifting money to things that really have impact and defunding the stuff that didn't.

To speed the arrival of that future, in the spring of 2016 the Arnold Foundation put up $15 million for the "Moving the Needle Competition," which sought to incentivize evidence-based policy-making by governments and nonprofits. The goal was to spur replication of social programs that seem to work and pay for the rigorous evaluations needed to ensure they really are effective, in different settings.

The competition brought a slew of proposals to the foundation. In another sign that this area of Arnold's work was gaining momentum, in early 2016, the U.S. Congress created the Evidence-Based Policymaking Commission. Its fifteen members were charged with determining how best to strengthen and expand the use of data to evaluate the effectiveness of federal programs and tax expenditures.

This effort was put together with bipartisan support, and you can see why: Whether they want to shrink government or expand it, everyone can agree that money should be going to programs that work. The Arnolds hope that this agreement can be a springboard to a public policy revolution.

APOSTLES OF REASON

As the Arnolds worked to make social programs more rigorous, they gave millions to two organizations that had been created during an earlier era of optimism about public policy. The Urban Institute had been set up in 1968 by the Ford Foundation, which in 1974 had also played a key role—along with government agencies—in creating the Manpower Demonstration Corporation, to evaluate anti-poverty programs.

In the 1980s and 1990s, though, technocratic pragmatism gave way to much more ideological debates over public policy. Places like the Urban Institute struggled for relevance as the Heritage Foundation and other values-driven think tanks took center stage, underwritten by an activist donor class. Again and again, policy innovators found themselves stymied by ideological forces at work in the public square—most notably, religious conservatism and a reflexive anti-statism. The entrenchment of a bureaucratic helping class, invested in certain approaches, was another obstacle to following social science wherever it led. An even bigger one has been the record sums of money flowing into politics.

All these problems remain, and in many ways have gotten worse, since the turn of the century. Political polarization is as bad as it's ever been in the United States, and even more striking has been a rising distrust in elites of all kinds. The tide of money in politics has risen even further since the 2010 Supreme Court ruling in *Citizens United v. FEC.*

In the face of these currents, the Arnolds' outlook—one that imagines experts armed with data guiding public policy—can feel quixotic. A case in point: the Arnold Foundation made $7.2 million in grants for research projects in early 2016 to address the "rising cost of pharmaceutical drugs" and reduce the "financial barriers that can make it difficult to obtain life-saving treatments." It also aimed at bringing more transparency to the prescription drug market, a strategy that has helped to fuel reform of other sectors like education.

Yet anyone familiar with Washington knows that Big Pharma is among the most powerful interest groups inside the Beltway. No industry has spent more on elections and lobbying over the past twenty years. That power goes a long way in explaining why prescription drugs are so much more expensive in the United States than in, say, Canada. As long as Big

Pharma has the clout it does, the findings of researchers won't matter very much.

The Arnolds are well aware that when it comes to drug prices, along with some of their other goals, they have embarked on an uphill climb. "It's not going to change overnight," John said. "But you have to have a vision, and a belief, that there's a chance, however small, that small victories will somehow lead to momentum. . . . It's about identifying these things that intuitively make sense, and are better alternatives to the status quo, and then trying to exert pressure from every direction."

That statement captures the mentality of many donors, past and present. A strength of philanthropists is that they can play the long game, without worrying about the next election or quarterly earnings report. They can chip away at a problem for years, against all political odds, waiting for a window of opportunity to finally open.

As relatively young donors, with decades of giving before them, the Arnolds are well positioned to take the long view. As it turns out, though, they have already seen the tide shift on one of the issues they care about most: criminal justice reform.

Perhaps nowhere has U.S. public policy become more unhinged from rational deliberation than in the area of crime and punishment. Draconian approaches embraced in the get-tough 1980s and 1990s kept hurtling forward in the early 2000s like a runaway train even as crime rates plummeted and studies piled up that such practices do more harm than good. The Arnolds worried about the many innocent people who were sucked into this system, but also about the way that minor offenders got ensnared in America's jails while more dangerous perpetrators were put back on the street.

The couple gave one of their earliest big grants to the Innocence Project, which works to exonerate wrongfully convicted people and fix the flaws in the system that allowed such people to end up behind bars. For a time, Laura Arnold sat on the group's board. As she began to think more about how philanthropy could improve criminal justice, Laura hooked up with Anne Milgram, a prosecutor who had risen to become New Jersey's attorney general, in which capacity she helped pioneer new strategies for reducing crime and lowering recidivism. Milgram became one of the early executives at the Arnold Foundation, with the mandate to help figure out the best way to reform the criminal justice system. "We spent a year looking at what might be the highest leverage points in criminal justice," Laura said, of the exploratory effort that Milgram led, which involved numerous conversations with people around the country.

Eventually Milgram zeroed in on the pre-trial process. This is the period after people are arrested and charged, but before their cases get to court—and it's a phase in which the U.S. criminal justice system is often at its worst. Because of bail requirements, many accused of minor offenses remain behind bars and are drawn deeper into the system, even though there is a negligible risk to public safety of releasing them. At the same time, some charged with serious crimes are let out on bail, possibly putting the public at risk. Milgram and Arnold came to believe there was a better way to do things and that the foundation could play a key role here. "It was a fruitful place to start," said Laura, because it was a focused area "where we were able to contribute to changing the conversation to a degree that wouldn't have happened absent our involvement."

One reform that was clearly needed to improve the pre-trial process was to replace an anachronistic bail system with new tools and data to assess who should be kept locked up until trial and who should be released. To her surprise, Milgram found that no such tool existed to help courts make quick decisions about pre-trial detainment, so the Arnold Foundation built one, using online technology and reams of data. Then it turned to getting its tool, called the Public Safety Assessment (PSA), adopted and tested by local governments. By 2016, thirty jurisdictions were using the PSA, with some reporting encouraging results.

This is the kind of solution that the Arnolds are drawn to. It pushes aside dated practices that hinge on guesswork in favor of better decision-making based on modern analytics—with results that could profoundly change people's lives and save truckloads of public dollars.

The Arnold Foundation also targeted other problem areas in the criminal justice system, like the shoddy ways that forensic evidence was collected and analyzed. And it poured money into big university data projects with the broad goal of helping "criminal justice officials make more objective, evidence-based decisions" in a number of areas.

The foundation's reform push has turned out to be well timed. The pendulum has been swinging away from the get-tough approach of the past, creating new openings for more rational policy-making. And as that window widened further—especially after a police shooting and civil unrest in Ferguson, Missouri—the Arnolds ventured into more political territory to push their agenda. Their foundation helped lead the charge to get police officers to wear body cams, and it backed efforts by nonprofit groups to curb the excessive use by courts of fines and penalties, a huge problem that had surfaced as a result of the protests in Ferguson.

A study by the U.S. Department of Justice had found that three-quarters of Ferguson residents were subject to arrest warrants, mostly for failing to pay fines or show up in court. "We are putting people behind bars for their inability to pay fines even when we wouldn't imagine throwing someone in jail for the underlying violation, which could be something as ordinary as jaywalking or driving with a broken tail light," said Sam Brooke of the Southern Poverty Law Center, after landing an Arnold Foundation grant to litigate against these practices, in partnership with the ACLU.

The Arnolds don't see the criminal justice issue in familiar ideological terms, as a left-right contest between more permissive or more punitive values. Rather, they see it in terms of smart policy versus dumb policy, and have looked for allies across the political spectrum who share their views—with notable success. In October 2014, the foundation convened an unusual meeting in Washington with some groups that are normally at each other's throats, most notably the Center for American Progress, the top liberal think tank inside the Beltway, and FreedomWorks, an organization close to the Tea Party. "It was really an experiment in terms of can people set aside their ideologies on everything else, and agree on this one narrow issue," Laura said. The foundation's president, Denis Calabrese—who had previously been a Republican staffer in Congress—made many of the calls that got this unusual cast of characters in the same room.

What came out of this meeting was a heightened awareness of how much common ground the Left and Right share when it comes to criminal justice reform. Libertarians see the overreach of the criminal justice system as yet one more example of government run amok, while progressives hate how these policies devastate communities of color and divert resources away from things like education.

In early 2015, a new Left-Right group emerged—the Coalition for Public Safety—the likes of which had rarely been seen in Washington, backed with $5 million in Arnold Foundation funding. The Ford Foundation and Koch Industries also put in money, the first time these polar opposite funders had ever worked on the same side. The coalition sought to advance bipartisan legislation in Congress, as criminal justice increasingly became one of the few areas where lawmakers could work across the aisle.

GRAND PLANS

By the end of 2016, John and Laura Arnold had given away over $600 million. That sum was equal to a sizeable slice of their fortune when John retired in 2012. Yet despite all the money going out the door, Forbes still pegged Arnold's net worth at $2.9 billion. Like many philanthropists intent on giving away big chunks of their wealth, the Arnolds found it wasn't so easy to make much of a dent in a multi-billion-dollar fortune, as investment gains piled up nearly as fast as grants could be dispensed.

During five years of hyperactive giving, the largest sums of Arnold money had gone for education reform—$186 million. The foundation became a well-known player in education philanthropy, but its giving was modest compared to funders like the Walton Family Foundation, which gave out more money for education reform in 2014 alone than the Arnold Foundation did in five years. The Bill and Melinda Gates Foundation is another giant player in this area, along with the Broad Foundation. All these foundations came to K–12 with a similar goal: to bring about large-scale changes in America's public education system.

Nowhere have philanthropists taken a more muscular approach to influencing public life than in education. And nowhere have they stirred more fears that philanthropy is becoming yet another tool for the wealthy to speak more loudly than anyone else.

Those fears are understandable. Funders have worked to reshape education in the past decade at multiple levels—with their influence reaching from Washington, D.C., to the new charter school down the street from you. Yet this crusade, marked by record levels of spending, also underscores the limits of philanthropic power. The new givers have made a lot of noise on K–12, the *Vergara* lawsuit in California being a good example, but it's not clear they've actually done much to improve outcomes for the vast majority of U.S. students.

America's public school system has famously been a graveyard for ambitious philanthropists. A first challenge is scale. As a $600 billion complex enrolling 50 million students, the K–12 system is hard for philan-thropists to sway given their comparatively limited resources. A second is decentralization: There are over 13,000 public school districts across the United States, and a victory in one city or state doesn't necessarily trans-late into gains elsewhere.

The philanthropist most famously humbled by education was the newspaper magnate Walter Annenberg, who gave a half-billion dollars to finance K–12 reform efforts in the 1990s. That effort channeled money to local groups trying to fix schools and was widely judged to have failed. For the funders who came next, like Gates, Broad, and the Waltons, a key takeaway from Annenberg's venture was that philanthropists needed to be more hands-on in orchestrating school reform, to ensure that their own vision of innovation wasn't compromised. "We didn't want to do what Walter Annenberg did," Eli Broad told me. "You can't just write a check and throw money at it."

A key trait of the new wave of education reform funders has been their muscular approach. Reform philanthropists have sought to change outcomes within this sprawling system by focusing on several leverage points—and along the way they have generated enormous backlash from critics who see these donors as usurping citizen control of public schools.

One of the biggest ventures of education funders in recent years has been to create the Common Core State Standards—with the goal of bringing sweeping changes in how children are taught.

In 2008 Bill and Melinda Gates were sold on the idea of raising the bar for U.S. education achievement through uniform standards. By this time, the Gateses had already given billions to improve U.S. education, backing reforms that often created wide disruption in school districts while yield-ing mediocre results.

Bill Gates sees education as the primary building block for equal opportunity. The issue has animated him since his earliest days of large-scale philanthropy. He's also found education maddening in ways that his foundation's global grantmaking is not. Partly his frustration is with the constraints imposed by democratic systems. "For me the most disap-pointing thing is that the work can go backwards," Gates once said. "In other areas where we work, if we come up with a new malaria drug or malaria vaccine, nobody votes to uninvent our malaria vaccine. So it's pretty steady progress." Education is different "because of its complexity, its political nature, the relationship between management and labor."

The Gates Foundation is often viewed as a nine-hundred-pound gorilla on the K–12 scene, bulldozing forward with ideas that have sometimes turned out to be half-baked. Critics see the foundation as wielding way too much power—and in way too cavalier a fashion.

Unsurprisingly, Bill Gates takes a wonkier view of his role in education, which he describes as financing the research and experimentation needed to improve schools. When he was building Microsoft, Gates put a huge emphasis on R&D, to the point that Microsoft came to outspend nearly every corporation in the world in this area. (In 2013 alone, Microsoft spent $10.3 billion on R&D.) Gates has also been a huge champion of government spending for research in fields like medicine and energy, which in recent years has totaled tens of billions of dollars annually. Meanwhile, though, Gates notes that funding of "what works in education . . . is tiny. The R&D percentage is the lowest in this field of any field of human endeavor, yet you could argue it should be the highest because this field is catalytic."

That's where Gates sees his foundation coming in, playing what he has called a "technocratic" role in testing what works to improve education and to "create more options" for public officials. Gates views this as one of the best ways to leverage K-12 philanthropic dollars. Among the foundation's most ambitious research efforts in the past decade has been investing hundreds of millions of dollars to determine what makes an effective teacher. This hugely critical question, it turned out, had never been answered in a rigorous way. The Gates project included analyzing videos of 13,000 lessons taught by some 3,000 elementary school teachers.

In public interviews, Gates plays up his foundation's R&D role and has denied that it is a political player. In fact, the foundation has often shaped policy in public school districts and in the nation as a whole. A case in point is its promotion of the Common Core State Standards.

That work got under way in the summer of 2008, after Bill and Melinda listened to a pitch for national standards from Gene Wilhoit, director of a national group of state school chiefs, and David Coleman, an education consultant. According to a later account by the *Washington Post*, "Coleman and Wilhoit told the Gateses that academic standards varied so wildly between states that high school diplomas had lost all meaning, that as many as 40 percent of college freshmen needed remedial classes and that U.S. students were falling behind their foreign competitors." In other ways, too, the U.S. education system was a fragmented mess.

The solution? To get all fifty U.S. states to embrace a common set of education standards, along with ways to assess teacher and student performance.

In many other advanced countries, the idea that all students should learn the same things in the same way isn't controversial. Places like France have centralized education systems, run by the national government. Not so the United States, which has favored more local control of schools and a diversity of approaches to education. The standards that Coleman and Wilhoit were proposing to Gates wouldn't be dictated by Washington, the way that Paris tells every school in France how to operate. Rather, the idea was to develop a single set of standards that each state would voluntarily embrace—hopefully sidestepping any firestorm about a federal "takeover" of education, but achieving a similar result.

After thinking about the pitch from Coleman and Wilhoit for a few weeks, the Gateses decided to get behind their idea in a big way, mobilizing the full resources of the foundation to help create and sell what became the Common Core State Standards.

The Gates Foundation is a colossus, at least in the world of philanthropy. It employs some 1,400 people, many working out of a modern headquarters in downtown Seattle that the couple financed with a one-time gift of $350 million and which opened in 2011, across the street from the Space Needle. The foundation spends nearly four times as much every year as the next largest foundation in the United States. Most of its grantmaking is focused overseas, but it gives over a half-billion dollars annually for education in this country, with most of that going to improve K–12.

Just for perspective, though, this is about as much money as the New York City public school system spends in a week. If the Gates Foundation were a corporation, it wouldn't make the Fortune 500 list. Back in his old life heading Microsoft, Gates commanded one of the biggest tech companies in the world, with over sixty thousand employees. And while nonprofit types often view the Gates Foundation as mammoth, the Gateses themselves are keenly aware of just how limited their resources are compared to the problems they are tackling. Gates has called the spending by himself and other education philanthropists "truly a rounding error" in the grander scheme of things.

Critics of education funders dismiss such humble claims as a smoke-screen, designed to obscure the real facts of just how much influence private money can buy in a public system, especially when it's strategically spent.

The Common Core offers evidence for both the power and the limits of philanthropists.

In pushing Common Core, the Gates Foundation pulled every lever it could think of, ultimately giving out several hundred million dollars in grants to a vast array of players who helped advance and implement the program—from associations of state officials to think tanks on both left and right to the U.S. Chamber of Commerce. Gates money also flowed during this period to the two top teachers unions. Over time, it became hard to think of many education groups that *weren't* getting Gates money. As one reporter commented: "Sooner or later, everyone works for Gates"—a situation that's not exactly conducive to honest debate about the foundation's ideas. Jay Greene, an education scholar at the University of Arkansas, put the problem this way: "Really rich guys can come up with ideas that they think are great, but there is a danger that everyone will tell them they're great, even if they're not."

By late 2010, forty-five states had adopted the Common Core, before the standards were even fully developed, with full implementation unfolding over subsequent years. This work was backed by a range of other foundations, such as Hewlett and Broad. But the lion's share of the credit for the initiative's adoption goes to Gates—a stunning victory for the foundation that, in a way, is hard to get one's mind around. In effect, Bill and Melinda Gates, two private individuals, have helped determine what tens of millions of American children in public schools will learn every year—and also how they will learn, with changes in the teaching of math and other subjects.

Less clear, though, is what effect the Common Core will ultimately have. While there is no question about the power that private money has played in ushering in the Common Core standards, experts remain divided as to whether they will actually do much to raise student achievement, and definitive answers to this question are unlikely to emerge for many years. Gates money may have changed policies and practices, but that's not the same as changing outcomes.

Charter schools are another area where private philanthropists have wielded enormous power over public life, with uncertain results to date.

Funders from the business world, like Bill Ackman, have viewed charter schools as the hot start-ups that would smash the public K–12 monopoly, forcing all failing schools to improve—just as market theory might predict. In this sense, bankrolling charters was seen as a highly leveraged investment, the kind of well-targeted philanthropy that would produce systemic change.

Things haven't worked out that way. Having charter schools in a city doesn't necessarily exert pressures on traditional schools to improve; it can even hurt such schools by draining away resources and students. Meanwhile, charters have proved hard to scale. By 2016, after billions of dollars in philanthropic outlays, just 5 percent of U.S. students were in charter schools. In some cities, with high concentrations of poor kids, that number is much higher, and charters have truly scaled in some places. But overall, this reform is far from ever reaching a significant percentage of K–12 students. Giving for charters has turned out to be more akin to funding direct services than instigating a revolution in American education.

In 2015, the Walton Family Foundation—the biggest charter champion of all—put out a new strategic plan that acknowledged that more competition wasn't delivering the change it had hoped for. The foundation said its "theory of change has evolved: choice is necessary, but schools of choice cannot stimulate systematic transformation and large-scale improvements on their own." Walton's proposed solution was to invest more heavily in trying "to create environments that support choice," an effort that entailed even more aggressive efforts to shape local school policies.

As charter funders absorbed hard-learned lessons, they began to concentrate resources more strategically in a handful of key cities, to increase the number of poor kids attending charters. Maybe charters couldn't produce systemic change, and maybe they were hard to scale nationally, but if funders could remake the systems of just those cities that contained the most poverty and the worst schools, that could make a huge difference. Or so went the thinking. This strategy entailed marshalling serious muscle to overcome the opponents of more charters in target cities.

Philanthropic spending was one tool, but campaign spending was another, as donors funneled electoral cash to pro-charter public officials and candidates in places like Los Angeles. In Washington State, a group of deep-pocketed donors—including Bill Gates, Alice Walton, Reed Hastings, and Connie Ballmer—gave millions of dollars to help narrowly pass a ballot initiative in 2012 authorizing charter schools. (It was later struck down by the Washington Supreme Court.) In New York, a small group of hedge fund billionaires poured some $10 million into campaign donations and lobbying in 2014 aimed at expanding charter schools in New York City. Across the river, in New Jersey, two wealthy hedge funders, David Tepper and Alan Fournier, created a PAC to influence state education policy, while also making steady philanthropic gifts aimed at boosting K–12 schools. Just to the north, in Connecticut, the hedge fund billionaire Stephen Mandel contributed heavily to elect a charter-friendly Democratic governor, Dannel Malloy, in 2010 and then gave charitable grants to nonprofits that backed a Malloy education plan that channeled more money to charters. Later, it was reported that one of Mandel's foundations was paying three fellows working on policy matters in Malloy's office and two state departments.

Thanks to Mark Zuckerberg's involvement, the troubled reform bid in Newark became a famous example of philanthropists focusing huge resources on a select number of high-poverty urban school districts. In fact, though, Washington, D.C., has attracted more money from funders, per student, than any other U.S city. The nation's capital became a top battleground for education funders in 2007, after Mayor Adrian Fenty appointed Michelle Rhee chancellor of the D.C. Public Schools. Rhee didn't just push charters, she rammed through a new teacher evaluation system that gave big bonuses for top teachers and penalized or fired ineffective ones. A group of foundations led by Walton and Broad helped shoulder the costs of the system to the tune of nearly $65 million. The retired billionaire hedge funder Julian Robertson also gave big to help Rhee.

Rhee's reign in Washington was highly controversial, and she was out of office by 2010, after Fenty was defeated in his reelection bid—in part because of criticism of Rhee. Still, her legacy lived on: In 2014–15, nearly half of D.C. school kids were enrolled in public charter schools. (Rhee went on to found the reform group StudentsFirst with start-up funds from the Arnold and Broad foundations, among other donors.) In fourteen other cities, including some of the poorest in the country, Gary, Indiana, and Flint, Michigan, 30 percent or more of students were enrolled in charter schools. In New Orleans, which the Arnolds and other funders embraced as a top proving ground of charters, 93 percent of students were in such schools. Just over half of Detroit's students now attend charters. In other words, the strategic choice of funders to push hard in certain places is paying off; charters may not be sweeping the entire education system, but they are greatly expanding choice in many poor cities.

It's hard to generalize about the effects of all these new charter schools on the students who attend them. Such impact is fiercely debated, with the jury still out in many cities, like Detroit, that remain in the throes of disruptive change.

The only thing that's really clear is that, compared to the systemic revolution that charter funders were hoping for, the results have been disappointing. Such schools haven't yet been the levers for broader change that many had imagined. Still, donors like the Walton family and Eli Broad aren't giving up. They've lately doubled down on charters and, with billions more to give, are ready for a long slog. "It's the toughest area," Broad told me.

Other top ed philanthropists, like Mark Zuckerberg and Priscilla Chan, are looking beyond the mantras of choice and accountability. The couple is now investing their greatest hopes in personalized learning, which Zuckerberg has described as a way for "teachers work with students to customize instruction to meet the student's individual needs and interests." Chan told me: "The charter numbers are great, but at the end of the day, we realized that a lot of kids are in district schools. We want to work with the people who are serving all those kids, too. We don't want to work for a few, special, activated families, or families that happen to be near charter schools. We want to be able to reach all kids. And to do that we need to be able to work with the current system and new systems."

Philanthropists may be the new social engineers of our time, but their efforts to orchestrate large-scale changes in society don't tend to attract much attention. Even your average reader of the *New York Times* probably can't name more than several of America's biggest donors, much less say what they're doing . Many philanthropists like it this way, working in the background to try to reorder American life without anyone knowing their names—or how powerful they really are. And while the media heavily covers the role of money in electoral campaigns, it rarely looks at how philanthropic dollars shape policy.

Education giving has been different. The role of these funders has drawn wide scrutiny, in part because some are so famous. Gates is well known because of his wealth, while the Walton family is known because of Walmart. The hedge fund industry, which has produced many billionaire education reform donors, is a high-profile lightning rod for criticisms of inequality.

In a populist age, with distrust of the wealthy growing, the new education philanthropists have taken withering fire for interfering with the proper workings of democracy. Diane Ravitch, a scholar who once aligned herself with reformers before she emerged as their fiercest critic, has warned about the undue influence of a "billionaire boys club" that has "decided that they know how to fix public education." About Gates and the Common Core, Ravitch said: "The idea that the richest man in America can purchase and—working closely with the U.S. Department of Education—impose new and untested academic standards on the nation's public schools is a national scandal. A congressional investigation is warranted."

Perhaps needless to say, there's been no investigation. It's rare for Congress to ask hard questions about how private philanthropy is influencing public policy. The last time it really did so was in the 1960s, when a populist congressman from Texas, Wright Patman, made it his business to probe what he saw as foundation misconduct in a series of hard-hitting reports. In 1969, foundation leaders—including Ford president McGeorge Bundy—were grilled by the House Ways and Means Committee on whether, as tax-exempt nonprofits, they had violated the law with their activist funding.

Since then, little has been heard on Capitol Hill about the overreach of philanthropy in democratic life. But lately, alarm about the growing influence of private donors in K–12 has spread beyond critics on the left to include some on the right, who share the view that Gates orchestrated the backdoor nationalization of education standards through the Common

Core, working in concert with the Obama administration to achieve a longtime dream of liberals. By the 2016 election, the conservative backlash to the Common Core had become so intense that it emerged as a major litmus test among GOP primary voters. Various wealthy philanthropists on the right, like the hedge funder Sean Fieler, stepped up to fight the initiative by backing grassroots activism nationwide that galvanized many Tea Party supporters.

In a rare media interview in 2014, in which he was pressed on his outsized influence in education policy, Bill Gates defended his foundation's role, reiterating his usual point that its work is aimed at expanding the "pool of ideas" available to policymakers—not to tell those officials what to do. He said: "Our voice is not there when the final choice of what to scale up is made. That's a governor or a superintendent or board of education that decide those things."

Bill Gates is not the first technocratic philanthropist to plead dumb when it comes to his or her political clout. The poise of expert neutrality has long been common across the foundation world. But if Gates is reluctant to admit his power over education policy, everyone else gets it; Gates is widely viewed as among the most influential people in education. One 2006 study ranked him as *the* most influential person, ahead of President George W. Bush.

Gates is also not the only mega-giver to defend himself by saying that he is expanding the scope of public debate, not narrowing it. The new large-scale giving, say Gates and others, is not a subversion of the Tocquevillean pluralist ideal, but rather an expression of it because the funds go to amplify many more voices and ideas so that they can inform policy deliberations.

Whether you think Gates is right or wrong on this point probably has a lot to do with how you feel about what he and his foundation have been up to. When donors hold views we detest, we tend to see them as unfairly tilting policy debates with their money. Yet when we like their causes, we often view them as heroically stepping forward to level the playing field against powerful special interests or backward public majorities.

These sort of à la carte reactions don't make a lot of sense. Really, the question should be whether we think it's okay overall for *any* philanthropists to have so much power to advance their own vision of a better society?

7

Advocates

Not every big-time philanthropist these days is out to disrupt existing systems with fancy strategies or breakthrough concepts. Many just want to have an impact, however they can, and will readily turn to old and familiar tools to get the job done. They see making change not as rocket science, but as an exercise in persistence and steady, high-level giving.

The ideological think tank funders we met earlier in the book are a case in point: They're pouring money into a proven strategy that's been used for decades to sway policy. Often, such think tanks don't advance many new ideas but rather just bang the drum for old ones, with a few tweaks and updates. Right-wing wonks have pushed for privatizing Social Security for thirty years; the Left's policy shops have been calling for a higher minimum wage for just as long. And lately, amid an influx of new cash, the tempo of all these familiar battles has been increasing.

Likewise, big philanthropy has meant boom times for traditional advocacy groups working such beats as the environment, LGBT rights, abortion, and guns. Nonprofits that have been around for decades—like the Sierra Club, the ACLU, Planned Parenthood, and the NRA—have pulled in record money in recent years as legions of new upper-class donors have mobilized to press their views in the public square.

The tug-of-war around some hot-button issues can be grueling, as advocates tap large donor bases to blast away at one another year after year, without much movement on policy. Abortion is a prime example.

Philanthropists on both sides of that issue give millions and millions annually, to be rewarded only with modest incremental gains.

Pro-life advocates have managed over decades to make it harder to get clinic abortions in many states, while pro-choice forces have greatly expanded access to medical abortion drugs. Big turning-point moments—such as when the U.S. Supreme Court struck down Texas's restrictive anti-abortion law in 2016—have tended to be few and far between. Public opinion on abortion hasn't changed much in a generation, despite various well-financed PR and messaging pushes by both sides.

On other issues, though, it's been a very different story, with wealthy donors bankrolling advocacy efforts that yield big shifts in public policy.

THE WAR ON COAL

Climate change is one area where deep-pocketed philanthropists have lately had a big influence by bankrolling advocacy, with Michael Bloomberg near the forefront of this push.

After the Bush administration rejected the Kyoto Protocol, in 2005 then-mayor Bloomberg joined a coalition of mayors who pledged to curb greenhouse gases at the local level. The following year, in a commencement speech at Johns Hopkins, he slammed those blocking action on climate change: "Despite near-unanimity in the science community, there's now a movement, driven by ideology and short-term economics, to ignore the evidence and discredit the reality of climatic change." During his second term as mayor, Bloomberg unveiled an ambitious plan to reduce the city's greenhouse gas emissions, and later became chairman of a group of mayors from major cities around the world fighting climate change.

In 2010, early in his third term, Bloomberg was looking to step up his philanthropy even as he spent his days governing Gotham. His fortune had soared during his years in office, as Bloomberg terminals proliferated ever more widely, and he had plenty of cash to spare for sideline pursuits. Bloomberg strongly considered a big push into education reform and asked his longtime advisor, Kevin Sheekey, to bring him ideas in that area.

At a meeting at Gracie Mansion, Sheekey floated an education idea that didn't go over well. "It was a terrible meeting in every way, and Mike was angry," Sheekey later told *Politico*. "I said: 'Look, if you don't like this idea, that's fine. We'll bring you another.' He said: 'No, I want another *now*.'"

Before the meeting, Sheekey had eaten lunch with Carl Pope, the head of the Sierra Club, who was starting a push to raise $50 million to expand the club's Beyond Coal campaign, which worked at the state and local level to shut down coal plants across the country. At the time, the campaign was only operating in fifteen states; Pope wanted to expand the effort to forty-five states. He saw this as a way to make progress on climate change even as efforts to pass a cap-and-trade bill were fizzling in Congress. But Pope also told Sheekey that closing coal plants could have a big impact on public health by lowering the number of deaths from air pollution. In other words, the Beyond Coal campaign aimed to advance not one, but two of Bloomberg's passions.

Bloomberg was sold on the idea of getting behind the campaign. "We'll just give Carl a check for the $50 million," he said. "Tell him to stop fundraising and get to work."

It didn't turn out to be that simple. Naturally, Bloomberg wanted metrics and data so that he could gauge the progress of the Sierra Club's work. He wanted detailed indicators to guide the effort, analyzing coal plants across the country. He "put us through the ringer," a Sierra Club executive said later. But thanks to Bloomberg's prodding, the group would go on to build a comprehensive database that tracked the retirement of coal plants and the gains from such closures in terms of public health and reduced carbon emissions.

Bloomberg's massive donation to the club, the biggest in its history, was announced in 2011 at a press event before a coal power plant on the Potomac River. Five years later, that plant was closed, and the Sierra Club was also taking credit for helping close an additional 232 coal plants. This success was accomplished largely through aggressive litigation work, with the club's lawyers using every strategy they could think of to shutter plants. Bloomberg's office received monthly reports on the work.

In 2015, Bloomberg dramatically upped his investment in Beyond Coal, committing another $30 million. With that money in the pipeline, the campaign set a new, more ambitious goal: to retire by 2017 half of all coal-fired power plants that had been in operation in 2010, a goal that Bloomberg would describe as once "almost unthinkable." Many millions of dollars had helped make it now nearly inevitable. In announcing this latest gift, Bloomberg called Beyond Coal "one of the most successful grassroots environmental efforts in this country's history."

That was something of a stretch, calling Beyond Coal a "grassroots" effort—since it was financed by a Manhattan billionaire, run by sophisticated advocates, and heavily staffed by lawyers. To the average coal miner in West Virginia, the effort might look like the very epitome of an elitist cabal. On the other hand, the director of Beyond Coal, Mary Hitt, had herself spent many years in Appalachia, with a grassroots group called Appalachian Voices that worked on the front lines to curb the damage to humans and the environment caused by coal mining, including the horrendous practice of obliterating entire mountaintops.

For decades, activists like Hitt had worked with limited success to challenge Big Coal, a powerful industry with clout at both the state and national level. Even as the industry took hits from the rise of natural gas in the early 2000s, it remained a major force, employing tens of thousands of people and devoting millions to campaign contributions and lobbying. Coal production actually hit an all-time high in 2008. Utility companies were also big coal boosters, looking to protect huge investments in generating plants that were designed to run on coal.

Quite apart from its effects on the climate, though, coal is bad news: It releases toxic particulates into the air when burned. A 2011 report by the American Lung Association estimated that such pollution accounted for thirteen thousand deaths a year, as well as huge numbers of cases of asthma and other respiratory problems, like emphysema. But the damage to human health went even further. As another report stated, "Coal pollutants affect all major body organ systems and contribute to four of the five leading causes of mortality in the U.S.: heart disease, cancer, stroke, and chronic lower respiratory diseases."

This was a high price for Americans to pay for relying on coal to generate electricity. But it was also a price widely dispersed across the country, given how coal pollution traveled in the air. That made it hard to organize those who suffered from coal. Many people didn't even know that coal pollution was to blame for their health problems, or the deaths of loved ones.

In contrast, those people who worked in the coal or power industries— from the miners to the truck drivers and up to the executives—were very aware of the critical role this fuel played in their lives. As a result, they were easily marshalled into a potent political force.

The scholar Mancur Olson would call this a collective action problem. As he described in his classic 1965 book, *The Logic of Collective Action,* large and disorganized groups of citizens have a hard time coming together to take action to advance their common interests. They are routinely bested in political combat by much smaller, but better organized groups who are ready to fight fiercely and with laser focus. There are lots of examples of this in American life, beyond coal—like the way that gun owners band together through the NRA in opposition to gun regulations that most Americans favor, but with far less intensity. Or how teachers unions are highly organized when it comes to defending job protections like "last in, first out"—policies that the public is only dimly familiar with. Or the way that the finance industry will fight much harder for looser rules on derivatives than ordinary people—most of whom don't know what derivatives are—will fight to impose such rules.

Collective action problems help explain any number of frustrating aspects of America's democracy. Again and again, it's hard to solve obvious problems because organized interest groups can thwart the broader will of the public.

Philanthropists can play a key role in overcoming such deadlocks. By writing checks and more, they can enable advocates to bypass the grueling—and perhaps impossible—work of rallying enough citizens to overcome narrow interest groups. This is one reason why philanthropy has been called "society's passing gear": it speeds along changes that otherwise might take much longer, or might never happen at all.

One obvious question, though, is whether it's okay that wealthy donors and foundations are the ones deciding when and where to use that passing gear. Also what happens when things accelerate too quickly, without enough careful thought? The answer, as we've seen, is that philanthropists applying the passing gear can end up in a ditch—which is what happened in Newark, when Mark Zuckerberg and other funders backed disruptive education reforms without buy-in from the community.

An even darker side of this picture is that the same advocacy tools that can engineer breakthroughs on behalf of the public interest can also be deployed by philanthropists to thwart the public interest. Indeed, who's to say what the public interest really is, anyway?

BETTER TOOLS, BIGGER CHECKS

These questions are growing more pressing as funders become savvier and more aggressive about influencing policy. Also, many more wealthy people are now engaged in such activist philanthropy than in the past, and richer ones, too. The total amount of money in play has lately exploded.

Green giving is a great example of this shift. Fifteen years ago, Michael Bloomberg's net worth was a fraction of what it is today and he didn't give any of it to environmental causes. Now he's one of the richest men on the planet and among the biggest backers of climate change advocacy. Bloomberg isn't just bringing his money to this fight. He's bringing decades of experience in business and government, and a global network of powerful contacts.

In turn, Bloomberg is just one of the new environmental mega-donors who had emerged in recent years and begun pouring money into large-scale advocacy. The former hedge fund manager Tom Steyer has drawn wide attention for his giving to curb climate change, much of it to his super PAC, NextGen Climate. Ten years ago, Steyer's pockets weren't nearly as deep as they are today and he was still immersed in building his San Francisco–based hedge fund. Thanks to shrewd bets in distressed assets, his fortune surged after the 2008 financial crisis, catapulting him onto the Forbes 400 list and ensuring he had ample money to play the influence game. After Steyer retired from his firm in 2012, he also had the time for such activism.

Nat Simons is another green philanthropist who's tapped a fast-growing pile of hedge fund wealth to become a major new force in environmental giving.

Nat is the son of Jim Simons, the mathematician and hedge fund pioneer who made billions in the markets, a fortune that tripled between 2005 and 2015, soaring to over $15 billion—creating plenty of spare cash to fuel family philanthropy.

Nat also works in finance, having joined his father's firm, Renaissance Technologies, in the mid-1990s, after getting his master's in mathematics from the University of California at Berkeley. He spent thirteen years there, before spinning off his own hedge fund, the Meritage Group, which is based in San Francisco.

While the older Simons has become very visible with his ambitious science giving (which will be discussed later), Nat operates very much in the background. In 2006, he and his wife, Laura Baxter-Simons, created a foundation called Sea Change, which has a small staff but little presence online. The couple are its only trustees.

Among climate advocates, Simons and Sea Change are well known. During the push to pass cap-and-trade legislation in 2009, the foundation wrote big checks to the top players in that battle, including the Environmental Defense Fund, the Natural Resources Defense Council (NRDC), and the Sierra Club. After the legislation failed, Sea Change kept up its spending. In just one three-year period, 2011 to 2013, the foundation made around $140 million in grants, with much of that money going to bankroll climate advocacy. Its biggest grants during that period went to the Partnership Project, an outfit started in 1999 to help unify America's top environmental groups so that they can have more impact. Other large, seven-figure grants went to top environmental groups, as well as the Center for American Progress, the liberal think tank, which pushes climate-friendly policies inside the Beltway.

Nat Simons is one of the single largest donors to environmental causes in the past decade. But he's rarely granted media interviews and seldom speaks in public, keeping a low profile that underscores how today's big philanthropy can feel shadowy and, to some, conspiratorial. Breitbart .com, the conservative news network, has attacked Simons for "waging war on affordable energy" by funding "hard-left environmental causes." The *Washington Free Beacon* has charged that he profits financially from his philanthropy by investing in clean technologies, and even criticized him as a hypocrite for commuting to work on a powerboat. Such attacks on donors who fund in contested territory aren't unusual, with critics often alleging that financial self-interest is the real motive for giving. (This is exactly why some donors choose to stay in the shadows, along with not wanting supplicants to line up at their door.)

For his part, Simons has described what he's up to in simple terms. Like other funders, he sees his giving as a way to speed up the pace of change toward a desirable, if not inevitable, future. He's said, "It's not really a question of whether we move to a low carbon economy. I think it's clear we're moving there. . . . The question is how quickly. The role of philanthropy is really to facilitate that process. . . . It's not going to be ramming something down the throats of certain people. We know that's not going to work."

Nat Simons's sister, Liz, also has a foundation bankrolled with their dad's hedge fund winnings, which she runs with her husband, Mark Heising. This couple, too, gives heavily for advocacy on climate change, although their interests range more widely to include science and education. Liz worked as a bilingual teacher in Oakland after getting her master's in education from Stanford; Mark trained as a computer scientist and worked in tech before going into finance.

Like her brother, Liz doesn't shrink from policy combat. In early 2015, the Heising-Simons Foundation teamed up with Bloomberg Philanthropies to lay out $48 million to help boost the Obama administration's ambitious effort to regulate greenhouse gas emissions at the state level. Operating through executive action, the administration was using the muscle of the Environmental Protection Agency (EPA) to push states toward renewable energy sources. The effort set off a furious backlash by Republican state officials—a backlash that funders like Bloomberg and Heising-Simons sought to counter by strengthening environmental advocates working in different states. In other words, a president who made an end run around Congress got critical backup from wealthy philanthropists elected by no one.

The Environmental Defense Fund was among the green groups that plunged into the running state battles over the EPA rules. EDF has been among the top grantees of the Heising-Simons Foundation in recent years, but has pulled in even bigger bucks from other funders, including many on Wall Street. EDF's funding has soared as big new donors have taken up environmental issues and existing ones have upped their giving. In 2010, the group had $64 million in revenue. Two years later, in 2012, that figure was up to $116 million. In 2014, it brought in $149 million, and it did nearly as well in 2015.

Who's giving all that money? It's hard to say, because EDF is not transparent about its funding. One of its biggest donors, though, is Julian Robertson, a retired hedge fund billionaire who's given EDF tens of millions of dollars, including around $33 million over just two years, 2013 and 2014. Among environmental groups, EDF has long had a reputation as a more moderate outfit ready to work with business. That may have drawn Robertson, a Republican, to the group. But make no mistake: EDF has been at the forefront of aggressive policy advocacy in recent years, often with work that bolsters the Obama administration's agenda.

Like Nat Simons, Robertson stays far out of the spotlight. Now in his eighties, he was once known as the "Wizard of Wall Street" for his uncanny investing skills. These days, Robertson places philanthropic bets, and beyond giving millions to curb climate change, he's put big money behind education reform. In the past fifteen years, Robertson's foundation has been deeply involved in two very contentious, and political, education battles. First, it backed efforts under Mayor Bloomberg to overhaul New York City's public schools and to dramatically expand the number of charters. Next, it supported Michelle Rhee's expensive push in Washington, D.C., to create a new teacher evaluation system—and also poured money into expanding the number of charter schools in that city. The Robertson Foundation has also supported key education reform groups at the national level.

Robertson isn't as well known as other education reform donors, but his giving underscores just how much new money has lately gone to a muscular philanthropy aimed at changing education policies—an area worth returning to for a moment, as we focus on how donors bankroll advocacy.

As with the environment, more donors with more money have embraced more aggressive approaches to effecting change in America's schools. One academic study found that two of the top education funders, the Gates and Broad foundations, more than doubled their giving to national advocacy groups between 2005 and 2010—with such giving rising to $60 million in the latter year. It has only climbed since then, with Walton also giving more funds to think tanks and advocacy groups as it ramped up its overall education-related giving to over $200 million a year by 2014.

Education funders have been very strategic in linking advocacy to their nuts-and-bolts work of creating new education institutions and practices. For example, Walton has spent the bulk of its education dollars on actually building charter schools, but it has also worked to create a policy climate where charters are embraced.

Education funders have also invested in media, giving a wide array of grants for reporting on these school issues. As mentioned earlier, grants by Broad and other funders went to the *Los Angeles Times* to cover education in that city. This funding has been modest compared to the $10 million that the Gates Foundation has given to support *Education Week,* the premier source of news on K–12 issues, or the $25 million in grants it made to National Public Radio and Public Radio International over many years, for reporting on both education and global issues. In 2015, many of the top education funders came together to support an online news site on education founded by Campbell Brown, the former CNN anchor turned education reformer. The site hit the ground running with a reported $4 million annual budget. Nearly every day it's banging the drum for charter schools and other reforms.

Do the consumers of education reporting know that it is supported by funders with a strong point of view who are behind that news? Sometimes yes, often not.

Funders in other issue areas have also invested heavily in media, in ways that complement their advocacy giving. Green donors have scaled up a number of media outlets, such as *Grist* and *InsideClimate News,* that are sounding the alarm about threats to the planet. The Google billionaire Eric Schmidt, along with his wife, Wendy, have been big backers of such environmental journalism, as has the Swiss billionaire Hansjörg Wyss. Health-care funders have given millions for reporting in their area, too. The Robert Wood Johnson Foundation has given over $10 million to National Public Radio since 2008, even as NPR covers highly charged health-care battles where the foundation is a key combatant, as the biggest funder promoting the Affordable Care Act. The Ford Foundation has bankrolled media outlets like the *Los Angeles Times* and Minnesota Public Radio to explore inequity in American life, which is also a major focal point of Ford's advocacy funding. Most recently, new philanthropic dollars have gone to underwrite reporting on criminal justice, and other issues have gotten attention, too. The PBS affiliate in New York City landed a grant of $3.5 million from the Arnold Foundation for a TV series that sounded the alarm about America's pension crisis, only to return the money after critical reporting on the gift by David Sirota.

That episode was unusual. Although you might think that a rising flow of so much interested money to major media outlets would attract scrutiny, this hasn't been the case. The larger point here is that, when it comes to influencing policy and public opinion, funders are pulling every lever they can think of. Many are rich enough to pull them all at the same time.

BRINGING IT ALL TOGETHER

If you want to see a prime example of how the different tools of philanthropic influence can change policy in one state, North Carolina is a great place to look. And Art Pope is the donor there to watch.

"I believe in trying to make North Carolina a better place for its citizens," Pope has said, in describing his years of philanthropy and political advocacy in that state. It's hard to argue with that sentiment, but many in North Carolina would hotly dispute Pope's vision of what "better" means. In 2016, nonprofits and elected leaders backed by Pope helped engineer the passage of a controversial law requiring transgender people to use bathrooms that match the sex on their birth certificate. The move triggered an uproar that cost North Carolina tens of millions of dollars in lost business.

More about the "bathroom bill" in a moment. But, first, a little about Art Pope.

Pope was born in Fayetteville, North Carolina, the son of an entrepreneur who built a corporate retail wholesaling business out of a few small stores after World War II. Pope studied law, eventually taking over the business, as well as becoming chairman of a family foundation that he established with his father, John Pope, in 1986.

The foundation funds a number of traditional causes, such as the arts, higher education, and human services. But it also devotes itself to supporting the ideals of free enterprise and limited government. "It's not enough to give a man a fish or even to teach a man how to fish," Pope has said. "We have to have a right to fish, to own the fish we catch, to sell the fish. . . . we need a free market economy under the rule of law."

Pope has explained his foundation's push into policy as being aimed at creating a more robust pluralism in his state, a familiar logic for controversial philanthropy, as we've seen. "We did not have much of a public policy debate in North Carolina," he said in 2013. "We needed a voice for those policies consistent with a free society."

Pope's strategy was simple enough. He created, at a state level, the same kind of policy network that conservative funders like Richard Mellon Scaife and the Kochs had built up nationally. Over the past quarter century, the John William Pope Foundation has given more than $60 million to finance a set of conservative institutions that have helped push North Carolina to the right—and made Pope one of the most influential people in the state.

One of the groups it created is the John Locke Foundation, which produces a stream of research and analysis aimed at influencing state-level policy on everything from taxes to health care to transportation. Another top Pope grantee, Civitas, plays a similar role, while the North Carolina Center for Constitutional Law uses legal strategies to advance conservative ideas. The Pope Foundation also finances centers that seek to reform education at all levels and to change policy on social issues like abortion and LGBT rights.

The foundation's main grantee working on social issues has been the North Carolina Family Policy Council (NCFPC), a small nonprofit in Raleigh. Among the group's various priorities over the years has been fighting an expansion of LGBT rights, as part of its broader "battle to retain the Judeo-Christian values that are the foundation of western civilization." In 2014, the Pope Foundation gave the council $150,000, or about a third of its total budget. In June 2015, it reportedly donated another $100,000 to the group, including $50,000 earmarked for NCFPC's 2016 voter guide. Such guides—carefully written to be nonpartisan, but clearly taking a point of view—are among the many ways that nonprofits, and the donors that back them, seek to legally influence elections.

NCFPC was strongly opposed to transgender people using bathrooms of their preferred gender, and celebrated when House Bill 2 was passed in March 2016, after the city of Charlotte adopted a transgender-friendly bathroom ordinance. During the ensuing uproar over the law, NCFPC became its main defender, pumping out statements and blog posts designed to combat "myths" about HB2. In an interview with NPR, Art Pope positioned himself above the fray, saying that both sides in the bathroom debate had legitimate concerns. But it's fair to say that few in the state had done more to precipitate this "political Category 5 hurricane," as *Charlotte Magazine* called the bathroom battle.

In turn, this was only the latest fight that Pope was at the center of. Even as he ramped up his policy network, Pope blazed a parallel path as a politician and top GOP donor in the state. He was first elected to the state legislature in 1988, serving nearly four terms. And he gave to numerous Republican politicians over many years, as well as to the party's state committee.

Pope's bid to buy influence in one state with both philanthropic and political money is unusual for its scope, but is otherwise not unique. In Missouri, the financial executive Rex Sinquefield has pursued a similar dual-track strategy—funding a policy think tank to push a broad conservative agenda that includes school choice while backing a ballot initiative to repeal the state income tax and showering campaign gifts on numerous politicians, from the governor downward.

Sinquefield, who spent some of his childhood in an orphanage and later went to the University of Chicago, made his fortune by pioneering stock index funds. Eventually, though, he said, he grew "bored" with just making money. Libertarian politics became his second career, with nearly all his efforts focused in Missouri—although he branched out to neighboring Kansas in 2012, to help push through a historic tax cut, one that blew a massive hole in the state's budget. "If you get involved at the local level," he once told an audience, "you will be amazed at how much influence you can have." That's especially true for wealthy donors who know how to pull all the levers of power.

Like Art Pope, Sinquefield also gives heavily to more traditional charitable causes, such as local music and chess programs in St. Louis. Those gifts have gotten positive press and helped Sinquefield position himself as a more traditional civic leader. Reading some of the media coverage of Sinquefield, you'd never know he had such extreme political views or was engaged in ambitious efforts to shape policy in the state.

Some liberal donors have also mixed heavy philanthropic and political giving at the state level. In Minnesota, Alida Messinger—an heiress to a Rockefeller fortune—has donated millions of dollars to local nonprofits working on environmental and energy issues, and has also given heavily to protect women's reproductive rights, fight poverty, and mobilize low-income voters.

Messinger's philanthropy goes back to the 1970s, when she fell in with a group of other young progressive donors, including George Pillsbury, after her father died in a car crash and she came into her full inheritance at age twenty-one—becoming one of the richest women in America. The checks for her donations flowed from an office in Manhattan that housed the philanthropic funds of the various descendants of John D. Rockefeller. That stream of funds to sway policy in Minnesota shows just how long the arm of old money can be, especially in the hands of an activist heir whose philanthropy is guided by the motto "change, not charity," as Messinger once explained it to me.

Meanwhile, Messinger became one of Minnesota's biggest Democratic donors, giving money to the state party committees and PACs, supporting dozens of candidates for office, and sinking $3 million into supporting a successful 1988 ballot initiative to raise money for environmental protection. This giving helped orchestrate a Democratic takeover of Minnesota's state government, and a burst of progressive legislation enacted in 2013 and 2014 with the support of Governor Mark Dayton—Messinger's ex-husband, who himself is an heir to wealth from the Target retail empire.

Wealthy liberal donors have used a combination of philanthropic and political giving to sway policy in other states, too, such as Colorado, where the billionaire medical instruments heiress Pat Stryker has been a key progressive funder. Along with three other donors, known as the "Gang of Four"—the others were Jared Polis, Tim Gill, and Rutt Bridges—Stryker is credited with bankrolling Democratic gains in Colorado. She's also been a major supporter of the Bell Policy Center, the state's top liberal think tank, as well as other liberal groups in the state, like Planned Parenthood. Pat's billionaire brother, Jon Stryker, has engaged in similar giving in Michigan, channeling a steady stream of philanthropic grants to local progressive organizations and giving millions of dollars to help elect Democrats.

Still, there's no question that conservative philanthropists have long been more attuned to swaying public policy in the states. Wealthy donors like Richard Scaife and the Kochs began to nurture a network of state think tanks, many modeled on the Heritage Foundation, in the 1980s. Thomas Roe, a southern building magnate and Heritage backer, was among those donors intent on capturing the high ground of ideas in state capitals. In 1992, he helped found and bankroll the State Policy Network, aiming to knit together an emerging set of local right-wing think tanks. When SPN launched, there were twelve such groups; now it reports there are sixty-five, across all fifty states. Many draw funding from a combination of national and local funders.

These investments by right-wing donors have paid big dividends. With a majority of governorships lately in Republican hands, and many key policy fights—over health care, education, climate change, and guns—unfolding in the states, local conservative policy shops have played a growing role in shaping choices that affect the lives of millions of Americans. Many progressive groups also exist in the states, mainly funded by foundations, but they don't have nearly as much capacity as their counterparts on the right. A basic law of fundraising is that nonprofits that can't build a strong stable of individual donors will find it hard to expand. So far, though, few major philanthropists on the left have focused on the states in any sustained way. "State policy work isn't sexy to donors," complained one advocate to a researcher.

Thomas Roe passed away in 2000, but the foundation he left behind still makes numerous grants every year to state policy groups. And other donors have emerged to carry on his work, including Robert Mercer, whose foundation has backed at least a half dozen such think tanks in recent years.

While Art Pope has fewer resources than many top national funders, his success in North Carolina underscores how far well-targeted giving can go in smaller state arenas. His political contributions helped Republicans win control of the North Carolina legislature in 2010, and then take the governorship in 2012. With total political control of the state, Republicans moved quickly to enact a range of policy proposals long touted by Pope-backed outfits for slashing taxes and social services, as well as restricting abortion, expanding gun rights, and much more, including the bathroom law. Pope himself played a hands-on role in some of these changes, after he was appointed the state's budget director by Governor Pat McCrory. As co-chair of McCrory's transition team, Pope also had a hand in choosing who occupied other key jobs in the administration.

The sweeping policy changes enacted by McCrory triggered a huge backlash in North Carolina, long before HB2 was passed, including an ongoing series of protests in the state capital called "Moral Mondays." This angry opposition softened a few elements of the governor's agenda, but what it couldn't easily change is the way a Republican advantage was increasingly baked into the electoral system. Pope's philanthropic dollars had played a role in orchestrating that tilt, by helping get a tough voter ID law enacted in North Carolina—one seemingly designed to suppress the state's black and Latino vote.

Pope's network of nonprofit groups started pushing hard on the voter ID issue in 2011—as conservative groups and Republican politicians took up this same issue in many other states. Compelling people to show ID at the polls is touted as a crucial safeguard to in-person voter fraud. Yet such fraud is negligible in the United States, and North Carolina was no exception. For example, of 3.79 million ballots cast in North Carolina's 2010 election cycle, only 28 cases of suspected voter fraud were referred to district attorneys. In 2012, 7 million ballots were cast, and only 121 alleged cases of voter fraud were reported.

Most electoral experts agree that the biggest threat to the integrity of U.S. elections lies not in individuals impersonating other voters, but rather in the manipulation of voter registration files by partisan public officials, as well as glitches in voting technology. Meanwhile, though, voter ID laws can serve to deprive citizens of the right to vote, since some of the electorate lacks proper ID. One analysis estimated that over 600,000 voters, or nearly 10 percent of the electorate in North Carolina, lacked state-issued photo identification in 2012. Many were poorer or older voters of color. People who can't afford to own a car are most likely to lack the ID needed to vote. They are also far more likely to pull the lever for Democrats when they do vote.

Pope-funded groups invested heavily in sounding the alarm over voter fraud and pushing for a photo ID law. "Realistically, voter ID requirements are an insurance policy against the possibility that an extremely close election might be stolen by voter fraud," John Locke Foundation president John Hood wrote in a December 2012 article. North Carolina enacted a new voter ID law the following year. Since then, Pope-funded groups have been closely involved in efforts to beat back efforts to repeal or modify the law, with the North Carolina Institute for Constitutional Law—the legal arm of Pope's nonprofit network—taking a lead in trying to squash litigation. Still, the law was struck down by a federal appeals court in 2016, holding that it was "passed with racially discriminatory intent."

You might think that Art Pope is an unusual philanthropist in that he directs money to restricting the franchise. You'd be wrong. In recent years, this cause has proven popular among a number of funders who have funneled millions to conservative groups that fan fears about voter fraud and press for ID laws—helping enact, and defend, such laws in numerous states since 2011. One leader in this work is True the Vote, which describes itself as "the nation's largest nonpartisan, voters' rights and election integrity organization."

True the Vote has been active in North Carolina's voter ID battles, among others. The Bradley Foundation has been one of its biggest donors in recent years, but it's impossible to identify the group's other top backers. Philanthropists giving money to sway electoral outcomes often hide their tracks, which is easy to do given the lax reporting rules for nonprofits.

One donor who wasn't so successful in this regard is Stephen Einhorn, a Wisconsin venture capitalist and major GOP donor. As the 2012 election approached, it emerged that the foundation Einhorn runs with his wife paid for dozens of anonymous billboards around Milwaukee and two Ohio cities, mainly in minority areas, that screamed "Voter Fraud Is a Felony!" with penalties of up to three and a half years in prison and fines of $10,000.

The Einhorns put out a statement through a PR firm that the billboards were a "public service" message aimed at Democrats and Republican alike. "By reminding people of the possible consequences of illegal voting, we hope to help the upcoming election be decided by legally registered voters." The director of a progressive group in Wisconsin, meanwhile, has this to say: "Perhaps their Chicago public relations firm could answer why the Einhorns only felt it was necessary to target legal voters in minority communities, and why they didn't feel the need to do this 'public service' throughout communities across Wisconsin where a majority of the residents are white."

What nobody mentioned amid this flap was just how elastic the definition of charitable activities is for tax-exempt outfits like the Einhorn Family Foundation. The IRS makes no distinction between funding minority voter suppression and, say, giving for civics education.

Efforts to gut the Voting Rights Act of 1965 also qualify as charitable, and have drawn generous philanthropic support in recent years, including by some of the same funders backing voter ID work. The main magnet for such donations has been the Project on Fair Representation, which was founded by Edward Blum.

A former Houston stockbroker, Blum is widely regarded as the most effective opponent of the Voting Rights Act; he has orchestrated a series of suits to weaken the law. Among his backers have been the Bradley Foundation and the Searle Freedom Trust. But the full story of Blum's support will probably never be known, since much money has come through DonorsTrust, an intermediary group that channels conservative giving in ways that leave no fingerprints. It's been called a "dark money ATM." (More about DonorsTrust later.)

Blum's crusade suffered a setback when the U.S. Supreme Court affirmed the dismissal of a suit in 2016, in *Evenwel v. Abbott*, that would have dealt another blow to the Voting Rights Act. But Blum has promised to keep working to demolish the cornerstone law of the civil rights era, and shown he can raise the money to do so. Meanwhile, Blum's group is also working hard to end affirmative action on college campuses, another cause that conservative funders have supported, going back to the 1990s.

NO ONE LEFT BEHIND

The charitable income tax deduction was created in 1917. It was included in a law to raise revenue for the U.S. war effort, and stipulated the exemption apply only for gifts made to groups "organized and operated exclusively for religious, charitable, scientific, or educational purposes, or to societies for the prevention of cruelty to children or animals." Remarkably similar language can be found a century later in the IRS tax rules that define a tax-exempt 501(c)(3) organization.

Much about the charitable sector has changed since 1917, and a lot has changed even since 1969, which was the last time that Congress took a close look at what activities foundations should be allowed to fund. Since then, there's been a huge proliferation of nonprofits driven by ideological goals that often track closely with those of partisan politicians. More philanthropic dollars are working to advance the same ultimate agendas as PACs and campaigns.

Why hasn't there been a clamor for a reform of the tax laws that govern nonprofits?

One reason is that groups across the ideological spectrum benefit from the status quo, and neither the Left nor the Right sees an interest in tightening the definition of what constitutes a tax-exempt nonprofit. You could argue that the *public* has a strong interest in tougher rules, since wealthy donors get a tax break when they buy megaphones that often drown out the voices of ordinary people. To date, though, few voters seem to have made the connection, and the media pays little attention to how much influence philanthropists can and do buy.

Progressives have generally led the charge to curb the role of money in public life. So it's notable that these advocates have been largely silent about how "charitable" dollars are influencing politics and policy—often with deeper impact than the campaign spending the Left so fervently wants to restrict.

You can see why progressives keep mum on this issue. Its advocates are especially dependent on philanthropy, and many see such giving as boosting democracy by empowering points of view that might otherwise be steamrollered by corporations or bigots. Sure, philanthropy can be used by the likes of Art Pope and other conservatives. But it can be used just as deftly by people like Tim Gill to help fast-forward America to a more enlightened state.

Gill has been engaged in large-scale giving for over two decades, with a laser focus on LGBT rights. By the summer of 2015, when the U.S. Supreme Court ruled in favor of marriage equality, he'd given over $300 million to the cause, and distinguished himself as one of the hardest-working, biggest-spending, and most creative donors in the fight for LGBT rights. He's been among the most political, too. Like Art Pope, Gill sees philanthropy as just one tool to press his agenda; he has also invested a fortune in campaign donations and rallied other LGBT funders to do the same through a 501(c)(4) organization, Gill Action, that he created in 2005.

Tim Gill grew up in Colorado and studied computer science at the state university in Boulder. After graduating he worked at Hewlett-Packard and a consulting firm. Then, in 1981, he got into the nascent personal computer revolution by starting Quark, a company that made page-layout software—including the hugely popular QuarkXPress. Gill's venture made him immensely wealthy. And so when the Christian Right in Colorado helped pass an anti-gay ballot initiative in 1992, Gill—the wealthiest openly gay man in that state—had the resources to fight back. He started the Gill Foundation two years later, which focused much of its early work on advocating for LGBT rights in Colorado. Later, after Gill sold a large chunk of his stake in Quark for a reported $400 million, he donated half of that to his foundation, which scaled up to become a top funder nationally of LGBT rights.

Gill worked closely with a handful of other LGBT donors, including David Bohnett, another tech winner; James Hormel, a food heir; and Henry van Ameringen, whose family wealth came from a flavor and fragrance fortune. As early as 2000, several of these donors staked out full marital rights for LGBT people as a long-term goal.

That year, at a political fundraiser at his home in Los Angeles that included a number of U.S. senators, Bohnett called for full equality for gays and lesbians, including same-sex marriage. "At the end of the day," he told the group, "all I really want is to marry the man I love, and live in our society with the same rights and privileges as everyone else."

Back then, marriage equality was quite controversial; as a goal it seemed far-fetched. "It was very challenging to bring the community along," Bohnett told me, of the reluctance many advocates felt about pushing this issue. "But I always believed it was possible." Bohnett thought it would take "twenty years."

Bohnett's guess proved overly pessimistic, and Tim Gill's money and savvy was a key reason history moved faster than anyone expected.

A galvanizing moment for Gill came in November 2004, when eleven states passed ballot initiatives barring same-sex marriage. Karl Rove had helped engineer these initiatives as a way to boost voter turnout by the religious right in key swing states. But a consequence was to trigger a big mobilization of LGBT activism—and funding—to fight for more rights, including marriage equality.

Gill recalls thinking, "We can't let this happen again." And one imperative that struck him as crucial was that everyone in the LGBT movement needed to be on the same page going forward, getting behind a winning strategy for securing marriage equality.

Because they write the checks, funders have a unique ability to convene nonprofits, which are often prone to turf battles. It's another way foundations wield power that is largely invisible to outsiders. Gill in particular had long pushed collaboration as a way to mold LGBT groups into a stronger fighting force—a role easy for him to play since he backed nearly every player in this space. So it was that after the 2004 election, leaders of top LGBT groups assembled in Denver, at the Gill Foundation, with a mandate to come up with a new strategy they could all get behind. "It was not us giving them the strategy," Gill told me. "It was us making them come up with one."

What emerged from the post-election retreat was a blueprint for pushing marriage equality called the "10-10-10-20 Plan." The goal was to achieve by 2020 ten states with marriage, ten with civil unions, and ten with a limited state of domestic partnership.

The theory of change here—a familiar staple of past movements—was to make progress at the state level, setting the stage for an eventual federal victory.

This was the kind of strategy that Tim Gill liked—one that set specific goals to be achieved in a realistic time frame. Though he had become a crusader for LGBT rights, Gill remained at heart an engineer who thought in mechanical and practical ways. Gill has described himself as happiest when he's writing code. And despite his huge Quark payday, he continued to tinker with tech ideas on the side, eventually launching another start-up related to artificial intelligence and home automation. Gill's role in the company is chief technology officer.

After 2004, the march to victory on marriage equality sped up considerably. A key breakthrough came when marriage advocates changed their messaging after losing on Proposition 8 in 2008. That was the California ballot initiative that barred LGBT people from marrying, and its passage forced Gill and other advocates to take a hard look at how they were talking about marriage equality.

Initially, they had focused on the rights and responsibilities involved in marriage, only to realize that this wasn't getting traction with the public. Gill said, "People had a feeling about what marriage was. And when we talked to them about rights and responsibilities, that didn't correlate with their feeling about what marriage was."

By investing in public opinion research, the same way that political campaigns do, the Gill Foundation discovered that another, more obvious message worked better: that marriage is about love and commitment, and nobody should be barred from this experience. "That is, in fact, what people think marriage is," Gill said. And when the LGBT movement shifted its focus in this way, "we saw a fairly radical shift in people's opinions."

After the U.S. Supreme Court made its final and definitive ruling in 2015 that ensured the right to marry in every state, Tim Gill might well have declared victory and turned to other pursuits, like his new tech start-up. He and his husband, Scott Miller, had also bought a huge historic mansion in Denver that would require years of renovation.

Instead, by the time of the Supreme Court ruling, Gill's foundation had already pivoted to its next big fight: eliminating all forms of discrimination against LGBT people, including in housing and in the workplace. In many states, such discrimination is perfectly legal. Gill aimed to change that. Once more, top LGBT leaders came together at his foundation to plot strategy. And once again, they emerged with a long-range plan for change, this time with a particular focus on states in the South and West, where discrimination against gays was the worst.

The shift to this next battle came after the Gill Foundation commissioned a study of how various rights movements had fared in the wake of major victories. It was a sobering exercise. As it turns out, euphoric high points not infrequently devolve into brutal slogs—like the unending fight over abortion rights after *Roe v. Wade* supposedly settled that issue, or how disabled people still struggle to get around and find jobs a quarter century after the Americans with Disabilities Act was enacted.

"I don't ever assume that we've won, that victory's inevitable, and that we don't have to do anything but mop up," Gill said after the Supreme Court victory. Those who work with Gill say this fight is intensely visceral for him. He just can't stand the idea that LGBT people everywhere don't have all the same rights as straight people. Nor is he content to trust that cultural and demographic change will gradually solve this problem in coming years. "Justice delayed is justice denied," he likes to say, quoting William Gladstone.

Gill has plenty of resources to carry the struggle onward for years. Like many of the newer philanthropists, he has no interest in creating a permanent foundation that would husband its resources for some future fight. Gill wants to see progress sooner rather than later, and has stipulated that his foundation spend all its assets—which now stand at over $200 million—by 2030 or so. "If you're talking about social change, your objective should be to improve the lives of people as dramatically and as soon as possible," Gill told me. "As long as you have a smart strategy, it makes sense to spend money more quickly."

There's something heroic about wealthy crusaders who aim to spend down their fortunes to improve society—that is, assuming you like what they're doing. If you don't, that sense of urgency can be unnerving. How many liberals, for example, would be thrilled if the Koch brothers announced that they intended to give away their vast fortune as quickly as possible to make "America a better place"?

The former billionaire Chuck Feeney, who earned his money in duty-free stores, has gotten loads of positive press for giving away all his wealth, $8 billion, through a foundation that officially concluded grantmaking in 2016. "When you've got the money, you spend it," Feeney once told the *New York Times*. "When you've spent it all, let someone else get going and spend theirs." He added: "I want the last check I write to bounce."

Feeney's rush to dispose of his riches made his foundation, The Atlantic Philanthropies, an especially forceful player in certain public policy arenas. It dispensed grants on a magnitude that wasn't common in the nonprofit world. In 2009, it became one of the biggest backers of a national advocacy group formed to ensure passage of the Affordable Care Act. The following year, it made an even bigger investment in an effort to temper harsh school discipline policy, which would help induce the Obama administration to issue guidance to school districts all over the country on this issue—yet another example of federal meddling in a sector that many believe should be governed locally.

Feeney was once something of a novelty because of his commitment to "giving while living." Now, though, more billionaires—some even richer than Feeney ever was—are embracing that same sense of urgency. This means the river of philanthropic money going to policy advocacy is likely to swell even further.

8

Networkers

In trying to grasp how philanthropy shapes society, it can be tempting to go with a "great man" theory: Titans of business harness piles of money to big visions of progress, at least as they define it, and forge ahead over years to have a major impact. Certainly there is much to that view, and you could imagine a Mount Rushmore of philanthropy that included the likes of John D. Rockefeller and Andrew Carnegie—along with contemporary figures like Bill Gates, Chuck Feeney, and George Soros. (People would fight like hell over who should be on such a monument, needless to say.)

Yet there's another big way that wealth is converted into power in the philanthrosphere, which is through networks.

Even donors with many billions of dollars tend to be acutely aware of how puny their resources are compared to the problems they seek to tackle. Bill Gates has often made this point. And if you're a more ordinary philanthropist, with mere millions to give away, or even less, the odds of having an impact can seem very long indeed.

One way to improve those odds is to hook up with like-minded donors who share your goals. If you pool your money with that of others, and direct it in a coordinated way, it just might be enough to make a difference. And elite networks of philanthropists can mobilize more than money. They can combine their social capital to push a cause to political leaders, the media, and corporations. They can make stuff happen in a big way.

NEW MONEY, NEW MUSCLE

It may come as no surprise that women have led the way in thinking out-side the "great man" approach to giving. Women have been the star net-workers in the philanthropy world, building up several strong outfits to pool contributions and direct them toward specific causes—often with a policy agenda.

One group at the center of this action lately is Women Moving Mil-lions (WMM). It's a network of several hundred high-net-worth women donors who have all given at least $1 million to support work for gender equality around the world. "We exist to promote women for women phi-lanthropy," Jacki Zehner told me. Zehner, who joined the network as a member in 2009, is the group's chief engagement officer as well as a donor.

Two ideas lie behind Women Moving Millions. One is that wealthy women are the most logical champions of gender equality, an issue that funders often ignore. The other idea is that there are many more such women today than ever before who can be mobilized to give, and at a high level.

Recent years have seen a jump in the number of women who have gotten wealthy through their own efforts, as opposed to through mar-riage. Research also shows that women often take the lead in family philanthropy—and in quite a few cases, end up controlling foundations when their husbands die before them. Two of the biggest foundations in the United States these days, the JPB Foundation and the Charles and Lynn Schusterman Family Foundation, are run by women who outlived their husbands. A third, the Susan Thompson Buffett Foundation, is run by Warren Buffett's daughter. A fourth, Margaret A. Cargill Philanthro-pies, is carrying out the detailed wishes of its benefactor, who was among the wealthiest women in the United States when she died in 2006.

Women Moving Millions has estimated that women control $13.2 tril-lion of wealth in North America alone. Jacki Zehner herself is an example of new women's wealth, as a former partner at Goldman Sachs. After leaving that firm, she and her husband, also a Goldman Sachs alumnus, started their own foundation.

Historically, total annual giving by women to charitable work aimed at empowering girls and women has been low. In fact, until sisters Helen LaKelly Hunt and Swanee Hunt started Women Moving Millions in 2007, few gifts of a million dollars or more had ever been given to women-led organizations. Just because women often controlled the purse strings of family philanthropy didn't mean they gave to women's causes.

The Hunt sisters got rich through inheritance. They are daughters of the silver tycoon H. L. Hunt, who was a well-known conservative Republican and, for a time, one of the richest men in America.

"My parents never talked about money," Helen Hunt told me, suggesting that "the greater the wealth of the family, the greater the incentive to keep the women disempowered." Hunt said there was the expectation "that I would marry someone who would join the family business. . . . The Southern belle culture hadn't caught up with second wave feminism." In Dallas, said Hunt, "you didn't use the terms women and money in the same sentence."

Hunt and her sister learned how wealthy they were by reading *Forbes* magazine. "Suddenly I learned I had money," she recalled. "There was all this net worth, but nobody had told me about it." As she came of age as a young woman, Hunt also developed strong ideas about how the world might work differently—and how her wealth might be put to good use. She had spent a stint teaching in a low-income part of Dallas, where she was exposed to poverty and injustice. She came away radicalized amid the social ferment of the early 1970s.

Hunt's journey away from her father's politics was not uncommon for young people of inherited wealth during this time. A number of them— with names like Pillsbury, Rockefeller, and Reynolds—were drawn to activist philanthropy, putting their trust funds behind the social movements of the era. They also networked together, bonding around their experience as "class traitors" and sharing ideas about how to give money to make change. Hunt and her sister established the Hunt Alternatives Fund in 1981, which funded progressive work in various areas, including international peace and security. (Swanee Hunt would eventually become the U.S. ambassador to Austria during the Clinton administration.)

Helen was determined to use some of her money to help women in Texas, but found that most nonprofits in the state were run by men and few thought about injustice in larger structural ways. Then Hunt came across the San Francisco Women's Foundation, one of the earliest local women's funds in the United States. The fund was powered by a network of savvy women, many from wealthy backgrounds, and Hunt remembers crying when she read its annual report. Here, finally, was a model for the kind of philanthropy she believed in—giving by and for women, with a keen eye on how the systems of society impeded equity and fairness. "I decided that's what I want to do with my life."

Hunt became one of the great builders of women's philanthropic networks. In 1985, she catalyzed the creation of the Dallas Women's Foundation. A few years later, she helped get the New York Women's Foundation off the ground. Also during the 1980s she helped create the Women's Funding Network (WFN), which aimed to knit together all the different women's funds emerging across the United States. Its first meeting, in 1985, drew leaders of twenty different funds. By 2000, the network, which by then operated globally, included ninety-four member funds and foundations, with over $200 million in assets and $30 million in annual grantmaking. It now has more than 120 members. WFN describes itself as "the largest philanthropic network in the world devoted to women and girls." Over the years, it has sought to marshal that power for such causes as reproductive rights, equal pay, and paid family leave.

Yet for all this activity, and the emergence of so many women's funds, Helen and Swanee Hunt found themselves disappointed in the early 2000s about the scope of giving for gender equity. They still saw a huge gap between the number of women who, like them, had access to significant resources, and how little money went to support work for women's issues.

An eye-opening moment for Helen came while doing research on the early history of the women's movement, before the Civil War. She came across a letter by the nineteenth-century women's rights activist Matilda Joslyn Gage, who vented about the lack of support for such work by wealthy women—many of whom gave generously for the arts and anti-poverty efforts, but never for women's suffrage. Thirty years into the push for women's voting rights, the movement still had only two major donors, both of whom were men. "Where are the women?" Gage wrote. "Why aren't women of means funding our causes?"

Hunt wondered the same thing in the early twenty-first century. Again and again, Hunt saw women's groups get only crumbs from top female philanthropists who gave away bundles of money. Typically, the biggest gifts—six figures and up—went to arts organizations or alma maters, while much smaller sums were given for gender-related issues. The leader of one major women's fund told her, "I can count all my million dollar donors on one hand."

That comment stuck with Hunt. She was excited to hear that at least some women *were* giving at a large level, and she became fixed on the idea of rallying many more to pass the million-dollar mark in their support of women's issues. Hunt wanted to reverse the usual formula of giving by female philanthropists, so that the opera would get the small checks for a change while these donors got serious about empowering women on a global scale.

With large initial pledges of their own, Swanee and Helen set out to "raise the bar on women's giving" through the Women Moving Millions campaign. Their initial efforts—which came at a moment of rising awareness of the dividends that come from empowering girls and women—yielded a flurry of donations for gender equity. Alida Rockefeller Messinger kicked in a million dollars. So did Abigail Disney and Barbara Dobkin. Other money would follow.

Since 2012, WMM has built a full-fledged organization to advance its mission of catalyzing "unprecedented resources for the advancement of women and girls." (Gifts go directly to nonprofits, not to WMM.) The group built up its staff and infrastructure to raise yet more money, putting on high-profile galas that one year featured the actress Meryl Streep (herself an active philanthropist) and the supermodel Christy Turlington Burns. By 2016, its 240 members in fourteen countries had made at least $600 million in gifts.

That's serious money, and it stands as impressive confirmation of the Hunt sisters' initial hypothesis: that there are huge latent resources waiting in the wings for women's issues—if you can just find a way to activate donors.

In a world that's awash in new wealth, this same idea is tantalizing for the leaders of any cause. Every nonprofit fundraiser dreams that their next sugar daddy—or momma, as the case may be—is out there somewhere, among the legions of zillionaires spawned by the second Gilded Age. So often, though, those dreams come to naught, since identifying and cultivating such folks is famously hard.

Which is why donor networks matter so much in twenty-first-century philanthropy. They provide a way to find and mobilize donors who might otherwise never swing behind a cause, tapping into mountains of money that are now sitting on the sidelines. This approach is an alternative to hustling for a bigger piece of a static pie of grantmaking dollars given out by known funders, all of whom have long lines outside their doors. If you want to get your cause or organization to the next level in an ultra-competitive fundraising environment, networking your way to new donors is key.

Women Moving Millions is a great case study of the potential of networks because it is tapping into one of the biggest reservoirs of latent giving capacity, wealthy women, and generating new dollars for the neglected area of gender issues.

But make no mistake: Building networks of wealthy donors is hard work. Finding members requires getting buy-in from busy people who may be quite guarded when it comes to giving away their money—or may be new to philanthropy altogether. The next step, marshalling them into a unified force that works together, isn't much easier. People with big money often have big egos and their own strong ideas of how things should be done.

As it turns out, though, women have been quite good at working collaboratively to pool money as donors. Women have long connected through so-called giving circles to combine their money and knowledge in ways that boost their impact—as Sondra Shaw-Hardy and Martha Taylor describe in their 2010 book, *Women and Philanthropy*. Many of America's early charities were the result of affluent women banding together to address social ills.

Why are women drawn to this model? Zehner offered a simple explanation: "Women like to do things together." Helen Hunt, who these days works with her husband, Harville Hendrix, to help couples and families improve their relationships, suggested that women think about building power in more collective ways—in other words, "power with"—while men think in terms of domination, "power over." Men are apt to like the idea of creating a new freestanding foundation named after them. Some women do, too, but others are more drawn to cooperative efforts to combine their money with that of other donors.

This can be especially true of women just coming to philanthropy. It's easy for new funders to be intimidated by the range of choices for giving away their money. Where Women Moving Millions adds value, said

Zehner, is by offering a way to "accelerate the process of getting up to speed. . . . It's a fast-forward." WMM brings together women who've long been giving away money with those who are new to the game. "We have the students and the teachers, and we're putting them all together."

GOING IT TOGETHER

Vanessa Kirsch also knows a thing or two about organizing wealthy donors so that they can have a bigger impact together than they could alone. Since the late 1990s, she's built up a Boston-based venture philanthropy group, New Profit, into a major conduit for giving to nonprofit entrepreneurs looking to make change in areas like education and public health. Much of this cash comes from philanthropists in the finance world who prefer pooling their funds with like-minded donors over going it alone with their own staffed foundations.

Kirsch describes herself as a "serial social entrepreneur." In the early 1990s, she had co-founded Public Allies, a national service group that sought to tap the idealism of young people and that thrived in the Clinton era, becoming one of the first recipients of funds from the White House's new AmeriCorps program. She also helped found the Women's Information Network, which sought to empower women looking to climb upward in Democratic Party politics. Kirsch is married to Alan Khazei, who had co-founded City Year in 1988, another national service group, and later started an advocacy group, Be the Change, and twice ran for the U.S. Senate in the Massachusetts Democratic primary. Despite the couple's partisan ties, they both embody a pragmatic idealism that defies ideological labels. The social entrepreneur movement they helped rev up in the 1990s took pains to distinguish itself from the cause-oriented mind-set of 1960s activism. The new do-gooders saw themselves as all about solving problems, regardless of established orthodoxies, and were agnostic about means. If government could get the job done, fine. If the free market could, that might be even better.

Philanthropy was among the systems that Kirsch came to believe was in need of new thinking. After years of raising money, she found herself frustrated by the traditional world of foundations. She noticed funders tended to give to achieve certain outcomes, what Kirsch calls "buy capital," doling out short-term program grants to pursue this or that goal. It was less common for them to put up "build capital," in the form of general support funds that help organizations grow. Meanwhile, financing for businesses tends to work in the exact opposite way: venture capital and private equity firms provide entrepreneurs chunks of capital because they know that "there's a real need for growth capital to help organizations build their capacity to scale," Kirsch told me.

Another problem that Kirsch saw with traditional foundations is that they tend to spread grants around too thinly, backing numerous nonprofits with modest support, as opposed to placing bigger bets on fewer groups. The result, as Kirsch saw it, was a social sector with "lots of innovations and solutions, but very few that had gotten to any significant scale." Again, venture capital and private equity firms worked quite differently—investing in just a handful of companies and then going all out to help them succeed. The other thing about this model is how venture firms pooled money from many investors, most of whom wouldn't be able to find winning bets if they were working alone.

Kirsch's simple idea was to bring the venture approach to philanthropy. She aimed to swing a network of wealthy donors behind top social entrepreneurs, so they could get the same financing and support that's the norm for business entrepreneurs. Her hunch in starting New Profit, at the height of the dotcom era of the 1990s, was that "if we bet on a few ideas and not only provided the programmatic support, but also the growth capital to scale organizations and support the social entrepreneurs, we would have some more home runs in our sector."

New Profit wasn't the first funding group to train its eye on helping innovative nonprofit leaders. Ashoka, founded in 1980 by Bill Drayton, also nurtured new talent, as did Echoing Green, with a fellowship program for early-stage social entrepreneurs. Kirsch saw New Profit as coming in further along in an organization's life span, helping already established nonprofits to grow. She imagined a future in which the most effective and innovative organizations quickly found the capital to scale their winning solutions—the way that groundbreaking new companies are able to get big fast. Kirsch believed that if she helped change how funding flowed in the social sector, she could help change the world.

Kirsch thought that New Profit would be an easy sell to the many business leaders who engaged in philanthropy. Why *wouldn't* they want their giving to track with strategies seen as elementary in the investing world? "To me this seemed intuitively like a good idea, that had really worked in the private sector—not only with venture capital, but with private equity." Kirsch imagined that once New Profit hung out its shingle, donors would be beating down its door.

Things didn't turn out that way. In fact, Kirsch faced long years of pick-and-shovel labor to build up a strong network of donors.

Before starting New Profit, Kirsch had worked for a spell with Peter Hart, the pollster. And as she got her new organization going, she asked Hart to help her understand the new philanthropists who would be so critical to her success. Hart convened a focus group in Boston of high-net-worth individuals to vet the thinking behind New Profit, with Kirsch watching from behind a one-way mirror. Many were quite intrigued by the plan and, at the end, Hart offered to put his client in touch with whoever wished to be contacted. This is how New Profit got its first major donor—Mark Nunnelly, a managing director at Bain Capital, the private equity group.

Nunnelly proved to be much more than a donor. He was a critical ally who opened doors and helped educate Kirsch on the strategies of the investment world. That advice proved crucial as New Profit curated a portfolio of grantees—mainly nonprofits working to improve education and boost economic mobility, using models that New Profit believed could be scaled to have major impact. Financing was only part of what Kirsch's shop offered. Like private investing firms, it also offered advice and technical support to the groups it invested in, help that could be very useful to young social entrepreneurs with a strong vision but often weak management skills.

New Profit's basic pitch to donors was similar to the pitch that professional investors make to clients: If you want to get a maximum return on your philanthropic dollars, let us do the work of identifying great investments and nurturing those bets to ensure they bear fruit.

Many of New Profit's early donors, like Nunnelly, came from venture capital and private equity, since these people quickly grasped what Kirsch was doing. Still, Kirsch's fantasy that donors would naturally flock to New Profit never materialized. Instead, she has spent years going to them, and estimated to me that she has pitched 1,800 people in fundraising meetings since founding New Profit in 1998.

Along the way, Kirsch has refined her appeal to stress the power of networked philanthropy. She often starts these conversations by asking prospects how happy they are about the impact they're having with their giving. If someone is satisfied with their own efforts, Kirsch doesn't see them as a likely donor to New Profit. Often, though, the philanthropists she meets *aren't* so happy with their impact.

Many major donors travel a similar trajectory, Kirsch has noticed. They make a few big initial charitable gifts and feel good about things. But, as their giving goes on, they may feel disappointed with how their money is used and how little change they can see happening. They start to realize that having impact is harder than they thought, and get frustrated that they aren't as effective at giving away money as they are at making it. At this point, some get curious about the mechanics of high-impact philanthropy and, among other things, may realize that they need a lot more help than they thought. One way to get that help is to work collaboratively, joining forces with like-minded donors in order to leverage their giving. This path is especially appealing to givers who don't want to staff up their own foundation, with the hassle and overhead costs that entails.

Kirsch sees the donors attracted to this model—those "who want to join others, not start a foundation, and act differently"—as a growing and important part of a new philanthropic ecosystem.

In part, the rising appeal of networked philanthropy reflects how similar thinking has swept the business world in recent decades. There, an older model of production—in which the large hierarchical organization was king—has given way to more decentralized approaches, whereby firms focus on their core competencies and rely on partners to handle everything else. As today's business leaders turn to giving, it makes sense that many might think differently—and more collaboratively—than philanthropists who made their fortunes in earlier eras. The fact that more major donors are giving at a large level while still in the prime of their careers, as opposed to leaving this to retirement, is another reason they might turn to an outfit like New Profit. The busier you are, the more sense it makes to let someone else ensure that you're getting the biggest bang for your philanthropic buck.

That said, New Profit's top donors have been anything but passive. They've often gotten quite involved in helping grantees with support and advice, and in 2008, two of these donors got together to give the organization a major boost in the form of eight-figure challenge grants. In one year, Kirsch raised $75 million, funds that helped catapult New Profit to a new level.

Network thinking hasn't just powered New Profit's fundraising model, it has also reshaped its theory of change. Initially, the group heavily stressed the role of empowered individuals in tackling society's problems—a worldview that, to some, underscored the naiveté of a youthful social entrepreneur movement that had yet to grasp how systemic most problems really are. Over time, though, Kirsch gravitated toward a more holistic view of how change needed to happen, co-authoring an article about the need to back "system entrepreneurs," not social entrepreneurs. "It's not just one actor with one solution," she told me. "It's a set of actors that has to work in concert. The more we understand the ensemble, the better."

Backing visionaries is still key to New Profit's model, but now Kirsch and her team are also putting money into a broader network of organizations—including investments in public policy research and advocacy. The group's evolution tells a broader story of how the social entrepreneur movement has grown up and gotten serious about jockeying for policy influence. Fueling that bid for greater power, in turn, has been a growing legion of like-minded donors who've become more collaborative and strategic.

MISSION DRIVEN

One trend of the past decade or two is that donors of nearly all stripes are getting better organized, recognizing that there's strength in numbers—whether they're trying to conquer Parkinson's disease or trying to make social change. The philanthropists behind Women Moving Millions and New Profit are examples of the latter kind of collaboration, but more examples can be found on both sides of America's ideological divide.

Earlier, I wrote about how progressive donors like Herb Sandler and George Soros had responded to the right's rise by building new policy and advocacy groups in the early 2000s, including the Center for American Progress and Media Matters. A network of wealthy donors, the Democracy Alliance, coalesced in 2005 to help fund and knit together a more robust progressive policy infrastructure.

This push, combined with the debacle in Iraq and a cratering economy, helped fuel the hottest burst of progressive energy in the United States since the 1960s. Democrats took control of Congress in 2006 and, a few years later, President Barack Obama, backed by a Democratic Congress, moved forward an agenda that included new taxes on the wealthy, new controls on Wall Street, and, that forever unrealized Holy Grail of liberalism, universal health insurance. Obama didn't get everything he wanted, but he got enough to trigger a full-scale panic among wealthy conservatives, who began writing more checks, and bigger checks, to roll back liberal gains.

Many of these checks went for campaign activities aimed at returning Washington to Republican control as well as capturing statehouses. The Koch political network began taking shape in 2010, emerging over the next six years as a unique new power player in American politics—a shadow political operation even larger than the Republican National Committee itself.

The other tributary in the mighty river of conservative money took the form of philanthropic dollars, with new funds boosting groups across the right-wing universe. Some of the wealthy donors upping their giving knew exactly what they were doing, like the hedge funder Robert Mercer, a big league philanthropist who used a family foundation, run by his daughter, to pump millions of dollars in grants into a wide array of think tanks, legal groups, and leadership training efforts. But other donors didn't have foundations, gave at a much smaller level, and didn't quite know where to put their money. They needed help to give, and to give wisely.

This is where DonorsTrust came in, a funding group started in 1999 that fully hit its stride during the Obama years. No organization has lately done more than DonorsTrust to marshal a large and diffuse array of conservative philanthropists into an organized ideological fighting force.

As the name might suggest, donor-advised funds lie at the core of DonorsTrust. These funds allow wealthy donors to put aside tax-deductible dollars for philanthropy without the hassle of setting up a foundation. The funds are housed at a larger organization that actually makes the grants. This arrangement is an ideal way to join together lots of small donors who want to have a big impact but can't do so alone.

Donor-advised funds were pioneered by the New York Community Trust in 1931, and for decades were mainly used by community foundations. Then, in the 1970s, an entrepreneurial activist named Drummond Pike teamed up with some of his wealthy friends to create the Tides Foundation, which used donor-advised funds to direct resources to progressive causes. In effect, Pike created a new kind of community foundation—one where the glue was a shared worldview rather than a particular place.

Over the years, Tides emerged as a key clearinghouse for liberal money backing a wide array of causes. Wealthy donors who wanted to see social change would write checks, and Pike and his veteran staff, who actually knew how to advance such change, would deploy the money through strategic grantmaking. It was a powerful model, and all the more so because donors could be anonymous. Tides had to report where its grants went, but it didn't have to reveal its donors. Which meant, among things, that young trust fund heirs could support the kind of lefty causes that might well get them disinherited if their parents ever found out. Tides also offered mainstream foundations a way to funnel grants to hot-button causes without leaving any fingerprints. By the 1990s, it was moving tens of millions of dollars every year.

Drummond Pike's success in organizing a shadowy phalanx of progressive donors through Tides didn't go unnoticed on the right. And, in the late 1990s, a movement conservative, Whitney Ball, set out to create the same kind of outfit for her team.

Ball had spent her entire career inside the policy world that right-wing funders like Scaife, Olin, and the Kochs had built up starting in the 1970s—except that she worked on the philanthropic side of things. Her first major job was raising money for the Cato Institute, where she got to know many of the foundations and individuals backing libertarian causes. Her next gig was helping build up the Philanthropy Roundtable, which was founded in the late 1980s by conservative foundations who broke away from the Council on Foundations, feeling that it had been captured by liberal orthodoxy. Ball helped turn the roundtable into an important community for funders on the right. Among other things, she took charge of creating the group's annual conference, which became a key forum for these funders to swap ideas and plot strategy.

Most foundations on the right aren't very large; none have the resources of such liberal leviathans as Ford or Kellogg. A key reason these funders have nevertheless been so effective is because they're good at sticking together. Starting in the 1970s, about a dozen or so conservative foundations—including Bradley, Olin, Scaife, Smith Richardson, and Searle—worked in close concert, backing the same network of organizations. (Olin closed its doors in 2005, after spending down its assets.) In turn, many other funders have joined the effort over time to support "liberty, opportunity, and personal responsibility," which is how the Philanthropy Roundtable describes the mission of its members.

The emergence of the roundtable was a major breakthrough for conservative philanthropy, but Whitney Ball had larger ambitions. Like Drummond Pike, she knew that many donors never get around to creating foundations and operate on a smaller, more informal scale. Organize a bunch of these donors, though, and you could create a powerful force. Also like Pike, Ball recognized how important anonymity could be for certain funders, as well as their grantees—as when corporations with a direct financial stake in policy debates support a sympathetic think tank working in that area, or when donors put money behind controversial efforts to limit voting rights, restrict abortion, or discriminate against LGBT people.

DonorsTrust, which Whitney Ball founded in 1999, would channel cash in all these specific ways, and many more. It became a place where ideologically committed donors could park their philanthropic dollars and be sure the money reached the causes they cared about. In fact, ensuring that "donor intent" is honored was a key reason that Ball created DonorsTrust. The conservative precincts of philanthropy are rife with stories of how liberal heirs or professional staff hijacked foundations and disregarded the donor's original vision—the Ford Foundation standing as the classic example. Preventing that kind of thing was (and is) a recurrent topic of conversation among members of the Philanthropy Roundtable, and one that Ball keyed into.

As she traveled the country building up her new organization, Ball stressed that any fund established at the trust would be used as intended—as the name itself, DonorsTrust, implied. "Greenpeace won't get a dime from us," Ball told the *National Review* in 2001. By contrast, she warned, conservative donors who set up foundations were taking a crapshoot with their money. In addition to DonorsTrust, Ball set up a related entity, Donors Capital Fund, which was designed to provide bigger donors with more services.

Ball's venture was hugely successful, tapping into the river of new wealth flowing to philanthropy from the top 1 percent. In 2002, her two fledging funds received $1.4 million and distributed grants totaling $1.2 million. In 2010, as alarm grew about Obama administration policies and the existence of liberty for "future generations," as DonorsTrust describes the stakes, $63 million went out in grants to myriad conservative groups. Just five years later, in 2015, Ball's operation gave out $124 million in grants. By 2016, the group reported that it had, in total, distributed $784 million to over 1,500 "liberty-minded charities."

Ball died from cancer in 2015, but not before convincing her long-time friend Lawson Bader to take over her position when she was gone. Bader was then head of the Competitiveness Enterprise Institute, one of the many policy shops pushing libertarian ideas inside the Beltway. He had raised millions in that position, and found himself again hustling for donors in his new role—trying to clear the bar that Ball had set. "Whitney Ball was a hell of a salesperson," Bader told me.

Bader has followed the script that Ball used to draw in new clients to DonorsTrust. He stresses the fund's ideological reliability, with its exclusive focus on backing groups that promote "liberty through limited government, responsibility, and free enterprise." And he underscores how, once money is locked up at DonorsTrust, it can't later be redirected by heirs or anyone else. "There are clients of ours that may love their kids," Bader said, "but perhaps the client and the kids differ in terms of political philosophy, or institutional support."

As Bader explained it, if a client of DonorsTrust passes away and, say, their daughter becomes the advisor to their fund, she will not have the authority to shift the money to a set of causes or organizations different from those the donor originally intended. As an added protection, all DonorsTrust funds are designed to sunset after a given period. None can exist in perpetuity, which would increase the risk that the money might someday reach causes not favored by the original donor.

Wealthy philanthropists who give through donor-advised funds are a mixed bunch. Some know where they want their money to go, and a place like DonorsTrust is simply a conduit. Others need guidance and advice. Part of Bader's job is to serve as a matchmaker between the many groups on the right looking for money and the funders who have a stash at DonorsTrust. It's a quietly powerful role, and a novel one for Bader after what he described as a career in nonprofits spent on "my hands and knees begging for money."

A reason that leaders of donor-advised funds have increasing clout is that so many of today's new donors are tough to identify and connect with. For every philanthropist who sets up a traditional foundation, complete with a website and contact information, there are many more who fly below the radar. The vast majority of America's 90,000-plus private foundations, which together hold more than $700 billion and assets, don't have any way for grant seekers to get in touch.

Donor-advised funds are even more secretive than foundations, in that they are housed anonymously in a larger entity. But because they are managed under one roof, by places like DonorsTrust or the Tides Foundation that have professional grantmaking staff, there is a clearer way for nonprofits to get at this money. In that sense, people like Lawson Bader are influential gatekeepers.

Bader doesn't have the power to be any kind of field marshal, telling funders where to put their money. What he does have is a bird's-eye view of who's doing what in the conservative policy world—and who's doing it well. Money from DonorsTrust flows to all the usual suspects on the right—Heritage, AEI, Cato, the Federalist Society, and the like—along with groups engaged in edgier activities. Because grants made through DonorsTrust can't be traced back to specific donors, it's a favored conduit for right-wing funders backing controversial causes.

Robert Bruelle, a sociologist who studied funding for work that denied climate change, found that a sizeable chunk of this money—some $78 million between 2003 and 2010—was moved anonymously through DonorsTrust and Donors Capital Fund. The amount of money going through these groups, Bruelle found, increased dramatically after ExxonMobil and Koch Industries pulled back from publicly backing policy work that questioned whether climate change was real. But he couldn't say whether it was these donors who fueled the surge of DonorsTrust with secret donations, since the group doesn't have to reveal who's using its services. Its donor-advised funds are like numbered Swiss bank accounts. "We just have this great big unknown out there about where all the money is coming from," Bruelle said.

Dark money moving through DonorsTrust has also fueled the Project on Fair Representation, the group seeking to dismantle the Voting Rights Act. And DonorsTrust has been the conduit for anonymous funding for groups sounding the alarm about Islamic threats within the United States. Some $18 million went to Clarion, a group that has been described as a leading purveyor of Islamophobia in the United States.

When she died of cancer in 2015, Whitney Ball was widely praised in conservative circles for her entrepreneurial vision. No one had ever done more to organize one of the most powerful constituencies that powers right-wing gains: wealthy philanthropists. Nor had anyone done more to help shroud their giving in secrecy.

HERDING CATS

Even as DonorsTrust hit its stride during the early Obama years, the Democracy Alliance was struggling.

The alliance had a lot of energy in its first few years, after emerging amid much fanfare in 2005. It galvanized many wealthy liberal donors, attracting scores of members, or "partners," who got together at high-profile retreats, and channeling tens of millions of dollars to liberal groups. But after Democrats retook Congress in 2006, and then the presidency two years later, the momentum flagged. Partners, who were required to give at least $200,000 a year to groups selected by the alliance, began to drop off. And new ones weren't joining at the same rate as before, when George W. Bush was scaring the hell out of people.

The other challenge facing the Democracy Alliance was the difficulty of managing a network made up of scores of very wealthy people. You rarely get rich by marching in lockstep with others, and the Democracy Alliance staff had a hard time telling its headstrong partners what to do—and where to put their money. The group was plagued by recurrent management problems and staff turnover. Dealing with the alliance could be maddening for progressive groups seeking funding.

But in late 2013, the Democracy Alliance finally hired a president with the gravitas to wrangle a large collection of wealthy donors. That was Gara LaMarche, a veteran foundation executive who had overseen George Soros's U.S. giving for many years before being asked by billionaire Chuck Feeney to run The Atlantic Philanthropies. All told, LaMarche had helped give away some $3 billion in those roles. He once commented that, if you command that kind of money, surrounded by supplicants, you end up feeling a "great deal smarter, wiser, funnier, and probably handsomer" than you did before.

In his new gig, though, LaMarche was both a gatekeeper to millions and something of a supplicant himself. When you head up an outfit like DonorsTrust or the Democracy Alliance, ensuring a steady influx of funds is as much part of your job as moving that money out into the field. You've got to rope in new wealthy donors, and ensure that existing ones don't drop out. LaMarche described his job to me as "a weird hybrid." But one thing was clear: After two decades of doling out grants in record sums, LaMarche was now a fundraiser.

LaMarche soon found himself spending a lot of time on the road rustling up new partners. There was no shortage of prospects, especially in places like Manhattan, Malibu, and Marin County. The ranks of the liberal rich have grown enormously in the past two decades as more fortunes have been minted in knowledge industries where creative types, often with progressive views, can earn vast rewards. The passing down of big inheritances is also moving the upper class to the left, since heirs tend to be more liberal than their parents in what might be called "Rockefeller syndrome."

The Democracy Alliance was not designed to be a holding pen for piles of money and act as a direct grantmaker, like DonorsTrust. Instead, its partners pay an annual membership fee, which goes to cover the alliance's overhead costs, and then give directly to those "portfolio" organizations that the alliance recommends. This remains the model, although over time the group has established several pooled funds that allow it to make direct grants.

When the Democracy Alliance was first formed, some veteran donors didn't see the point in joining, since they already knew where to put their money. Herb and Marion Sandler were the most notable liberal megagivers who opted not to enlist. "We never saw the point," Herb said. (His daughter, Susan, would later join the group's board.)

But the organization's advisory role was helpful for less experienced donors who needed strategic guidance—and who also liked the idea of amplifying their impact by teaming up with other funders. Just having other donors to talk with proved very appealing to some partners, much as many Giving Pledge members loved the annual retreats. "A lot of these people felt a lot more isolated than we knew," Rob McKay, a Taco Bell heir who chaired the Democracy Alliance early on, told me. "Rich people are people, too, and actually like community. . . . The chance to be in a room with peers, to be able to think strategically, gave a number of people the impetus to do more than they did previously."

When LaMarche came on, he also found that the alliance's community was a big selling point for would-be partners. The group's retreats are unique shindigs, where philanthropists, political leaders, and top policy experts come together to plot progressive strategy. The year LaMarche started his job, the featured speakers at the alliance's winter meeting were Senator Elizabeth Warren and Vice President Joseph Biden. That's heady stuff if you're a wealthy software entrepreneur who's new to the world of politics.

The Democracy Alliance had around 90 partners when LaMarche arrived, and he quickly pumped up that number to 100. He also launched what he described as a "highly participatory process" to chart a new strategy for the group. Taken individually, the partners had an array of interests, and getting them to focus on a few priorities had been a major challenge for past directors of the group. LaMarche's approach was to pull partners closely into the work of crafting a sharper game plan for pushing progressive change in America. If they had real buy-in, they'd embrace the Democracy Alliance's new direction.

That strategy worked, and by late 2015, the Democracy Alliance had zeroed in on just three core issues: strengthening democracy, creating a more inclusive economy, and fighting climate change. The group also agreed to focus grants heavily in the states, where progress seemed more possible than in deadlocked Washington.

Funding in the states can be daunting for individual donors, in terms of figuring out which organizations to support across a wide and diverse playing field. On the right, the State Policy Network and DonorsTrust help funders find their way around this terrain. The Democracy Alliance now offers similar help. "It provides a vehicle for individual donors to get involved in state-level campaigns," LaMarche said.

The alliance also offers in-depth guidance to donors on how to combine political and philanthropic contributions in ways that advance the same goals. Whether you're drawn to building better databases of Democratic voters or funding policy reports, the DA is sure to have ideas about where to put your money.

One of LaMarche's projects at the Democracy Alliance was to get more institutional funders involved. He cultivated foundations as members, as well as labor unions. And he worked to engage funders who weren't ready to become partners but were open to supporting specific projects—including some new donors in Silicon Valley who were wary of associating with such a partisan group. The resulting mix of players orbiting around the Democracy Alliance created a new and unique hub that connected nearly everyone giving money for liberal causes. Two years after LaMarche took over, the alliance had over 120 partners and described itself "as the largest network of donors dedicated to building the progressive movement in the United States." It moved as much as $60 million annually.

Rich liberals may still be in the minority in the far upper class, but there are now enough of them to constitute a powerful force in politics and policy—and they've become much better at sticking together.

The broader point here is that philanthropists of all kinds are getting more organized. And those pushing a policy agenda have been especially keen to team up with one another so that they can collectively wield more clout. On the one hand, donors are building overarching power networks that knit together philanthropists who broadly share the same ideological worldview. On the other, they are coming together around particular causes, as we saw with those focused on women's issues.

Name a cause, and you can probably find an outfit that is helping donors pool their funds together to have more impact. Some intermediaries, such as NEO Philanthropy, the Proteus Fund, and the New Venture Fund, run multiple pooled funds at a time—often combining money from large donors with contributions from many smaller donors.

Through its Piper Fund, for example, Proteus has long been one of the leading aggregators of philanthropic gifts to campaign finance reform. That fund has moved over $31 million in grant money since 1997. Meanwhile, another Proteus fund, the Security and Rights Collaborative, has organized donors to address hate crimes, profiling, and xenophobia.

Education reform funders are yet another group that coordinates closely and have created new mechanisms to jointly deploy money. During the early 2000s, as the push for more charter schools was gaining steam, some of the biggest funders behind this movement—including the Walton family and the Fisher family (whose fortune came from Gap stores)—came together to start the Charter School Growth Fund (CSGF), with the goal of pooling their financial muscle to increase the number of charters around the country.

After its founding in the early 2000s, CSGF emerged as a critical hub in the efforts of funders to support the growth of charter schools. Beyond Walton, the Gates Foundation backed the group, as did the Arnold Foundation, the Broad Foundation, the Michael and Susan Dell Foundation, the Charles Schwab Foundation, and others. The small board includes not just Carrie Walton Penner, a third-generation Walton, but John Fisher, a billionaire heir whose parents chose charter schools as their top cause after retiring from building the Gap.

The Charter School Growth Fund is a classic philanthropic middleman, operating at a powerful level in highly contested terrain. It's been a place for funders to come together and plot how to increase the number of charters, helping out with financial, technical, and political support. The fund has marshalled tens of millions of dollars for over fifty charter school networks that now run over 500 schools enrolling a total of 250,000 students. In effect, it's a network of funders that support a network of charter school networks. A venture capital approach has been key to CSGF's model, with grants often going to entrepreneurial charter founders still at an early stage of starting schools.

Opponents of charter school funders see them as an anti-democratic cabal, channeling the fortunes of billionaires to privatize public education. The CSGF might seem to reinforce this view of shadowy power. What this group of funders is up to, though, is no different from what so many other philanthropists are doing: joining together more strategically to push a shared agenda.

Regardless of what you may think about this or that network of funders, what is striking is how much more organized private money has gotten at a time when many ordinary citizens are feeling less empowered. Some of the key civic institutions that used to amplify the views of average people have famously declined, like labor unions and political parties. Polls show that citizens have little confidence that their voices matter in civic life.

That growing public cynicism, and the apathy that comes with it, is often cited in connection with the increasing role of super PACs and mega-donors in electoral politics. There's far less awareness of the private philanthropists who have also mobilized in new and powerful ways, but this phenomenon reaches into just as many parts of American life as the growing clout of campaign donors. And, as we've seen, political and philanthropic funds often operate hand in hand to sway policy outcomes.

Alexis de Tocqueville famously praised civil society as a conduit for myriad people's voices. And while that remains so, there's no denying the role of top philanthropists in shaping just which of these voices speak most loudly.

9

Heirs to Influence

George P. Mitchell was born to Greek immigrants in Galveston, Texas, in 1919 and went to Texas A&M, where he studied petroleum engineering and geology. He graduated as valedictorian, and later started his own oil company. The timing couldn't have been better. Mitchell's operation thrived, drilling thousands of wells, as demand for petroleum products surged during the postwar boom.

Mitchell had a keen understanding of the rock and shale formations that lay underground, and in the late 1980s, his company began experimenting with a new process to capture natural gas locked within those formations. They drilled deep into the earth, through the rock, and pumped in water, sand, and chemicals to force out gas. Hydraulic fracturing, as the process became known, took years to perfect but eventually paid off big for Mitchell's company. He became a billionaire and was known as "the father of fracking." *The Economist* would say that "few businesspeople have done as much to change the world as George Mitchell."

Mitchell had ten children and twenty-three grandchildren and lived to the age of ninety-four. He and his wife, Cynthia, gave away hundreds of millions of dollars over the years, often through a foundation they created in 1978. Much of their giving was quite traditional—mostly staying local, with big money going to the arts in Houston, medical research centers, human services, and education. But Mitchell was also interested in issues of sustainability, unusual for an oil baron, and gave millions for research in this area. His particular concern was how the earth would sustain a growing population with finite resources.

Mitchell signed the Giving Pledge in 2010. And when he died, in 2013, most of his remaining fortune—over $800 million—was bequeathed to the Cynthia and George Mitchell Foundation. By that time, the foundation was run by one of Mitchell's granddaughters, Katherine Lorenz, who came to lead the family's grantmaking outfit in 2011, while still in her early thirties.

Lorenz's background had prepared her well for overseeing millions of dollars in annual giving power. During a good part of her twenties, she lived in Oaxaca, Mexico, where she co-founded a nonprofit working on food and agricultural issues in poor farming communities. Earlier, she had spent two summers living in rural villages in Latin America through the volunteer program Amigos de las Américas. Lorenz had also spent years thinking broadly about philanthropy, starting in 2003, when her family joined the Global Philanthropists Circle, a network of wealthy families from around the world committed to reducing poverty.

Lorenz connected strongly with the founder of that group, Margaret "Peggy" Dulany, David Rockefeller's daughter, who had co-founded the global anti-poverty group Synergos in 1986. As a Rockefeller, with numerous siblings and other relatives involved with giving, Dulany had long wrestled with big questions about family philanthropy. She had started the Global Philanthropists Circle to help families look beyond traditional forms of giving to be more strategic about making "lasting change in the lives of poor and marginalized people." It is one of several networks that help mold heirs into more effective philanthropists for social change. (Another such group is Resource Generation, an organization of progressive heirs that "organizes young people with wealth and class privilege in the U.S. to become transformative leaders working towards the equitable distribution of wealth, land and power." For a time, Lorenz sat on the group's board.)

Dulany became an inspiration for Lorenz because she, too, had started out living and working in rural communities in poor countries, only to decide over time that she could have more impact through philanthropy. "That path really resonated," Lorenz told me.

Lorenz was also tired of searching for grants after six years of running a small nonprofit. While she saw herself as someone who liked getting her hands dirty, working close to the ground, she found fundraising to be brutal work. "You have to pitch every foundation differently," she said. "And you don't know who to talk to, and who's making the decision." Another frustration was the various reporting requirements that funders demanded of grant recipients. "The whole process was just really difficult." Equally eye-opening to Lorenz, though, were the benefits of having truly supportive funders who acted as partners. Lorenz wished that more foundations could be like that.

Through the Global Philanthropists Circle, Lorenz learned about the Philanthropy Workshop, which offers intensive training to emerging philanthropists. Lorenz went through the workshop in 2007–2008, and it was a major turning point in her life. She realized that she really belonged on the grantmaking side of things, while also working to improve philanthropy as a whole. Meanwhile, Lorenz was becoming more involved in her grandparents' foundation, which was going through major changes as it evolved into an organization that was collectively run by two generations of George and Cynthia Mitchell's offspring.

That transition began in 2004, when all ten children and many of the grandchildren came together in an extended strategic planning process designed to chart a new future for the foundation. The process moved at a slow pace, involving retreats and many discussions. Paying close attention to the wishes of George Mitchell, who stayed on the sidelines, the family first hammered out a vision for the foundation that centered on sustainability. Then, in 2005, it agreed on a new governance structure, one that included all family members. And in 2006, it began mapping out specific grantmaking priorities. The first issue area it decided to focus on was clean energy, launching that program in 2008. Next came a program on water management, and then one on fracking and shale.

Lorenz was named president of the foundation in 2011 through a vote of the board. And after her grandfather died in 2013, she oversaw the foundation's expansion into more issue areas, including land conservation and anti-poverty work in Galveston, where Mitchell had grown up.

Creating new programs at the Mitchell Foundation always involves a similar process. The family comes together for a planning retreat with experts on a particular issue for two to three days. The idea is to engage in intensive learning and then set a vision as a family. Everyone is welcome to weigh in at this stage. "It's very much an open process where all family members have an equal voice whether they're board members or not," Lorenz said.

Once the vision is set, the board and foundation staff work together to translate it into measurable long-term goals, as well as short-term grant-making strategies.

Today, the George and Cynthia Mitchell Foundation describes itself as working to secure the "long-term human and ecosystem well-being for the planet." Among other things, this means pushing the conservative state of Texas to embrace clean energy and finding ways to reduce the environmental risks of fracking. Lorenz is well connected in green circles—sitting on the board of the Environmental Defense Fund and the National Academies' Roundtable of Science and Technology for Sustainability.

As one of the richest men in Texas, and a pioneer in the oil industry, George P. Mitchell wielded one kind of power. Now, leveraging his legacy and wealth, Mitchell's ambitious granddaughter is on her way to being quite powerful in her own right.

Katherine Lorenz is hardly alone among heirs who have spent their formative years working on social causes and networking widely. This is a way that the next generation can be quite different from the forebears who made the family fortune. Wealth creators are businesspeople, and tend to be more conservative. Heirs grow up in privilege, with the kind of post-materialist worldview that lends itself to progressive concerns about poverty or ecology.

At the same time, next-generation philanthropists are often drawn to a more rigorous approach to giving. They're less interested in so-called relationship giving, whereby donations flow to alma maters, community institutions, and the causes championed by friends. Like younger donors in tech and elsewhere, next-generation funders are often thinking about impact and breakthroughs. As Lorenz put it once: "This generation will ask for more metrics, and want to know the impact they are having more than previous generations. I think this group will also be open to taking more risks as they search for innovative solutions. In taking more risks, there will be more failure but also potential for more significant social change if the risk pays off."

INHERITED POWER

With ten children and twenty-three grandchildren, George Mitchell had plenty of descendants to leave his fortune to. That he chose instead to leave the bulk of that money to a foundation is a reminder that great dynastic wealth has never been a very popular idea in America, even among some of the super-rich. Andrew Carnegie famously called for curbing large inheritances through an estate tax, with an eye on recycling this wealth to ensure opportunity for future generations. An estate tax was established in 1916, and has since withstood fierce efforts at repeal.

One reason the estate tax has survived is because it has defenders across the nonprofit sector, who point out that it's a boon to charitable giving. Faced with the prospect of seeing nearly half their wealth go to the IRS, many rich people choose to instead make large bequests or endow foundations. The estate tax also has powerful friends in the far upper class, most notably Warren Buffett, who once gave Bill Gates a copy of Carnegie's essay "The Gospel of Wealth." (To be sure, plenty of America's rich loathe the estate tax, including a handful of ultra-wealthy families, the Waltons among them, who've secretly bankrolled efforts at repeal.)

When the estate tax was battling for its life against a GOP attack in Congress, Buffett helped lead the charge to save it. William Gates Sr. even co-authored a book with Chuck Collins defending the estate tax. Among other things, they wrote: "We share a concern with our nation's founders that the existence of a powerful economic aristocracy distorts our democracy and negates equality of opportunity . . . these fears were realized during the Gilded Age of the late 1800s, and the estate tax was part of our country's remedy." In a new Gilded Age, went the argument, the estate tax remained a key bulwark against an American aristocracy. A range of other wealthy people have also defended the estate tax, including George Soros and members of the Rockefeller family.

When Bill Gates and Warren Buffett developed the Giving Pledge, making new resources available for social good was the top priority. But another was to promote Carnegie's vision that great wealth should be recycled to create opportunity and not be used to entrench dynastic power in the United States. As Buffett told Charlie Rose on *60 Minutes*: "I don't really think that, as a society, we want to confer blessings on generation after generation who contribute nothing to society, simply because somebody in the far distant past happened to amass a great sum of wealth."

As good as all this sounds, a thought that seems not to have crossed the minds of Gates and Buffett is that dynastic power and privilege in America can take different forms—one of which is inheriting the influence that comes with controlling a foundation. In fact, there may be no better way for the super-rich to ensure lasting clout for their heirs than to dedicate their wealth to philanthropy.

If George Mitchell had just divvied up his fortune among his many offspring, you probably wouldn't be hearing the Mitchell name very often in twenty or fifty years, much less a century from now. Studies show that most inherited family wealth disappears by the third generation. As things stand now, though, the Mitchell family is poised to wield influence for many decades to come through one of the larger private foundations in Texas.

The early tech titan David Packard may be long gone, but today his offspring control a foundation with nearly $7 billion in assets that gives away around $300 million annually. Do Packard's descendants wield more power in society through this institution than he ever did through Hewlett-Packard? Maybe so. Do they wield more influence than they might have as wealthy private citizens who inherited fortunes? Absolutely.

The examples could go on and on. Many philanthropists stipulate that the foundations they create remain in family control—a setup that can endure for generations. A full century after John Emory Andrus created the Surdna Foundation, its twelve-member board remains controlled by his descendants, including members of the fifth generation. The Nathan Cummings Foundation is a far newer family foundation, endowed by the founder of the food company Sara Lee, and some of its younger board members had barely been born when the family patriarch died in 1985. Yet here they are today, sought after for coffee dates by nonprofit leaders anxious to get grants. While that kind of popularity may not sound like it confers "blessings on generation after generation," as Buffett described it, whether important people seek you out is a key indication of influence in our society. Even more so, the ability to effect real change with cash grants is a form of hard power.

In contrast to inherited wealth, which typically shrinks over time, philanthropic wealth that is locked in a foundation with conservative pay-out rates tends to grow—along with the influence heirs can have. Heirs can also have influence when the plan is to give away family wealth on an accelerated timetable, within one generation, as is sometimes the case. Bill and Melinda Gates have stipulated that their foundation will close within 20 years of their deaths. That timetable could place vast grant-making resources in the hands of their three children.

However it plays out, is inherited power through philanthropy a bad thing? It's an important question right now, with trillions set to flow across generations in coming decades. Such power feels deeply at odds with America's egalitarian ideals—and all the more so given the growing scope of this phenomenon. An ever larger number of heirs are coming to populate the philanthrosphere, with many of them taking an activist approach to making change. This class of super-citizens have come to their position through birth, and they can speak in the public square with a volume unimaginable to most people born to ordinary families. The resources at their disposal are swelling at a time when government faces mounting constraints.

Yet even as a new kind of aristocracy emerges, rooted in philanthropic wealth, it's unlikely to be an enforcer of upper-class privilege. Since heirs tend to be more liberal than the business leaders who create family fortunes. Most famously, a number of fourth-generation Rockefellers became involved in activist causes, starting in the 1960s. The Hunt sisters, mentioned earlier, tapped the wealth of their notoriously conservative father to bankroll liberal groups. There are plenty of similar examples, including from the past few years. When the GOP mega-donor Harold Simmons died in 2013, he left his two daughters in control of the family foundation named after him, which was slated to receive some of his $8 billion fortune. Neither of these women shares their late dad's world-view, and some foundation grants in recent years have flowed to progressive nonprofits. Rob McKay also grew up in a Republican household, in Southern California, where his father started the Taco Bell chain. McKay has used his inherited wealth to back activist efforts on the left, helping build the Democracy Alliance and supporting work to raise the minimum wage. Other heirs who've been involved in the Democracy Alliance since its founding include Rachel Pritzker, Pat Stryker, Jonathan Lewis, Patricia Bauman, Farhad Ebrahimi, and Anne Bartley, Winthrop Rockefeller's daughter.

Like Katherine Lorenz, Bartley is a great example of someone born to wealth who's spent her entire career in the social sector, going back to the late 1960s. Which is another point about heirs: many have prepared well to be philanthropists, readying themselves to one day command major resources. And the ones who've prepared most carefully are keenly aware of the limits of their power. They know that their funds are modest relative to the size of the problems they're tackling and that the odds tend to be long in terms of achieving real change. They're not waving the checkbook around in a hubristic way. Rather, they're committing to the long slog of grantmaking year after year in pursuit of gains that may never actually materialize, or be modest at best if they do.

Many of these heirs aren't spinning when they speak of their involvement in family philanthropy using terms like "responsibility" and "service." Sitting through hours of board meetings and planning sessions, or making site visits and reviewing grant proposals, is not everyone's idea of fun. There are a lot of other ways the youthful rich can amuse themselves with fancy toys and exotic travel. Plenty of heirs make exactly such choices, leading private lives of extreme luxury. Yet a growing number are more like Katherine Lorenz or Farhad Ebrahimi, who inherited part of a tech fortune at a young age and started his own foundation. These people are aware of the power that comes with their privilege and want to "leverage it in the best way possible," as Ebrahimi has said.

Ebrahimi told me that inheriting a big pile of money was confusing and more difficult than one might imagine. "I was intimidated. I didn't know how to think about it. I didn't know how I *wanted* to think about it." Over time, he came to believe that this kind of large private wealth transfer—and the vast inequality that made it possible—was simply wrong. "In my opinion nobody should be given this kind of financial resource," he said. And so, as Ebrahimi set out as a philanthropist, he sought to use his wealth to move society "further and further away from the world we live in right now, where there are very large consolidated piles of capital where small numbers of people decide what will happen to it."

In the 1970s, an earlier generation of progressive heirs who turned to philanthropy, such as George Pillsbury—whose family was made rich from food products—had thought along similar lines. "I felt it was not my money," Pillsbury said, of his trust fund, seeing it as wealth that should rightly have gone to workers but instead had been "skimmed off." Oscar Meyer heir Chuck Collins was so uncomfortable with his trust fund that he gave the money away to progressive foundations when he was twenty-six.

Ebrahimi grew up in an affluent neighborhood of Denver, where his father was CEO of Quark, the software firm that Tim Gill started. His parents, originally from Iran, talked about global politics around the house, imbuing their kids with a worldliness that's not so common. Ebrahimi went on to attend college at MIT. Like many heirs who tend to grow up in sophisticated families and get first-rate educations, Ebrahimi moved into adulthood with a huge head start in terms of understanding the workings of society and being prepared to influence it.

Michael Bloomberg's daughter, Emma, is an even better example of an heir who knows her way around the realms of power and policy. After attending an elite private school in New York City, she went to Princeton and later earned a joint MBA from Harvard Business School and MPA from Harvard's Kennedy School of Government. She spent nearly three years working for New York City government, and then nearly seven years working for the Robin Hood Foundation, the anti-poverty group heavily backed by Wall Streeters. Emma sits on the board of Bloomberg Philanthropies and will likely have a major hand in giving away one of the greatest fortunes of our time, through a foundation with an explicit goal of influencing government policy. That's a lot of power to hold because of who your dad is—but you can't say she hasn't been preparing to exercise such power.

The swelling ranks of capable do-gooder heirs almost calls to mind the "Guardians" that Plato imagined in *The Republic*—an elite leadership class chosen at birth and rigorously educated to selflessly serve the common good. These days, it's easy to see the appeal of Plato's vision, given the failings of a flawed political class, and the frequent rapacity of the business class. A philanthropic elite groomed for service and empowered with loads of cash doesn't sound half bad given what a mess of things other elites have made. Maybe we *want* the Emma Bloombergs of America to be amassing as much power as they are.

Or maybe not. The Enlightenment thinkers who invented modern democracy firmly rejected Plato's ideal of beneficent elite rule. And most Americans champion the idea of governance by the everyman, at least in principle. We don't like the idea of having our destinies shaped by a bunch of trust fund kids, most of whom are only faintly acquainted with the real-life struggles of ordinary people or the challenges faced by small businesses or how key parts of society—like, say, public education— actually work on the ground.

The pros and cons of having a new inherited philanthropic elite captures the larger debate over wealth being deployed for social good: The world desperately needs both new resources and new ideas focused on its biggest problems. But it's unnerving to watch rich people, however smart or well meaning, amass even more power through giving after three decades of rising inequality.

SOCIETY'S RISK CAPITAL

Big picture questions aside, who exactly are the most empowered heirs in philanthropy, and what are they up to?

A place to start a deeper dig is with the Buffett family. As one of the richest people in America, Warren Buffett is among the most scrutinized billionaires of our time. But the large-scale philanthropy of his three children—who, together, give away more than $750 million annually— and the influence that comes with it, are only dimly understood.

Over many decades, as Buffett built his conglomerate Berkshire Hathaway, and piled up a historic fortune, he always had a philanthropic plan: His wife, Susan, would be in charge of giving away that money.

Buffett's thinking was not uncommon. The wives of super-wealthy men often are the ones who take command of family philanthropy, identifying the causes to support and overseeing the day-to-day work of moving money out the door. (Still, in a maddening pattern, it is nearly always their husbands who get all the public credit.)

Buffett himself had little interest in giving away money, only in making it. But Buffett did believe strongly in philanthropy, calling it the "risk capital of society." And Susan, or Susie as she was known, had specific ideas for how to affect the world with Warren's wealth. She had liberal views and an urge to help people in need. She was active in civil rights work in Omaha in the 1960s, pushing for an end to segregation in housing, along with other changes. Later, she embraced reproductive rights as her top cause. Nuclear disarmament was another issue that animated Susie.

When the Buffetts set up a foundation in the 1960s, Susie served as its president. Planned Parenthood was among the top beneficiaries of the Buffett Foundation, and in the 1990s the foundation—now managed as well by the Buffetts' daughter, also named Susie—played a key role in bankrolling the research that created RU-486, the so-called abortion pill.

Warren generally shared his wife's liberal views, if not her desire to work in a hands-on way to improve society. He strongly rejected the Horatio Alger view of success so popular among conservative-minded business types and instead talked often of how the "ovarian lottery" determined people's fate. As he's said: "For literally billions of people, where they are born and who gives them birth, along with their gender and native intellect, largely determine the life they will experience."

Buffett had always assumed that his wife would outlive him, and imagined her as the one "who oversaw the distribution of our wealth to society." In his will, Buffett left his entire fortune to Susie, even though the couple had lived in separate cities for years.

But Susie died of cancer in 2004, rendering moot Buffett's philanthropic endgame. Buffett was then in his mid-seventies, with a net worth of $41 billion. By this time, Buffett's three kids—Susie, Howard, and Peter—all were developing foundations of their own. And his late wife had left her shares of Berkshire Hathaway stock—eventually worth over $2 billion—to the Buffett Foundation, which was renamed in her honor. That foundation started scaling up after her death under the direction of daughter Susie and her ex-husband, Allen Greenberg. The natural thing for Buffett would have been to revamp his philanthropy plan to leave his fortune to the four family foundations controlled by his kids.

Three of those foundations had been set up in 1999, when Warren and Susie Buffett created a foundation for each of their children, endowed with $10 million. "They wanted us to clearly understand that we should do what we wanted to do," Howard Buffett told me. "And the biggest reason was because if you do something you love you'll do it with passion. And if you do it that way, you're way more likely to do a good job than not."

Other billionaires have had the same insight. When Jim Simons started thinking harder about giving away his vast hedge fund fortune, he originally had the idea that his children might work with him on that project through one family foundation. Then it became clear that not everyone had the same interests. So while Jim and his wife, Marilyn, developed a major foundation focused on science, the three Simons children went their separate ways as philanthropists, running their own foundations each with its own distinctive priorities.

Warren Buffett's stunning success with Berkshire Hathaway had made him many times wealthier than most other billionaires, which compounded the challenges of wisely giving away a lot of money. According to his biographer, Alice Schroeder, Buffett didn't have the natural confidence in his kids that he did in Susie. He wasn't sure they could handle wealth on such an epic scale. So, two years after his wife's death, in June 2006, he announced that he would leave the bulk of his fortune to the foundation run by his long-time friends Bill and Melinda Gates.

The deal, which had taken months to work out, sent shock waves through the philanthropy world. It was unprecedented for one billionaire to turn to another to give away his money. Yet the move seemed logical to the no-nonsense Buffett, who thought he knew a good investment when he saw it. "Bill Gates is the most rational guy around in terms of his foundation," Buffett once said. "He and Melinda are saving more lives in terms of dollars spent than anybody else."

This part of the story about Buffett's philanthropy—the massive gift to the Gates Foundation—is well known. What is less known is that Warren Buffett's wealth grew dramatically after he made that gift in 2006, standing at around $65 billion a decade later, and the amount of his money that *isn't* slated to go to the Gates Foundation is far larger than most people realize—or maybe than Buffett himself ever anticipated.

Under the terms of his pledge to the foundation, Buffett is handing five out of every six shares of his stock holdings to Gates. Yet given his wealth, the spare change left over after meeting that pledge is a great fortune itself, all of which will eventually make its way to philanthropy.

Where will this money go? Buffett said as part of his 2006 announcement that most of it will go to the foundations controlled by his kids. Since then, along with the Gates Foundation, these family foundations have also been getting large annual gifts of Berkshire Hathaway stock from Buffett. And thanks to those infusions, the three younger Buffetts have quietly emerged in recent years as among the top philanthropists in the world.

This was a turn of events that none of them had expected. Along with his siblings, Peter Buffett had been tipped off about his father's plan a few months before it was publicly announced. At the time, the pledged stock was worth around a billion dollars. But that value would soar in coming years.

Buffett's children take after their mother, with each intent on helping people in need—and ready to try to reshape public policy if that's what it takes. Peter is probably the most radical of the bunch, questioning capitalism itself in a 2013 *New York Times* op-ed. In the piece, he inveighed against how "lives and communities are destroyed by the system that creates vast amounts of wealth for the few." Too often philanthropy, or the "charitable-industrial complex," as Peter called it, worked to perpetuate such inequities. The real goal of giving, he said, should be to "shatter current structures and systems that have turned much of the world into one vast market." (Peter later said that his dad read the piece before it ran and loved it.)

A professional musician with a new age bent, Peter had initially been ambivalent about focusing his time on philanthropy after his parents set up foundations for their children. He liked his quiet private life, with its calm routines. His wife, Jennifer, though, jumped into the work of running a small grantmaking operation and handled the many administrative details.

Warren's massive 2006 gift, what Peter dubbed the "big bang," would take their foundation, which they named NoVo, to an entirely different level. The couple has used their windfall of annual gifts of Berkshire Hathaway stock (worth $185 million in 2014 alone) to champion some of the most marginalized people in the world. Operating out of offices in Midtown Manhattan, not far from the New York Public Library, NoVo has made empowering women and girls—particularly those of color—its primary cause.

Peter has explained how this focus came about. When he and Jennifer started NoVo, they weren't fixated on specific issues, as many philanthropists are. Rather, they were driven by a few basic instincts. One was a desire to avoid what Peter called "philanthropic colonialism," which he described in his memoir, *Life Is What You Make It*, as the tendency of well-meaning outsiders to "imagine that they understand the challenges facing local peoples better than the local people themselves." Peter and Jennifer wanted to do things differently: "Our approach would be to provide support for people who identified *their own* needs and evolved *their own* solutions."

A second idea was to challenge a world "based in domination and exploitation" and help "move it to a world of collaboration and partnership." That led the couple to think about "what we would call feminine values," said Peter, where the focus is less on "power over" and more on "power with" and collaboration.

More concretely, as the Buffetts talked to experts in philanthropy and beyond, trying to sort out their giving priorities, they came to see that empowering girls and women had all sorts of multiplier effects in terms of changing how communities and entire national economies worked. Warren Buffett has made his fortune by investing in undervalued assets, and Peter came to think of the world's female population in this light. He said: "If their voices aren't heard, of course you're missing half the population—but more importantly when you support them, they support their families, and their communities, and it starts to transform how the world is taken care of." By 2016, the NoVo Foundation was one of the top U.S. funders for gender equity.

This is also a focus of the much larger Susan Thompson Buffett Foundation, which is based in Omaha, and chaired by daughter Susie. In 2014, the foundation gave out $416 million in grants, nearly all of it to further sexual and reproductive health and rights. Just a decade earlier, it gave out a fraction of that amount—a testament to how quickly new philanthropic powerhouses can emerge these days, pouring game-changing amounts of money into certain issues.

The Buffett Foundation remains a top supporter of Planned Parenthood and other groups that back abortion access, as it was when the senior Susie ran it. Yet now it's writing even bigger checks. One of its largest impacts has been around contraception, where the foundation has played a key role in battling unwanted pregnancies by helping bankroll new birth control options. Its grants have helped revolutionize the use of IUDs, a long-acting form of contraception. A reason that IUDs are so effective is because, once these tiny T-shaped devices are inserted into the uterus, there's no room for user error. The Buffett Foundation invested heavily both in research to improve IUDs and programs to spread their use. "Quietly, steadily, the Buffett family is funding the biggest shift in birth control in a generation," according to one media account.

In the United States, more than half of pregnancies are unintended—some 3 million such surprises every year—with poorer women most likely to get accidentally pregnant. Around 1.5 million births result from these pregnancies annually, with most of the costs covered by Medicaid.

Yet while Medicaid picks up the tab for unplanned births, government funding for contraception is in short supply, especially in certain states where religious conservatives wield influence or fiscal pressures are mounting. The Buffett Foundation has often stepped in to make a difference. One foundation-backed effort to provide long-acting birth control to teenagers in Colorado helped lower the birthrate among teenagers across the state by a stunning 40 percent from 2009 to 2013, and sharply cut the number of abortions, too. Despite this success, the Colorado legislature refused to provide ongoing funding for the program—at which point a group of private funders stepped in ensure it would continue, including Ben Walton, an heir to the Walmart fortune who lives in Denver.

Buffett funds don't just make contraception more widely available; this cash is also crucial to ensuring that abortions are accessible in many places in the United States. The foundation is the single largest funder, by far, of the National Abortion Federation (NAF), the professional association of abortion providers. It's given the group tens of millions of dollars in recent years, money that, among other things, helps train doctors to perform abortions, a skill no longer taught at most medical schools. In 2014, it gave the group $23 million to support its national telephone hotline, which NAF describes as the "only toll-free source of information about abortion and referrals to providers of quality care in the U.S. and Canada." Other big checks have gone to an array of pro-choice groups that are deep in the policy fights over abortion access, like the National Abortion Rights Action League (NARAL) and the National Women's Law Center.

Meanwhile, the Buffett Foundation is also the single largest private funder of family planning services at an international level. Much of this money finds its way to distant parts of the world, where women are battling not just for control over their reproductive choices, but for a range of basic rights. One of its biggest grantees, Ipas, is the global equivalent of NAF—advocating for abortion rights while training providers in numerous countries, especially in Africa, where some 6 million unsafe abortions occur every year, killing nearly 30,000 women. Ipas has pulled in nearly $150 million in grants from the Buffett Foundation in the past decade.

In recent years, the Buffett Foundation's giving has grown steadily as it absorbed an influx of ever more valuable Berkshire Hathaway stock—an influx that promises to continue for years to come, bestowing billions on this institution and allowing it to expand its push for reproductive rights.

How many people know that one of America's richest men is pouring a fortune into one of the world's most contested issues? Not many.

HOWARD'S CRUSADE

Even less well known is how Buffett money is being used to fight hunger worldwide, as well as the conditions that lead to hunger—like war and political instability. Those are the priorities of Howard Buffett, whose foundation has lately been giving away upwards of $175 million a year, often backing ambitious and risky projects in sub-Saharan Africa.

Like his two siblings, Howard attended integrated public schools in Omaha growing up, and like both of them, he never finished college, a fact that didn't bother his parents, who had always told their children to chart their own path. In an affectionate foreword to Howard's memoir, *Forty Chances,* Warren joked of his kids: "If the three combine their college credit, they would be entitled to one degree that they could rotate among themselves."

That book, published in 2013, explains Howard's unusual life choices. He became a farmer in his twenties, eventually owning 1,500 acres in central Illinois. This experience led him to be keenly aware of the challenge of producing enough food for an ever more populous world, especially in places with poor soil or a lack of water. Buffett visited many such places after he took up wildlife photography and traveled the world taking pictures of exotic animals. He came to see how widespread hunger and malnutrition were in many places, especially Africa, where he traveled extensively, often to remote corners of little-known countries. When Warren Buffett began shoveling big chunks of Berkshire Hathaway stock into Howard's foundation, after 2006, Howard moved to tackle food issues on a large scale.

Buffett strongly embraces his father's adage that philanthropy is society's risk capital. He told me Warren passed along huge wealth with exactly that attitude, saying: "You go take risks, you try to do things. You can fail as many times as you need to fail to get to some of those big wins." Howard estimates that he'll give away a total of $8 billion before his foundation shuts its doors in 2045. That's a lot of risk capital to work with.

Howard and his small staff have bankrolled projects in Africa, Latin America, and South Asia—getting behind local efforts to help farmers boost their yields and incomes. The foundation is making its biggest investment in Rwanda, where it's putting up $500 million for a push to transform that country's agricultural sector in ways that can serve as a model for the rest of Africa. Buffett has also created three research farms, to explore how to raise crop productivity in adverse settings. One is in Arizona. Another is in South Africa.

Not everything he's tried has worked out so well. "I'm sure we have more failures than we have successes," Buffett said, "and that doesn't bother me. We've tried to do things in a lot of difficult places, and we've tried to do a lot of new things." That's the whole point of philanthropy, as he sees it. Buffett told me: "It's the private foundations in the world that should take risks. . . . We don't have to stand up at our annual gala events to show our successes because we need more people to write checks."

Warren has said that, as a small child, Howard was "a force of nature, a tiny perpetual motion machine," and that he grew up to have "boundless energy," operating on only one speed: "fast-forward." As a philanthropist, Howard has given away huge amounts of money with just a few staff to help him, operating in a very hands-on way. "I go charging ahead. I want to go see stuff, look at stuff, and try to figure it out." He estimates that he's been to 130 countries.

No part of the world has preoccupied him more than the Great Lakes region of Africa. That spectacular area includes two of the biggest lakes in the world, Victoria and Tanganyika, along with some of its greatest biodiversity. It's also home to three deeply troubled countries, the Democratic Republic of Congo, Rwanda, and Burundi.

In his work on agriculture in the region, Buffett came to see just how important peace and stability are to ensuring food supplies and preventing hunger. When farmers are driven from their land by warlords, or can't get their crops to market because of conflict, people go unfed. And so it was that Buffett became involved in trying to stop the cycle of brutal conflicts in eastern Congo, where multiple armies have been fighting since the 1990s, in wars that have claimed five million lives.

This effort has taken different forms, including supporting efforts to stop poaching in the beautiful Virunga National Park, where rebels slaughtered elephants and sold the ivory to buy arms and supplies. The Howard Buffett Foundation gave funds to the park's courageous director, Emmanuel de Merode, to build up a stronger force of rangers, helping bolster a small army that goes up against armed poachers.

Buffett also helped fund the hunt for Joseph Kony, the notorious Ugandan leader of the Lord's Resistance Army (LRA), which is known for kidnapping children and for its psychopathic brutality. Black-market ivory is among its chief sources of revenue. Buffett knew the LRA all too well; his foundation had made grants for work to undo Kony's damage by reintegrating child soldiers, counseling rape victims, and more. After consulting with lawyers, Buffett gave money to support helicopters and planes searching for the LRA. He even spent a night at the forward base in the Central African Republic. Buffett would tell the *New Yorker* about backing the Kony hunt: "Why would you not jump at the chance to stop the core problem? If I can spend my money stopping it so I don't have to spend more money in the future on the victims?"

Smart philanthropists often think this way, casting an eye upstream to where problems get started. While Buffett's giving can seem chaotic and impulsive at times, he's also a strategic thinker. He wants to fund permanent solutions that stick, not to just keep reapplying Band-Aids. After years of watching recurrent warfare in the eastern Congo, Buffett had come to the conclusion that most of what NGOs were doing in the region wasn't getting at the underlying causes of conflict. Relief projects didn't deal with a key problem, which was that a lot of men had no other livelihoods beyond warfare. "The missing piece was you couldn't reintegrate people because there were no jobs." There was no magnet pulling fighters into more productive endeavors. "We felt we needed to do something different," Buffett said. "You've got to provide the jobs, provide alternatives to what people are doing today."

The quest for a breakthrough led Buffett to bet big on building hydroelectric plants in the Great Lakes region. Electricity, Buffett knew, is an important driver of prosperity. "It provides the power to establish businesses." And so the foundation undertook a pilot project, financing a small hydroelectric plant in Congo. Sure enough, after the new electricity was flowing, two new businesses popped up, one of them making soap, that eventually came to employ hundreds of people. Buffett decided to double down, next backing larger hydroelectric plant in North Kivu, in eastern Congo, that would cost $20 million and provide power to 130,000 people. Another benefit he saw from this electricity, beyond powering businesses, is that it would reduce the number of trees that people had to cut down in Virunga National Park to make charcoal for cooking. That activity didn't just hurt the forest, it helped rebel groups who often forced charcoal harvesters to pay a tax to them. Buffett saw how a new, bigger power plant could have "a very far-reaching impact in terms of a single project. That's what sold us on it."

The plan was for the Howard Buffett Foundation to put up half the cost of the new plant, with other partners laying out the rest. After those partners pulled out, Buffett still went forward. He and his staff also did a feasibility study of funding six more power plants in the area. The study found that 800 to 1,000 jobs would be created for each new megawatt of electricity. That seemed like a bargain to Buffett, who had enough money to actually back an effort on this scale and saw growing hope that economic development could eventually crowd out conflict in eastern Congo.

Yet he always knew that things could go wrong. "It's a huge bet," he said of the power plants. "It's also a really big risk. There is a lot that can go wrong. . . . We're doing this in the middle of active conflict." But the alternative—doing the same things NGOs had always been doing—was a dead end. This wasn't the time to play it safe, as many funders prefer to do. "The risk doesn't faze me in terms of what we're trying to do. If you don't do something different, nothing's going to change."

As for the standard metrics of success that foundations obsess over, Buffett said to forget them all. "You really can't set up metrics in a conflict zone. Everything changes all the time. The goalposts change, the players change. . . . If we sat back and tried to analyze these on a set of metrics, we would never do the project."

The new hydroelectric plant opened in December 2015. Buffett pledged nearly $40 million to build two more such plants in North Kivu.

NOT FAR FROM THE TREE

Not every billionaire has kids ready to put the family fortune to good use. Some children of top philanthropists aren't keen on carrying on their giving. Eli Broad, who is in his eighties with a $7 billion fortune to dispose of, told me that neither of his children was interested in one day piloting the Broad philanthropic operation. The foundation instead will spend down and close within fifteen or twenty years of Broad's death. Gordon Moore's sons sit on the board of his foundation, but neither has emerged as a very active figure in philanthropy. Some billionaires, like David Geffen and Paul Allen, don't have any heirs.

Other families, though, are more like the Buffetts, with the next generation eagerly taking on the job of large-scale philanthropy. Three out of four of George Soros's kids back different causes and sit on the board of the Open Society Foundations. His daughter, Andrea, has focused on Tibet and global development issues. His son Jonathan has pushed to reform the campaign finance system. The youngest son, Alexander, has taken up human rights and other challenges facing marginalized peoples. Jim Simons's three kids are even further along in their own giving. Pete Peterson's son, Michael, is the president and CEO of the foundation named after his father. He's led the foundation's influential work on fiscal policy and in years to come is sure to be a key figure in giving away many hundreds of millions of dollars that his father has pledged to philanthropy. Shari Redstone, the daughter of the media mogul Sumner Redstone, has played a central role in that family's philanthropy and is set to play an even bigger role down the line. Dave Peery is now piloting the Silicon Valley foundation set up by his billionaire parents with their real estate fortune, just as Lisa Sobrato Sonsini, the daughter of another Bay Area real estate billionaire, John Sobrato, has been a driving force in scaling up her family's philanthropy over the past eighteen years. The list could go on.

Probably no heirs in America wield as much influence as the Walton family, which still has a dominant ownership stake in Walmart, the largest private employer in the United States. Arguably, though, these heirs wield nearly as much clout through the family's foundation, which has nearly $3 billion in assets and gave out $374.7 million in 2015 alone, with the largest share of that money going to reshape America's K–12 system.

The foundation has a professional staff, but its board is controlled by family members. Among them is board chair Carrie Walton Penner, a third-generation Walton who has long been a major player in the foundation's K–12 giving. Penner has a profile similar to that of other heiresses who've groomed themselves for leadership in philanthropy, like Katherine Lorenz and Emma Bloomberg.

After graduating from prep school in 1988, Penner went to Georgetown University, where she studied economics and history. At college, she volunteered to tutor high school students in Anacostia, a poor neighborhood of Washington, D.C. She found the experience deeply disturbing. "I have no idea why they were going to school at all because, frankly, they weren't being educated," she later said. By the mid-1990s, Penner was immersed in education issues and finished her master's degree in education policy and program evaluation at Stanford University. Afterward, she served as a program officer at the Walton Family Foundation, among other jobs working on education.

Penner is more than a funder of the school choice movement: She's actively directing it by serving on the boards of the top groups leading the reform charge. She is on the board of the KIPP Foundation, America's largest charter school organization, which runs 125 schools. One reason KIPP has such reach is that the Walton Family Foundation has pumped over $60 million into it. For a time, Penner sat on the board of the Alliance for School Choice, an advocacy group that not only supports charter schools but has also backed vouchers. Walton has been by far the largest funder of this group, with grants totaling over $20 million. As well, Penner is on the board of the Charter School Growth Fund, a pivotal player in the charter movement, as mentioned earlier. The Walton Family Foundation has given it over $100 million.

Penner is active in several education organizations in California, where she lives, most notably the California Charter Schools Association, which seeks to expand and defend charter schools in America's largest state. The Walton Family Foundation is this group's largest funder by far, with grants totaling over $40 million. Penner has been deeply involved in key charter school fights in California, both as a philanthropist and as a campaign donor. The Walton Family Foundation is helping fund the Broad Foundation's ambitious quest to expand charter schools in Los Angeles, while Penner and her uncle, Jim Walton, have sought to create a more politically friendly climate in LA for charters by donating over $1 million for local school board races in 2014 and 2015.

Penner's husband, Greg, who is the chairman of Walmart's board, is also immersed in the education world. He previously served as co-chair of the Charter School Growth Fund, and is a board member of Teach for America. The Waltons are the single largest funder of Teach for America, with cumulative grants totaling more than $100 million. In late 2015, their foundation announced it would make a $50 million grant to the organization.

The Penners are one of the top power couples in education reform circles right now, with huge resources and major clout. They have worked hard to master K–12 issues and make things happen. But make no mistake: Carrie has so much influence over education policy in America because of the family she was born into; Greg has it because of who he married.

These private citizens, with such outsized power over public institutions, illustrate the new face of dynastic wealth in America. Get ready for a future with many more philanthropic heirs who operate in the same activist style.

There's enough hostility to inherited wealth in America that even some of the nation's richest people see it as a bad thing. But their solution, to give away the money, turns out to be not much of a solution at all—at least not if you're worried about civic inequities getting baked more deeply into American life amid the disposal of today's historic fortunes. Indeed, as we've seen, leaving a foundation to your kids actually gives them *more* influence in society than passing down the wealth directly.

The fact that many heirs take philanthropy so seriously is good news and bad news. It's good news in that we're unlikely to see a bunch of empty-headed rich kids giving away billions, or at least this hasn't been the pattern so far. It's bad news in that we're seeing a marked expansion of the kind of sophisticated elite power that so many Americans find unnerving. In this case, though, we're not talking about expert leaders who at least ascend to their influence through quasi-meritocratic systems. We're talking about elites who are born into that power and come to exercise it at considerable expense to U.S. taxpayers, who help foot the bill when new family foundations are created.

So far, most Americans are unaware of the huge power that heirs are coming to wield through philanthropy, and there has been minimal backlash to this trend. But there *has* been pushback lately to elites in general, as seen in social movements like the Tea Party and the presidential campaigns of Donald Trump and Bernie Sanders—not to mention years of polls showing declining public faith in most institutions.

One reason so many Americans chafe at being ruled by experts and rich people is the sense that such elites are out of touch with their own life experiences. There's a lot of truth to that. For all their training and expertise, as well as their obvious empathy, people like Emma Bloomberg and Carrie Penner Walton—raised in wealth and privilege—can't possibly understand what it's like to live in certain circumstances. And, yet, as philanthropists they have the ability to powerfully intervene in ordinary people's lives, both in America and around the world. That doesn't seem right in a country founded in opposition to dynastic power. And it doesn't seem sustainable in an America that has often distrusted elite rule.

Even if philanthropic heirs use their power wisely much of the time, it's hard to imagine that this situation—if fully understood—will sit well with the American public in a coming future where many more heirs exercise ever growing influence in society.

10

The New Medicis

The aviator and industrialist Howard Hughes spent his final years living in a luxurious hotel suite in Acapulco, a recluse who indulged in the heavy use of codeine and Valium. After he died in 1976—on his private plane, fittingly—it was said that Hughes had lost his mind long before.

One piece of business Hughes badly bungled in his final years was estate planning. He died without a valid will.

This was ironic, since Hughes had created his first will at the young age of nineteen, in 1925. In it, he stipulated that a portion of his estate go to a medical institute bearing his name. Later, in a bid to outwit the IRS, Hughes formally created such an institute and gave it all the stock of the Hughes Aircraft Company. It was an epic tax dodge, but Hughes's interest in medical science was very real. Both his parents had died from medical problems early in his life, when he was still a teenager, and he himself sustained major injuries in a plane crash in 1946. The charter Hughes signed in 1953 creating the Howard Hughes Medical Institute (HHMI) stated that its purpose was the "promotion of human knowledge within the field of the basic sciences (principally the field of medical research and medical education) and the effective application thereof for the benefit of mankind."

Hughes reportedly had intended to leave his entire estate to the medical institute, since he had no heirs. But his death without a valid will set off years of litigation, fragmenting his estate among many claimants.

Eventually, though, a court ruled that HHMI was at least entitled to all shares of the Hughes Aircraft Company and appointed a group of trustees to oversee the institute. In turn, the board sold the company to General Motors in 1985 for $5.2 billion, which created one of the largest nonprofit endowments in the United States. In the past thirty years, that endowment has more than tripled, to over $18 billion.

These days, the Howard Hughes Medical Institute employs 2,500 people and gives out over $700 million a year. It makes grants to scientists all over the country from its sprawling brick headquarters in Chevy Chase, Maryland. The institute also hosts hundreds of researchers in the Janelia Research Campus, a vast modern research complex that sits on rolling farmland in Virginia. It features a 900-foot-long arc-shaped laboratory, with a design inspired in part by AT&T's fabled Bell Laboratories. Janelia is a mecca for researchers, who are given full funding for six years, freeing them from the demands of teaching or chasing grants or ensuring that their research has commercial applications. Their work ranges across areas such as computational neuroscience and structural biology. Janelia even provides housing and childcare, and there's also a pub on this campus without students. It's a utopia for scientists, made possible by a man who's been dead for over forty years.

The Howard Hughes Medical Institute is governed by a small board, operating in complete independence from legislative oversight or shareholders. It receives little scrutiny from the media and is beholden to neither a bottom line nor much of a constituency. It is designed to exist in perpetuity, and barring some catastrophe, it is likely to be funding research for centuries to come, growing ever richer and larger in a future where no one remembers who Howard Hughes was. Such is the long arm of philanthropy.

J. Paul Getty died the same year that Hughes did, in 1976, also leaving behind a fortune that now powers a fabulously wealthy institution offering a haven to researchers. The Getty Center sits high in the hills overlooking Los Angeles and the ocean. It cost over $1 billion to build, including construction of a train that brings visitors up to an extravagant travertine-encased complex that conjures up the Acropolis in Athens. While the Getty is best known as an art museum, it also houses a research institute "dedicated to furthering knowledge and advancing understanding of the visual arts," and a foundation that pumps out millions in grants each year. Backstopping it all is the $12 billion J. Paul Getty Trust, which describes itself as the "world's largest cultural and philanthropic organization dedicated to the visual arts." The trust is run by a board of sixteen people. This institution, too, is designed to last in perpetuity. Since 2005, its endowment has more than doubled.

The Getty Center and the Howard Hughes Medical Institute have long stood out for their enormous resources and large footprint in the arenas in which they operate. But both institutions are becoming less unique as a new wave of wealthy patrons of the arts and sciences arrives on the scene.

Not far away from the Getty Center, in the Santa Monica Mountains, a think tank is being built, one that its iconoclastic founder, Nicolas Berggruen, has endowed with an initial gift of $500 million. Set on 450 acres, with endless views, the Berggruen Institute will expand its current work of exploring social and political ideas, convening leaders and thinkers from around the world. Berggruen has said that his vision is of a "society where people can flourish in harmony with one another." The institute also works on more prosaic fronts, like reforming dysfunctional governance in California. Berggruen, who made his fortune from investing, has plans to eventually increase the institute's endowment to a billion dollars. That's not big money in science, where research is very expensive, but it's a huge sum for a think tank—twice the endowment of the Brookings Institution, one of the largest and most influential think tanks in the world. It's yet another reminder of the kind of game-changing wealth that is arriving in philanthropy, including in the most rarefied of arenas. Such wealth is coming to more fields faster, and in larger chunks.

When J. Paul Getty died forty years ago, he was among the very richest people in America, with a net worth of $2 billion, the equivalent of $8 billion in 2016. Hughes had a similar net worth. Both men drew enormous attention for fortunes whose size seemed to defy comprehension. Very few other Americans of their time were nearly as rich. (When the Forbes 400 list debuted in 1982, it had just thirteen billionaires on it.) Yet today, neither Getty nor Hughes would rank among the wealthiest hundred Americans. And that top tier of today's super-rich includes quite a few billionaires who have embarked on ambitious projects to shape the realms of culture and science.

Consider Alice Walton. In 2011, Walton—long among the top twenty richest Americans, with a net worth of over $30 billion—presided over the opening of one of the most expensive new art museums ever built, Crystal Bridges Museum of American Art in Bentonville, Arkansas. She'd been interested in art all her life, buying her first painting at the age of ten—a reproduction of Picasso's *Blue Nude*.

Since its founding, Crystal Bridges has amassed a nearly unmatched collection of American art, spending hundreds of millions of dollars of Walton money in an acquisition spree that has roiled art markets. Its prizes include Andy Warhol's *Coca-Cola (3)*, snatched up for $57 million, and *Jimson Weed*, by Georgia O'Keeffe, bought at Sotheby's in 2014 for $44.4 million. It's not known how much the museum paid for *Rosie the Riveter*, the classic painting by Norman Rockwell.

Crystal Bridges has also ramped up its research and scholarship functions, building the kind of highbrow back-office operation that you'll only find at the world's top museums. It wouldn't be surprising to see grantmaking added to the mix. While Crystal Bridges cost around $1.6 billion to build and endow, there is plenty more where that came from: Alice Walton's net worth is five times larger than J. Paul Getty's was when he died. Is Alice Walton destined to one day emerge as the biggest arts philanthropist in American history? It's quite possible.

Meanwhile, in Cambridge, Massachusetts, hundreds of scientists are pursuing breakthroughs in genomic medicine at the Broad Institute of MIT and Harvard, which sprawls across three large buildings. Despite its name, the Broad Institute is actually a free-standing entity with its own governing board that doesn't answer to either MIT or Harvard. Since its founding in 2004, it's pulled in nearly $2 billion in private donations—mostly from its founders, Eli and Edythe Broad, and another mega-donor, Ted Stanley, who gave it $650 million in 2014, one of the largest gifts ever for scientific research.

Stanley, who made his fortune in collectibles, became interested in biomedical research after his son had a manic episode as a college junior, running through the streets of New York until the police found him naked in a deli. In total, Stanley would give $825 million to the Broad Institute before he died in 2016. Eric Lander, the founding director of the institute, told the *New York Times* that these funds had enabled scientists there to make breakthroughs in identifying DNA associated with schizophrenia.

BENEFACTORS

Giving like this reflects one of the oldest strains in philanthropy: the wealthy as benefactors to the creative class, a tradition that long predates government support for the arts and sciences. Half a millennium ago, the Medici family famously supported Galileo and Leonardo da Vinci. The railroad tycoon John Johnson helped create the Metropolitan Museum of Art in New York City in 1870. John D. Rockefeller created the Rockefeller Medical Institute in 1901, the first biomedical research center in the United States, and also the University of Chicago. His son, John Jr., underwrote the creation of the Museum of Modern Art, starting in the late 1920s.

Still, in terms of scale there is no comparison between past patronage of the arts and sciences, as well as higher education, and what is happening today.

Just as ever more donors are crowding into areas like education or the environment, more are showing up in the arts and sciences, covering the paychecks of molecular biologists, curators, neuroscientists, art conservationists, geneticists, professors holding endowed chairs, and on and on. Pick nearly any disease, and you'll find a deep-pocketed donor who's hot on the trail of a research breakthrough. Name a leading cultural institution, and chances are it's lately received new infusions of cash from billionaire backers. Get lost in a top hospital, and you'll find yourself wandering from one named wing to another. Visit any major university, and it will be hard to find a big building on campus that doesn't bear the name of a mega-donor. In some cases, these names have been painted over those of earlier philanthropists whose gifts, huge at the time, seem rather paltry now.

Between 2005 and 2014—a period in which the combined net worth of the Forbes 400 nearly doubled—over 14,000 gifts of $1 million or more were made to colleges and universities. At least 100 of these were worth over $100 million. Health institutions pulled in nearly 5,000 gifts of a million dollars or more, with at least two topping a half-billion dollars.

Arts and cultural institutions received 4,000 gifts of $1 million and up each during this same period. One of the largest of these was $400 million to the Dallas Museum of Art—a gift that underscores how today's bene-factors are now operating in more places, well outside the usual coastal orbits of yesteryear's wealth elite, even including Bentonville, Arkansas, a city of just 40,000. If you're a neuroscientist, you'll probably find your-self in Seattle at some point, where a brain science institute financed by Paul Allen has grown by leaps and bounds since 2003. If you're a molecu-lar biologist or a geneticist, you may find yourself in Kansas City, Mis-souri, visiting the Stowers Institute for Medical Research, a huge facility that houses several hundred biomedical scientists. The money behind the institute, some $2 billion, has come from a mutual fund pioneer, Jim Stowers, and his wife, Virginia.

Wealthy local donors are also pumping up universities across the heartland. After Harvard and Yale, the University of Texas system has the largest endowment in the United States. The University of Minnesota now has a larger endowment than Brown University, thanks to the rise of new wealth in the Upper Midwest. The University of Michigan's endow-ment is bigger than that of three Ivy League schools. None of this is much of a surprise given that some 70,000 Americans now have a net worth of $30 million or more, and not all of them live on the East or West coasts.

I'll say more in a moment about what today's Medicis are up to, but first let's consider what's at stake here. We are all affected by the direction of the arts and sciences, as well as of higher education. What cultural work gets valued and shared can shape how we understand the human experience, while the nature of cultural institutions themselves can influ-ence how communities interact and evolve. The impact of science is far more tangible: Which problems researchers are funded to attack can determine which diseases people die from or what breakthrough tech-nologies emerge. Top universities influence what ideas get traction and how tomorrow's leaders think.

For a period, beginning in the 1950s and 1960s, the United States seemed headed toward a future in which these critical parts of society would be shaped by democratic governance. We wouldn't depend on the munificence and preferences of millionaires to chart scientific and artis-tic progress, or to fund our universities. We'd do it together as citizens, through public agencies like the National Science Foundation (created in 1950) and the National Endowment for the Arts (created in 1965). Or through the great public university systems that were greatly expanded after World War II.

Now, that vision is dimming, as governments face new fiscal constraints and as vast resources are mobilized behind an earlier model of private patronage. To be sure, we are still early in this story. In science, even the biggest private funders still deploy minuscule funds compared to what government spends every year. "It's a drop in the bucket," Marilyn Simons told me, talking about the annual grantmaking budget of the Simons Foundation, which gave out $230 million in a recent year—compared to the nearly $40 billion that the National Institutes of Health (NIH) and the National Science Foundation (NSF) give annually.

Simons is right. Still, signs abound that the locus of influence in science funding is indeed shifting toward private benefactors. The new donors are often supporting younger scientists coming up and getting behind riskier or neglected areas that government agencies won't touch. The choices of philanthropists are increasingly shaping which researchers are able to apply for government funding. In higher education, a torrent of new private money has flooded onto campus during the same period that has seen many states cut spending for public universities, even as academic researchers faced declining federal support. Meanwhile, in the arts, the pendulum has now swung far away from public influence after years of budget cuts to the NEA and state arts agencies. Here, philanthropic dollars dominate the funding landscape, both for individual artists and for arts institutions.

As further budget cuts kick in over the coming years, and megadonors step up their giving, the shift toward private financing for scientific exploration, cultural expression, and advanced learning is likely to accelerate.

This is not a conscious power grab by the new Medicis, many of whom favor more public funding for the arts, sciences, and higher education. The wealthy can often be found leading the charge to defend the NSF or NEA from deficit hawks. Bill Gates has testified before Congress, calling for more science research funding, while Jim Simons has been a strong proponent of more public investment in math education. In some cases, private donors have stepped forward to write big checks to public universities only after watching in dismay as these institutions were hurt by budget cuts.

On the other hand, today's era of austerity didn't come about by accident. It was orchestrated in part by an upper class keen on reducing its taxes, along with the size of government. In some states, cuts to higher education have specifically helped finance tax reductions for the wealthy and corporations.

Donors from the far upper class have also underwritten the conservative policy groups that have been whacking away at public support for science and—especially—the arts since the 1980s. The Cato Institute, backed heavily by wealthy libertarians, has long called for the total elimination of government science funding. Scholars at the more moderate American Enterprise Institute, supported by a slew of billionaires, would never go this far, but many advocate sharp cuts in federal spending. Even more influential, as we saw, was Pete Peterson's targeted philanthropy during the early Obama years to help move deficit reduction to the top of the national agenda. As a result of the Budget Control Act of 2011, government-funded scientific research through the NIH and the NSF will be on a downward slide for years to come. Veteran scientists have described the cuts so far as devastating. Further cuts lie ahead.

For its part, the NEA has never recovered from earlier attacks, when some Republicans—including President Reagan—worked to eliminate all government funding of the arts, a position championed by the Heritage Foundation and its wealthy donors. Heritage has kept up the attack on the NEA for over three decades now, publishing dozens of policy briefs attacking its funding. If the NEA's budget had kept pace with inflation since 1981, it would now be over $400 million a year. Instead, in 2016, Congress appropriated just under $150 million to the NEA. State arts funding has also been in decline in many places, especially California. A web of right-wing think tanks in the states, modeled on Heritage and Cato, has been at the forefront of attacking local arts funding. Cutting such spending, for example, has been among the priorities of the North Carolina policy groups backed by Art Pope. Following the political revolution engineered by Pope in 2010, government funding for the arts in North Carolina fell sharply.

Many of the billionaires who underwrite efforts to reduce taxes and government also are big donors to the arts and biomedical research. Some, like David Koch, are libertarians who believe as a matter of doctrine that government shouldn't be involved in funding such research. Others, like Bruce Kovner, may take a softer stance, but nevertheless favor fiscal policies that virtually guarantee cuts to the arts, science, and higher education. Hedge fund billionaires like Kovner or Kenneth Griffin get lots of praise when they write big checks to arts institutions (Kovner is the biggest donor ever to the Juilliard School of Music), but few observers connect the dots and realize that some of these same figures have been writing checks for years to groups and politicians that seek to downsize government, including spending for the arts.

To be sure, quite a few wealthy people have been on the other side of this debate, financing think tanks and Democratic politicians who have pushed for higher taxes on the wealthy and a more robust government. But in recent decades the overall weight of the donor class has been behind a fiscal conservatism that has left government with diminishing discretionary cash.

Critics of the public sector often argue that it has usurped roles that are better played by civil society, pointing out that philanthropy accomplished plenty of good before the era of big government. The Metropolitan Museum is just one of philanthropy's greatest hits prior to the New Deal and the Great Society. Advanced medical research centers, great museums, top universities—you could find all these institutions a century ago, when Washington, D.C., was still a sleepy southern city that commanded just a small sliver of the nation's GDP. What's so wrong with a shift back to a time when nonprofits, as opposed to public agencies, charted the direction of culture, science, and higher learning? Also, as a practical matter, with government short on cash and vision, shouldn't we be celebrating the arrival of new donors who can fill the vacuum? Haven't these generous benefactors come along just in the nick of time?

Indeed, they have. And many are doing great things. But it's important to keep in mind the backstory of why private philanthropists and their money now loom so much larger. What's happening in the cultural and scientific realms tracks with what's happening in other areas like education and public parks. As the great twentieth-century tide of public money recedes, in an era in which "big government is dead," as Bill Clinton famously declared, a new tide of private money is flowing in—heralded by headlines about huge gifts to hospitals, museums, universities, and research centers.

Most of the donors behind these gifts simply want to do some good in the world. For every donor like David Geffen, who gave $100 million to Lincoln Center in 2015 in what struck many as a naked bid for status, there are many others who would just as soon duck the spotlight. In fact, since 2005, there have been at least ten philanthropic gifts of $100 million or more that have been made anonymously.

Yet whatever their motives, or their humility, donors do get something for their money, beyond mere satisfaction. They get influence over our culture, along with the arc of progress. And as the United States shifts back toward an earlier model of achieving big things, where civil society takes more of the lead, that influence is growing. Maybe in earlier times one could talk about ordinary people driving civil society forward; now it's the givers who are the main drivers, and that's especially true in the rarefied realms of the arts, science, and higher learning.

In short, what we have here is another complicated story about philanthropy and influence in a new Gilded Age. It's hard not to be inspired by the vision and achievements of many donors—and equally hard not to be troubled by the bigger picture of more power shifting into private hands.

KNOWLEDGE QUEST

The Simons Foundation exemplifies the pace and scale of today's new philanthropy. In just over a decade, it has emerged as one of the leading private funders of basic science in the United States, pushing forward the frontiers of knowledge about mathematics, physics, the life sciences, and more. The Manhattan-based foundation has also revolutionized autism research, spending hundreds of millions of dollars to draw new talent into a once-neglected field and helping orchestrate a series of breakthroughs on a condition that afflicts millions.

These are big accomplishments for a foundation that for many years was no more than a filing box in the dressing room of Marilyn Simons, the second wife of hedge fund billionaire Jim Simons. Jim got his PhD in mathematics and then worked in the defense sector in Washington before pursuing a successful academic career. He became the chair of the math department at SUNY Stony Brook and, in 1976, won the prestigious Oswald Veblen Prize in Geometry. His career took yet another turn when he started his hedge fund, Renaissance Technologies, in 1982. There, Simons and his teams created mathematical models to predict the behavior of financial markets. The firm was phenomenally successful. For a twenty-year period, from 1994 through mid-2014, Renaissance averaged a 71.8 percent annual return. In some of those years, Simons personally made over $1 billion. Eventually his net worth climbed to over $10 billion, and it has kept growing.

Jim and Marilyn started their foundation in December 1994. "We had always given to charity, since I had any money to give away," Jim told me. The Simonses usually made those gifts around the holidays. Marilyn had the idea of formalizing things with a foundation, which was seeded with an initial gift of a million dollars. In 2001, Marilyn—who'd gotten a PhD in economics but never went into academia—rented a small office down the street from Gramercy Park and hired a few part-time staff. Still, the foundation was a pretty informal operation, and mostly it operated passively, fielding requests for money. "They were coming to us," said Jim. "We didn't sit around and say, 'Oh, why don't we do x or y or z.' We were being reactive." Then, one day, Marilyn recalled, Jim had an idea: "We should give to things we want to give to."

That basic insight led the Simonses to think more carefully about where they might give money—and to start building a real foundation. Their main interests were math and science, but they were also keen on doing something about autism and learning disabilities. They pulled together a roundtable of experts for a day to learn about the research in this area. Jim said of that meeting: "We came away with the conclusion that there were two things we could do: one, bring better people into the field because the quality of the research was not all that good. And two, to focus at least initially on genetics, where it was clear that this was caused at least in part by one's genes."

The Simons Foundation made a few grants along these lines, but felt out of their depth when giving out money at this level. "We were lucky we picked a couple good people to support, but we didn't really know how to do that," Jim said. So he and Marilyn looked around for someone to help them, and soon hooked up with Gerald Fischbach, a neuroscientist who had spent years at NIH and also two medical schools before becoming a dean at Columbia, where he continued advanced research. In 2006, he joined the Simons Foundation as the scientific director overseeing its autism research funding.

It's worth pausing here to point out that top foundation jobs can be very attractive, especially to academics or nonprofit executives who get tired of always hustling for grants. Moving to the other side of the funding game can be a nice break, not to mention hugely empowering since now you're the one waving the magic funding wand to bring new projects to life. And it's all the better if you're getting in on the ground floor of a billionaire's young foundation. The appeal of these jobs means that donors can easily recruit first-tier talent to advance their philanthropic dreams—in effect, building private brain trusts, a powerful asset in a society where expertise is a key currency of influence.

Hiring Fischbach was a paradigm shift, said Jim Simons, because he "introduced these methods of learning about the field, learning about the investigators, opening up an application process and reviewing." The Simonses were so thrilled with this step forward that they decided to also professionalize their giving for basic math and science, which had tended to be haphazard as well. Within a few years, the Simons Foundation had top directors building up all its grantmaking areas. As the operation evolved, Marilyn stayed on as president, leading the work to scale up an outfit that soon occupied several floors in a lower Fifth Avenue office building not far from Madison Square Park. Along the way, the couple moved ever bigger chunks of money into the foundation's endowment, which had risen above $2 billion by 2013. Annual grantmaking soared, too, and even doubled in some years. "It just grew," Jim said.

Many new philanthropists these days are reluctant to build large foundations, fretting about the overhead costs and the dreaded thought of their philanthropy becoming "bureaucratic."

Jim and Marilyn Simons never had any doubt about the need to hire a sizeable staff. "What we're doing is very technical," Jim said. "You can't just give money to mathematics by throwing it out on the street and letting the mathematicians pick it up. You need to know who's doing what, how good they are, what's the likelihood they will use the money wisely, and so on. We're giving a lot of money. Hundreds of millions of dollars every year. So we want to do it in a professional way."

The Simons Foundation grew even larger in 2016, when it took over an eleven-story building near its headquarters and began populating the new space with several hundred researchers working in-house at a new operation called the Flatiron Institute. Like the Howard Hughes Medical Institute, the Simons Foundation is embracing a hybrid model of making millions of dollars in grants while also providing a cushy home for researchers. In time, Simons may well rival HHMI in size and influence. Jim and Marilyn Simons said in their Giving Pledge letter that "the great majority of our wealth will be devoted to philanthropic purposes." As of 2016, the combined assets in their foundation and private investments totaled around $18 billion.

In March 2014, the *New York Times* published a front-page article ominously headlined "Billionaires with Big Ideas Are Privatizing American Science." It named the many deep-pocketed donors that have moved into this space in recent years, including Jim Simons. "For better or worse," said one analyst in the article, "the practice of science in the 21st century is becoming shaped less by national priorities or by peer-review groups and more by the particular preferences of individuals with huge amounts of money." The age of grand federal research endeavors, the *Times* suggested, was winding down as science became "a private enterprise."

Jim and Marilyn Simons were pleased with the piece, because it drew attention to the alarming decline of government funding for science. Jim knew firsthand how important such funding is, because he'd gotten his math PhD under a new federal program begun after the Soviets launched Sputnik in 1957. But they thought the *Times* claim that American science was becoming "privatized" was an overreach, given the modest resources of philanthropists compared to those of government.

Ironically, the keen awareness among science philanthropists of just how puny they are relative to the Feds has lately helped drive their influence to new heights. That's because these funders have zeroed in on where they're likely to make the biggest difference, which is in backing young researchers and those engaged in riskier work. "The NIH is a conservative outfit," said Jim Simons. "The grants they give are for work that's been mostly done already. . . . They don't want to give you money unless they're pretty darn sure that you're going to succeed. Well, if you're doing great science, maybe you'll succeed and maybe you won't. . . . For people who are think-ing well outside the box, to do something that's riskier, philanthropic sup-port is much more likely than government support in many cases." The Simonses have sought to operate at this edgy frontier of science.

Another funder who thinks the same way is Paul Allen, the Micro-soft billionaire who is also among the big science funders to emerge in recent years. Allen has directed hundreds of millions of dollars to risky and experimental research areas, such as artificial intelligence and gene editing. Big chunks of that money could be wasted—or maybe transform life on earth.

Beyond flowing to safe bets, government research funds rarely go to anyone under forty who doesn't already have a long track record. The result is that, for today's younger scientists, private funders have become all-important gatekeepers.

Yes, philanthropy only accounts for a fraction of overall science fund-ing, but the balance has been changing. One study charting this shift found that if you factor in endowment income, "science philanthropy provides almost 30% of the annual research funds of those in leading universities." That figure offers a window into the growing role of private money in deciding which new ideas and young researchers get support.

NEW TALENT

The wealthy also play an ever larger role in deciding who lives and who dies. Or, more specifically, which medical problems get conquered versus which are neglected.

That ultimate power is not hard to understand. If donors take an inter-est in a particular disease or condition, moving new money into research, cures are more likely to be found and lives to be saved. Yet the pet health interests of rich people may or may not line up with what society overall should give priority to in seeking medical breakthroughs. As the *Times* warned: "The philanthropists' war on disease risks widening that gap, as a number of the campaigns, driven by personal adversity, target illnesses that predominantly afflict white people—like cystic fibrosis, melanoma and ovarian cancer."

Giving for health and medicine is among the most personal areas of philanthropy. Many wealthy donors make huge medical donations because they've had a brush with a particular disease or been helped by a specific hospital. Just look at how Memorial Sloan Kettering Cancer Center has thrived in recent years. Strategically located on the Upper East Side, it caters to some of the wealthiest cancer sufferers in the world—who, in turn, have shown their gratitude. David Koch, who lives in the neighborhood and was treated at Sloan Kettering for prostate cancer, has given it over $200 million. Another Upper East Sider, Henry Kravis, the private equity billionaire, gave $100 million to support "precision oncology" at Sloan Kettering that taps insights from genomic medicine.

Walk around in the vast labyrinth of New York Presbyterian Hospital, located a few blocks from Sloan Kettering, and you'll find one pavilion and specialty center after another named after wealthy donors—some of whom live a short cab ride away. David Koch has also given to this hospital, helping finance an ambulatory care center named after him with a $100 million gift. In turn, that center will be the home of the new Alexandra & Steven Cohen Hospital for Women and Newborns, paid for by a $75 million gift from the hedge fund billionaire and his wife. Both these operations are housed in the hospital's Weill Cornell campus, named in part after Sanford Weill, a philanthropist who once ran Citigroup.

Meanwhile, a few miles north in the Bronx, men have the lowest life expectancy of nearly anywhere in New York State—often dying from causes that could have been prevented if only they had access to basic health care. But helping out the hospitals and health clinics in the city's poor neighborhoods has never been of much interest to wealthy donors. Nor do these donors tend to back work on pedestrian health problems like hypertension, one of the top killers stalking poor black men.

Such disparities in health funding make it tempting to settle on another simple storyline about self-serving, elitist philanthropy. As usual, things are more complicated. Many of the biggest health donations that go to name-brand institutions like Sloan Kettering or the Mayo Clinic, another strong money magnet, are for research that can potentially benefit everyone. David Koch's huge gifts for cancer research are a case in point. Koch was drawn to this area after he survived a plane crash in the early 1990s, only to learn at the hospital that he had prostate cancer. He's given millions for this cause, which is a big focus of the research he's backed at Sloan Kettering. Koch has said: "Once you get that disease . . . you become a crusader to try to cure the disease not only for yourself but for other people." In the case of prostate cancer, many of those other people are African American men, who are nearly 1.6 times more likely to get prostate cancer than Caucasian men and 2.4 times more likely to die from it.

The health giving of Herb Sandler, whom we met earlier in the book, also offers a counterpoint to the notion that such philanthropy favors the more affluent.

After Sandler and his wife, Marion, grew rich from banking, they didn't give heavily just to progressive causes, like the Center for American Progress and the ACLU. They also began investing in medical research, in ways that would have a major effect on poor kids.

Marion suffered from severe asthma, which led the couple to research this chronic disease that affects millions of Americans, and which can be terrifying. "We wanted to know more about it," Herb told me. The Sandlers learned two things as they dug in: First, that low-income kids of color were among the top sufferers of asthma, which is linked to pollution and cockroaches—both of which are found in abundance in many poor urban areas. The damage to these kids is enormous. Asthma is among the leading reasons that poor kids miss school; they are home with inhalers instead, or in the hospital, at a huge cost to Medicaid.

Second, the Sandlers learned that asthma research was a backwater within biomedicine. Very few breakthroughs had been made on asthma in the past half century, and few talented scientists were entering this area. Americans may have been suffering from several million asthma attacks a year, with a few thousand people dying annually, but the world of medical research—and health philanthropy—didn't seem to much care.

The Sandlers set out to change that. They saw a unique opportunity: to boost asthma research up into the big leagues and, just maybe, mitigate a health challenge tormenting kids who already had the odds stacked against them.

Marion had the unusual thought of injecting big money into the asthma field—but only making grants available to researchers who had never worked on this problem before. "It was a wild idea," Herb recalled, for bringing in "new blood." It was also an idea that only people with huge financial resources might even have considered, given how much it cost to do medical research. An ordinary person could never imagine using their checkbook to get top-tier MDs and PhDs to shift their career path in a new direction. But billionaires like the Sandlers could imagine that, just as the Simonses—who had even more money—later had the same thought for pushing forward autism research.

Still, Marion's idea was risky, and the couple was nervous as their project got under way, soliciting research proposals on asthma from newcomers to the field. "Nobody knew whether it would work," Herb said. All doubts lifted once the applications started rolling in, including many from impressive scientists who'd never worked on asthma. In time, the organization the Sandlers helped start, the American Asthma Foundation, became the largest private funder of asthma research in the United States as the Sandlers pumped in $100 million that went out as grants. The foundation has brought over four hundred new researchers into the field, including at least three dozen who made major breakthroughs, such as advances that led to the development of new drugs. Its emergence has helped transform asthma research, with benefits for people of all economic levels.

Even greater universal gains may flow from a rising torrent of gifts for brain research. Paul Allen has been a leader here, pumping more than $500 million into the Allen Institute for Brain Science since 2003, but many other donors have followed. The Simonses' giving for autism research, which has totaled hundreds of millions of dollars, has mainly sought to understand this complex disorder of brain development. Likewise, much of the $450 million in grants that the Michael J. Fox Foundation has given to cure Parkinson's disease has gone to unlock the workings of the brain. Google co-founder Sergey Brin has been the single largest donor to the foundation, giving it at least $160 million. In late 2015, Chuck Feeney gave $177 million to the University of California, San Francisco (UCSF), for neuroscience research. Just a few months later, Sandy and Joan Weill gave even more for UCSF's brain work, $185 million.

Well before these donors came along, Herb and Marion Sandler had given more than $25 million for neuroscience at NCSF. That giving wasn't on par with the Sandlers' backing of work on asthma, but it could have a greater impact, along with all the other money flowing for brain research these days. Why? Because few health challenges will inflict a greater toll on America in the twenty-first century than the explosive rise of neurodegenerative diseases. Already, the costs of caring for five million Americans with Alzheimer's runs more than $250 billion a year, according to one study. Absent new medical breakthroughs, our society will be spending over a trillion dollars a year to care for thirteen million Alzheimer's sufferers. The global costs will be far higher.

When you hear that billionaires like Paul Allen are funding experimental brain research, it can sound like a perfect example of elite philanthropy unmoored from most people's day-to-day concerns. Allen, after all, is the same guy who's spending big for private space travel and also financed the world's largest airplane. His $200 million yacht, *Octopus*, has a ten-person submarine.

In fact, though, backing neuroscience is yet one more way that today's mega-givers may be changing the lives of millions of Americans, in this case for the better.

CAMPUS CASH

The vast money pouring into already-wealthy elite universities would seem to offer up a more clear-cut storyline of the upper class feathering its own nests—and amplifying its own influence. The gifts to such institutions have become ever larger in recent years and, in some cases, ever harder to justify.

Consider the $400 million donation that Nike founder Phil Knight made to Stanford University in early 2016. The money will be used to cover tuition and living expenses for just one hundred grad students a year at Stanford, which has one of the largest endowments in the United States, over $20 billion. The idea is to train the next generation of leaders who will go on to "address society's most intractable problems, including poverty and climate change."

Of course, though, there are plenty of talented leaders who are already in the trenches working on these problems—and could sure use some help from the likes of Phil Knight. It's hard to think of Stanford grad students, many of whom already get a tuition-free ride, as a needy bunch.

Since 2005, Stanford University, as well as the eight schools of the Ivy League, have received over thirty-five gifts of at least $100 million. (Stanford received four such gifts in 2015 alone.) During this same period, state funding for public universities and community colleges has fallen by 20 percent, according to some estimates, resulting in tuition hikes that put college out of reach for more low-income students. The value of Pell

Grants has also been falling for decades. Once, these federal grants for needy students covered most of the cost of attending a public university; now they cover just a third of that cost.

It's not surprising that the fortunes of elite schools have been soaring. A great many billionaires and multimillionaires have graduated from these schools. Knight got his MBA from Stanford, as did over 20 other billionaires. Harvard Business School has produced at least 64 billionaires, while one analysis found that 3,000 graduates of Harvard College were worth at least $30 million. Now richer than ever, the alums of wealthy universities are giving back in record-breaking ways. America's universities raised over $40 billion in 2015, with 28 percent of that money going to just 20 top universities, much of it donated by rich alums.

Unfortunately, the ranks of financial winners include few graduates of community colleges, and as a result big gifts to such institutions are rare. When LaGuardia Community College in New York City received a $2 million donation from Goldman Sachs in 2015, it doubled the school's endowment. The gift was unusual enough to make the *New York Times*. By comparison, Harvard raised an average of $3.1 million *a day* during 2015.

The richer schools are getting richer; the poor are getting poorer. Three-quarters of the $516 billion in endowment wealth held by U.S. colleges and universities in 2014 was concentrated in the hands of just 11 percent of schools. These numbers mirror broader inequalities in society.

The wealthy get a lot of credit for boosting the fortunes of higher education with their big gifts. But if you look at all their giving, philanthropic and political, the record is mixed. Many donors who give generously to their alma maters also give to conservative politicians and policy groups that have orchestrated cuts to public higher education. John Paulson, the hedge fund billionaire, is a great example. He's been a huge backer of a Republican Party that has repeatedly sought to cut Pell Grants nationally and has cut spending to public universities in the states. Paulson also became, in 2015, the biggest donor in Harvard's history when he made a $400 million gift to the school. That gift, to a university with a $36 billion endowment, could ultimately cost the U.S. Treasury more than $200 million, assuming this money would otherwise have been captured by estate taxes.

As it turns out, though, that huge Paulson gift shows why one should be wary of too quickly casting mega-giving to elite universities as another sign of emerging plutocracy.

Harvard isn't just a place where the already privileged are groomed to tell everyone else what to do. It also advances research in multiple disciplines, especially science, and has produced forty-seven Nobel laureates. Harvard spends around a billion dollars on research every year, with more than half that money coming from the federal government, and the lion's share going to studies in the life sciences aimed at yielding biomedical breakthroughs.

These numbers are a reminder that much of the advanced research that goes on in the United States is conducted at universities. Harvard isn't even a leader in this regard. Johns Hopkins spent $2.2 billion on research in 2014, with the bulk of that money coming from the federal government, and especially the National Institutes of Health.

Federal funding for medical research has fared better than most government programs in the past two decades because Congress is besieged by constituents demanding cures to diseases that kill hundreds of thousands of Americans every year. There's a lobbying group for every major disease you can think of. In contrast, funding for research on engineering, physics, and computational science has far fewer supporters, although breakthroughs in these areas are more likely to produce new inventions that drive economic growth. At most universities, including Harvard, researchers working outside the life sciences are more likely to struggle for funding, especially as the National Science Foundation gets hit with budget cuts.

This is where John Paulson's gift came in. The money went to bolster engineering and applied sciences at Harvard. Such research taps the building blocks of basic science—the sort of research backed by the Simons Foundation—to invent stuff, like nanotechnology, robotics, and artificial intelligence.

Paulson's gift was unusual in its size—and the ridicule it drew from critics—but otherwise it was similar to many of the largest gifts flowing to elite universities, many of which go to fund research. This has also been the focus of three other top higher education donors of our time: Michael Bloomberg, Gordon Moore, and Chuck Feeney.

Bloomberg has given more than $1 billion to Johns Hopkins, with most of that money going for research, including big investments in what became the Bloomberg School of Public Health. One gift, of $125 million, went to establish the Malaria Research Institute. Another, for $69 million, went to create the Institute for Cell Engineering, to advance stem-cell research. Yet another massive donation, in 2013, endowed fifty distinguished professors—the kind that mainly devote their time to research, not teaching.

Gordon Moore, the billionaire co-founder of Intel, has given $700 million to Caltech over the past fifteen years, helping turn this small school into one of the world's top research universities. He's been by far the biggest donor to a school that has fewer than 2,400 students—but has produced thirty-four Nobel laureates. As with other research universities, a steady stream of new inventions and new companies emerge from Caltech every year. Over 2,300 U.S. patents have been issued to Caltech researchers since 1985, and since 1995, 130 start-up companies have had their genesis on campus.

Chuck Feeney has spread his higher education gifts around more widely, but with a similar focus on research—like that $177 million gift for neuroscience he made to UCSF in 2015. Feeney gave his single biggest gift, of $350 million, to help finance a new Cornell science school on Roosevelt Island in New York City. Cornell Tech, as it is called, focuses on a "deep inquiry into many of the core disciplines of the digital age, including Computer Science, Electrical Engineering, Information Science, Operations Research and Business." The new school also landed a $133 million gift from Irwin Jacobs, the founder of Qualcomm, and $100 million from Michael Bloomberg, who as mayor championed the idea of turning Roosevelt Island into a tech center. Bloomberg saw his big private gift as helping along a project that would become a huge economic driver for New York, bringing new scientific talent to the city and producing new start-ups, jobs, and growth.

Meanwhile, the generosity of campus givers means that some of the nation's wealthiest schools are now able to offer a free ride to students from lower-income families. That practice was first started by Princeton in 2001, and since then the school has notably increased the economic diversity of its student body—although, overall, elite schools have made little progress on this front over the past few decades. And while more assistance may be flowing to needy students on these campuses, thanks to philanthropy, such giving also is a way that affluent alums transfer class privilege to their children, helping ensure "legacy" slots at elite schools that might otherwise go to more gifted students. It gets even worse. As Daniel Golden showed in his book, *The Price of Admission*, the kids of big donors who aren't alums often receivable favorable treatment at admission time. It's no secret that parents with wealth can buy their offspring a big head start in life. Less well known is how tax-deductible philanthropic gifts can be a means to this end.

Private money has long played a huge role in higher education. Now that role is growing, and this growth is especially striking at the state level, where there's been a surge of new philanthropic dollars flowing into public universities even as their state funding has been cut back. Between 1992 and 2010, state appropriations for public research universities dropped from 38 percent to 23 percent of the universities' total revenues.

Along the way, state schools got much better at currying favor with private donors. In 2015, six of the top twenty fundraising universities were public schools. In some cases, major donors have stepped forward in recent years to help public universities hit by budget cuts. Giving like this offers reassurance that it isn't just the Princetons pulling in big money these days, as the great wealth boom in recent decades has spread far beyond elite coastal enclaves. Rich people are everywhere, and many have fond memories of their alma maters.

Yet anyone who knows how campuses work also knows that donors have influence—especially when their money is viewed as indispensable. Today, America's public universities are being more heavily shaped by the wealthy than at any time since these institutions were created.

That clout can play out in troubling ways. At the University of Virginia, a cabal of wealthy donors forced out the school's president, Teresa Sullivan, in 2012, causing an uproar. She was later reinstated, but the underlying conditions that made the failed coup possible haven't changed. In 1990, the Virginia state government provided about a quarter of the university's budget. Two decades later, that proportion had dwindled to under 7 percent, which meant the school relied far more on the goodwill of major private donors—donors who often have strong opinions as to how a public university founded by Thomas Jefferson should be run.

In another case, documented by the *Los Angeles Times*, major donors to the University of Illinois reportedly pressured the school's leadership in 2014 to fire a professor, Steven Salaita, for a series of provocative tweets on Israel and Gaza. You can see why the university's officials might be so attuned to private donors, given that the Illinois university system has faced punishing cuts in public funding that began well before the 2008 recession. Between 2002 and 2015, state appropriations for higher education in Illinois fell by 20 percent.

Public universities in Michigan have also been hit by spending cuts in recent years, including Wayne State in Detroit. Between 2011 and 2016, with fiscal conservatives led by GOP governor Rick Synder in total control of Michigan's government, the school had been forced to accept $75 million in budget cuts. That battering may explain why leaders at Wayne State University in Detroit eagerly accepted a $40 million gift in 2015 from a wealthy local couple that came with controversial strings attached. Among other things, the donors were given input on the curriculum and strategic plan of the university's business school, as well as "aspects of the educational experience."

In his book *Unmaking the Public University,* Christopher Newfield documents the rising influence of private donors over state schools since the 1980s, and what it's meant to have these schools increasingly catering to the "preferences, and sometimes the narrow-minded whims, of powerful outside figures." The clout of donors on campus has risen in conjunction with that of corporations, which have also come to exercise new influence on campus through research funding and contracting, as Jennifer Washburn documented in her 2006 book, *University, Inc.: The Corporate Corruption of Higher Education.*

Some philanthropists have seen campus donations as a way to try to shape the ideology of students and the direction of academic research. After the so-called Powell memo of 1971 called on businesses to challenge liberalism on campuses, the Olin and Bradley foundations, both started by wealthy industrialists, poured money into campus work to promote free-market ideas. They underwrote research centers, endowed professorships and graduate scholarships. Charles Koch is another funder that moved aggressively to fund on campuses. In 2014 alone, his foundation directed $27 million in grants to some three hundred universities to back libertarian ideas that stress the virtues of markets and the downsides of government.

Koch has been interested in these ideas all his adult life. In his twenties, after graduating from MIT, he read lots of political theory at night while working as an energy consultant. He was deeply influenced by writers such as Friedrich Hayek and Michael Polanyi. He started making donations to think tanks and academic centers as early as the 1960s, and has so far channeled at least $200 million to universities alone. That's a big stream of funding, but Koch has said he plans to expand such giving down the line.

State schools have been among the biggest beneficiaries of Koch largesse—which has occasionally caused controversy. Florida State University was embroiled in a flap after it was alleged in 2011 that a Koch grant had come with stipulations about what faculty could be hired and fired by the school's economics department. The controversy caused a stir, and made national news. But it didn't dampen FSU's willingness to take $800,000 in additional Koch grants in 2016. Far bigger sums are flowing to other schools, like Montana State University, which landed a Koch $5.7 million grant the same year to fund research critical of government regulation.

It's not uncommon for donors to make various demands in return for campus cash. In one case, the foundation of BB&T Bank offered $1 million for business education to Western Carolina University, a public state school in Cullowhee, North Carolina. Among the reported stipulations of the gift was that the university's College of Business make *Atlas Shrugged* by Ayn Rand required reading for students. The school took the money.

This was not an isolated episode. The donor behind the offer, John Allison, the former chairman of BB&T and later the president of the Cato Institute, had offered similar deals to at least sixty-three schools going back over a decade. After Guilford College accepted a half-million dollar grant, with little consultation with faculty, a professor there wrote: "This deal with BB&T was simply an egregious case of the college administration deciding to sell a chunk of the curriculum."

Allison framed his goals in terms strikingly similar to how Lewis Powell had in 1971: as a pushback against the pervasive liberal orthodoxy on campuses. "It's really a battle of ideas," he told a reporter. "If the ideas that made America great aren't heard, then their influence will be destroyed." Allison said in 2011 that he hoped to extend his grants to two hundred schools, but by 2015, BB&T claimed that it was no longer making such grants.

Meanwhile, plenty of liberal donors also bankroll campus work. Williams Institute at UCLA's law school, initially underwritten by Chuck Williams and then backed by other top LGBT funders like Tim Gill, played a key role in formulating the legal ideas behind the quest for marriage equality and other anti-discrimination efforts. Thomas Piketty's treatise on inequality, *Capital in the Twenty-First Century,* was partly informed by research done at the Center for Equitable Growth at the University of California at Berkeley, which has been supported by Herb Sandler, among other donors. Sandler has funded a similar institute in Washington, D.C., that makes grants to academics who are exploring how to reduce inequality and boost growth. A research outfit fueled with $75 million from George Soros and tech leader Jim Balsillie, the Institute for New Economic Thinking, has been backing economists in the United States and around the world to challenge "free market fundamentalism."

The hedge fund billionaire Tom Steyer has donated millions for campus work on clean energy and climate change. Separately, through his NextGen Climate organization, Steyer has given money to register college students to vote.

In short, higher education is yet one more venue where more philanthropists are giving more money than ever in an effort to shape the direction of U.S. society.

Given the size of the federal budget, which totaled around $4 trillion in 2016, you might think that elected leaders would have plenty of leeway to increase spending on things like science, the arts, and education. Yet only about a quarter of the federal budget can be used in such discretionary ways, and far less if you don't count defense spending. The rest is committed by law to mandatory outlays, chiefly for entitlements like Medicare and Social Security, but also to pay interest on the national debt. This mandatory spending is projected to grow dramatically in the next few decades as the boomers retire and more debt payments come due. Budget analysts say that without big changes in current policies, federal mandatory spending will equal 21 percent of GDP by 2046—which is as much as *all* federal spending in recent years. The squeeze on discretionary outlays will only grow more intense as time goes on.

Even a major boost in revenue through higher taxes, along with entitlement reform—both of which would be heavy lifts in a polarized Washington, D.C.—may do little to lessen that squeeze. We're likely to see the steady shrinking of a pot of money that goes to not only science, education, and the arts, but also to NASA, the EPA, housing and community development, infrastructure, national parks, the Department of Energy, and so on. Already, according to one analysis, "the share of national income going to these programs . . . is rapidly approaching the lowest level (measured as a share of the economy) in at least five decades."

The upshot is that we're moving into an era in which dreamers who want to see big advances in areas like the arts, science, and higher education often feel they should be talking to people like Elon Musk, Paul Allen, or Alice Walton—the billionaires who actually have the resources to make stuff happen.

When philanthropists step into the breach left by a hollowed-out public sector, one reflex is to feel gratitude. I certainly felt that way, for example, when Jim Simons told me the story of how he had sounded the alarm for years about the decline of U.S. math education, an area he knew well, only to be ignored by Washington. Finally, he started funding a new program with his own money, Math for America (which now draws some state funding). That's obviously a good deed. And, just as obviously, it's troubling that it takes the wealth of a private citizen to tackle a problem that affects the entire U.S. economy.

The new mega-givers are not the villains in this story. Simons and other high-minded donors like him are coming along at a very fortuitous moment, and we should indeed be thankful as more of them step forward. Most are just trying to do a good thing. But as their power grows, so, too, must the scrutiny grow of how that power is used, along with the larger changes in U.S. society that are acting to amplify that power.

11

Agents of Wealth

In the 1985 movie *Brewster's Millions,* Richard Pryor played a bewildered heir who has to spend $30 million in thirty days in order to inherit a fortune ten times that size. Brewster gets to work, moving into a luxurious hotel suite and hiring staff at exorbitant rates. But he finds the job is much harder than he thought, especially after he accidentally makes his pile of money even bigger from business investments.

Any number of philanthropists have learned the same lesson that Brewster did in the movie: Giving away large amounts of money isn't easy. And the more money you have, the tougher it is to get rid of.

"Let's say you have $10 billion," one donor told me. "And you stick it in municipal funds that earn 3 percent. That's still $300 million a year you're making." Of course, many wealthy investors make much higher returns, and any number of billionaire philanthropists have seen their fortunes rise by huge leaps in the past decade.

Giving away lots of money is especially hard for donors who are gunning to make systemic changes in society—and aren't interested in tossing big chunks of wealth overboard by writing nine-figure checks to Harvard or the Met. If you want to have that deeper kind of influence with your money, you need a strong vision and strategy; you need to find the right leverage points and identify the best people to invest in.

Few major philanthropists can do this alone. They need help, which often means building a foundation.

Much has been written about the American foundation since it was invented over a century ago. One way to think about such institutions, at least early in their life cycle—when the original donor is still alive—is that they are incomparable vehicles for amplifying the influence that wealthy private citizens can have over society.

You don't fully appreciate this until you walk around a foundation created by a living donor, and see rows of offices filled with people working to advance that person's vision. It's hard for most of us to imagine hiring dozens, or hundreds, of professional staff to carry out any grand ideas we may have for reshaping society. (Bill and Melinda Gates now have some 1,400 people working at their foundation.) Yet the super-wealthy are setting up new institutions like this all the time, with enough money to hire top executives and experts from different fields. That's another thing unfathomable to most of us: that we could have former university presidents or cabinet secretaries or award-winning scientists on our own payroll.

Major philanthropists aren't just empowering themselves; they are empowering those who work for them—people who suddenly find themselves in charge of big resources that can be used to make things happen. These new agents of wealth have a unique kind of power, insulated from the whims of voters or shareholders, even as they wield influence on a par with some elected officials and corporate CEOs.

Foundation executives and program officers have long been familiar figures in the nonprofit world. Most have typically worked at legacy operations, where the original donor is long gone. And while that remains true today in raw numbers, more of these people now work for living donors who are involved in a hands-on way.

PARADIGM SHIFT

When wealthy people first get involved in philanthropy, they often spend some time floundering around. They tend to give reactively, as Jim and Marilyn Simons did at first. They put money here and there. They get advice from different people. They experiment. "We just sort of noodled it out ourselves," Jim said about the early years of the Simons Foundation. Some philanthropists never move past this stage. Their giving may remain pretty informal even as the dollar amounts get bigger and bigger, and some actively resist institutions that could become "bureaucracies," as the hedge fund billionaire Bruce Kovner put it.

Other philanthropists, though, find themselves hankering for more help getting money out the door in a smart way. They start looking for somebody who can turn a grab bag of giving into a real philanthropic operation, one that is focused and strategic. For the Simonses, that person—and a "paradigm shift"—came in the form of Gerry Fischbach, the research veteran who knew how to deploy money in search of scientific breakthroughs.

For John and Laura Arnold, it was Denis Calabrese.

Calabrese first met John Arnold at an event on education in 2010, and later got to talking to the couple about funding in this area. "What became clear to me is that they were dissatisfied with investments in education which were not going to produce systemic change," Calabrese told me. They weren't jazzed by the idea of building one charter or even ten charter schools. They "were wondering if there was a way to do something more lasting and systemic."

The Arnolds had started their foundation two years earlier, and their giving was pretty uncomplicated. They were big supporters of KIPP charter schools, and among the biggest backers of the Houston Food Bank. But when they met Calabrese, they were already starting to think more strategically—and ambitiously—about philanthropy, with an eye on grantmaking that could foster permanent changes. "I don't think they had terminology for it. They just had this instinct," said Calabrese

Calabrese has a diverse background. He'd gone to Rice University in Houston, and then been drawn into politics. "I wanted to change the world," he said. Calabrese worked in Congress, eventually becoming chief of staff to Republican representative Dick Armey in the 1990s. He grew jaded on Capitol Hill, coming to believe that Beltway politics "was not the way to change the world." So he returned to Texas and became a consultant, working with a range of clients, both corporate and nonprofit, on policy and communications. He became adept at pulling different levers of power—from lobbying and grassroots advocacy to litigation and advertising campaigns. Often, he was a hired gun for business clients fighting regulation—or prosecution. When Enron collapsed in 2001, Calabrese led the PR effort for ex-CEO Jeffrey Skilling, serving as his spokesman. (Skilling would later be convicted on federal felony charges related to Enron's demise.)

There are no standard qualifications for becoming a foundation president. While some such leaders emerge from the inside, after years climbing upward in foundations, the majority are recruited from outside philanthropy. Calabrese had never worked in a foundation, but he knew this universe. Some of his clients over the years had been foundations and major donors, and usually he was the guy telling these funders to think more strategically. What he liked about the Arnolds is that they already got it, and the couple and Calabrese began a series of conversations about how they could focus their giving more sharply to advance systemic changes. One criteria for such change, the three agreed, was that it would have to be scalable, so that it could have a large impact on society. Another is that it would have to be sustainable, to endure without ongoing philanthropic support.

The next big question, though, was how the Arnolds should pursue this goal. Was a traditional grantmaking foundation even the right vehicle? And, if it was, "would it be possible to assemble a group of people who would think about things in a more structural way as opposed to an incremental way?"

These conversations led to Calabrese's being named the first president of the Arnold Foundation in September 2010. He also became the third member of its board. Tightly held governance is not uncommon for foundations, even big ones. The Gates Foundation has just four trustees: William Gates Sr., Bill, Melinda, and Warren Buffett. In the early twentieth century, when John D. Rockefeller was petitioning Congress for a charter to create the first foundation, a top nonprofit leader of that time, Edward Devine, argued the charter should only be granted if public officials had some say over the selection of board members. The idea never went anywhere and has rarely been raised since. Foundations answer only to themselves.

With Calabrese in place as president, the Laura and John Arnold Foundation began to take shape. Within a year, it had a growing staff and swanky new offices in an office tower in downtown Houston. "I'm not the person who figures out what the ideas are," Calabrese said about what he brought to this effort. "I'm the one who if you tell me what the status quo is, and where you're trying to get to, I try to figure out the strategy to get there. The communications needs. And all the other stuff."

As the new president of the Arnold Foundation, Calabrese saw his job as advancing the overall goal of systemic change, while other senior staff brought expertise in specific issues. Three years into the job, he was making nearly $700,000. That level of pay is common for the head of a midsize foundation—and arguably quite generous for running an entity with no real bottom line, no competition, and no fear of ever going bankrupt. On the other hand, as the philanthropy expert Fay Twersky has written, after interviewing dozens of foundation CEOs, these jobs are harder than they look. Such executives must be able to "tend to their board of directors, to manage their organization internally, and to drive their foundation to make an impact externally. By their own reckoning, few CEOs are equally successful in all three domains."

After John Arnold closed his hedge fund, he and Laura were both in the office all the time. The Arnolds see their active role as an advantage. "It allows the staff to take more risks, ironically," John told me. "Foundations get very conservative after the founder passes, and you have a professional staff that answers to a third party board." He went on: "Our role is to push the staff to take risks. We'll sign off on it. So whenever we have projects that aren't successful, we'll have our name on it, too. . . . So it's not 'you're fired.' It's 'Okay, that didn't work. Let's add that to the feedback loop and figure out how to do this better next time.'"

When he was managing a hedge fund, Arnold's job was to carefully monitor the risk-taking of his traders—to make sure that hungry staff paid on commission didn't get reckless in their pursuit of big gains. "On the foundation side, it's the opposite," he said. There are few big upsides to risk-taking in a grantmaking environment for staff, in terms of rewards—but some obvious downsides if things go wrong. Along with Calabrese, the Arnolds wanted to ensure a different dynamic, one in sync with their belief that philanthropy "should think big, take risks, and be aggressive and highly goal-oriented."

As the Arnold Foundation expanded, it was soon staffed with a core group of experts. Philanthropists have a major edge in recruiting talent, offering salaries higher than what nonprofits or academic institutions pay. The biggest allure for those joining foundations is having the resources to help advance causes they care about. The initial focus was education, criminal justice, and pension reform—issues that the Arnolds were already interested in before Calabrese came along. But the agenda quickly expanded to include other issues, including health care, scientific integrity, and inequality. The foundation opened an office in New York City, and eventually one in Washington. More staff were hired. In 2012, the foundation gave out $40 million. In 2014, it gave out $85 million. In 2015, it gave out $185 million.

Foundation expansion can take on a momentum of its own, once more senior staff start to come on board. With new people come new ideas for doing more things and giving away more money. Initiatives proliferate, along with people to carry them out. Was the growth of the Arnold Foundation an example of what many donors, like Bruce Kovner, fear—that staff would create their "own agenda," with a result of "mission drift"? Calabrese didn't think so. The expanding agenda had its own logic, he said, which was pretty simple: "As we learned more, and talked to more people, we started to get interested in other areas."

Philanthropists with ambitious, complex goals for influencing society are likely to feel the strongest need to build up major foundations. If you're trying to achieve breakthroughs in science, as the Simonses are, you need expert help. The same is true if you're on a quest for paradigm-shifting solutions to stubborn public policy problems, as the Arnolds are—although even as their foundation added staff, it remained lean compared to some older foundations that, over time, have developed ever more infrastructure.

Then there's a donor such as Bill Ackman, who—like the Arnolds—is looking for the big score, impact-wise, with his philanthropy but has still resisted creating much of an infrastructure. Ackman does his giving with the help of just a few staff working at his hedge fund offices overlooking Central Park in Manhattan. He echoed Kovner's fear that foundations can "become horrible bureaucracies." Ackman's day job involves managing billions of dollars and making frequent bets that hinge on understanding complex issues and data. The key to success, he believes, isn't having staff studying things to death—but asking the right questions to see whether an idea, and the person behind it, can succeed. "I don't think overhead is particularly productive," he told me.

Eli Broad is another philanthropist with large ambitions who hasn't built a large organization. "I don't believe in huge staffs," he said. One reason he cited is that it's easier for a donor to shift direction, pulling the plug on certain lines of grantmaking, if you don't have to deal with internal constituencies. Quite a few other top philanthropists who've emerged in the past decade or two think the same way, including Herb Sandler, who's hired few staff at the Sandler Foundation even as it gives tens of millions of dollars away every year. Sandler talks about the formula for high-impact philanthropy in ways similar to Ackman: It's all about betting big on the right people working the right leverage points with the right ideas.

Like many new philanthropists who focus their giving narrowly and strategically, Sandler tends to scratch his head at how many big legacy foundations operate: slicing and dicing their grantmaking budgets across hundreds of nonprofits, most of which never achieve the scale that's needed to have impact. In fact, that approach is really not so surprising at foundations with large program staff who develop their own agendas, forming attachments to certain work and grantees. Also, when a foundation has a lot of staff, each with their own pet interests and professional networks, more nonprofits have routes to land a grant—as well as an ally inside to defend that grant at renewal time. There are good reasons that newer philanthropists worry about creating bureaucracies.

Many top philanthropists don't have foundations at all. Sanford Weill and Denny Stanford, for example, have both given away over a billion dollars without much help from permanent staff. A proliferation of consulting firms, along with full-service donor-advised funds and intermediaries like New Profit, makes it easier than ever to engage in large-scale grantmaking without building up a foundation of one's own.

On the other hand, some lean funders have run into big problems with their approach. Ackman put $25 million into the bid to reform Newark schools based on a pitch from Cory Booker. He believed in Booker and saw the bet as about "investing in a person." Some better staffing might have been helpful here.

The Arnolds' operation, as it evolved, landed in between the poles of bureaucratic and lean. It's a substantial organization, yet one determined to remain nimble—and to keep up the momentum. This is not a foundation designed to exist in perpetuity. The Arnolds' goal, along with so many younger donors, is to give away all their money while they are still living.

IMMORTAL INFLUENCE

Plenty of living donors still favor traditional foundations that have limitless lifespans and embrace an ethos of stewardship. Amos and Barbara Hostetter are a case in point. They are part of the Boston Brahmin elite, or what's left of it—a world that frowns on big egos and brash pronouncements. Amos attended a prestigious private school before going on to Amherst and Harvard—and then making his fortune in cable television. Barbara became a pillar of Boston's nonprofit world, sitting on multiple boards. The couple live in a mansion on stately Beacon Hill and embrace a more restrained vision of how philanthropists should operate. They aren't in a rush to deploy their multi-billion-dollar fortune in an urgent push for systemic change. Rather, they have aimed to endow a foundation that will exist in perpetuity, providing a steady flow of resources to improve life in Boston and New England.

The Hostetters started their Barr Foundation in 1987 and for years moved slowly in their giving. That pace is common for many older donors who accumulate their wealth over decades and, as they age, gradually ramp up their philanthropy. An advantage of this approach is that there's plenty of time for trial and error. "We didn't start with being the smartest people in the room," Barbara once said. "We knew we had a good learning curve ahead of us."

For many years, the Hostetters kept their giving anonymous, quietly becoming one of the biggest funders in Boston as they funneled grants to the arts, education, and more. Even after they went public with their giving, the foundation kept things quiet, with a modest staff overseen by low-key executive directors who reported to the couple. But the foundation steadily grew in size, adding more staff and programs. By 2013, it had assets of $1.6 billion, making it the biggest foundation in New England.

Barr became more influential in Boston as its money flowed everywhere. It was among the city's biggest private funders of education, as well as the arts. In 2010, emerging from behind the scenes, it announced a $50 million initiative to reduce carbon emissions by backing work on energy efficiency and public transportation. All the while, Amos Hostetter cultivated other levers of influence as a mover and shaker in local business circles, as well as a campaign donor and advisor to politicians. He and Barbara were prototypical super-citizens.

The Hostetters' path to influence may have been low-key and modest (they rarely spoke to the media), but it was highly effective. Among other things, their wide power network made it easier for the Barr Foundation to do things in collaboration with partners, such as city government or other foundations. Barr would come to forge an especially close relationship with the Klarman Family Foundation, a more recent arrival to Boston philanthropy, which is piloted by the hedge funder Seth Klarman and his wife, Beth—who share the Hostetters' keen interest in the local arts. In 2013, *Boston Magazine* ranked Amos and Barbara Hostetter among the twenty-five most powerful people in the city.

At some point, the couple decided it was time to take their foundation to the next level. For all the money they'd given to Barr, they had even more sitting on the sidelines, another $3 billion or so. While they never commented on their plans for that wealth, the foundation was an obvious destination—assuming it had the capacity to handle such an expansion.

The Hostetters began to scout around for a top-tier executive to run Barr. One candidate who emerged was Jim Canales, then president of the James Irvine Foundation in California. Canales, still in his forties, had spent almost his entire career at Irvine. He'd ascended the ranks quickly at the foundation, a top regional funder, becoming its CEO in 2003. Along the way, he'd become a subtle thinker about foundations, and saw their CEOs as leaders who manage key "tensions" within the institution. There is a natural tension, Canales told me, between "constancy and change"— having staying power on a set of issues, but also taking on new things. As well, there's a tension between tackling urgent challenges and having a long-term perspective. A foundation needs to be focused and strategic, Canales believes, but also flexible.

When he was first approached about the Barr job in 2013, Canales wasn't interested. He was happy at Irvine and a lifetime native of San Francisco. Canales had grown up in the city in a lower-middle-class family, with divorced parents. His father was a cab driver, his mother a waitress. He was raised mainly by his great-grandmother, who was from Nicaragua and spoke only Spanish. As a student at a Jesuit high school, Canales got interested in public service, but even through college and graduate school, at Stanford, he never aspired to work in foundations. "I don't think it's necessarily a career path that one thinks about: 'Oh, I'm going to become a professional philanthropist.'" Few young people—and, indeed, few Americans—know the first thing about the rarefied realm of grantmaking.

Canales went into teaching after Stanford and, in his mid-twenties, stumbled into a job at Irvine by accident, through a connection with its president, Dennis Collins, who hired him as a special assistant in 1993. Within ten years, after holding several positions at Irvine, Canales was running the place.

Beyond feeling settled in his life in the Bay Area, Canales wasn't interested in the Barr job because he'd heard stories about the difficulties of working with living donors or family members. Over half of all U.S. foundations are controlled by families, and "crazy," is how one veteran consultant described to me the dynamics at some of these institutions. Canales was more diplomatic, a trait he's known for, referring obliquely to "the history, and the relationships that exist" at foundations controlled by living donors and/or their heirs. He preferred working in a more professionalized setting where there "aren't other layers or agendas or relationships at play."

Still, Canales agreed to meet the Hostetters for lunch when the couple was on a visit to San Francisco, to offer advice about Barr's governance. During that conversation, and in more talks that followed through the fall of 2013, Canales found the Hostetters "thoughtful and strategic," and grew excited about their vision. For one thing, they didn't want Barr to be a family foundation; rather, their goal was to gradually expand the board, beyond just the two of them, to include a majority of outsiders. Barr's new president would be the first addition, and that was a second thing that excited Canales: the Hostetters were really looking for a partner, one who could take the foundation to the next stage, past its adolescence, as Barbara described it.

The Hostetters also liked Canales, with his seasoned views on how foundations should operate. The couple had been funding in the same core areas for many years and weren't looking for a radical makeover. What they wanted was a more strategic foundation that delivered higher impact—but in a style consistent with how the Hostetters had long operated. Here, too, the couple felt confident about Canales. "His values are akin to our own," Barbara would tell a reporter. "He believes in humility and collaboration and partnerships in philanthropy."

Given Barr's big footprint in Boston's civic life, these values aren't just a matter of personal taste. They help reduce the chance that the foundation's growing local power will invite a backlash. After all, who are Amos and Barbara Hostetter, whatever their good intensions, to have so much influence in a city that led the way in rejecting dynastic rule by Britain's royal family?

The more Canales thought about leading Barr, the more he was drawn to the idea. "It was really about building something," he told me. "It wasn't a start-up, but it was about taking something . . . to its next level as an institution." Canales' husband, a doctor, would have plenty of opportunities in Boston, with its many hospitals. So, finally, Canales said yes. A press release announcing the hire said he would "lead a strategic planning process to explore how Barr might grow over time, leveraging its local work, taking good ideas to scale, and extending its impact regionally, nationally, and internationally." His salary was $700,000 a year, a nice bump up from what he'd been making at Irvine.

As it turned out, Canales's first order of business after arriving at Barr in 2014 was streamlining its work, not expanding it.

Foundations can evolve haphazardly in their early years, especially if the donors behind them circulate widely and aren't good at saying no. Also, once a nonprofit starts getting support, and comes to rely on that money, it becomes hard to cut the cord. Grantees can accumulate over time, spreading a foundation too thin and dissipating its impact. By the time Canales arrived at Barr, it seemed as though it was funding every major nonprofit in Boston—sometimes without a strong strategy driving that blizzard of grants. The foundation had also started a global program, jumping into a vast new area.

Canales launched a planning process aimed at getting a handle on things. The global work was the first to go, with that program soon shutting its doors. As the internal discussions went on, Barr decided to really double down on Boston and New England, rather than expand nationally. That was an important choice, and a disciplined one, since many funders hanker to operate on a grand stage where they can shape federal policy. Even with over a billion dollars in assets, though, the Hostetters and Canales saw that the foundation would likely have a larger impact by remaining a big fish in a small pond.

The streamlining continued. Barr was especially overextended in its education giving, and Canales worked to sharpen the focus in that area. Here, he said, "we really did take a step back. We wanted to see if there was some particular zone where Barr could have a unique impact." The new strategic plan called for helping young people develop the skills and critical thinking needed to succeed in future careers, a grantmaking strategy Canales had earlier brought to Irvine.

As Barr's planning was wrapping up, Canales wrote in a blog post that education would be the "area of biggest transition" for the foundation. That kind of language strikes terror in grantees. And, sure enough, some education-related nonprofits that had long gotten Barr grants soon discovered that this support would be "winding down"—another phrase that stalks the nightmares of nonprofit executives.

The foundation world is famously genteel, even as strong disagreements roil beneath the surface. Canales embodies that civility, and he wielded a scalpel and anesthesia, not a meat cleaver, as he streamlined and professionalized Barr. As a foundation lifer, Canales also exhibits the cautious instincts that philanthropoids often are criticized for. The new Barr, like the old, wouldn't be gunning for disruptive or systemic changes. Instead, Canales talks soothingly about the foundation's melding the roles of "steward" and "catalyst"—language that very much reflects the Hostetters' sensibilities.

That approach might not yield the kind of big near-term impacts that many younger funders aim for these days, but it's attuned to the downsides of billionaires treating society as guinea pigs as they throw around money in search of breakthroughs. While new entrepreneurial funders talk with pride about their willingness to take risks, veteran funders like Canales know that such risk-taking can jerk people around. At one point, Canales wrote a blog post saying that while Barr embraced risk, it was mindful that screwups by the foundation could "burden the very people it is our mission to serve." To Canales's careful way of thinking, the key in pushing the envelope is "balance."

Another difference between Barr and a place like the Arnold Foundation is that it's being designed to exist in perpetuity. This choice tends to be more common among donors who are loyal to a place, as the Hostetters are to Boston—where, presumably, extra resources to address problems will always come in handy. The perpetuity model also syncs up with the couple's stewardship view of philanthropy—one that stresses the need to nurture key institutions and people over long periods of time.

This model means that Barr will be limited in its ability to place truly big bets, since it has to husband its resources. But perpetuity offers a path to influence that's compelling in its own way. In decades to come, or centuries, Barr's endowment is likely to grow many times.

The Hostetters may be powerful in Boston today. But long after they are gone, their money might be speaking even more loudly in the city and region than it does now. In effect, Barr is immortal.

LEGACY

In the 1990s, when he had a net worth of several billion dollars, George Soros—already a major philanthropist—often said that he wouldn't leave a foundation behind when he died. Soros shared the common fear that such institutions tended to grow bureaucratic and ineffective. His goal was to give away all his money during his lifetime—or even sooner, at one point saying that he'd wind up his philanthropy by 2010.

This turned out to be overly ambitious. Even as Soros gave away more and more money, with grants going to every part of the world, he kept getting richer at an even faster rate. His legendary Quantum Fund averaged annual returns of over 25 percent. By 2005, with a net worth of $7 billion, Soros announced at his seventy-fifth birthday party that he wouldn't try to give away all his money after all and would leave a foundation behind. It was a wise decision—since a decade later, even with Soros's annual giving running over $900 million a year, his fortune had grown larger still, to $24 billion.

Soros's sprawling Open Society Foundations (OSF) is the largest and most complex foundation ever created. It has branches in thirty-seven countries and is involved in an endless array of issues. Although Soros is best known for his activities in the former communist bloc, his foundation now operates throughout Africa, as well as in the Middle East, Latin America, and parts of Asia. OSF also funds throughout the United States.

Soros started giving in the late 1970s, and greatly stepped things up in the 1980s as he sought to weaken totalitarian rule in the Soviet bloc. Once communism collapsed, he pivoted to the next challenge of making sure the new nations that arose embraced the ideals of an open society, which to Soros meant that everyone should be heard in public life and no one should have a monopoly on the truth.

In 1993, Soros hired Aryeh Neier to run his foundation and to lead its expansion into other parts of the world, too, including the United States. For nearly twenty years, Neier and Soros were a dynamic duo, divvying up the planet's problems, with Soros charting OSF's work on economic development and higher education, while Neier—who had co-founded Human Rights Watch—took point on rights and political development. Together, the two men built a formidable philanthropic organization— but one also known for its fragmentation and maddening, jerry-rigged qualities. Outsiders found it hard to understand the place; grantees and staff often had the same complaint. Even board members didn't always know where grant money was going. In fact, no single board had full authority over the entire foundation.

Soros knew there was a problem. And when he named a new president in 2011, after Neier retired, he told the *New York Times*: "We have a very complex organization. It has become too complicated, and it needs to be streamlined, to become more unified."

The stakes were high in taming OSF. Soros, now in his eighties, wouldn't be around forever, and it was critical to build a foundation where he wasn't the glue holding things together. One bleak scenario was that Soros's far-flung philanthropic operation could splinter after he dies. "It could be like the former Yugoslavia," a former OSF executive told me.

The larger picture was that Soros's life work of advancing open society wasn't going so well. During the 1990s, Soros had been widely celebrated for his foundation's role in bringing down communism and encouraging the spread of democracy. By the early twenty-first century, though, history was moving in the opposite direction, with many countries led by authoritarian rulers. In the former Soviet bloc, OSF grantees were coming under new pressure from repressive regimes. Hard-fought gains by the foundation were slipping away.

Soros, who became more active in his foundation after retiring from his hedge fund, had no intention of ceding the fight in whatever time he had left.

The new president of OSF was Chris Stone, whom Soros called an "outsider insider." Stone had come to know OSF well, as both a grantee working on criminal justice reform and an advisor to the foundation. When he was tapped to lead OSF, he was teaching at Harvard's Kennedy School, and he came across more as a brainy academic than as the guy you'd hire to wrangle an organizational octopus, much less to go up against, say, the thugs who run Turkmenistan.

But Stone was a seasoned nonprofit leader, who earlier ran the Vera Institute of Justice, and while at Harvard, he had spent much time thinking about management as director of the Hauser Center on Nonprofit Organizations. Stone's mission at OSF was to build a foundation that, as he told me, was "working with a meaningful budget" designed to advance "a meaningful strategy that is clear and expressed," which the board had "a meaningful role in shaping." While those goals were elementary, they'd be a huge step forward for a foundation well known for its creative chaos. And they'd ensure that OSF could carry forth Soros's vision when Soros himself was no longer active.

That vision has always included a strong appetite for policy combat, along with a willingness to engage in controversial causes that other funders steer clear of. For example, no philanthropist has done more than Soros to soften America's drug laws. Soros got behind that cause in the mid-1990s, funding a new drug policy think tank and bankrolling the push for medicinal marijuana, widely seen as a bridge to legalization. Today, two decades after Soros began his push—and many tens of millions of dollars later—several states have legalized pot, and more are likely to follow.

OSF was also the first major foundation to get behind same-sex marriage. From 2000 to 2005, a pivotal period in the marriage equality fight, OSF invested millions in LGBT rights organizations. This early money, some of which went to back state-level fights, like a 2005 legal challenge in Iowa, was arguably more important than the bigger money that came in from other funders later on. OSF grants also went to frontline activist groups fighting for immigrants and, later, to Black Lives Matter.

As early as 1996, before Soros had become a bogeyman of the American right, the *New York Times* would write: "While other foundations and philanthropists are more comfortable healing the sick, housing the poor or feeding the hungry, Mr. Soros is unabashed in pursuing a political agenda." The *Times* described Soros as a billionaire who "redefines charity," but it couldn't have predicted just how influential his model would come to be over the next two decades. In some ways, Soros's activist giving marked the start of today's modern era of big philanthropy by living donors.

OSF's biggest focus has always been overseas, where it's backed efforts to attack government corruption, support dissidents, and champion the right of persecuted minorities, like the Roma of Europe and the Rohingya of Burma. It's funded Palestinian groups challenging Israeli policies in the Occupied Territories, and financed a long-running effort to combat the immense graft and abuses around extractive industries, such as oil. Endless grants have flowed to youth activists, human rights lawyers, and documentary filmmakers. At some point or another, nearly every justice and rights group on almost every continent has gotten OSF money.

And the plan, as George Soros faced his mortality, was to keep that spigot open forever. Embracing a perpetuity model, OSF would be a lifeline for contrarian voices until, potentially, the end of time.

Soros had never endowed his foundation. It was always a pay-as-you-go operation, which is not uncommon among living donors. Soros preferred to keep his money in his hedge fund, which kept scoring huge gains even after he officially retired. In 2013, the first year after Soros stepped down from actively running it, his fund—now basically an outsized family office, led by his son Robert—returned gains of 24 percent. Soros himself made $4 billion that year.

While Soros has not signed the Giving Pledge, Chris Stone said that the board and staff have "every expectation that the bulk of his fortune will be left, one way or the other, to the foundation. And we are building an organization capable of governing and deploying that resource as responsibly as possible to fulfill his mission." Assuming all goes as planned, though, OSF will someday have one of the biggest foundation endowments in the world.

After three years in what was surely one of the toughest jobs in philanthropy, Stone had made good progress toward unifying OSF and streamlining its operations. The foundation has put in place a stronger system of board governance, as well as a unified budgetary process. Soros himself was more involved with the foundation than he had been in years, talking with Stone nearly every day and traveling to the foundation's local offices.

Even in his mid-eighties, Soros thought nothing of setting off to Ukraine or some other faraway place to see for himself what was happening. Still, Soros didn't micromanage Stone and remained committed to the long-term shift of authority to OSF's governing board. While his children sat on that board, they didn't have a majority voice. The idea was that the post-Soros OSF would be run by a collection of eminent leaders, not the Soros family.

After Stone's hard labor, the foundation was still a place where, occasionally, the left hand didn't know what the right hand was doing, but those days were coming to an end. For all its past achievements, OSF was being bolstered and reshaped to possibly wield even more influence in coming decades—and maybe for centuries beyond.

ENDGAME

Not long before George Soros abandoned his quest to give away his fortune while still living, Chuck Feeney got serious about doing exactly that. In 1984, Feeney had transferred all his business assets to his foundation, The Atlantic Philanthropies, which operated anonymously for years with a small staff. In 2002, the foundation announced it would cease all grant-making within a finite period of time—2016 to be exact. At the time, its endowment stood at $3.5 billion, which was hardly an insurmountable amount of money to dump overboard.

Flash-forward to 2015. With the clock ticking down, Atlantic still had hundreds of millions to dispose of. And the man charged with getting rid of the money, Chris Oescheli, Atlantic's CEO, was under a lot of stress. "To do this well is not an easy job," he told me.

By this time, Atlantic had long ago emerged from the shadows and Feeney himself had become an iconic figure in modern philanthropy. He'd been the subject of a biography, *The Billionaire Who Wasn't*, and of numerous articles about the odd rich guy "trying to go broke," as *Forbes* put it. For years, Feeney had stood out as an evangelist for "giving while living," in his catchy phrase. "I see little reason to delay giving when so much good can be achieved through supporting worthwhile causes today," Feeney once said. Now that same logic was being widely embraced by many new funders, especially in the tech world. Young philanthropists like Dustin Moskovitz and Sean Parker share Feeney's belief that a donor could have the most impact by front-loading their giving in the form of big bets—and that foundations were most effective when the clock was ticking. Tim Gill, the LGBT funder, is also among those tech funders who have set a sunset date for his foundation. "If you're talking about social change, your objective should be to improve the lives of people as dramatically and as soon as possible," Gill told me. His husband, Scott Miller, added: "It's given us the mind-set that we need to act fast. These foundations that go on in perpetuity—where do they get a sense of urgency?" The Gill Foundation's own impatient, forward-looking posture is a key reason it's been so effective at advancing LGBT rights faster than anyone had once thought possible.

Eli Broad is another funder who's been in a hurry and can't think of any reason to leave the job of giving away his billions to someone else. He told me: "If you have the resources, and you have the talent, you should use it—rather than leaving it in a foundation, with people who don't have any idea of what the founder wanted."

The debate between continuing in perpetuity and spending down sooner is almost as old as modern philanthropy itself, although it's been getting a lot more attention lately as new funders sort out their plans. At one of the annual convenings of the Giving Pledge members, the staff organized a panel that featured voices on either side of this issue.

Long before Feeney popularized giving while living, the early-twentieth-century philanthropist Julius Rosenwald preached the same gospel—with a remarkably similar slogan, "Give While You Live." The founder of Sears, Roebuck, Rosenwald's name is now largely forgotten precisely because he didn't emulate contemporaries like John D. Rockefeller and Andrew Carnegie in creating a permanent foundation. Yet Rosenwald may have had as much impact as either philanthropist because of what he did do, which was to sink a lot of his fortune into helping build 5,300 schools for black children throughout the South. It was the kind of huge up-front capital investment that a more cautious foundation, mindful of preserving its endowment, would never have made. But Rosenwald's cash and boldness had a transformative effect on African-American chances in the Jim Crow South, where his schools educated the likes of John Lewis, who helped lead the civil rights movement long after Rosenwald was gone.

Chuck Feeney never found a leverage point quite that profound. But the staff at Atlantic was very focused on systemic change, and the imperative to spend down meant they had the resources to put lots of money behind bold efforts to redirect public policy—and society. In 2009, Atlantic became the single biggest backer of hard-hitting advocacy to help enact the Affordable Care Act, with a $27 million gift to the progressive coalition Health Care for America Now (HCAN). That grant was made by Gara LaMarche, the foundation's CEO at the time, who'd perfected the art of using money to shape policy during his many years leading George Soros's U.S. giving.

Chris Oechsli, who succeeded LaMarche in 2011 as Atlantic's CEO, had spent time in the U.S. Senate, as a top aide to Democrat Russ Feingold. His main background, though, was in business—as well as in working with Feeney and Atlantic over many years.

Oechsli found the job of winding down Atlantic difficult not just because the clock was ticking ever more loudly by 2015, but because the foundation had grand ambitions for how to deploy its final millions. It aimed to make a series of big "culminating grants" to nonprofits that could keep achieving important gains long after Atlantic was gone—what Oechsli called "champion organizations." According to one planning document, Atlantic's goal was to build on its previous grantmaking with the hope of "catalyzing transformative, systemic change" in the fields and countries where it had worked for years, including the United States. The overall aim of such change was greater equity, and to "enhance opportunity for people who have unfairly been denied that opportunity," Oechsli said.

The culminating grants would be on the order of $10 million to $20 million, the kind of money that most nonprofit CEOs could never even dream of getting. But how would Atlantic decide which groups got these transformative gifts? "There are more champions than we can possibly support," Oechsli sighed. "But we're trying really hard to identify those institutions that can make a lasting impact."

That challenge—of who to bet on—is a familiar one for foundation CEOs. Few such executives, though, had ever faced such an intense deadline for deciding where to put their chips. "It's complicated and stressful," Oechsli told me.

Some choices were easy. A large culminating grant went to the ACLU, which was founded nearly a century earlier and was widely admired by funders for its skill at engaging legal and policy contests. Atlantic's big infusion of cash, $10 million, would specifically aim to bolster the ACLU's advocacy powers, including at the state level, where so many key issues were decided.

Another culminating grant went to the Center for Budget and Policy Priorities, for over thirty years a stalwart defender of U.S. government programs to aid the poor. Few Beltway groups had done more to beat back conservative efforts to "drown government in the bathtub," as Grover Norquist famously put it. Yet the center did have a major weakness: It had never been very good at generating new policy ideas or reframing debates over the long term. It was more of a finger-in-the-dike operation than an effort to redirect the river, which is what places like Heritage and Cato were focused on. Atlantic's huge grant aimed to help the center do a better job playing offense—promoting new ways to reduce poverty, as opposed to just blocking the latest round of Draconian cuts.

To transform America's health-care system in a more equitable way, Atlantic gave a culminating grant to Community Catalyst, a Boston-based group known for its advocacy of progressive health-care policies, including its extensive work to help implement the Affordable Care Act in the face of fierce GOP opposition. The money would fund a new push to empower consumers using the health system. Much of it would go for investments in advocacy and leadership. Separately, Atlantic gave over a million dollars to Community Catalyst's 501(c)(4) arm, which could engage more directly in political battles.

Atlantic's big grants kept flowing through 2015 and into 2016, when it announced $200 million in investments to create a community of leaders that can promote equity on a global scale. Nearly half of that money went to establish a new Atlantic Fellows program at the London School of Economics and Political Science. The larger half, $106 million, was a fifteen-year grant to create the Atlantic Institute, which the foundation said will be a "nexus" for the fellows to collaborate as they work to make the world a better place.

"Change is always about people," Oechsli told me about this new effort, launched as the foundation got ready to finally wrap up its grant-making. The idea, he said, is to create a "community of actors" that will have a big impact on equity challenges worldwide. Oechsli said Atlantic hoped to help shift the global narrative on this issue, "retelling the story about what's unfair and biased."

That's a lofty goal, even for a funder as aggressive as Atlantic. Will Feeney's billions ultimately have as much impact as Julius Rosenwald did, or as contemporaries like George Soros do? It's too early to say. But it's hard to recall a more urgent quest for influence than Atlantic's spend-down push over the past decade.

In 1910, when Edward Devine argued that the proposed Rockefeller Foundation should have to abide by certain constraints, one of them was a limited lifespan: He said the foundation should have to dissolve after one hundred years. That idea, along with a limit on the foundation's size and a public role in selecting its trustees, was incorporated into a bill put before the U.S. Congress in 1911. Such was the hostility to Rockefeller, though, and the fears of a powerful foundation, that Congress rejected the proposal. The Rockefeller Foundation would later be incorporated in New York State with none of the conditions that Devine had proposed. Nor would such stipulations be applied to the tens of thousands of foundations that were subsequently created.

Today's critics of philanthropy fixate often on perpetuity, which some see as prime evidence that foundations are accountable to no one—not even, eventually, to the people who created them. Rather, they become shadowy entities on autopilot—amassing ever greater wealth and wielding enormous clout even as they answer only to themselves.

All that may be true. But forcing foundations to spend down is hardly a way to limit the influence of private money over public life. On the contrary, as we've seen, living donors in a hurry can be far more aggressive in trying to reshape public policy. If all philanthropists were compelled to act as Chuck Feeney has, it's likely that philanthropy's influence in U.S. society would actually be much greater. That could be a good thing, to the extent that more resources are focused on big problems, like climate change or poverty. Or it could be a bad thing, as public debates increasingly become a clash of philanthropic titans, with ordinary Americans sitting on the sidelines.

As for which model of giving the majority of new donors will actually embrace, that remains to be seen. The spend-down approach is certainly popular right now, especially among younger tech philanthropists like Mark Zuckerberg. Down the line, though, as these donors find out how hard it is to unload big money quickly and effectively, they may revisit the idea of leaving behind foundations—just as George Soros did.

Whatever the case, one thing is clear: It's not just the new philanthropists who are wielding more power these days. It is those they are deputizing to dispose of their wealth, a group whose ranks are fast expanding as more foundations are born and grow. In coming decades, this segment of America's elite class will loom ever larger in national life.

Epilogue:
Balancing Act

In the summer of 2015, a fierce debate played out in Washington, D.C., and across the media, over a proposed deal to curtail Iran's nuclear program.

It was hard to recall a foreign policy fight quite like this one, with donors opening their checkbooks to finance millions of dollars in advertisements, lobbying efforts, and policy reports aimed at shaping not just what Congress did, but how elites and the public thought about the deal.

Just how much money were we talking about? Nobody could say for sure—and they still can't—since the nonprofits leading the charge on both sides don't have to reveal the identity of their donors or the amounts they gave. But estimates ranged in the tens of millions of dollars, with a good chunk of that anonymous money flowing through 501(c)(4) groups that opposed the deal, like Citizens for a Nuclear Free Iran. In this way, the Iran fight was another reminder of the lax regulation of nonprofits, even as they have become ever more powerful bullhorns for wealthy donors.

This doesn't seem quite what Alexis de Tocqueville had in mind when he famously opined about how U.S. civil society gave voice to the everyman. To be sure, nonprofits still do that, and in myriad ways, but there's been a big change in recent decades in who's orchestrating public conversations. The mass membership organizations of earlier eras, which were fueled by the dues of ordinary citizens, have become less important, while wealthy philanthropists have grown more numerous and empowered.

This shift has occurred alongside a parallel shift in electoral politics, where the donor class has come to wield greater clout as political parties have declined and voter turnout has remained anemic.

The swollen river of money coming into America's democracy has drawn attention for years. Less understood is how philanthropic dollars make up a key tributary in that river—often helping set the agenda on key policy issues well before they come onto the radar of elected officials or voters.

The Iran nuclear debate showcased that. Years of tax-deductible gifts to think tanks and advocacy groups helped to shape the larger terms of the Iran debate long before negotiators reached a final deal. For example, scholars at the American Enterprise Institute, heavily backed by Wall Street donors, had endlessly pounded the point—in op-eds, congressional testimony, and TV appearances—that Iran couldn't be trusted, as did other outfits like the Center for Security Policy.

On the other side, the peace group Ploughshares, backed by foundations and major donors, played a key behind-the-scenes role in pushing forward U.S.-Iran dialogue starting in the early 2000s. The Rockefeller Brothers Fund was among the top funders of this work, a reminder of the long reach of old money into current debates. Another key player was J Street, which describes itself as the "political home for pro-Israel, pro-peace Americans who want Israel to be secure" and was founded in 2007. Bringing a less hawkish Jewish voice to debates over the Middle East, J Street would emerge as a leading proponent of the deal with Iran—acting as a counterweight to the more conservative American-Israel Political Action Committee (AIPAC), which had long dominated Beltway debates over Israel's security.

Like so many policy groups these days, J Street is a hybrid creature. It is a 501(c)(4) that has a 501(c)(3) arm, the J Street Education Fund, which can receive philanthropic contributions. It also has a political action committee, JStreetPAC.

J Street's breadth was a crucial asset in the Iran debate. When the finalized nuclear deal reached Washington, heavy political spending through 501(c)(4)s, PACs, and lobbying firms took center stage amid efforts to influence lawmakers—even as J Street kept pumping out policy analysis. That kind of tag-team influence push is common these days. As we've seen in other areas—education, LGBT rights, climate change—donors who care deeply about causes often work all the levers they can to press their agenda. Meanwhile, the rest of us can write our congressional representatives. Or maybe start a petition.

When it comes to who gets heard in the public square, ordinary citizens can't begin to compete with an activist donor class that has grown exponentially in the new Gilded Age. Grassroots movements like the Tea Party or Occupy Wall Street can and do spring up to wield strong influence at certain moments, but—on a day-to-day basis—the deck is stacked in favor of those who have the money to amplify their voices. This helps explain why so many Americans have disengaged from civic life. Why bother?

At least with the Iran nuclear deal there was a clear entry point for average voters, given that Congress had a say in the deal. Often, though, philanthropists are shaping agendas in ways that never entail a roll-call vote by elected representatives. That's especially true as funders expand their role in areas where government leadership is waning, such as creating new schools, building public parks, setting the priorities of state university systems, and funding scientific research.

Many of the things philanthropists are doing are inspiring, depending on your point of view. And it's hard to argue with new resources and imagination at a moment when government seems less able to solve problems, because of either a lack of political will or money. Still, the overall picture here is unsettling: Private funders have been pushing more energetically into public life even as many ordinary people have been withdrawing—and even as a key means by which citizens do things together, government, is foundering.

It can be tempting to blame the wealthy for this situation, reinforcing a neat narrative about creeping plutocracy. And for sure, some elements of the far upper class have pushed hard for an America where government is smaller and weaker, while philanthropy and business call more of the shots. Since the 1970s wealthy donors have heavily financed efforts to cut taxes and public spending. The success they've had helps explain why government now can't do as many things, which gives private funders new leverage in shaping society.

It's hardly far-fetched to think we've witnessed a brilliant power grab: First, the wealthy helped knock out government. Now, they're taking more direct charge of society themselves, using philanthropy as one tool.

Yet if you get to know wealthy donors, you'll quickly realize that most don't think in sweeping terms like this. Instead, they're focused on solving specific problems, and they tend to think in practical ways about how to do that. Their engagement in policy and politics often comes reluctantly, with many steering clear of this area for fear of controversy. Also, quite a few of today's philanthropists are prone to see government more as a partner than as an enemy. In fact, many believe in expanding government's role—whether to protect the environment or civil rights or to help more poor kids go to college. Many would happily pay higher taxes.

There is no plutocratic plot behind today's big philanthropy—at least not that I've uncovered. Very few of the new donors are doing anything sinister. You may or may not agree with the ends they seek, but their means reflect a feature of our society that has made it better and stronger since Tocqueville's day.

That said, we still have a problem: that an ever larger and richer upper class is amplifying its influence through large-scale giving in an era when it already has too much clout. Things are going to get worse, too. Which is why now is a good moment to reform philanthropy so that it's more aligned with American values—and especially the egalitarian ethos so core to our national identity.

WHO'S GETTING HEARD

Economic inequality has risen sharply in the past four decades and, in some ways, philanthropy's fingerprints are all over this trend. Waves of funders, as we've seen, have donated billions to push economic policies that favor the owners of capital and to downsize government programs for lower-income Americans. In other ways, though, philanthropy has fought inequality—by defending the social safety net, helping the poor build assets, promoting universal health insurance, paying for college scholarships, and much more. Overall, the net impact of philanthropy in regard to *economic* inequality seems limited.

The story on *civic* inequality is quite different, and troubling.

Here, we find a glass more half empty than full. Philanthropy has famously helped enfranchise marginalized groups starting in the 1950s, and still finances a large legal and advocacy infrastructure to advance the rights of minorities, women, and LGBT Americans. It has also worked to offset the clout of corporate interests, like the fossil fuel industry. Yet much of what we've seen in this book suggests that philanthropy now acts as a driver of the growing divide in America in who gets heard in the public square—along with who sets the agenda—both nationally and locally. Giving by the wealthy is amplifying their voice at the expense of ordinary citizens, complementing other tools of upper-class dominance.

Not everyone agrees with that analysis, or worries about this trend. One line of thought is that funders put their money behind so many different causes that such giving more or less tracks with the overall diversity of viewpoints in America. "Philanthropy doesn't act as one voice and one actor," John Arnold told me. "There are many different philanthropists, many different foundations, that have different ideologies, different philosophies, different interests. And they are all trying to win in the marketplace of ideas." This competition, the logic goes, helps amplify an informed public debate and strengthens pluralism and democracy. "This is civil society flourishing," the scholar Paul Schervish told me, in discussing the recent upsurge in activist philanthropy backed by the wealthy.

A number of philanthropists told me the same thing: that their giving was opening up debates, not shutting them down. I certainly heard this argument in regard to K–12 education, an area that's sparked the most alarm about private funders meddling in public life. As donors like Eli Broad tell the story, their philanthropy has finally created a real debate over how to improve schools after decades in which the education establishment and teachers unions squelched certain kinds of ideas and experiments, enforcing what Broad has called a "tired government monopoly."

The rise of J Street is another example of donors broadening public debates. The days when AIPAC dominated discussion of Israel inside the Beltway are now over, thanks partly to philanthropists like George Skoll and Soros. One can think of plenty of other places, such as drug policy, where funders have expanded the range of views that are getting heard.

Another defense of philanthropy is that government isn't so good at exploring new ideas and taking risks. Precisely because it is a democratic institution—beholden to fickle voters with limited patience—government can be a weak tool for tackling certain challenges that are critical to the public interest. "There are absolute constraints on what a political entity can do, just because of the nature of how politicians are elected, and the incentive systems that most politicians have," John Arnold told me. So it's good to "have some small amounts of money that are outside of political oversight." Arnold went on to add that, ultimately, "the check on the system is you still have to convince the political system that a certain idea is better and should be adopted. That is the correct and reasonable check." In other words, representatives elected by citizens still make the final decisions.

Bill Gates has said the same thing, presenting his foundation as an R&D shop that engages in experiments that government can't or won't fund and thus expands the "pool of ideas" available to decision-makers. He's insisted that "our voice is not there when the final choice of what to scale up is made. That's a governor or a superintendent or board of education that decide those things."

Meanwhile, it's often said that philanthropy boosts civic equality by empowering voices that would otherwise be bulldozed aside by business interests. Recall how Chuck Feeney gave millions to ensure that advocates of the Affordable Care Act had a fighting chance against industry opponents. Philanthropists also stress that it's not their ideas that are being heard; it's that of their grantees. "Mark and I aren't in some ivory tower making up all these strategies on our own," Priscilla Chan told me. "We are deeply connected to experts. We are in touch with the front lines. . . . We are amplifying the voices of the people who are doing great work out there."

The claim that philanthropy advances pluralism is largely persuasive. But pluralism is not the same as civic equality. While philanthropists may support lots of different views and ideas, we're still talking about an America where public debates have become heavily choreographed by wealthy actors without real constituencies.

The Gates and Arnold foundations may very well do an excellent job of teeing up new ideas that get a hearing in our political system. That's different, though, from such ideas percolating upward by more democratic means. These foundations, controlled by billionaire couples and answerable to no one, have put themselves in an influential position to shape what moves higher on the to-do list of public officials. Yes, elected leaders make the final call on which ideas get enacted. But their power—exercised at the *end* of the policy-making funnel—may actually matter less than what's being fed into the *front* of the funnel. In the case of the Gates Foundation, which has dangled many millions of dollars before school districts to enact certain policies, the hard power of the purse has supplemented the soft power of ideas.

Agenda setting by wealthy donors might not matter so much if their views truly tracked with those of the general public. But the wealthy really are different from other Americans in their ideology. They are more fiscally conservative and socially liberal than the population as a whole. They have a stronger belief in market solutions and technocratic fixes, and don't share the public's rising concern that the system is "rigged."

This book has shown the various ways such divergences have played out. A phalanx of donors has helped put any number of economic ideas on the political agenda in recent decades that are unpopular with most Americans, like reducing taxes on the wealthy, cutting Social Security, and prioritizing deficit reduction over job creation. Likewise, the donors behind the marriage equality movement—operating far out in front of public opinion—helped bring about policy changes that would have taken far longer to happen if left up to ordinary voters. Education donors have often polarized debates over public schools with experimental, market-oriented approaches that are introduced in a top-down fashion without community buy-in.

The other problem with the pluralism defense of big philanthropy is that, these days, it's hard to know what solutions really *do* have authentic public support. Any nonprofit can say they speak for some group of Americans—the working poor or inner-city parents or coal miners—and hit the fundraising circuit, possibly with great success. Then it's easy to use that money to generate a lot of buzz and "momentum." The rise of "grasstops" or "Astroturf" groups is well documented—that is, organizations mainly sustained by major backers, not ordinary citizens.

Nonprofits that draw minimal financial support from ordinary Americans are common these days as deep-pocketed donors line up behind different causes. While philanthropists like John Arnold talk about a more robust marketplace of ideas, many of the groups that are hawking ideas nowadays—fueled by gifts from the wealthy—would wither overnight if they had to win support from large numbers of citizen donors giving at a small level.

The growing dominance of wealthy donors over civil society is seen in data on charitable gifts that I mentioned earlier in the book. From 2003 to 2013, itemized charitable contributions from people making $500,000 or more increased by 57 percent; at the same time, such gifts from donors making less than $100,000 declined. Those figures aren't so surprising given that nearly all of the nation's income gains of recent years have gone to a sliver of top households while most Americans have treaded water or seen their net worth decline.

There's been no shortage of analysis lately of how today's vast wealth chasm affects various parts of U.S. society. Yet the distorting effects of inequality on civil society remains only dimly understood—even as the ranks of nonprofits sustained almost exclusively by rich donors keeps growing and speaking ever more loudly.

Education is one area where it's hard to know which nonprofits have a real constituency. Reform funders often argue that they're empowering minority parents in the face of entrenched bureaucrats and teachers unions. And there's now a pretty loud echo chamber of parent groups calling for more charter schools or questioning teacher tenure. Yet if you follow the money, you'll find that some of these groups rely heavily on just a handful of funders. Take the Black Alliance for Educational Options, a pro-charter-school group that says it pushes reform policies that "empower low-income and working-class Black families." In 2014, nearly half its annual revenue came from just one funder, the Walton Family Foundation. Or consider Parent Revolution, another activist group largely financed by funders like the Walton, Broad, and Arnold foundations. Do either of these groups really speak for parents? It's hard to say.

In an earlier era of civic life, you typically could only mobilize money if you really *did* speak for real people, and got them to pay dues. As the sociologist Theda Skocpol has shown, mass-membership groups were once the most powerful players in civil society. That has changed in an America awash in new philanthropic dollars and where "checkbook activism" is pervasive. "A civic world once centered in locally rooted and nationally active membership associations is a relic," Skocpol wrote in 1999. "Vital links in the nation's associational life have frayed, and we may need to find creative ways to repair those links if America is to avoid becoming a country of detached spectators." In the years since Skocpol penned those words, though, things have only gotten worse. Power in civil society has become more concentrated in the hands of the wealthy. In turn, that clout is shaping how public debates, large and small, unfold, as well as policy outcomes.

How many very rich people need to care intensely about a cause to finance megaphones that drown out the voices of everyone else? Not many, given the resources they can deploy. The Iran debate showed how just a few wealthy super-citizens can crank up a whole new infrastructure to wage policy warfare—leaving the rest of us to watch these gods throwing lightning bolts at one another.

Battles like this will only become more common as new mega-donors arrive on the scene with big ambitions to shape society. We're fast moving toward a future where private funders, not elected officials and the citizens they answer to, choreograph more of public life.

A BETTER BALANCE

What, if anything, can be done to stop the further erosion of civic equality in an age of big philanthropy?

This is a tough challenge, because it pits two important American values against each other. Along with egalitarianism, we also care deeply about freedom—and especially the freedom to express oneself in civic life. Even more specifically, there's long been consensus around "philanthropic freedom"—the idea that government should only minimally regulate civil society and how Americans use their money to support different causes.

In recent years, the Philanthropy Roundtable, which was started by conservative foundations in the 1980s, has offered some of the most robust arguments in favor of philanthropic freedom. It argues that civil society is an extension of our deep belief in freedom of association and that private charitable dollars are a key to ensuring that freedom. The roundtable and others see a robust civil society as an all-important counterweight to the power of the state, and it's precisely because it plays this role that we can't let government meddle with the lifeline that keeps this sector strong and independent.

Rethinking philanthropic freedom is a Pandora's box that almost nobody wants to open. Nearly every foundation and nonprofit trade group is dead set against any new restrictions on giving for policy and advocacy, while progressives—the usual critics of money's political sway—have their own reasons for staying silent, given how dependent their organizations are on philanthropy.

I get these concerns. But it will be hard to stop a further erosion of civic equality without putting some new curbs in place on how the wealthy can use their charitable dollars to shape public life. Yesterday's mantras about philanthropic freedom, and the dated regulations that uphold it, are out of step with a new set of challenges arising in a second Gilded Age.

The charitable tax exemption was created a century ago. And the last big regulatory changes to philanthropy were made in 1969. Since that time, though, nearly everything has changed in terms of how private funders wield influence, and the pace of change has notably accelerated in just the last decade, with even bigger changes on the horizon. Now it's time for reformers to play catch-up with new thinking—and yes, new rules—about how much influence we allow philanthropists to have over our shared destinies.

In many ways, the tension between philanthropic freedom and civic equality is a familiar one. Similar tug-of-wars have played out through U.S. history. America has struggled mightily with how to balance economic freedom with greater equity, as well as with other goals, like environmental and consumer protection. We've also struggled with how to balance personal freedom and civil liberties with concerns for social order, national security, and the common good.

If we can navigate those challenges, as we have in the past, we should be able to figure out a way to impose reasonable limits on philanthropic freedom so that it doesn't bulldoze the egalitarian ideals we hold dear—ideals, by the way, that impressed Tocqueville far more than America's robust nonprofit sector.

The key here is striking the right balance, and regulating economic freedom offers a helpful parallel. Ideally, efforts to soften the harsh edges of capitalism don't kill the goose that lays the golden egg of dynamic wealth creation. In the case of curbing philanthropic freedom, we should be thinking about nips and tucks that don't undermine the overall vibrancy of civil society. We want to target the philanthropic behavior that's most troubling, not hobble the sector as a whole. And, mindful of the dangers of the state meddling in civil society, we want to find ways to insulate the mechanisms of philanthropic oversight from the political pressures of the moment. None of that sounds so impossible, since we've done it all before in regulating other sectors of U.S. society.

Ideas for Reform

What kinds of changes might bring more democratic oversight to philanthropy? Plenty of experts have weighed in on that question over many decades, offering up various ideas for reform—most of which have gone nowhere. I can't pretend to have found any new silver bullets in my own explorations, but I will say this: The stakes are rising as private donors become more powerful in American society and, at the same time, existing oversight becomes less able to keep up and to protect the public interest.

What follows are a few suggestions for updating and strengthening the rules that govern philanthropy.

MORE TRANSPARENCY

When wealthy people and foundation staff use philanthropy to shape our society's direction—and especially public policy—their fellow citizens should know what they're up to. Yet often that is not the case. There is no legal requirement by funders to reveal where they are making grants. Nor do most nonprofits have to reveal their donors.

Private foundations have to report their grants in annual tax returns. But it can be several years before those returns are available to the public.

Some established foundations do a great job of being transparent. Most do not. Data available through the Foundation Center on the top eighty or so U.S. foundations reveals that just twenty-six of them share timely information about their grantmaking through online grant databases. These include some of the biggest players in philanthropy.

The Susan Thompson Buffett Foundation, one of the top five grantmakers in the United States, is a case study in non-transparency. This leading funder of reproductive health work, including abortion services around the United States, has no real website, and the information available on its grantmaking through tax returns is always a few years out of date.

But if you really want to peer into a black hole, take a look at donor-advised funds, which reveal where grants go on annual tax returns—but not who gave that money. In 2015, more than $13 billion in grants moved through donor-advised funds. Among these entities are some of the largest grantmakers in the United States, like Fidelity Charitable, as well as leading funders of ideological policy groups, such as Tides and Donors-Trust. As more new donors turn to DAFs, instead of traditional foundations, philanthropy is becoming less transparent.

Other kinds of giving vehicles can also hide the tracks of funders.

When Mark Zuckerberg and Priscilla Chan announced they would give away nearly all of their Facebook stock, they also unveiled a new limited liability company, the Chan Zuckerberg Initiative, which directs their giving and isn't subject to the same disclosure rules as nonprofits and foundations. Laurene Powell Jobs also does her philanthropy through an LLC, the Emerson Collective, making it hard to know what causes one of America's richest women is getting behind.

Some mega-donors have used anonymous private foundations, funded and controlled by LLCs, to do their giving. Among them has been David Gelbaum, who along with two other hedge fund colleagues, used a complex network of secretive entities to give away hundreds of millions of dollars. Some of his biggest gifts went to the ACLU and Sierra Club, groups actively seeking to sway public policy. Another donor in this trio, Andrew Schectel, was revealed in 2014 to control two anonymous charitable trusts that hold $9.7 billion in assets.

These are all examples of how yesterday's nonprofit disclosure rules are being rendered moot by changes in the sector amid an explosion of new giving.

Why is transparency, along with the timely reporting of grants, such a big deal? Because without it, citizens don't know who's shaping decisions that affect their lives, or what their motives might be. The Iran nuclear debate is a perfect example: Millions in philanthropic and political gifts sought to influence one of the most important national security debates of recent years, yet it was hard to get any real-time information on who was writing the checks. We'll probably never get a full picture of the funders involved, given how easy it is to keep donations anonymous forever. A similar veil of secrecy shrouds other important recent debates. We'll likely never know, for example, the full extent of philanthropic giving to help enact and implement the Affordable Care Act, or to try to block and weaken that law, which was among the most consequential policy changes in a generation.

There's plenty of hard-to-trace philanthropy happening locally, too, around crucial public debates. In early 2015, for example, a school reform group in Philadelphia offered $35 million to help that city close a funding gap, but it demanded the right to open more charters as a condition— all without disclosing who was putting up this money. Also that year, a new nonprofit in New York began a legal push to weaken tenure laws for teachers in the state. It refused to disclose its donors. As mentioned earlier, funds from the Walton Family Foundation make up a big chunk of the revenues of the Black Alliance for Educational Options. Who are the alliance's other top donors? That information isn't public, and the same is true of numerous other advocacy groups, on both the left and the right.

Dark philanthropic money has also become a more potent tool for partisan political gains, financing efforts to mobilize or suppress targeted groups of voters, as well as to investigate and attack politicians. But while there is a big push to bring more sunlight to campaign money in the wake of the 2010 U.S. Supreme Court ruling in *Citizens United*, there have been few calls to crack down on secretive charitable giving or to require more timely reporting of gifts. That doesn't make much sense. Among other things, if campaign finance reformers ever do succeed, philanthropy will likely become an even more popular means by which the wealthy pursue policy change.

Today's shadow giving system is strongly defended by champions of philanthropic freedom, who say a right to privacy in giving is a key part of such freedom. And certainly donors can have some good reasons for anonymity. Maybe you don't want to be hit up by other fundraisers or you believe donors should be humble. Or maybe you're worried about serious retaliation, as was the case with donors to the NAACP in the Deep South during the 1950s—and is sometimes the case today, such as for donors giving to restrict LGBT rights.

These privacy concerns are understandable, but ultimately should not trump the public's interest in greater transparency at a time when a wealthy minority exerts growing influence over public policy—and people's lives. This is an area where the value of philanthropic freedom can't be absolute. Donor-advised funds should be required to disclose their donors just as private foundations must, and most nonprofits engaged in policy or advocacy work should also have to reveal their donors. Transparency should be the default expectation.

LIMITING POLITICIZED PHILANTHROPY

If I donate to a politician who I believe will help enact certain public policies, I don't get to deduct the gift on my tax return. That's how it should be. My fellow taxpayers shouldn't help foot the bill of promoting my political beliefs. On the other hand, if I donate to a think tank or advocacy group for the exact same reason—to influence public policy—I can deduct the gift on my tax return.

That may not sound like it makes much sense, but it reflects current law. A century ago, the War Revenue Act of 1917 provided a tax deduction for gifts made to "corporations or associations organized and operated exclusively for religious, charitable, scientific, or educational purposes, or to societies for the prevention of cruelty to children or animals." This is one of the oldest breaks in the tax code, and while it's evolved in various respects, the basic idea hasn't changed much. The IRS broadly defines what activities tax-exempt 501(c)(3)s can engage in that are deemed "charitable"—a wide menu that includes "relief of the poor, the distressed, or the underprivileged," as well as "defending human and civil rights" and "lessening the burdens of government."

This definition is broad enough that the IRS makes no distinction between what most of us would think of as charity—say, donating to a food bank—and activities that are more political, like donating to an effort to abolish food stamps. I would get the same tax break for contributing to an emergency fund to help unemployed coal miners as I would for contributing to a push to shut down coal-fired energy plants. I'd get the same deduction for giving to a local health clinic as I would for donating to a policy group that wants to strip that clinic of funding.

Today's vast world of nonprofit groups with strong policy agendas didn't exist a century ago. This world didn't even exist a half century ago, when Congress last revisited charitable tax law in a major way. It has emerged largely since the 1970s, financed by a new breed of activist philanthropists like Richard Scaife on the right and George Soros on the left. The past decade has seen a notable acceleration in money flowing to this world.

Yet charitable tax law has remained largely unchanged.

Nobody knows for sure the scope of tax-subsidized giving that flows every year to 501(c)(3) nonprofit organizations that expressly aim to shift public policies that affect the lives of Americans. It's hard to tally up all contributions made to thousands of policy and advocacy groups at both the national and the state levels given the limitations in data on where charitable donations go. As well, not everyone who donates to such groups takes advantage of the charitable deduction. Typically, only affluent people itemize deductions on their tax returns, which is the only way to make use of the exemption.

What might be a ballpark estimate of the total tax-deductible charitable contributions made to policy and advocacy groups every year? We're probably talking about a sum in the low billions, less than $10 billion. That number doesn't sound huge, but it's much more than the combined annual political giving to candidates, party committees, 501(c)(4)s, and super PACs.

Just the top five environmental groups in the United States pulled in more than $500 million in 2015 in charitable contributions. The Right's biggest think tank, the Heritage Foundation, pulled in a record $129 million in contributions that same year. Most policy groups raise much less than these organizations, but there are huge numbers of them. As we've seen, nearly every state now has smaller versions of the ideological think tanks that have become so influential in Washington.

Some policy and advocacy groups raise significant funds from minor donors. But the bulk of such money tends to come from the wealthy and foundations. For example, the American Enterprise Institute, which raised $55 million in 2015, has fewer than 1,500 donors, who contribute, on average, $35,000 each to have their values expressed in national policy debates, as Arthur Brooks described it. That's more money than most U.S. workers earn in a year.

Whatever the exact numbers, the bottom line is that all taxpayers are subsidizing the efforts of the wealthy to influence public policy. It's not just that the megaphones operated by 501(c)(3) groups and financed by a sliver of rich donors have gotten louder and louder, making it harder for ordinary citizens to be heard. It's that these citizens are helping foot the bill for those megaphones.

The charitable tax deduction has long enjoyed strong support, because there's an assumption that those donations help better society. Most of us don't mind paying a little bit extra in taxes every year to make up for the money lost to the deduction, which was around $47 billion in 2016. But most of us probably *would* mind helping foot the bill for gifts to the Republican or Democratic parties. There are big, obvious differences between political parties and nonprofits like Heritage or CAP. What they share in common is the goal of making changes to public policy. In fact, policy groups and political parties often work in close concert with each other, as we've seen.

Given the politicization of nonprofits over the past half century, it's time to rethink which groups really should qualify for tax-exempt status. One obvious solution here is to redraw the line that now separates 501(c)(3) nonprofits from their cousins, the 501(c)(4)s, donations to which are not tax-deductible.

Such nonprofits have famously become political powerhouses—the NRA, the AARP, and the NAACP are all 501(c)(4)s—although there are also many that have nothing to do with public policy. The IRS defines them as "civic leagues or organizations not organized for profit but operated exclusively for the promotion of social welfare." The reason tax-exempt dollars can't flow to 501(c)(4)s is that many often engage in what the IRS refers to as "nondeductible lobbying and political expenditures," with goals that include "influencing legislation" or trying to "influence the general public with respect to elections, legislative matters, or referendums."

Today, plenty of 501(c)(3)s that can receive tax-exempt donations are pursuing the same goals, only a few steps further upstream. Such groups do things like write reports that argue for or against a higher minimum wage, whereas 501(c)(4)s publish reports that argue for or against passage of legislation or ballot initiatives that actually would raise the minimum wage. The differences are often meaningless, a fact that the donor class well understands. Indeed, the most savvy donors know they can often have the greatest influence by funding upstream, shaping what ideas get on the legislative agenda in the first place.

The time has come for the IRS to define more narrowly what constitutes charitable activities by 501(c)(3) groups, with the result that many of these policy and advocacy organizations would be reclassified as 501(c)(4)s and contributions to them would no longer be tax-deductible.

To be sure, this would be quite disruptive to such groups, and likely fatal to quite a few. Foundations that now fund lots of policy and advocacy work would have to shift away from it, leaving big gaps in nonprofit budgets.

Still, it's hard to argue that this step would infringe on anyone's freedom. Wealthy donors could still give all the money they want to places like Heritage or CAP. The important thing is that we'd end the charade that such gifts are "charity" and thus that taxpayers should help foot the bill.

GREATER ACCOUNTABILITY

One of the great strengths of philanthropy is that donors and foundations are only minimally accountable to any outside authority or constituency. It allows funders to take risks without worrying about losing their jobs, unlike politicians or the CEOs of public corporations.

This part of philanthropic freedom is mostly a good thing, and we don't want to mess with it by imposing too much new oversight. What I think the public can and should demand, though, is to know what society is getting in return for billions in charitable tax breaks.

The U.S. Treasury has estimated that the cost of such breaks over the next decade will total around $740 billion. That's serious money in an age of fiscal austerity when we're kicking people off food stamps, cutting science funding, yanking away housing vouchers from the poor, and so on. But despite frequent discussion of the charitable deduction, it's hard to say whether the cost of these breaks is worth it, in terms of the public benefits, compared to other priorities. Nor, for a growing share of tax-exempt gifts, do we know *when* such benefits will start to flow, since donor-advised funds have no annual payout requirement, unlike foundations. While donors get an immediate tax deduction for contributing to DAFs, they have no near-term obligation to make gifts out of such funds.

The easiest reform to enact here is to compel donor-advised funds to distribute money at the same rates as foundations. Even though DAFs already do a good job on such payout, today's lax rules create too great a risk that, over time, piles of untaxed wealth will grow ever higher without society seeing commensurate returns. The same can be said, by the way, about foundation endowments, which will grow much larger at the same time that government coffers grow emptier. That's unlikely to sit well over time with the public, and there's a strong case for increasing the required foundation payout rate beyond 5 percent.

The thornier question is what the public is getting in return for tax breaks granted for philanthropy, which mainly go to the wealthy. The way the tax code helps amplify upper-class power seems problematic on its face—unless we can easily agree that the benefits are overwhelmingly positive and fairly distributed. Right now, though, no independent authority—like, for instance, the Congressional Budget Office or the Government Accountability Office—works to analyze how these benefits play out.

To take one example: John Paulson's $400 million gift to Harvard in 2015 will cost the Treasury tens of millions of dollars at a time that Pell Grants for needy college students are being cut. Is that okay? Maybe or maybe not, depending upon the projected public benefits of that subsidy to America's richest university. Perhaps the cost of Paulson's gift is actually a bargain for taxpayers because the applied science research he is supporting will produce major economic gains for society.

We don't have a clue one way or another, since no effort is being made to analyze the benefits of charitable tax breaks. What's more, some people are wary of even asking the question, since that could lead down the slippery slope of government making choices about what forms of charity are worth subsidizing, which would infringe on philanthropic freedom.

I agree that, beyond limiting tax breaks for politicized giving, government shouldn't take a heavy-handed approach to deciding which nonprofits should be able to accept tax-exempt gifts. Who's to say whether funding for the arts, for example, is valuable to society?

On the other hand, plenty of people are already arguing that Congress should limit the charitable exemption because it doesn't deliver enough value to society. Some say that in an era of dire fiscal choices we could put that lost revenue to better use.

It's hard to know how to evaluate such claims without more information on the benefits of tax-exempt charitable giving. Who's getting what, here? Broadly speaking, while we know it's largely the wealthy who make use of the charitable tax deduction, we don't know which communities or groups benefit from those gifts and how. We *are* able to answer these crucial questions in regard to other huge tax breaks, like for mortgage interest and health-care costs, but we're flying blind on the charitable tax deduction. What's more, we're flying blind into the biggest giving spree in history, with a slew of billionaires likely to die in the next few decades. The total of tax revenues lost due to charitable gifts will become ever more eye-popping—even as every tax break comes under closer scrutiny as the fiscal screws tighten in Washington. It doesn't help matters that we also can't answer basic questions about the efficiency of the charitable sector.

Take the matter of foundations' administrative costs. How much such spending is too much? Right now, we don't have a clue.

The Ford Foundation's overhead costs in the past decade have been running at over 20 percent of its annual spending and have totaled over $1 billion in the past decade. Many other top foundations have similar costs, with staff at the top ten foundations paid some $600 million annually.

Maybe that money is well spent because all those smart program officers work to leverage foundation dollars and achieve more impact. Or maybe it's an outrageous waste, since plenty of foundations achieve comparable impact with much lower overhead costs. Your guess is as good as mine, since no one actually knows which foundations get the most bang for their buck. This means there's no real way to shame spendthrift funders that live high on the hog with tax-subsidized money while delivering poor performance—or to praise models of efficiency that should be replicated.

The philanthropic sector has simply never devoted enough resources to evaluating its own performance in a rigorous way. The work that now goes on to evaluate foundations, by the Center for Effective Philanthropy, the National Committee for Responsive Philanthropy, and other groups, is excellent but limited in scope. Also, all these organizations are dependent on foundation funding, which may crimp their watchdog role. Meanwhile, no government agency is on the case either.

Should we be worried about the lack of independent oversight in regard to the efficiency of foundations and philanthropy writ large? A purist on philanthropic freedom would likely say no—that it's the funders' own money and how well they spend it is no one else's business. Others might say that many questions are basically unanswerable and the last thing we need is to flood the social sector with more bean counters.

Ultimately, though, it's not okay to settle for a status quo in which the foundation world remains forever a black box, filled with an expanding array of wealthy tax-exempt institutions that are of uncertain effectiveness and ever more costly to the U.S. Treasury. The public has a right to know more about the efficiency of this sector.

It's even less okay that the government watchdogs that are supposed to enforce charitable laws are notoriously feeble. The United States has some 1.5 million tax-exempt nonprofits, and just over a million of them are eligible to receive deductible contributions. Policing these myriad groups, which together hold $2.7 trillion in assets, is a big job—and one that neither federal or state agencies are equipped to handle.

That's true of the IRS, which saw cuts to its nonprofit division during the early Obama years. It had less than 900 employees in 2012 to ensure compliance with tax law across a vast nonprofit sector that's been growing ever more politicized and complex. The job of reviewing some 60,000 nonprofit applications every year fell to just 200 low-level employees at a regional IRS office in Cincinnati. After accusations that the agency had unfairly scrutinized Tea Party groups seeking tax-exempt status, Congress responded by curtailing the IRS's oversight powers and making it easier for groups to get nonprofit status—exactly the wrong response. As for keeping an eye on foundations, one expert estimated in 2016 that the IRS scrutinizes less than 1 percent of all 990 tax forms these nonprofits file ever year. This lax oversight is an invitation to abuse.

Things aren't much better at the state level. A recent study found that even as the number of nonprofits has grown in recent years, the enforcement capacity of the public watchdogs overseeing nonprofits—most notably, offices of state attorneys general—has largely remained flat. This weak oversight helps explain a steady stream of charity fraud cases, including one involving a bogus anti-cancer group that raised nearly $200 million. State officials cracked down on that scam, but who knows what other abuses have gone undetected—or what new scandals may emerge down the line.

Stronger watchdogs are a must if the charitable sector wants to ensure the trust of the American public. Likewise, if the wealthy are going to get ongoing public subsidies to set up yet more foundations and donor-advised funds—and ever bigger ones—it's reasonable to ask for more evidence that all of society is benefiting from this setup.

Stronger accountability for philanthropy, through expanded regulatory oversight and new research on the benefits and efficiency of charitable giving, won't come cheap. Who should foot the bill? And how should such an effort be organized?

The first question is easy to answer:

Private foundations already pay a 2 percent federal excise tax on their annual investment income that generates more than $500 million a year in revenue. The tax is supposed to cover the costs of IRS oversight of charities, but it stopped being earmarked for this purpose in the 1990s, and it's fair to say that the nonprofit sector isn't getting its money's worth. Far more should be done with the excise tax income. Beefing up the IRS enforcement capacity is an obvious need, and it would also make sense to grant out some of these funds to the states, given their front-line role in policing charities.

More intriguing is the idea of devoting a portion of excise tax revenue to research philanthropy and nonprofits, analyzing the benefits of charitable giving as well as the sector's performance. Such an effort could be orchestrated by a new U.S. federal office of charitable affairs, which could contract out much of the work to nonprofits and universities. Just as the federal government has spent many millions assessing various social programs, relying on groups like the Urban Institute and Manpower Demonstration Corporation, it makes sense to devote public resources to studying how well philanthropic dollars are spent—since every taxpayer has an interest in answering these questions, too.

A new office of charitable affairs could also help orchestrate partnerships between government and philanthropy—work that's been growing in recent years. In addition, it could provide help to people seeking to start nonprofits and foundations, or running them, just as other agencies, like the Small Business Administration and U.S. Department of Agriculture offer a wealth of how-to information and services. With the nonprofit sector accounting for over 5 percent of GDP and 10 percent of the private-sector employment, it makes sense for government to get more organized about supporting it.

A new U.S. office of charitable affairs could also assist with some of the compliance challenges that have overwhelmed the IRS in recent years. These issues can be complex and nuanced, requiring an expertise on nonprofits unlikely to be nurtured at the IRS.

One last point: To insulate a new charitable affairs agency from political pressures, its governance might resemble that of the Federal Reserve, or other independent agencies, whose leaders serve extended terms to reduce their dependence on partisan patrons.

GETTING AHEAD OF THE CURVE

Many leaders in philanthropy and the nonprofit sector have zero interest in the kinds of reforms I'm proposing, however modest they may be. They fear government meddling in a hugely successful American experiment that has thrived with few outside constraints. I understand those fears; we don't want to mess up a good thing.

But there's a larger principle involved here: In a democracy, all powerful institutions that affect our lives need vigilant oversight. Philanthropy is no exception. Right now, it's one of the last major sectors of U.S. society that gets to basically do as it pleases, answering to no one. That can't last. We live in an age of skepticism, remember, and public trust in all institutions has fallen in recent decades. The charitable sector is doing better than most others, but it hasn't been immune from the overall trend. Judging by some of what we've seen in recent years—the backlash to Mark Zuckerberg's outsized philanthropy, the intense criticism of charter school funders, the allegations about the Clinton and Trump foundations—more Americans are getting nervous about how the wealthy are using philanthropy as a tool of influence in an age of inequality. Those fears have risen even though most people are in fact clueless about just how much influence philanthropy really *does* wield in U.S. society. As I've shown in this book, the power of the givers is much greater than many people realize.

Public concern is likely to grow as private giving gets bigger in coming years. This is one reason why, instead of fighting more oversight, leaders in philanthropy should embrace it. They shouldn't make the same mistake their peers in other sectors have made: insisting that yesterday's level of oversight is still fine even though conditions have dramatically changed. Think of how that kind of denial has played out in recent years for higher education, the National Football League, or the accounting and mortgage industries.

And, yes, things really have changed in philanthropy in just the past decade or two. We're seeing a historic influx of new wealth that is bringing more activist living donors into the sector, and at times they throw their weight around in troubling ways. We're seeing the rise of powerful giving networks like the Democracy Alliance and the one organized by the Koch brothers. We're seeing the growing popularity of donor-advised funds that are part of a shadow giving system that has made philanthropy less transparent in recent years.

The backdrop for all these shifts is the decline in the resources and problem-solving capacities of government. Power seems to be shifting away from elected public officials, who face growing fiscal constraints, to unelected private funders with ever deeper pockets. This is happening at a time of growing public unease about the wealthy and elites generally.

These are big changes, and philanthropy's leaders need to accept that now new oversight is needed to catch up. Otherwise, they risk ceding the initiative to outside reformers. That's a movie we've seen before, a bunch of times. An insular sector defends a badly dated oversight regime, even as conditions change and new problems emerge, along with new public concerns. It reflexively fights every reform that comes along, however modest. The sector thinks it's different, and special, and that its free pass is good forever. Then, because of some scandal or investigation or citizens' movement or shift in culture, everything changes and the result is a massive loss of public trust and more heavy-handed government regulation than might otherwise have been the case.

Philanthropy's leaders need to get ahead of this curve—while they still can.

The Mindful Philanthropist

None of the reforms I've suggested will substantially limit the influence of wealthy philanthropy over public life. Perhaps the best we can hope for is that funders bring greater self-restraint and mindfulness to giving that affects the lives of their fellow citizens.

Some of the donors I've spoken with seem to have given little thought to the obvious question of how their influence squares with America's egalitarian values—as if I were broaching an unfamiliar subject. Donors must do more to engage this question and reflect on how they operate. Otherwise they're just asking for trouble, both in regard to maintaining public trust and achieving impact.

A few high-profile philanthropists, like Mark Zuckerberg and Priscilla Chan, are already engaged in reflection and are now listening more closely to the communities they're trying to help. The Gates Foundation has also begun to change its style, after various missteps in which it failed to bring along key stakeholders. But there's room for much more self-awareness among funders, and especially on such local issues as education and community development, where Americans are rightly sensitive to being bulldozed by wealthy super-citizens who parachute in acting like they have all the answers. If we've learned anything in a century of modern philanthropy, it's that few donors actually *do* have all the answers and, often, the people who can help them most are those they're trying to help.

The good news is that lots of thought has already been given, over many years, to how funders can be better listeners and more responsive to what they learn. Some of that thinking came together in 2014 in a new initiative called the Fund for Shared Insight, which is backed by over half a dozen foundations. This effort seeks to help nonprofits better listen to the people they seek to help, and also to ensure that foundations do a better job of listening to nonprofits. Along these same lines, many foundations now hire the Center for Effective Philanthropy, a Boston-based group, to survey their grantees on what it's like to work with them. The most transparent of those funders make public the findings of these reports. The center has drawn on this work and other research to offer valuable guidance to funders that want to build respectful partnerships with grantees. Other groups, like Grantmakers for Effective Organizations, offer advice along the same lines.

Meanwhile, some individual foundations have been breaking new ground in seeking feedback from the people they serve. In Los Angeles, the Weingart Foundation has turned to its grantees, which are mainly community-based groups, for input on its grantmaking priorities—and then actually acted on that guidance. The Chicago Community Trust has an initiative called "On the Table," holding an annual one-day event to get thousands of Chicagoans talking about the challenges the city faces, with the goal of generating actionable funding ideas. Other experiments are also under way around "participatory grantmaking," with the goal of making sure that funders don't get stuck in a bubble.

So far, though, it's mainly older, established foundations that are keying in to the new push for better listening and stronger feedback loops—as opposed to the mega-donors who've more lately arrived on the scene and have often used tactics that feel high-handed. In any case, it remains to be seen whether all the new attention to creating more respectful partnerships between funders and grantees can ultimately do much to offset the power imbalances that seem inherent in philanthropy. Too often, inequities in the charitable sector mirror those of society at large, with the people controlling most of the wealth calling most of the shots.

Some of the boldest thinking on how to offset this dynamic can be found in the more radical zones of the philanthrosphere. One group with an eye to fostering authentic equity between those who give and receive is Resource Generation, which organizes rich young people to become leaders in social change philanthropy. A key premise of the group's work is that donors need to be ever mindful that their giving doesn't replicate the same unequal power arrangements in society that they're hoping to curb. It's easy for that to happen when donors put themselves in the driver's seat, deciding on their own what solutions will work best or how to enact plans for change. Some 2,200 wealthy heirs have been engaged by Resource Generation since its founding in 1998.

Among them Karen Pittelman, who created a foundation in Boston to help low-income women. Pittelman put up the money, but the "ultimate intended beneficiaries" of her philanthropy ran the foundation and decided where grants went. She told me: "I wanted to transfer power to the people on the front lines, and I didn't want to define it more than that." Other foundations have been designed in a similar way, like Bread & Roses in Philadelphia, which is fueled by wealthy donors but where grantmaking decisions are made by a committee that includes neighborhood people most directly affected by the grants. The foundation's motto is "change, not charity."

Or consider the Chorus Foundation, run by Farhad Ebrahimi, the heir to a tech fortune we met earlier in the book. This foundation focuses on climate change, working in communities that are directly affected by the issue—such as coal country in Kentucky and Inuit areas in Alaska, where people's homes are sinking as permafrost melts. While its structure is quite traditional, it bends over backward to really listen to the people on the front lines of the climate crisis. Ebrahimi told me: "We enter into conversations with grantees and potential grantees always as a line of inquiry and not as 'we're the very smart foundation that has identified the very smart strategy and now we're going to put out an RFP to see who wants to implement this strategy for us.'" That process, he said, means "we go spend time with those folks and hear how they're thinking about the problem and what they need to be able to advocate for the solutions that they know are going to work for them."

The Chorus Foundation also pays out grants with an eye to empowering nonprofits, giving community-based organizations long-term general support over a period of years so they don't fear that Chorus will "turn off the faucet." In contrast, many foundations dole out one-year project grants that can leave grantees feeling like supplicants on a short leash. "We're not going to come once a year to course correct and check, and try to tweak, and tell them what we would need to see for a grant renewal," said Ebrahimi. "We're saying that we trust them and we want to give them the capital to do what they need to do. . . . Then we can start really building real relationships with them and we can talk about all the other ways we can be helpful."

Some wealthy donors aren't keen to share too much power with grant recipients, since they often see their own skills and ideas as a prime asset that they bring to solving tough problems. They may also believe that long-time players on an issue have run out of creative steam and aren't able to think outside the box. Newer education reform funders have operated in such a top-down fashion in part because Walter Annenberg's huge initiative to fix schools in the 1990s—which ceded power to local groups—failed to achieve much change. Viewing insiders as entrenched in a failing system, education donors have seen empowering disruptive outsiders as a key to overturning the status quo.

There's a logic to that thinking. On the other hand, the heavy-handedness of K–12 funders in recent years has offered a showcase of big philanthropy's dark side. Their grandiose plans have often failed to anticipate realities on the ground, created intense polarization, and alienated the stakeholders who are essential to successful schools—like teachers.

There's plenty of room for a middle ground, whereby philanthropists do pursue bold efforts at systemic change—but in ways that are inclusive and don't run roughshod over people with less money and power. Certainly any donor with a business background should grasp why they'd want to be great listeners and truly engage the end users of philanthropic dollars.

Corporations are rightly obsessed with understanding consumer preferences so that they can improve their products and services (which is why we're all bombarded with surveys from hotels, airlines, banks, and so on). Philanthropists should be equally fixated on pressing their ear to the ground in the communities in which they operate—and listening with a humble readiness to learn. Ebrahimi noted: "A mistake that folks in philanthropy can make is, just because you get to sit in a privileged position to hear about more things, doesn't mean that your reaction to those things is any more strategic—or even, frankly, *as* strategic—as folks who are completely focused on one place and the work they do in that place."

To ensure communities get heard, some philanthropy reformers have suggested that foundations be mandated by law to have inclusive governing structures. For example, Michael Edwards, a former executive at the Ford Foundation, has argued that no "foundation or social enterprise should receive tax-exemption unless its board is fully representative of the communities it claims to serve." That proposal sounds hard to operationalize, but there is a strong case that foundation boards should, as a norm, include outsiders—as opposed to just being composed of family members or other insiders.

Research on corporate boards has found that having independent directors improves the bottom line; it stands to reason that foundations would also benefit from this approach, and many of the top major foundations do have professional boards. Gordon Moore and George Soros are two examples of living mega-donors who have ceded significant power to outside board members—and, in return, have attracted top-tier talent to help guide their philanthropy. Meanwhile, the Gates Foundation has just four board members: Bill and Melinda, William Gates Sr., and Warren Buffett. Perhaps this institution could have avoided some of its mistakes in the past decade if it had had less insular governance.

Likewise, greater diversity on foundation boards is also important. Such boards tend to be far whiter, more male, and older than the U.S. population as a whole—which puts philanthropy at a disadvantage in understanding an America undergoing rapid demographic change. The privileged status of this leadership class feeds into a larger problem, which is that philanthropy is not as responsive to poor and marginalized communities as it ought to be. Too many charitable dollars go to elite institutions that mainly cater to the affluent; too few go to alleviating poverty or fighting injustice—a point that the National Committee for Responsive Philanthropy has been making since its founding in 1976.

Here, again, you'll find proposals for mandating change by law. In his book *Born on Third Base,* Chuck Collins—the Oscar Meyer heir who gave away his fortune—argues that Congress should establish two types of charitable entities and give them different tax benefits. Donations to groups that "alleviate poverty, reduce inequality, and address urgent social problems" would be fully deductible; donations to other nonprofits would not get the full benefit. Others have made similar proposals.

As a practical matter, it seems difficult—if not impossible—to define which nonprofits deliver a public benefit worthy of a full tax break and which do not. One can only imagine the arguments over, say, symphonies. On the other hand, if philanthropy really is as tilted to feathering the nests of the wealthy as critics charge (a question that needs further research, as I've suggested), then some kind of reform along the lines Collins proposes may be needed.

Regardless of whether new rules are the answer, philanthropy better start listening more closely to its social justice critics. Quite apart from doing the right thing, if this sector doesn't deliver more to the least fortunate, it may be only a matter of time before the tax breaks that help fuel it will come under fiercer attack in an era of lifeboat fiscal choices.

The modest changes I've suggested would produce a philanthropoic sector that is more transparent, accountable, and responsive—and also less aggressively political. Still, these changes are unlikely to do much to reduce the influence of private donors over public life in coming decades. As long as activist giving keeps growing while government keeps declining—against a backdrop of vast inequality—power in society will likely keep shifting to the hands of unaccountable donors. This power, as we've seen, will be used for purposes that some of us will cheer and others will fear. My own sense is that the new big philanthropy is likely to be a net positive in its substantive effects on U.S. society—and, yet, at the same time, a force increasingly at odds with America's egalitarian values, as we're seeing already.

How do we get off this path to benign plutocracy? One answer lies in rebuilding the capacity of citizens to solve problems together through government, as opposed to ceding that work to billionaires. This requires a public sector that is better financed, more nimble and effective, and more responsive to average people. It also means reviving lost ideas about economic democracy.

For starters, government needs more resources. To pay for the retirement of baby boomers and still have a public sector that enables us as citizens to tackle big problems will require higher revenue in coming years. That means reversing years of historically low tax rates ushered in during the Reagan years. The wealthy can and should pay more—for instance, through higher taxes on capital gains—but mobilizing greater resources requires that middle- and upper-middle-class households also pay more. One path forward is reducing tax breaks for mortgages, health insurance, and retirement savings that mainly benefit the affluent. Another is finding revenues through new taxes on financial transactions or carbon emissions, as many have suggested. Ideally, our tax system would rely more on taxing bad behavior, like pollution and speculation, and less on taxing good things, like work and investments.

Of equal importance is controlling entitlement spending on seniors—and particularly health-care costs, which threaten to consume a growing portion of public spending in future decades. This will require limiting the power of market actors in the health-care system, as most other advanced countries have done. Reducing national security spending is another imperative. Just maybe, for example, we don't still need a nuclear triad that costs over $30 billion a year to maintain—much less sixteen different intelligence agencies.

Many of these steps won't be easy or popular. But the alternative is a broke government and citizenry that can't afford to solve problems together—and thus come to rely ever more heavily on private funders to lead the way.

Of course, more resources alone will not be enough to revive government as a dynamic agent of change. We also need reforms to make public agencies more flexible, which will require curbing the scope and complexity of regulatory law, updating civil service systems, and limiting the collective bargaining power of some government workers. We can't solve today's problems with yesterday's calcified institutions. In many cases, as we've seen, philanthropy has moved into a void created by ineffective government. If public agencies are going to compete with nonprofits as change agents, attracting the brightest and the most idealistic problem solvers, they need to improve how they operate.

One other thing: Government certainly should work closely with philanthropy in coming decades in a mix that also includes business. The history of such partnerships goes back to the earliest days of modern philanthropy, and they often have been a key to progress. Just in the past decade, we've seen exciting new initiatives of this kind to tackle an array of challenges, such as creating more opportunities for young men of color, helping veterans, cutting teen pregnancies, and enrolling people in the Affordable Care Act.

Looking ahead, public-private partnerships will only grow more important as the squeeze on government funding grows. The tricky thing will be to ensure that, in these relationships, the public sector doesn't find itself on bended knee, as a supplicant, which sometimes happens now—with donors occasionally abusing their power by demanding changes in policy. Government needs to embrace philanthropy as a partner, now more than ever, but it can't do so in a way that compromises democratic decision-making.

A last point is that big changes are needed to ensure that government actually speaks for most Americans. This means limiting the role of money in politics even as we expand the voice of ordinary voters. Making it much easier to vote is one way to do the latter, as well as eliminating electoral practices that protect incumbents and ensure that the most ideological candidates prevail at election time. None of this is rocket science, although the political obstacles to such reforms are formidable.

A more effective, better financed public sector that really speaks for Americans would do much to limit the shift of too much power into the hands of private philanthropists, as well as corporations. Still, as long as economic inequality remains so entrenched, with the rich getting richer and richer—while everyone else treads water—we can also expect high levels of civic inequality. Such inequities always go hand in hand.

There are no easy ways to close today's economic chasm. More progressive taxation will make only a limited dent in a problem that's also driven by globalization and technological change—two trends that have greatly strengthened the power of capital vis-à-vis labor.

The good news, though, is that some changes in the economy now favor the ability of workers to demand, and get, a fairer share of the bounty generated by American capitalism. The fastest-growing jobs in the U.S. are service jobs that can't be outsourced or so easily done by machines. Recent successes by the new labor movement, including the fight for a $15 minimum wage, show the limits of capital's playbook of shipping jobs to Mexico or China.

A new era of economic democracy hasn't dawned yet, but we're getting glimpses of it. And if our government institutions were not dominated by money and special interests, always tilting the rules toward capital, we'd see ordinary workers get a bigger share of the pie. Along with higher taxes on the rich, this shift would limit the size of the fortunes at the top of our society—along with the philanthropic power that can come with such wealth.

Given the trajectory of American life over recent decades, it's easy to feel fatalistic about a future ever more dominated by wealthy people, as well as their money and ideas. But it doesn't have to be that way. There's lots of room for a major course correction.

In the alternative future I've just sketched out, philanthropy—one of America's greatest inventions—would remain a powerful force for solving problems and improving society. But it wouldn't come to trump this nation's more important invention: democracy.

Acknowledgments

My biggest thanks go to those philanthropists who made time in their busy schedules to speak with me. Their names appear throughout these pages. As well, I owe a debt to the many others—including foundation presidents, leaders of donor networks, and philanthropy experts—who spoke with me, both on and off the record, for this book. I'd also like to thank the many communications people and assistants who patiently helped schedule these interviews.

Beyond my own reporting and research, this book is deeply informed by several years of researching donors and foundations by the writers for *Inside Philanthropy,* the digital media publication I launched in 2014. I'm grateful for their persistence in working to pull back the veil on a highly opaque world, looking at the giving of a wide array of funders across multiple issues. Special thanks to Ade Adeniji, Michael Gentilucci, Paul Karon, Kiersten Marek, Sue-Lynn Moses, Alyssa Ochs, Mike Scutari, and Tate Williams. As well, many thanks to Kristin Castle and Christopher Packham.

There are a large number of philanthropists doing interesting things these days, and I regret that I've only been able to focus on a select few in this book. This sampling is in no way scientific, and instead was driven by my own interests and contacts, along with the book's focus. There are many more donors whose funding deserves to be spotlighted and analyzed. Readers hungry for a wider and deeper exploration of what the new mega-givers are doing should check out *Inside Philanthropy,* which seeks to provide such coverage every day.

Andrew Stuart has been my literary agent for nearly twenty years and, once again, has proved a great ally and friend in making this project happen. He helped me to shape the book's idea and then connected me to a talented editor, Andrew Miller, who was a strong champion of the project from the start. Also at Knopf, Stephanie Kloss and Katie Schoder brought strong ideas and enthusiasm to building an audience for *The Givers.*

I should also mention a debt of gratitude to my father, Daniel Callahan, who first got me interested in philanthropy and public policy, back in the mid-1990s, with ideas that sparked some of my earliest writing on this topic. This is a world he came to know well from decades of raising money for a bioethics think tank, the Hastings Center, and even as a kid, I picked up quite a bit about philanthropy by osmosis. I also learned much about the funding world during my five years at the Century Foundation, and my fifteen years helping to build Demos, a national think tank, where I was lucky to meet various foundation executives and individual donors, starting with Charles Halpern who incubated Demos while serving as president of the Nathan Cummings Foundation.

In recent years, I've learned a great deal about philanthropy by reading the work of researchers, scholars, and practitioners who have been immersed in this subject for a lot longer than I have. The ranks of people who write on philanthropy aren't very large compared to the size and impact of the sector. But this is a growing field, and I'm grateful to those who've devoted their careers to understanding and explaining the rather curious world of foundations and major donors.

Finally, Susan Barnett has been listening to me talk about philanthropy for over four years now. If any of this has gotten tiresome to her, she's never let on for a moment. Instead, she's been a great booster of the book, and *Inside Philanthropy,* from the start. For that I'm grateful. As anyone who knows Susan can attest, she is a superstar in many ways. I'm lucky to have her on my side.

Notes

This book is based on numerous interviews I conducted with major donors and others who work in the field of philanthropy. As well, it is based on several years of research, reporting, and writing by myself and the team behind *Inside Philanthropy*, which has published profiles of hundreds of philanthropists, including both well-known figures and many people who are still new to giving.

Of necessity, this book has focused on just a handful of these donors, but my overall observations draw from *IP*'s deep research on today's philanthropists, which covers many different kinds of donors, diverse in age, background, and the focus of their giving. Not every philanthropist featured in this book would agree to an interview, or had time to schedule me in, and I make clear in the text where I've spoken to people by using the phrase "told me." Otherwise, I identify the sources of many quotes below, as well as data and studies cited in the chapters.

These notes also seek to guide readers to important books and resources that inform my points. I generally do not provide citations when citing data for giving by different foundations and individuals, or the budgets of nonprofits, which change often as new annual reports, audited statements, and tax returns are released. Readers looking for the most up-to-date-numbers for particular funders will be able to find that information with a little bit of digging.

Prologue: The Great Power Shift

3 **bottom fifth of American households:** Edward N. Wolff, "Household Wealth Trends in the United States, 1962–2013: What Happened over the Great Recession?" National Bureau of Economic Research, December 2014. http://www.nber.org/.

3 **In their letter to Max:** "A letter to our daughter," by Mark Zuckerberg, Facebook, December 1, 2015.

3 **"Wow," wrote Bill and Melinda Gates:** "Mark Zuckerberg and Dr. Priscilla Chan announce Chan Zuckerberg Initiative, inspired by the birth of their daughter," press release, December 1, 2015.

4 **ProPublica's Jesse Eisenberg, writing:** Jesse Eisenberg, "How Mark Zuckerberg's Altruism Helps Himself," *New York Times*, December 3, 2015.

4 **Other critics echoed these points:** Gillian B. White, "Assessing Mark Zuckerberg's Non-Charity Charity," *Atlantic*, December 3, 2015.

5   **Another U.S. official criticized:** Oliver Zunz, *Philanthropy in America* (Princeton, NJ: Princeton University Press, 2011), 21.

5   **The subtitle of a 2008 book:** Matthew Bishop and Michael Green, *Philanthrocapitalism: How Giving Can Save the World* (New York: Bloomsbury Press, 2009).

6   **point that the Forbes 400:** Chuck Collins and Josh Hoxie, "Billionaire Bonanza: The Forbes 400 and the Rest of Us," Institute for Policy Studies," December 2015. http://www.ips-dc.org/.

1. The Coming of Big Philanthropy

11   **He also said he wanted to:** Michael Barbaro, "As the Clock Ticks Down, Mayor Bloomberg Experiences 12 Years of Gratitude," *New York Times,* December 31, 2013.

12   **In a 2010 public statement:** Michael Bloomberg Giving Pledge Letter, Givingpledge.org.

13   **Data shows the world's:** "Bloomberg Philanthropies Launches the Vibrant Oceans Initiative, a $53 Million Commitment to Reverse Declining Fish Supply," press release, Bloomberg Philanthropies, January 29, 2014.

13   **His foundation also rolled out:** 2014: Annual Update, Bloomberg Philanthropies, April 2015.

14   **"Some still see philanthropy":** 2015 Annual Update, Bloomberg Philanthropies, April 2016.

16   **Buffett added $25 billion:** All figures in this book on the net worth of billionaires come from Forbes. The Forbes 400 lists for past years can be found at Forbes .com. The best source of current billionaire wealth is its "World's Billionaires," which is updated continuously in the "Real Time Rankings" section of the list. The net worth of billionaires changes often. All numbers in this book are the latest available, but may not match figures after publication.

17   **boosting the wealth of the Forbes 400:** Agustino Fontevecchia, "There Are More Self-Made Billionaires in the Forbes 400 Than Ever Before," *Forbes,* October 3, 2014.

18   **From 2003 to 2013, according to one study:** Chuck Collins, Helen Flannery, and Josh Hoxie, "Gilded Giving: Top Heavy Philanthropy in an age of Extreme Inequality," Institute for Policy Studies, December 2016, 2.

18   **Some 30,000 new private foundations:** All data on the number and assets of foundations in this book come from the Foundation Center. Data and numbers of donor-advised funds come from the National Philanthropic Trust.

18   **One study has predicted:** John J. Havens and Paul G. Schervish, "A Golden Age of Philanthropy Still Beckons: National Wealth Transfer and Potential for Philanthropy," Center on Wealth and Philanthropy at Boston College, May 2014. https://www.bc.edu/research/cwp/.

18   **Another study estimated:** "Giving in Retirement: America's Longevity Bonus," Merrill Lynch, February 2015. https://mlaem.fs.ml.com/.

18   **A 2015 study found that:** "American Ultra Wealth Rankings 2014–2015," Wealth X, 2015. http://www.wealthx.com/.

19   **Meanwhile, community foundations:** "2015 Donor-Advised Fund Report," National Philanthropic Trust, 2015. https://www.nptrust.org.

20   **"I didn't do much philanthropy":** "A Conversation on Philanthropy with Bill Gates and Sir Michael Moritz, Sequoia Capital," November 2013. http://sequoia capital.tumblr.com/. On the early days of Microsoft, see James Wallace and Jim Erickson, *Hard Drive: Bill Gates and the Making of the Microsoft Empire* (New York: Wiley, 1993).

20 **Later, though, Gates would regret:** Bill and Melinda Gates, "Why Giving Away Our Wealth Has Been the Most Satisfying Thing We've Done," transcript of TEDx interview, April 2014.

21 **But once he read that report:** "Warren Buffett with Bill and Melinda Gates," transcript interview, *Charlie Rose*, May 26, 2006.

22 **"So Bill can look at the big data":** Bill and Melinda Gates, "Why Giving Away Our Wealth Has Been the Most Satisfying Thing We've Done," transcript of TEDx interview, April 2014.

22 **Meanwhile, in the same year:** Carol Loomis, "The $600 Billion Challenge," *Fortune*, June 16, 2010.

23 **"There are a lot of reasons why people":** "Bill and Melinda Gates Talk About the Giving Pledge," ABC News, June 5, 2015.

23 **Singer had even gone after:** Peter Singer, "What Should a Billionaire Give—and What Should You?" *New York Times Magazine*, December 17, 2006.

27 **Oracle founder Larry Ellison:** All facts and quotations from Giving Pledge letters in this book come from the text of those letters, which can be found online at Givingpledge.org.

28 **Gifts by living wealthy donors:** "Giving USA 2016: The Annual Report on Philanthropy in the Year 2015," Giving USA, 2016. http://givingusa.org/.

28 **One analysis by the scholar Kristin Goss:** Kristin Goss, "Policy Plutocrats: How America's Wealthy Seek to Influence Governance," *PS: Political Science & Politics*, July 2016, 442–48.

28 **When the smoke had cleared:** Richard Kogan and William Chen, "Projected Ten-Year Budget Deficits Have Shrunk by Nearly $5 Trillion Since 2010, Mostly Due to Legislative Change," Center for Budget and Policy Priorities, March 20, 2014. http://www.cbpp.org/.

29 **One analysis stated:** David Reich, "Non-Defense Discretionary Programs Have Seen Large Cuts and Face More Cuts in 2015," Center for Budget and Policy Priorities, November 18, 2014.

29 **Non-defense discretionary spending:** Office of Management and Budget, FY 2016 Budget, "Summary Tables."

29 **Second, interest payments:** "The President's Budget for Fiscal Years 2017," 120. https://www.whitehouse.gov/.

29 **By 2046:** "The 2016 Long-Term Budget Outlook," Congressional Budget Office, July 2016, 2. https://www.cbo.gov/.

29 **Things won't be much better at the state level:** "The State Pension Funding Gap: Challenges Persist," Pew Charitable Trusts, July 14, 2015. http://www.pewtrusts.org/.

29 **Top cities are also in the red:** Sally Goldenberg, "City Pension Liabilities Top $46 billion," *Politico*, October 31, 2014.

29 **States and localities have loads:** "The State of the Municipal Securities Market," U.S. Securities and Exchange Commission." https://www.sec.gov.

30 **In Rauch's telling:** Jonathan Rauch, "Demosclerosis," *National Journal*, September 5, 1992.

31 **As Philip Howard has written:** Philip Howard, *The Rule of Nobody: Saving America from Dead Laws and Broken Government* (New York: W. W. Norton, 2014), 3.

32 **In his 2012 book:** Martin Gilens, *Affluence and Influence: Economic Inequality and Political Power in America* (Princeton, NJ: Princeton University Press, 2012), 1.

32 **In his 2008 study:** Larry Bartels, *Unequal Democracy: The Political Economy of the New Gilded Age* (Princeton, NJ: Princeton University Press, 2008), 258.

32 **One 2016 survey found:** Hannah Fingerhut, "Most Americans Say U.S. Eco-

nomic System Is Unfair, but High-Income Republicans Disagree," Pew Research Center, February 10, 2016. http://www.pewresearch.org/.

32   **One survey, funded by the Russell Sage Foundation:** Benjamin I. Page, Larry M. Bartels, and Jason Seawright, "Democracy and the Policy Preferences of Wealthy Americans," *Perspectives on Politics* 11, no. 1, pp. 51–73.

33   **One other thing:** Collins, Flannery, and Hoxie, "Gilded Giving: Top Heavy Philanthropy in an Age of Extreme Inequality," 2.

2. Who Are These People?

34   **There weren't many big funders:** For more on the history of philanthropy and foundations, see Mark Dowie, *Foundations: An Investigative History* (Cambridge, MA: MIT Press, 2001); Joel Fleishman, *Foundations: A Great American Secret* (New York: PublicAffairs, 2001); Karl Zinsmeister, *The Almanac of American Philanthropy* (Washington, DC: Philanthropy Roundtable, 2016); and Oliver Zunz, *Philanthropy in America* (Princeton, NJ: Princeton University Press, 2011).

38   **One global study of high-net-worth individuals:** "The Wealth Report 2016," Knight Frank, January 2016. http://www.knightfrank.com/wealthreport.

39   **The psychological returns from:** Arthur Brooks, "Why Giving Makes You Happy," *New York Sun*, December 28, 2007. See also Arthur Brooks, *Who Really Cares* (Basic Books, 2006).

41   **Schervish describes this:** Paul G. Schervish, Platon E. Coutsoukis, and Ethan Lewis, *Gospels of Wealth: How the Rich Portray Their Lives* (Santa Barbara, CA: Praeger, 1994), 3; and Paul G. Schervish, "Hyperagency and High-Tech Donors: A New Theory of the New Philanthropists," Boston College Social Welfare Research Institute, November 13, 2003.

42   **But Melinda Gates has described:** "Bill and Melinda Gates Talk About the Giving Pledge," ABC News, June 5, 2015. http://abcnews.go.com/.

43   **As early as 1986, Buffett told:** Richard Kirkland, "Should You Leave It All to the Children," *Fortune*, September 29, 1986.

43   **Later, when Buffett pledged:** Jeremy Peters, "Buffett Always Planned to Give Away His Billions," *New York Times*, June 26, 2006.

43   **Bill has written:** Bill Gates, "Why Inequality Matters," *GatesNotes.org*, October 13, 2014.

43   **Mike Bloomberg has been even:** Michael Bloomberg, *Bloomberg on Bloomberg* (New York: Wiley, 2001), 236.

44   **Ostrower detailed the many ways:** Francie Ostrower, *Why the Wealthy Give: The Culture of Elite Philanthropy* (Princeton, NJ: Princeton University Press, 1995).

49   **One analysis found that Apple's:** Charles Duhigg and David Kocieniewski, "How Apple Sidesteps Billions in Taxes," *New York Times*, April 28, 2012.

54   **Instead of primarily serving:** See, for example, Wallace Turbeville, "Financialization and Equal Opportunity," Demos, February 10, 2015. http://www.demos.org.

3. Grandmasters

63   **The *Washington Post* would:** Don Eggen, "Many Deficit Commission Staffers Paid by Outside Groups," *Washington Post*, November 10, 2010.

64   **Peterson wasn't pleased with:** Kai Ryssdal, "Pete Peterson: The Man Who Focused Washington on the National Debt," *Marketplace*, February 26, 2013.

65   **Even better, such spending:** For a look at the history of philanthropists supporting think tanks, see James A. Smith, *The Idea Brokers: Think Tanks and the Rise of the New Policy Elites* (New York: Free Press, 1991). See also Andrew Rich, *Think*

Tanks, Public Policy, and the Politics of Expertise (New York: Cambridge University Press, 2004).

65 **At least nine billionaires:** David Callahan, "Which Washington Think Tank Do Billionaires Love the Most? And Why?" *Inside Philanthropy*, February 5, 2015.

66 **In a long piece in Commentary:** Arthur Brooks, "Be Open-Handed Toward Your Brothers," *Commentary*, February 1, 2014.

70 **He was a young Democrat:** "Interview with Bruce Kovner," *Philanthropy*, Fall 2015.

71 **AEI scholars have even:** Alan D. Viard, "Understanding Carried Interest," *National Review Online*, January 31, 2012.

71 **But AEI scholars have contested:** Peter J. Wallison, "Does Shadow Banking Require Regulation?" American Enterprise Institute, June 14, 2012. http://www.aei.org.

74 **Now, tired of being publicly vilified:** Tim Alberta and Eliana Johnson, "Exclusive: In Koch World 'Realignment,' Less National Politics," *National Review*, May 16, 2016.

77 **The Mercer Family Foundation:** Eric Lichtblau and Alexandra Stevenson, "Hedge-Fund Magnate Robert Mercer Emerges as a Generous Backer of Cruz," *New York Times*, April 10, 2015.

78 **The Heritage Foundation:** Lee Edwards, *The Power of Ideas: The Heritage Foundation at 25 Years* (New York: Jameson Books, 1997).

79 **In 1997, a philanthropy watchdog group:** Sally Covington, "Moving a Policy Agenda: The Strategic Philanthropy of Conservative Foundations," National Committee for Responsive Philanthropy, July 1997. http://www.ncrp.org.

79 **A follow-up report:** David Callahan, "$1 Billion for Ideas: Conservative Think Tanks in the 1990s," National Committee for Responsive Philanthropy, March 1999. http://www.ncrp.org.

84 **So it was that, in the early spring:** Josh Richman, "Silicon Valley Types Launch D.C. Think Tank," *Political Blotter*, March 31, 2015.

85 **Just two years earlier, Conway:** Norimitsu Onishi, "A Silicon Valley Vision for San Francisco," *New York Times*, April 18, 2013.

85 **Parker said that Silicon Valley's:** Nick Gass, "Tech Bigwigs Help Launch Economic Policy Group," *Politico*, March 31, 2015.

88 **Hanauer wrote in a widely read:** Nick Hanauer, "The Pitchforks Are Coming . . . for Us Plutocrats," *Politico*, June 2014.

4. Super-Citizens

90 **Not long before Thanksgiving:** Charles V. Bagli and Robin Pogrebin, "With Bold Park Plan, Mogul Hopes to Leave Mark on New York's West Side," *New York Times*, November 17, 2014.

91 **One journalist wrote:** Peter Schjeldal, "High Line Rhapsody," *The New Yorker*, October 7, 2014.

94 **One housing advocate:** Miriam Axel-Lute, "Will Columbia Take Manhattanville," *Shelterforce*, Spring 2008.

95 **Robert Moses, who famously:** Robert Caro, *The Power Broker: Robert Moses and the Fall of New York* (New York: Knopf, 1974).

96 **Between 1982 and 2007:** Margaret Walls, "Parks and Recreation in the United States: Local Park Systems," Resources for the Future, June 2009. http://www.rff.org/.

97 **Among its powerful opponents:** Nicholas Loris, "Land and Water Conservation Fund: Wrong Solution for Public Land Management," Heritage Foundation, November 12, 2015. http://www.heritage.org.

97 **Bloomberg said in his final speech as mayor:** Jill Colvin, "Bloomberg Sounds Alarm Over 'Labor-Electoral Complex' in Final Speech as Mayor," *Observer,* December 18, 2013.

99 **At least two hundred parks around New York:** Michael Kimmelman, "Mayor de Blasio's Plan for Parks Needs to Grow," *New York Times,* October 28, 2014.

102 **"The number of people who really want":** Chuck Taylor, "Skeptics Deem Proposed $40M Fieldhouse a 'Masquerade That Doesn't Belong in BB Park,'" *Brooklyn Heights Blog,* July 26, 2012.

103 **Emily Lloyd, the head of:** Michael Powell, "Reducing Some City Parks to the Status of Beggars," *New York Times,* May 27, 2013.

104 **Broad later went on:** Eli Broad, *The Art of Being Unreasonable: Lessons in Unconventional Thinking* (New York: Wiley, 2012).

106 **The city, he has said:** Connie Bruck, "The Art of the Billionaire," *The New Yorker,* December 6, 2010.

106 **The state now ranks:** "State Arts Agency Revenues: Fiscal Year 2014," National Assembly of State Arts Agencies, February 2014, 11. http://www.nasaa-arts.org/

106 **In August 2015, readers of the *Los Angeles Times*:** Howard Blume, "Major Charter School Expansion in the Works for L.A. Unified Students," *Los Angeles Times,* August 7, 2015.

108 **A memo outlining the plan:** Howard Blume, "$490-Million Plan Would Put Half of LAUSD Students in Charter Schools," *Los Angeles Times,* September 21, 2015.

108 **It was among several pro-charter funders:** Paul Fahri, "Foundations Fund L.A. Times' Education Reporting. A Conflict?" *Washington Post,* October 29, 2015.

108 **The donations by pro-charter funders:** Howard Blume, "PAC Shielded $2.3 Million in Donations by L.A. Charter School Backers," *Los Angeles Times,* December 2, 2015.

109 **In recent years, pro-charter funders:** Sarah Reckhow, Jeffrey Henig, Rebecca Jacobsen, and Jamie Alter, "Outsiders with Deep Pockets: The Nationalization of Local School Board Elections," *Urban Affairs Review,* August 10, 2016.

109 **Caputo-Pearl also told the *Times*:** Mike Szymanski, "LA Teachers Planning Campaign to Oppose Charter Expansion," *LA School Report,* August 26, 2015.

109 **Some observers questioned the rush:** Craig Clough, "Charters with Broad Support Show Only a Mixed Return on Investment," *LA School Report,* September 30, 2015.

109 **"The really important question":** Diane Ravitch, "Eli Broad Releases Plan to Take Over and Privatize Public Education in Los Angeles," DianeRavitch.net, June 15, 2015.

111 **The *New York Times* reported:** Michael Barbaro, "Bloomberg Is Quietly Ending a Charitable Program," *New York Times,* March 28, 2010.

5. Disrupters

112 **Parker saw the transformative potential:** Steven Bertoni, "Sean Parker: Agent of Disruption," *Forbes,* September 21, 2011.

113 **He said about food allergies:** Steven Bertoni, "Why Sean Parker Gave $24 Million to Build a Stanford Allergy Research Center," *Forbes,* December 17, 2014.

113 **"A huge amount of costs":** Stephanie M. Lee, "The Story Behind Sean Parker's $10 Million Donation to Autoimmune Research," *BuzzFeed,* November 16, 2015.

115 **In a *Wall Street Journal* essay:** Sean Parker, "Philanthropy for Hackers," *Wall Street Journal,* June 26, 2015.

120 **Moskovitz decided early on:** "PandoMonthly: Fireside Chat with Dustin Moskovitz," May 6, 2012. https://pando.com.

126   **Ackman has had some major ups and downs:** Katrina Brooker, "Love Him or Hate Him, Ackman Now Runs the World's Top Hedge Fund," Bloomberg, January 5, 2015.

126   **In an interview with *Vanity Fair*:** William D. Cohan, "Billionaire Bill Ackman's Ill-Fated Bike Ride: 'His Mind Wrote a Check That His Body Couldn't Cash,'" *Vanity Fair*, February 2013.

127   **Even with the steep loss:** Antoine Gara, "Pershing Square's Investment Team, Led by Ackman, Made $509 Million in Down 20% Year," *Forbes*, March 24, 2016.

130   **Much has been written about the Newark effort:** Dale Russakoff, *The Prize: Who's in Charge of America's Schools?* (New York: Houghton Mifflin Harcourt, 2015).

6. Leverage Points

137   **In 2011, the Optical Society of America:** "2011 John Tyndall Award Winner Announced," OSA: The Optical Society, 2011. http://www.osa.org/.

139   **For years, the California Teachers Association has:** Campaign contribution data is from National Institute on Money in State Politics. http://www.followthemoney.org.

140   **Joshua Pechthalt, president of the:** Vergara Lawsuit Just an 'AstroTurf' Attempt to Dismantle Teachers' Rights," *Sun Mercury News*, February 12, 2014.

140   **Dana Goldstein wrote:** Dana Goldstein, "Will California's Ruling Against Teacher Tenure Change Schools?," *The Atlantic*, June 11, 2014.

140   **"Instead of working to erode":** Jack Schneider, "Making It Easier to Fire Bad Teachers Won't Get You Better Ones," *Los Angeles Times*, June 10, 2014.

140   **In June, the court ruled:** Teresa Watanabe, "Judge Says Effect of Bad Teachers 'Shocks the Conscience,'" *Los Angeles Times*, June 10, 2014.

140   **"The ruling opens a new chapter":** "In California, a Judge Takes on Teacher Tenure," editorial, *New York Times*, June 11, 2014.

141   **Lawsuits started gestating in other states:** Laurence Tribe, "Why Progressives Should Defend 'Vergara v. California' Ruling," *USA Today*, September 24, 2014.

141   **As the unions saw it:** David Bacon, "Why Is Silicon Valley So Bent on Destroying Public Education," *Alternet*, October 10, 2014.

142   **That study was supported by the Carnegie Corporation:** "The Lasting Legacy of an American Dilemma," Carnegie Corporation, Fall 2004. https://www.carnegie.org/.

143   **Conservative philanthropists have embraced:** Steve M. Teles, *The Rise of the Conservative Legal Movement: The Battle for the Law* (Princeton, NJ: Princeton University Press, 2010).

143   **Bolick moved fast to diversify:** John J. Miller and Karl Zinsmeister, *Agenda Setting: A Wise Giver's Guide to Influencing Public Policy* (Washington, D.C.: Philanthropy Roundtable, 2015), 116.

145   **Bradley has been one of the top funders:** Brian Mahoney, "Conservative Group Nears Big Payoff in Supreme Court Case," *Politico*, January 10, 2016.

146   ***The Advocate* has called:** "The Most Important LGBT Group You've Never Heard Of," *The Advocate*, August 15, 2011.

146   **To change minds, Williams said:** "Chuck Williams: The Focused Funder," Rockefeller Philanthropy Advisors. http://www.rockpa.org/.

148   **But he distinguished himself:** Telis Demos, "The Wunderkind Gas Trader," *Fortune*, November 24, 2009.

158   **Reform philanthropists have sought:** Sarah Reckhow, *Follow the Money: How Foundation Dollars Change Public School Politics* (New York: Oxford University Press, 2013); Frederick M. Hess and Jeffrey R. Henig, eds., *The New Education*

Philanthropy: Politics, Policy, and Reform (Cambridge, MA: Harvard Education Press, 2015); and Megan E. Tompkins-Stange, *Policy Patrons: Philanthropy, Education Reform, and the Politics of Influence* (Cambridge, MA: Harvard Education Press, 2015).

159 **Education is different:** "Conversation with Bill Gates, Melinda Gates, and Gwen Ifill," U.S. Learning Education Forum, October 9, 2015. http://www.impatient optimists.org.

159 **According to a later account:** Lyndsey Layton, "How Bill Gates Pulled Off the Swift Common Core Revolution," *Washington Post*, June 7, 2014.

161 **Gates has called the spending:** Jason L. Riley, "Was the $5 Billion Worth It?," *Wall Street Journal*, July 23, 2011.

161 **As one reporter commented:** Layton, "How Bill Gates Pulled Off the Swift Common Core Revolution."

162 **Walton's proposed solution:** "2015–20 K–12 Education Strategic Plan," Walton Family Foundation, 2015. http://www.waltonfamilyfoundation.org/.

163 **In Washington State:** Joanne Barken, "Charitable Plutocracy: Bill Gates, Washington State, and the Nuisance of Democracy," *NPQ*, April 11, 2016.

163 **In New York, a small group:** Zephyr Teachout and Mohammad Khan, "Corruption in Education: Hedge Funds and the Takeover of New York's Schools," *The Washington Park Project*, December 2, 2015.

163 **Later, it was reported:** Don Michak, "Hedge Fund Founder Buys Leadership 'Pipeline' in Malloy's Office," *Journal Inquirer*, February 3, 2014.

163 **In 2014–15, nearly half:** America's Largest Charter School Communities," National Alliance for Public Charter Schools, November 2015, 3. http://www .publiccharters.org/.

165 **Diane Ravitch, a scholar who:** Valerie Strauss, "Ravitch: Billionaires (and Millionaires) for Education Reform," *Washington Post*, November 15, 2011.

165 **About Gates and the Common Core:** Valerie Strauss, "Ravitch: Time for Congress to Investigate Bill Gates' Role in Common Core," *Washington Post*, June 9, 2014.

165 **The last time it really did so:** Waldemar Nielsen, *The Big Foundations* (New York: Columbia University Press, 1972), 7–11.

166 **In a rare media interview in 2014:** Layton, "How Bill Gates Pulled Off the Swift Common Core Revolution."

166 **One 2006 study ranked him:** Christopher B. Swanson and Janelle Barlage, "Influence: A Study of the Factors Shaping Education Policy," Editorial Projects in Education Research Center, December 2006. http://www.edweek.org/rc/.

7. Advocates

168 **At a meeting at Gracie Mansion:** Michael Grunwald, "Inside the War on Coal," *Politico*, May 26, 2015.

170 **In announcing this latest gift:** Andrew Restuccia, "Michael Bloomberg's War on Coal," *Politico*, April 8, 2015.

170 **A 2011 report by the American Lung Association:** "Toxic Air: The Case for Cleaning Up Coal-Fired Power Plants," American Lung Association, March 2011. http://www.lung.org.

170 **As another report stated:** Alan H. Lockwood, Kristen Welker-Hood, Molly Rauch, and Barbara Gottlieb, "Coal's Assault on Human Health," Physicians for Social Responsibility, November 2009. http://www.psr.org/.

171 **They are routinely bested in political combat:** Mancur Olson, *The Logic of Collective Action: Public Good and the Theory of Groups* (Cambridge, MA: Harvard University Press, 1971).

171   **Again and again, it's hard:** For an updated take on Olson's argument, see Jonathan Rauch, *Demosclerosis: The Silent Killer of American Government* (New York: Crown, 1994).

173   **Breitbart.com, the conservative news network:** James Delingpole, "Exposed: Sea Change—the Shadowy One-Percenter Foundation Waging War on Affordable Energy, Breitbart.com, July 30, 2014.

173   **The *Washington Free Beacon*:** Lachlan Markay, "Dem Mega-Donor Commutes to Work on Gas-Guzzling Yacht," *Washington Free Beacon*, November 3, 2014; and Lachlan Markay, "How Dem Moneyman Nat Simons Profits from Political Giving," *Washington Free Beacon*, November 4, 2014.

174   **Two years later, in 2012:** "Annual Report, 2012," Environmental Defense Fund, 2013; and "Annual Report, 2015," Environmental Defense Fund, 2016. https://www.edf.org/.

175   **One academic study found that:** Sarah Reckhow and Megan Tompkins-Stange, "Singing from the Same Hymnbook as Gates and Broad," in Frederick M. Hess and Jeffrey R. Henig, eds., *The New Education Philanthropy: Politics, Policy, and Reform* (Cambridge, MA: Harvard Education Press, 2015), 61.

177   **Pope has explained his foundation's push:** "Public Policy Support," John William Pope Foundation. https://jwpf.org/.

178   **Over the past quarter century:** Jane Meyer, "State for Sale," *The New Yorker*, October 10, 2011.

178   **During the ensuing uproar over the law:** Alex Kotch, "The Money Behind HB2: How Art Pope Helped Create North Carolina's 'Bathroom Bill,'" *Facing South*, May 6, 2016.

178   **But it's fair to say that:** Greg Lacour, "HB2: How North Carolina Got Here," *Charlotte Magazine*, May 9, 2016.

179   **"If you get involved at the local level":** Lee Fang, "King Rex," *Politico Magazine*, July/August 2014.

181   **So far, though, few major:** Alexander Hertel-Fernandez, "Explaining Liberal Policy Woes in the States," *PS: Political Science & Politics*, July 2016, 461–65.

182   **In 2012, 7 million ballots were cast:** Jake Seaton, "Widespread Voter Fraud Not an Issue in NC, Data Shows," WNCN News, July 25, 2013. http://www.nbcnews.com/.

182   **Pope-funded groups invested heavily:** John Hood, "No Controversy About Voter ID," *Carolina Journal*, December 3, 2012.

183   **The director of a progressive group in Wisconsin:** Daniel Bice, "Venture Capitalist Einhorn Paid for Voter Fraud Billboards," *Journal Sentinel*, October 29, 2012.

184   **But the full story of Blum's support:** Andy Kroll, "Exposed: The Dark-Money ATM of the Conservative Movement," *Mother Jones*, February 5, 2013.

189   **"When you've got the money, you spend it":** Jim Dwyer, "Philanthropist Wants to Be Rid of His Last $1.5 Billion," *New York Times*, August 7, 2012.

8. Networkers

195   **Women have long connected:** Sondra Shaw-Hardy and Martha A. Taylor, *Women and Philanthropy: Boldly Shaping a Better World* (San Francisco: Jossey-Bass, 2010).

200   **Over time, Kirsch gravitated:** Vanessa Kirsch, Jim Bildner, and Jeff Walker, "Why Social Ventures Need Systems Thinking," *Harvard Business Review*, July 25, 2016.

203   **"Greenpeace won't get a dime":** The Dark-Money ATM of the Conservative Movement," *Mother Jones*, February 5, 2013.

205 **Robert Bruelle, a sociologist:** Alex McKechnie, "Not Just the Koch Brothers: New Drexel Study Reveals Funders Behind the Climate Change Denial Effort," *Drexel Now*, December 20, 2013.

206 **Some $18 million went:** Matthew Duss, Yasmine Taeb, Ken Gude, and Ken Sofer, "Fear, Inc. 2.0: The Islamophobia Network's Efforts to Manufacture Hate in America," Center for American Progress, February 11, 2015, 57. https://www.americanprogress.org/.

207 **He once commented:** Gara LaMarche, "Democracy and the Donor Class," *Democracy*, Fall 2014.

207 **The ranks of the liberal rich:** David Callahan, *Fortunes of Change: The Rise of the Liberal Rich and the Remaking of America* (Hoboken, NJ: Wiley, 2010).

9. Heirs to Influence

212 *The Economist* **would say:** "The Father of Fracking," *The Economist*, August 3, 2013.

215 **As Lorenz put it once:** "NextGen Family Philanthropy: An Interview with Katherine Lorenz," Social Velocity, December 19, 2013. http://www.socialvelocity.net/.

216 **To be sure, plenty of America's rich:** "Spending Millions to Save Billions: The Campaign of the Super Wealthy to Kill the Estate Tax," Public Citizen and United for a Fair Economy, April 2006; and "Billionaire's Bluff: How America's Richest Families Hide Behind Small Businesses and Family Farms in Effort to Repeal Estate Tax," Public Citizen, June 25, 2016. https://www.citizen.org.

216 **Among other things, they wrote:** William H. Gates Sr. and Chuck Collins, *Wealth and Commonwealth: Why America Should Tax Accumulated Fortunes* (Boston: Beacon Press, 2004).

217 **As Buffett told Charlie Rose:** "The Giving Pledge: A New Club for Billionaires," CBS News, July 20, 2014.

217 **Studies show that most inherited:** Missy Sullivan, "Lost Inheritance," *Wall Street Journal*, March 8, 2013.

219 **These people are aware:** Tate Williams, "The Chorus Foundation's Radical Philanthropy," *Inside Philanthropy*, February 2, 2016.

220 **"I felt it was not my money":** Susan Ostrander, *Money for Change: Social Change Movement in Haymarket* (Philadelphia: Temple University Press, 1995), 9.

220 **Oscar Meyer heir:** Chuck Collins, *Born on Third Base: A One Percenter Makes the Case for Tackling Inequality, Bringing Wealth Home, and Committing to the Common Good* (White River Junction, VT: Chelsea Green Publishing, 2016), xiv.

222 **He strongly rejected the Horatio Alger:** Howard G. Buffett, *Forty Chances: Finding Hope in a Hungry World* (New York: Simon and Schuster, 2013), xiv.

223 **According to his biographer:** Alice Schroeder, *The Snowball: Warren Buffett and the Business of Life* (New York: Bantam Books, 2008), 662–63.

225 **One was a desire to avoid:** Peter Buffett, *Life Is What You Make It: Find Our Own Path to Fulfillment* (New York, NY: Three River Press, 2010), 240.

225 **"If their voices aren't heard":** Tracy L. Barnett, "Peter Buffett: Shifting the Balance," Esperanza Project, September 3, 2012.

225 **One of its largest impacts has been:** Karen Weise, "Warren Buffett's Family Secretly Funded a Birth Control Revolution," *Bloomberg Businessweek*, July 30, 2015.

226 **One foundation-backed effort:** Sabrina Tavernise, "Colorado's Effort Against Teenage Pregnancies Is a Startling Success," *New York Times*, July 5, 2015.

227 **In an affectionate foreword:** Buffett, *Forty Chances: Finding Hope in a Hungry World*, xii.

232 **At college, she volunteered:** Alex Daniels, "3rd Generation of Walton Family Makes Sharp Turn in Giving," *Chronicle of Philanthropy*, February 29, 2016.

10. The New Medicis

238 **Eric Lander, the founding director:** Sam Roberts, "Ted Stanley, Whose Son's Illness Inspired Philanthropy, Dies at 84," *New York Times*, January 8, 2016.

239 **Between 2005 and 2014:** Data is from Million Dollar List, a database of charitable gifts of $1 million or more, created by Lily School of Philanthropy, at Indiana University–Purdue University, Indianapolis. http://www.milliondollarlist.org/.

242 **As a result of the Budget Control Act:** Kwame Boadi, "Erosion of Funding for the National Institutes of Health Threatens U.S. Leadership in Biomedical Research," Center for American Progress, March 25, 2014. https://www.americanprogress.org/.

242 **If the NEA's budget had kept pace:** "National Endowment for the Arts Appropriations History," National Endowment for the Arts, 2016. https://www.arts.gov/.

242 **Following the political revolution:** "Current State Arts Agency Revenues: North Carolina," National Assembly of State Arts Agencies. http://www.nasaa-arts.org/.

247 **The age of grand federal research:** William J. Broad, "Billionaires with Big Ideas Are Privatizing American Science," *New York Times*, March 15, 2011.

248 **One study charting this:** Fiona Murray, "Evaluating the Role of Science Philanthropy in American Research Universities," National Bureau of Economic Research, 2013. http://www.nber.org/.

249 **He's given millions for this cause:** Ade Adeniji, "This Koch Brother Is Also a Crusader Against Cancer," *Inside Philanthropy*, October 6, 2014.

250 **In the case of prostate cancer:** Dan Zenka, "African Americans: At Higher Risk for Prostate Cancer," Prostate Cancer Foundation, October 5, 2012. http://www.pcf.org/.

251 **Already, the costs of caring:** "Changing the Trajectory of Alzheimer's Disease: How a Treatment by 2025 Saves Lives and Dollars," Alzheimer's Association, 2015, 5–6. http://www.alz.org/.

252 **During this same period:** Michael Mitchell and Michael Leachman, "Years of Cuts Threaten to Put College Out of Reach for More Students," Center for Budget and Policy Priorities, May 13, 2015. http://www.cbpp.org/.

252 **The value of Pell Grants:** Tyler Kingkade, "Pell Grants Cover Smallest Portion of College Costs in History as GOP Calls for Cuts," *Huffington Post*, August 29, 2012.

253 **Harvard Business School has produced:** Will Yakowicz, "Want to Be a Billionaire? Apply to Harvard Business School," *Inc.*, November 11, 2014.

253 **America's universities raised:** "Colleges and Universities Raise Record $40.30 Billion in 2015," Council on Aid to Education, January 27, 2016. http://cae.org/.

253 **Three-quarters of the $516 billion:** Molly F. Sherlock et al., "College and University Endowments: Overview and Tax Policy Options," Congressional Research Service, https://www.loc.gov.

254 **Harvard spends around a billion dollars:** "Harvard University: Total R&D Expenditures, by Source of Funds and R&D Field: 2014," National Science Foundation. http://www.nsf.gov/.

255 **Over 2,300 U.S. patents:** "Innovation at a Glance," Caltech. https://www.caltech.edu/.

256 **As Daniel Golden showed:** Daniel Golden, *The Price of Admission: How America's Ruling Class Buys Its Way into Elite Colleges—and Who Gets Left Outside the Gates* (New York: Broadway Books, 2007).

256 **At the University of Virginia:** Andrew Rice, "Anatomy of a Campus Coup," *New York Times Magazine*, September 11, 2012.

256 **In another case, documented:** Michael Hiltz, "The Salaita Case and the Big Money Takeover of State Universities," *Los Angeles Times,* September 15, 2014.

257 **punishing cuts in public:** "Fiscal Year 2017: Higher Education Budget Recommendations," State of Illinois Board of Higher Education, December 2015. http://www.ibhe.org/.

257 **Public universities in Michigan:** David Jesse, "Illitches' Wayne State Gift Comes With Strings," *Detroit Free Press*, August 28, 2016.

257 **In his book:** Christopher Newfield, *Unmaking the Public University: The Forty-Year Assault on the Middle Class* (Cambridge, MA: Harvard University Press, 2008), 164.

257 **The clout of donors on campus:** Jennifer Washburn, *University, Inc: The Corporate Corruption of Higher Education* (New York: Basic Books, 2006).

257 **In 2014 alone, his foundation:** Jim Tankersley, "Inside Charles Koch's $200 Million Quest for a 'Republic of Science,' " *Washington Post*, June 3, 2016.

258 **Among the reported stipulations:** Julie Ball, "Universities Grapple with Donor Influence," *Citizen-Times*, April 2, 2016.

258 **The donor behind the offer:** S. Douglas Beets, "BB&T, Atlas Shrugged, and the Ethics of Corporation Influence on College Curricula," *Journal of Academic Ethics* 13(4) (2015): 311–344.

258 **After Guilford College accepted:** Seth Lubove and Oliver Stanley, "Schools Find Ayn Rand Can't Be Shrugged as Donors Build Courses," Bloomberg, May 4, 2011.

258 **Allison said in 2011:** Colleen Flaherty, "Banking on the Curriculum," *Inside Higher Education*, October 16, 2015.

259 **Budget analysts say that:** "The 2016 Long-Term Budget Outlook," Congressional Budget Office, July 2016, 2. https://www.cbo.gov/.

260 **We're likely to see the steady shrinking:** David Reich, "Non-Defense Discretionary Programs Have Seen Large Cuts and Face More Cuts in 2015," Center for Budget and Policy Priorities, November 18, 2014. http://www.cbpp.org/.

11. Agents of Wealth

264 **While some such leaders:** Fay Twersky, "Foundation Chief Executives as Artful Jugglers," Center for Effective Philanthropy, 2014. http://www.effectivephilanthropy.org/.

265 **Such executives must be able to:** Fay Twersky, "The Artful Juggler," *Stanford Social Innovation Review*, Summer 2014.

268 **An advantage of this approach:** Patti Hartigan, "Who's Behind the Barr Foundation," *Boston Magazine*, February 2016.

268 **In 2010, emerging from behind:** Erin Ailworth, "Big Gift for Local Climate Efforts," *Boston Globe*, February 14, 2010.

274 **Soros knew there was a problem:** Stephanie Strom, "Criminal Justice Expert Named to Lead Soros Foundations," *New York Times*, December 7, 2011.

275 **As early as 1996:** Judith Miller, "With Big Money and Brash Ideas, A Billionaire Redefines Charity," *New York Times,* December 17, 1996.

278 **But Rosenwald's cash:** Peter M. Ascoli, *Julius Rosenwald: The Man Who Built Sears, Roebuck and Advanced the Cause of Black Education in the American South* (Indianapolis, IN: Indiana University Press, 2015).

280 **Atlantic's big grants kept flowing through 2015:** Christopher G. Oechsli, "Atlantic Fellows: Advancing Fairer, Healthier, More Inclusive Societies," The Atlantic Philanthropies, May 31, 2016. http://www.atlanticphilanthropies.org/.

281   **In 1910, when Edward Devine:** Judith Sealander, *Private Wealth, Public Life: Foundation Philanthropy and the Reshaping of American Social Policy from the Progressive Era to the New Deal* (Baltimore, MD: JHU Press, 1997), 220.

Epilogue: Balancing Act

287   **Another defense of philanthropy:** For a deeper discussion along these lines, see Rob Reich, "On the Role of Foundations in Democracies," in Rob Reich, Lucy Bernholz, and Chiara Cordelli, *Philanthropy in Democratic Societies: History, Institutions, Values* (Chicago, IL: University of Chicago Press, 2016), 64–85.

290   **As the sociologist Theda Skocpol:** Theda Skocpol, "Associations Without Members," *American Prospect*, July–August 1999. See also: Theda Skocpol, *Diminished Democracy: From Membership to Management in American Civic Life* (Norman: University of Oklahoma Press, 2003).

293   **Data available through:** "Foundation Transparency 2.0," Foundation Center. http://foundationcenter.org/.

294   **Some mega-donors:** Zachary Mider, "The $13 Billion Mystery Angels: Who Is Funding the Fourth-Largest Charity in the U.S.," *Bloomberg Business*, May 14, 2014.

297   **was around $47 billion in 2016:** "Briefing Book: Tax Expenditures," Tax Policy Center, 2016. http://www.taxpolicycenter.org/.

299   **The U.S. Treasury has estimated:** U.S. Department of Treasury, "Tax Expenditures FY2017," 33. https://www.treasury.gov/resource-center/tax-policy/Documents/Tax-Expenditures-FY2017.pdf.

301   **The Ford Foundation's overhead costs:** David Callahan, "Ford Sinks Over $1 Billion a Decade into Overhead. Is That Money Well Spent?" *Inside Philanthropy*, April 10, 2015.

301   **Many other top foundations:** David Callahan, "Top Philanthropoids Are Paid Over $600 Million a Year. Is That Too Much?" *Inside Philanthropy*, May 7, 2015.

302   **That's true of the IRS:** Dave Levinthal, "IRS Nonprofit Division Overloaded, Understaffed," Center for Public Integrity, May 14, 2013. https://www.public integrity.org/. See also: Kim Barker and Justin Elliott, "How the IRS's Nonprofit Division Got So Dysfunctional," ProPublica, August 17, 2013.

302   **As for keeping an eye on foundations:** Ruth McCambridge and Virginia Gross, "Changes in the IRS Oversight of Nonprofits: A Conversation with Virginia Gross," *Nonprofit Quarterly*, August 8, 2016.

302   **A recent study found:** Alex Daniels, "Nonprofits Proliferate But Not the Regulators, Says Report," *Chronicle of Philanthropy*, October 5, 2015.

302   **The first question is easy to answer:** "Domestic Private Foundations: Number and Selected Financial Data, by Type of Foundation and Size of End-of-year Fair Market Value of Total Assets, Tax Year 2012." https://www.irs.gov/.

306   **The center has drawn:** See, for example: "Working Well With Grantees: A Guide for Foundation Program Staff," Center for Effective Philanthropy, June 2013. http://www.effectivephilanthropy.org/.

306   **Too often, inequities:** For a good overview of this problem, see Courtney Martin, "The Trouble With Philanthropy Is That Money Can't Buy Equality," *The Guardian*, September 2, 2017.

309   **For example, Michael Edwards:** Michael Edwards, *Just Another Emperor? The Myths and Realities of Philanthrocapitalism* (New York: Demos and the Young Foundation, 2008), 88.

310   **Donations to groups that:** Chuck Collins, *Born on Third Base* (White River Junction, VT: Chelsea Green Publishing, 2016), 124.

Index